JOHN ROBINSON

STURTON-LE-STEEPLE CHURCH AT THE PRESENT DAY.

JOHN ROBINSON

PASTOR OF THE

PILGRIM FATHERS

A STUDY OF HIS LIFE AND TIMES

BY

WALTER H. BURGESS

WIPF & STOCK · Eugene, Oregon

Wipf and Stock Publishers
199 W 8th Ave, Suite 3
Eugene, OR 97401

John Robinson, Pastor of the Pilgrim Fathers
A Study of His Life and Times
By Burgess, Walter H.
ISBN 13: 978-1-60608-513-4
Publication date 12/7/2009
Previously published by Williams and Norgate, 1920

"There is no creature so perfect in wisdom and knowledge but may learn something for time present and to come by times past."

JOHN ROBINSON.

FOREWORD

THE following pages give an independent study of the work of the Pastor of the Pilgrim Fathers and those associated with him. Robinson and his companions loved England with a passionate love, yet they were compelled to leave the land of their birth to secure freedom to worship according to the dictates of their conscience. Two sentences from Robinson's writings will explain the position : " For the commonwealth and kingdom, as we honour it above all the States in the world, so would we thankfully embrace the meanest corner in it, at the extremest conditions of any people in the kingdom." Again he says, " For our country we do not forsake it, but are by it forsaken, and expelled by most extreme laws and violent prescriptions, contrived and executed by the prelates and on their own behalf." To say, as has recently been said, that it was their own intolerance which drove these pilgrims to Holland is a gross misinterpretation of the facts.

Besides the identification of the early home and the parentage of John Robinson, these pages throw a little fresh light upon the Southworths and Carvers and others connected with the Pilgrim Father movement. Gervase Neville is identified, and the anonymous opponent of Robinson in one of his earliest controversies is named. The history of the obscure Church in the western parts of England is unfolded, and an attempt made to settle the vexed question of the identity of John Smith. The Appendices give illustrative extracts from contemporary documents.

Given time and means, no doubt further facts concerning members of the Pilgrim Church could be recovered. It should be possible to identify the actual site of the Robinson homestead—or toftstead, to use the old word—at Sturton. But sufficient is known now to set the story out in fair proportions.

I desire to thank all who have helped in my work of research, and to express my deep obligation to the writings of the late Dr. H. M. Dexter and his son Morton Dexter, on whom I have mainly relied for the Leyden period of this narrative. To the Hibbert Trustees I am also much indebted. It is in great part due to their encouragement and support that the publication of this volume has been made possible.

WALTER H. BURGESS.

Plymouth,
England.

CONTENTS

CHAP.		PAGE
I.	THE BIRTHPLACE AND PARENTAGE OF JOHN ROBINSON	1
II.	JOHN ROBINSON'S WIFE	17
III.	ROBINSON'S BOYHOOD	27
IV.	LIFE AT CAMBRIDGE	32
V.	RELIGION IN ENGLAND IN THE DAYS OF ELIZABETH AND JAMES	42
VI.	DISPUTATIONS ON RELIGION AT CAMBRIDGE AND LEYDEN	49
VII.	JOHN ROBINSON AT NORWICH	58
VIII.	SEPARATION FROM THE CHURCH OF ENGLAND—ROBINSON AND BERNARD—GERVASE NEVILLE—WILLIAM BREWSTER	67
IX.	"AN ADVENTURE ALMOST DESPERATE" . . .	82
X.	RELIGIOUS REFUGEES AT AMSTERDAM . .	85
XI.	CONTROVERSIES WITH JOSEPH HALL AND JOHN BURGESS	94
XII.	THE PILGRIMS AT LEYDEN	100
XIII.	"JUSTIFICATION OF SEPARATION"	110
XIV.	ROBINSON'S INTERCOURSE WITH AMES, PARKER AND JACOB	123

CONTENTS

CHAP.		PAGE
XV.	INFANT BAPTISM, FLIGHT IN PERSECUTION AND THE OFFICE OF MAGISTRACY DISCUSSED BY ROBINSON	143
XVI.	THE PILGRIM CHURCH IN RELATION TO THE CIVIC AND UNIVERSITY LIFE OF LEYDEN	156
XVII.	THE PILGRIM PRESS AT LEYDEN	164
XVIII.	INTERCOURSE BETWEEN LEYDEN AND AMSTERDAM—RICHARD CLIFTON—FRANCIS JOHNSON—HENRY AINSWORTH	187
XIX.	ROBINSON'S PLEA FOR LAY PREACHING	204
XX.	"THIS WEIGHTY BUSINESS ABOUT VIRGINIA"	209
XXI.	THEY PREPARE FOR THE VOYAGE—THE "MAYFLOWER"	236
XXII.	THE SAILING—ROBINSON'S LETTER OF ADVICE—ROBERT CUSHMAN'S LETTER — THE "MAYFLOWER'S" VOYAGE	248
XXIII.	ROBINSON AND THE PLYMOUTH PLANTATION	267
XXIV.	OPPOSITION TO ROBINSON'S MIGRATION—HIS CONCERN FOR THE INDIANS—HIS LAST LETTERS	273
XXV.	ROBINSON'S HOUSEHOLD AT LEYDEN—LATER CONTROVERSIES—ROGER WHITE	282
XXVI.	LETTERS OF THE LEYDEN CHURCH—ROBINSON'S ESSAYS—HIS DEATH	290
XXVII.	AFFAIRS IN PLYMOUTH COLONY—A BRIEF CATECHISM	314
XXVIII.	THE INFLUENCE OF ROBINSON ON THE THOUGHT AND LIFE OF HIS AGE	322
XXIX.	THE FORTUNES OF THE ROBINSON FAMILY AND THE AFTER-HISTORY OF THE PILGRIM CHURCH—A PARALLEL RELIGIOUS DEVELOPMENT IN OLD AND NEW ENGLAND—CONCLUSION	348

APPENDICES

PAGE

I. SUITS AT LAW OF TUDOR AND STUART TIMES ILLUSTRATING LIFE AT STURTON IN ROBINSON'S DAY 369

II. RESIDENTS IN STURTON IN THE SIXTEENTH AND SEVENTEENTH CENTURIES 395

III. STATEMENT BY JOHN BURGESS, DATED JULY 2, 1604 407

IV. DID JOHN SMITH THE SE-BAPTIST AND SEPARATIST LEADER SPRING FROM STURTON? 409

CHRONOLOGICAL TABLE OF THE WRITINGS OF JOHN ROBINSON 418

INDEX 421

LIST OF ILLUSTRATIONS

Facing page

STURTON-LE-STEEPLE CHURCH . . . . *Frontispiece*

SKETCH PLAN OF CORPUS CHRISTI COLLEGE, CAMBRIDGE . 32

LETTER FROM THE FELLOWS OF CORPUS CHRISTI COLLEGE, BEARING ROBINSON'S SIGNATURE, PRESERVED AT HATFIELD HOUSE 40

GREASLEY CHURCH 46

SKETCH MAP OF THE PILGRIM DISTRICT 74

STURTON-LE-STEEPLE CHURCH AS ROBINSON KNEW IT . 84

FACSIMILE OF A DOCUMENT, BY AN ANONYMOUS OPPONENT OF ROBINSON, IN THE BODLEIAN LIBRARY . . . 99

ST. WILFRID'S CHURCH, SCROOBY 187

THE "MAYFLOWER" STONE AND MEMORIAL TABLET AT PLYMOUTH, DEVON 263

THE OLD CHAPEL AT GAINSBOROUGH 322

A LIST OF PREACHERS TO THE GAINSBOROUGH PROTESTANT DISSENTERS, 1698–1700 354

HANDWRITING OF JOHN BURGESS, FROM A DOCUMENT IN THE PUBLIC RECORD OFFICE 408

JOHN ROBINSON

PASTOR OF THE PILGRIM FATHERS

CHAPTER I

THE BIRTHPLACE AND PARENTAGE OF JOHN ROBINSON

On the last day of May 1919, Lieutenant-Commander A. C. Read, the first man to cross the Atlantic entirely by air, landed at the historic Barbican jetty in Plymouth. He and his gallant companions brought their seaplane down in a graceful sweep to the mouth of the Cattewater, and after a welcome from their compatriots, on board a naval vessel of the United States, they were received, as they stepped ashore, by the Mayor of the ancient borough, at the "*Mayflower* stone." One's thoughts naturally turned to the little company of Englishmen, known as the Pilgrim Fathers, who sailed from that spot three hundred years ago on a venture scarcely less daring. It is of the Pastor of the Pilgrim Fathers, his life, his times, his work, his friends and his influence, that we tell in the following pages.

The men of the *Mayflower*, who made the first effective settlement on the shores of New England in 1620, were sustained and inspired by religious convictions arrived at under the guidance of John Robinson, their pastor. Robinson was a remarkable man. He left the impress of his thought upon much of the religious life of America and England. In the tenacity of his nature and the solidity of his judgment, he was essentially English. In the depth and range of his spiritual experience he was essentially

Christian. Though his life only extended to a bare half-century, it was crowded with incident and marked by an unwearied industry. He came into contact with many men and women, who took an active and decided part in the religious movements of his age. He himself tells us, in one of his latest writings, how, in the days of his "pilgrimage," he had enjoyed "special opportunity of conversing with persons of divers nations, estates and dispositions in great variety." [1] This gave a wider range to his outlook than was usual amongst the Puritans. We find him domiciled at Cambridge, at Norwich, at Amsterdam, at Leyden, in each case in the midst of a stimulating environment, each a centre where the principles of political and religious liberty were brought under discussion and hammered into practical shape. Any one desiring to gain a thorough understanding of the religious history of England in the Stuart period, or of the origin of the Free Churches of the English-speaking world, cannot afford to ignore the personality of John Robinson or the books which came from his pen.

When the "first collected edition of the Works of the Pastor of the Pilgrim Fathers" [2] appeared, in 1851, Robert Ashton, the editor, prefixed a Memoir, which claimed to contain "all that can be learned respecting Mr. Robinson." He justly remarked that "the parentage, education, youthful predilections, and exploits of a distinguished man, are important to be known; they give an interest and specificness to his biography, and take it out of the mere generalizations of an everyday memoir," but he went on to say, "unhappily, none of these things can be learned respecting Mr. Robinson." [3] Even so recently as 1910 a writer on this subject says, "considering [4] all the time

[1] *Observations Divine and Moral*, 1625, preface.

[2] *The Works of John Robinson*, 3 vols., preface, p. vii. This edition is referred to in these pages as *Works*. I have consulted original editions on vital points.

[3] *Ibid.*, vol. i. p. xiii.

[4] Burrage, *New Facts Concerning John Robinson*, 1910, p. 5.

that has been spent in studying Robinson's life, it is surprising how slight is our present knowledge of his early years."

In the following pages something will be done to fill in the gaps in the biography of John Robinson. The time has arrived for a fresh study of his life and work. We must consider him in connexion with the men and movements of his time. We must picture him against the background of rural, academic, civic, social and religious life in the midst of which he lived. We must look at his works in due perspective, and judge them in relation to the controversies of the time in which they appeared, remembering that the topics handled were then of living interest, though in these days they may seem to be remote and moribund.

Hitherto the Scrooby district of Nottinghamshire, and the village of Austerfield in the adjoining county of Yorkshire, have received special attention as the cradle-home of the church of the Pilgrim Fathers. In the former parish lived the Brewster family, and in their roomy house the early religious meetings of the society were held; in the latter parish William Bradford,[1] the historian and "governor" of Plymouth Plantation, was born. To Joseph Hunter belongs the credit of identifying the homes of these two eminent lay leaders in the "Pilgrim movement," and he fondly designated the district as *maximæ gentis incunabula*. But for the early home of John Robinson, the "Pilgrim pastor," the clerical leader of the movement, we must journey a few miles to the eastward from Scrooby, to the little town of Sturton-le-Steeple. In this part of Nottinghamshire there is a range of hills running north and south, almost parallel with the Trent, a few miles to the westward of that noble river. These hills slope down gently to the broad Trent Valley, and from their heart flow many streamlets of clear, sweet water to join the brimming river. The

[1] Bradford was baptized in the Chapel of St. Helen, Austerfield, March 19, 1589–90; died at New Plymouth, May 9, 1657. Both he and Brewster were on the *Mayflower*.

soil is fertile, and the firm ground of the foothills between the marshy lands nearer the river and the more exposed hill-tops was early chosen as a desirable place of habitation. The earth is here friable and easily worked, and the pasturage is good for cattle. The Trent afforded a fine waterway, giving access down-stream to the ports of the north and the Humber, and up-stream to Newark, Nottingham, and the heart of England.

The old Roman road from Lincoln to Doncaster crossed the river by a ford at Agelocum, now known as Littleborough, and passed in a north-westerly direction over the water-logged ground near the river. Two miles from the ford, the Roman "ramper," as it is still called, joined the road connecting the homesteads and hamlets lying north and south along the foot of these hills that form the watershed between the Trent and Idle valleys, and here a village grew up, to which the name Estretton—the town on the Street—was given. In due course a fine parish church was built and dedicated to St. Peter and St. Paul. It was embellished with a magnificent pinnacled tower, which serves as a landmark for miles around. This striking feature of the village gives the definitive term to its present title, Sturton-le-Steeple, and so distinguishes it from other Sturtons in that part of England. The village, geographically, was in the North Clay [1] division of the wapentake or hundred of Bassetlaw. Its position, like that of the neighbouring manors, was fairly well defined even at the time of the great survey embodied in Domesday Book. The Archbishop of York held large estates in the neighbourhood, granted to his See before the Conquest, and represented to-day by the "Liberty of Southwell and Scrooby." [2]

The district was well peopled, and there were many small freeholders. I am inclined to think, from a

[1] Hence the alternative designation—Sturton-in-the-Clay—which was sometimes used.

[2] The Charter by which King Edgar made this grant may still be read in the *Liber Albus* at York.

perusal of Subsidy Rolls for the locality, that Sturton and its neighbourhood carried a larger population in the days of Henry VIII and Elizabeth than it does to-day. Three of the old parishes adjoining the Sturton of John Robinson's time have in modern days been merged in neighbouring parishes, and the churches of West Burton, Habblesthorpe and South Wheatley, on which Robinson's eyes must often have rested, have fallen into ruin, and were long ago dismantled.

In mediæval times, if resident incumbents were not available for these small parochial cures, they were served by priests from the neighbouring religious houses, of which there was an abundance. At Mattersey stood the Gilbertine Priory of St. Helen, granted at the Dissolution of the Monasteries to Anthony Nevill and Mary his wife,[1] members of a family to whom we shall have further occasion to refer. Blyth was the seat of a Benedictine settlement, while Worksop had an active colony of Augustinian monks, with a noble priory church. The trouble was that these religious houses engrossed for their own purposes the Church revenues of such parochial "livings" as were granted to them. The tithes, levied in the first instance for the maintenance of a resident parish clergyman, were in these cases collected for a distant monastery, and the parish had to be content with the perfunctory services of a visiting priest, or depend on an ill-paid vicar. If these revenues had been restored to parochial Church uses at the Dissolution of the Monasteries, as the Puritan clergy later on desired them to be, the smaller parishes would not have languished. Their position in respect to religious services was often rendered worse than before, because the rectorial and vicarial tithes held by the monasteries were now granted for the most part to laymen, and diverted altogether from ecclesiastical uses.

The tithes of Sturton itself were farmed out by the

[1] Grant of the house and monastery of the Priory of Mattersey and the manor of Mattersey, as Thomas Norman, late prior, held the same. November 1539, *Letters and Papers of Henry VIII*, vol. xiv. p. 220.

Dean and Chapter of the cathedral church at York, the clerical patrons of the living, and it must have been necessary for the parishioners to supplement the scanty revenue assured to their vicar by substantial voluntary offerings.

The social life of Sturton in Robinson's boyhood was still largely conditioned by feudal ideas and practices. The "great family" was that of the Manners, the Earls of Rutland, whose seat was at Belvoir Castle. They had a finger in the affairs of Sturton and Littleborough in virtue of holding the Manor of Oswaldbec Soke (which extended into those two parishes) and owning rights in Littleborough Ferry. They appointed bailiffs to look after their interest in the Soke.

In Sturton itself, with its dependent township of Fenton, there were three leading families—Lassells, Fenton and Thornhagh, with a goodly sprinkling of yeomanry of lesser rank, such as the Whites, Smyths, Sturtons, Flowers, Dickons, Bellamys and Eatons.

The Lassells Family

The lord of the Manor of Sturton in the earlier part of the reign of Henry VIII was Thomas Lord Darcy (1467–1537), appointed, June 18, 1509, as warden of the forests beyond Trent. He took a prominent part in public affairs in the North, but brought himself into trouble through his support of the rebellion known as the Pilgrimage of Grace, which broke out in Lincolnshire in the autumn of 1536 owing to dissatisfaction at the suppression of the religious houses. He was charged with treason, and executed on the last day of June 1537. A scramble for his lands at once ensued. We find that George Lassells was in London in the early days of 1539 suing for "the late Lord Dersy's lands in Stirton." His brother, John Lassells, was in the service of Thomas Cromwell, and the family gained some pickings from the confiscated monastic lands. George Lassells had been busy in March 1538, with Sir John Markham, Sir John Hercy of Grove, and John Babyngton of Rampton, in suppressing Lenton Priory and bringing the Prior to trial and execution in accordance with the powers of a commission from the King. It was he who carried the report of their proceedings to London.[1] A letter from Sir John Hercy to Thomas Cromwell, dated from Grove, October 31, 1538, has survived, in which Hercy refers to his "cousin John Lassells," and then goes on to say, "I beg you will remember your servant Lassells to have the preferment of Beyvall Abbey for the setting forward of a faithful brother, and you shall command me, having no children, to help him."[2]

Beauvale Abbey will come into our story again, as it was thence that John Robinson took his bride to be married in 1604.

A landmark in the township of Sturton was "Mr. Lasseles wyndmylne."[3] Some of his lands in Sturton and Fenton were sold away by George Lassells on August 10, 1545, for £68 to "Anthony Thorney."[4] In Robinson's time the Lassells family moved to Gateford, near Worksop, but they continued to exert an influence as landowners in Sturton. The ancestors of Robinson's wife bought their homestead in Sturton from this family.[5]

The Fenton Family

The Fentons of Fenton Hall were of good old stock long settled in the parish of Sturton, and supplied their country with several men who did good work in the public service. Two branches of the family appear in the Heralds' Visitations of the county, one descended from Sir Richard Fenton, Knt., Lord of Fenton, to which belonged Captain Edward Fenton,

[1] *Letters and Papers of Henry VIII*, vol. xiii. Pt. I. pp. 225, 294, 388.

[2] *Ibid.*, vol. xiii. Pt. II, No. 726. This request was not granted. Beauvale Abbey was allowed to continue another two years, and was surrendered by the Prior, Thos. Woodcock, July 18, 1540.

[3] *Vide* Will of Wm. Flower of Sturton, husbandman, 1602.

[4] Add. MS., Brit. Mus. 30,997, f. 17.

[5] Exchequer Depositions, Notts. Mich. 5, xi., Chas. I.

who commanded the *Mary Rose* with gallantry in the great Armada fight, and won distinction as a navigator and explorer. Tales of his adventures and the strange lands he visited would filter through to his old home and be talked over round the winter firesides in Sturton, and so reach the ear of young John Robinson. Another member of this branch was Sir John Fenton, who filled the difficult post of Secretary for Ireland with credit. This family of Fentons intermarried with the Disneys and Nevilles.

The second branch, of humbler station, looked to Thomas Fenton, of Fenton, Notts., as its founder. One of its members, Lawrence Fenton, married Catherine Leggatt of Sturton, a sister of George Leggatt, the first husband of Catherine Carver. There is evidence that the Robinsons also were in some way connected with these Fentons, for John Robinson, the father of the "Pilgrim Pastor," appointed William Fenton, his "lovinge Cozen," as one of the "overseers" of his will.

The Thornhagh Family

The Thorney or Thornhagh family[1] were also of old local stock. They acquired land in Fenton by the marriage of John Thornhagh with Katherin, the daughter of Francis Paine of Fenton before the year 1440, and continued to add to their possessions in the locality by purchases from various small yeomen and landowners. In the period with which we are concerned the family was further enriched by the marriage of John Thornhagh with Elizabeth, the daughter and heiress of Brian Bailles, who had made a fortune in Yorkshire as a merchant by dealings in Leeds, Wakefield and Hull, to which towns he left bequests. With their rising fortunes a grant of arms was applied for and secured, and the son, John Thorn-

[1] An excellent account of the Thornhagh family, drawn up by B. G. in the year 1683, based on "their old Evidences. and other Authorities," is contained in Add. MS. 30,997 in the British Museum.

hagh the younger, served as a cadet in the Manners household at Belvoir Castle, and was knighted. When John, the fourth Earl of Rutland, died, John Thornhagh the younger was in attendance on the family. The Countess Elizabeth was then in residence at Winkburn.[1] There she gave birth (October 17, 1588) to a posthumous daughter, who was baptized twelve days later as Frances. In the same church, on the following February 5, "Francis, son of John Thornhaighe, gentleman," was baptized.

The elder John Robinson was brought into close association with John Thornhagh. The will of Richard Worsley of Sturton, 1588, contains this clause, "I desyere Mr. John Thornhaghe esquier, John Robinson, and William Hunter of Fenton, yoman, to be the supervisors of this my last will." [2] As a Justice of the Peace, Thornhagh had much of the public work of the locality to attend to, and in this he was assisted by a young ward of his, Edward Southworth [3] by name, between whom and young John Robinson a firm and fast friendship grew up. Young Sir John Thornhagh went on the grand tour to Italy in 1596, and became member of Parliament for Retford in 1603. His son Francis went up to Cambridge about the year that the "Pilgrims," under Robinson's lead, were leaving their old homes for Holland. He was there in April 1608, and subsequently travelled, writing home from Orleans September 4, 1611, to his father. His life crosses the thread of our story in later years.

We may note that when Roger, Earl of Rutland, was made Chief Justice of Sherwood Forest, he appointed John Thornhagh, senior, his Deputy and Lieutenant for the forest by a deed dated June 18, 1600.

Old John Thornhagh lived on till 1614, and so long

[1] Winkburn was a Donative, and had been a Cell or Camera of the Knights Hospitallers, dependent on their Commandery, at Newland, Yorkshire.

[2] Wills at York, vol. xxiii. f. 735.

[3] His widow, Alice, and his sons Constant and Thomas Southworth, subsequently went to Plymouth, New England.

as he lived he rather overshadowed his son Sir John. He directed that his body was to be buried "within the Chancell of the parish church of Sturton," and left the bulk of his property to his "beloved son, Sir John Thornagh, Knight," with £1000 to his grandson Francis, and £700 and £500 respectively to the grandchildren Elizabeth and "Brigett" Thornhagh. The vicar, Christopher Fielding, witnessed the will, along with Gregory Starky and Wm. Webber, "my man."

At the *Inquisition Post Mortem*, held at East Retford September 28, 1614, the jury presented that he held Fenton Hall "as of ye King's Manor of Oswaldbeck Soke in free Socage by Fealty and Suit of Court to ye said Manor and by ye rent of 15*s*. 7½*d*. p. annum." Other of his lands in Sturton were held of "the King's Manor of Bassetlawe parcell of his Duchy of Lancaster by fealty and suit of Court to the said manor twice a yeare."

The Robinsons of Sturton

Perhaps it was in connexion with some of the changes resultant upon the forfeiture of the Darcy estates or the enclosure of fresh lands in the locality that the Robinson family became established in Sturton. There were those of the name among the landholders of several parishes within easy distance of Sturton, but I do not find it among the names of the "Archers" and "Billmen" of Sturton and Fenton in the thirtieth year of King Henry's reign (1537), nor does it occur in the list of Sturton residents who contributed to a "Benevolence" for that monarch in 1543. When we turn to a list of Sturton taxpayers for the next year, however, we find Christopher Robinson amongst those assessed on the value of their lands. The nominal annual value of his holding is given as £1 6*s*. 8*d*., while that of Anthony Thorney, the highest in the parish, is £10. In 1571 Christopher Robinson still held his place in the parish, and under a new assessment he paid his subsidy on lands then valued at £2.[1] When we reach the year 1585 Christopher Robinson has dropped out, and "John Robinson" takes his place, paying the same tax of five shillings and fourpence on lands of the same value as Christopher Robinson had held. It is natural to infer that in the intervening time Christopher had died, and that John Robinson, who declared in 1603 that he was born at Sturton, was the son who succeeded to his farm.

One glimpse we have of Christopher Robinson in his lifetime which shows him in touch with the Fenton family. This was at the signing of the will of Thomas Fenton, July 25, 1552, when Christopher Robinson, Alexander Nevell and Wm. Wollay attended and signed the document as witnesses.

I take it that John Robinson the elder, as we must call him, to distinguish him from his gifted son, was born about 1550,[2] and had come to man's estate and married shortly after the death of Christopher Robinson. Soon a son was born to him and his good wife Ann, and the young father settled down to steady work to win a livelihood for his growing household. To the eldest son the name John was given. Doubtless he was taken to the parish church for baptism in the ordinary way by the vicar of the parish. The registers of Sturton are not extant for this period, in fact they do not begin till the year 1638, so we gain no help from them, and can only say that young John Robinson was born about the year 1576. Other children came to brighten the home of this Nottinghamshire yeoman: a son William, a daughter Mary and another daughter. These lived to manhood and womanhood, surviving their parents. When the future Pastor of the Pilgrims was about seven years old, Sturton was afflicted with an infectious sickness, which swept away many of its inhabitants, but he and his father's family happily survived.

[1] Lay Subsidies in the Record Office, Bassetlaw, Notts. Roll 160–206. See Appendix A.

[2] He deposed in 1591 that he was "thirty-six years or thereabouts"; in 1603 that he was fifty-three years of age, and in 1609 that he was sixty. There was no exactitude.

I have found several contemporary references to the elder John Robinson which go to show that he was a man of probity and dependable character, winning the regard and esteem of neighbours and fellow-parishioners. Richard Worsley, yeoman, of Sturton, in making his will, March 26, 1588, appointed this John Robinson as "supervisor," that is to say, he trusted him to see the provisions of the will duly carried out. Three years later we find Robinson giving evidence at East Retford on behalf of the Dowager Countess of Rutland.

In 1599 he and Robert Poole were nominated as "supervisors" of the will of Ellen White of Fenton, one of whose sons appears to have crossed in the *Mayflower*. Then in the will of William Flower of Sturton, dated June 29, 1602, "John Robinson, yeoman," was appointed, together with "John Quippe, Clerk, our vicar," to receive a bond from Margaret Flower as an assurance that she would keep her son and his houses and lands "sufficientlie according to the order of the lawe" till he was of age. Flower refers in a codicil to "my lovinge neighbour, John Robinson." The will itself concludes with these terms—

> "I desire John Quippe, Clerk, and John Robinson to be the supervisors of this my last will and testam^t to see all things p'formed in it to the pleasure of god and my soules healthe. These being witnesses John Quippe, George Smyth, John Bate." [1]

If Margaret Flower declined her obligation, then William Flower directed that "John Quippe, Clerke, and John Robinsonne shall have the tuicon of my sonne."

In 1604, the year of his son's wedding, old John Robinson witnessed the will of Thomas Sturton of Sturton, signing the document along with "Christopher ffieldinge, clerke, George Diccons, Willm Haworth, Thomas Lassells, Robert Heppenstall, and Dennis

[1] Probate Registry at York, vol. xxviii. f. 830.

Barmbie." Six years or so later he did a similar service, together with "Christofer ffeildinge, Cler.," and Robert Bishop, for one of his humbler neighbours, John Cawthorne. I also find him mentioned in connexion with the vicar of Sturton in the will of Anne Padley, which was executed March 11, 1610–11. Both of them sign as witnesses to this document.

"*Itm* I give unto Christopher ffeildinge, clerke, tenne shillings and unto John Robinson three shillings fourepence and I do desire the said Christopher ffeilding and John Robinson that they would be the supervisors of this my last will and testament to see the true performance thereof."

Now it is clear from these references that John Robinson the elder was held in good esteem by those amongst whom he lived, and was accustomed to act in close association with John Quipp, who was vicar of the parish in the boyhood of young John Robinson, and with Fielding, his successor in the benefice of Sturton. In all likelihood young Robinson received some of his early education under the guidance of John Quipp. Moreover, he had the priceless advantage of having constantly before him the example of the industry and integrity of his father—a man whose judgment was sought and trusted in the valuation of the cattle and effects of his neighbours, and whose testimony was recognized to be of weight in affairs concerning the interest and welfare of the locality.

The wills of both parents of the Pastor of the Pilgrims I found registered in York. They give us authentic information as to the family, and throw fresh light on the position it held in the Sturton district.

The Will of John Robinson's Father

Extracted from the District Probate Registry at York attached to His Majesty's High Court of Justice.

"In the Name of God Amen the fourteenth daye of March in the yeare of o^r^ Lorde God one thousand sixe hundred and thirteene I John Robinson of Sturton in the Countie of Notts Yeoman beinge weeke of bodie but of good and perfect memorie praise bee given to God therefore doe make and ordaine this my last Will and Testament in manner and forme followinge That is to say First I bequeathe my soule to Almightie God my Creator and to Iesus Christ my Redeemer by whose precious blood sheading I have an assured hope of salvation and my body to the earth from whence it came.

Itm I give to the poore of Sturton and Fenton sixe pounde thirteen shillinge fourpence to bee payed w^th^in one yeare after my decease

Itm I give and bequeathe unto John Robinson my eldest sonne five marks and his wife xx^s^ and to John theire sonne fourtie shilling*es* and to everie of their other children xx^s^ apiece.

Itm I give and bequeath unto William Robinson my Younger sonne one hundred and five pound*es* and to the wife of the said William xx^s^ to everie of their children xx^s^.

Itm I give to my sonne in lawe Roger Lawson xx^li^ wch he owed me upon condicon that he performe a will and a guifte wch he made to William Pearte.

Itm I give to William Pearte my sonne in lawe xx^s^ to his wife xx^s^ and to everie one of theire children xx^s^.

Itm I give and bequeath to Richard Barke and his wyfe x^s^.

Itm I give and bequeath to John Mytton my servant tenne shillinge and to Joane Greene ij^s^ vi^d^.

Itm I give to my Cosen William Fenton x^s^ and to his Daughter my Goddaughter ij^s^ vj^d^.

Itm I ordaine and make my lovinge wyfe Anne Robinson my whole and sole Executrix of this my last Will and Testament to whome I doe give and bequeath all the residue of my Goods and Cattels not before by me given and bequeathed she to see my debts and legacies satisfied and my funerall expenses discharged And lastly I desyre my lovinge Cozen William Fenton my lovinge sonne William Peart to bee overseers of this my last Will and Testament in Witness whereof I have hereunto set my hand the daye and yeare above written. Red signed and acknowledged in the p'nce of William Fenton Robert Bishopp."

On the 19th day of August 1614 the Will of Iohn Robinson late of Sturton in the County of Nottingham Yeoman deceased was proved by the oath of Anne Robinson the Relict and sole Executrix.

Will of John Robinson's Mother

"In the name of God, Amen, the sixteenth day of October in the yeare of our Lord God 1616. I Ann Robinson of Sturton in the countye of Nottingham widowe beinge aged and weake in body but whole and sound in mynd and of good and p'fect remembrance thankes be to Almightye god and perceiving and consideringe the instabilitye of this vaine and transitory world and the shortness of mannes lyfe therein doe ordaine and make this my last will and testament heareby revoking and absolutely adnullinge thereby all and everye former will and testament by me in anywise heretofore made in manner and forme followinge that is to say ffirst and principally into the hands of Allmightye Godd my creator redeemer and sanctifier I commend my soule assuredly hope-inge and trustinge in and by the meritts death and passion of his deare sonne Jesus Christ my onely lord and Saviour to be one of his electe and blessed Companye in the kingdom of heaven and by noe other way or meanes whatsoever.

And my body I committ to the earth to be interred or buried in the p'ish church of Sturton beforesaid or else wheare it shall please God to call me to his mercy.

Itm I give and bequeath unto the poore people of Stourton and ffenton fortye shilling of lawfull money of England to be given and bestowed at my funerall at the disposition of my sonne in lawe William Pearte.

Itm I give unto my sonne John my sonne and heire apparent the some of fortye shillings of lyke lawfull money of Englande.

Itm I give and bequeath unto Bridgett Robinson wife to my said sonne John one paire of lynninge sheets and one silver spoon.

Itm I give and bequeath to John Robinson sonne of my said sonne John Robinson the some of fortye shillings and to every one of my said sonne John his children the some of xx^{s}.

Itm I give and bequeath unto my said sonne John Robinson all the pailes railes stoupes gates and all fences round about the messuage or Toftstead wherein I now dwell wth all and singular rackes and maingers beastes houses and plowhows wth all the glasse about the said messuage to remaine and be to him and his heires for ever.

Itm I give and bequeath unto Ellen my sonne William his wife one paire of lyninge sheets and a silver spoone and to every one of his children twenty shillings.

Itm I give unto fower of the children of my sonne in law

William Pearte that is to say to William, Thomas, Originall and John Pearte everye of them the some of xx^{s}.

Itm I give and bequeath unto Mr. Charles White of Stourton ten shillings And I appoint and make him (as I trust he will be) to be superv^{r} and overseer of this my said last will and testament.

Itm I give and bequeath to Marye my daughter and wife to the said William Pearte all my wearinge app'ell wolle and lynnen.

Itm I give and bequeath unto John Robson ijs & vj^{d}. *Itm* unto Jone Greene s'vante other two shillings and sixpence

Itm I give and bequeath unto my said sonne William Robinson, my debts legacies and funerall expenses pd and discharged all and singular the motye [moiety] and halfe p'te of all my goods cattalls and chattles quicke and deade moveable and unmoveable of what kynd quantity or quality soe^{r} they be and unbequeathed.

And I make and ordaine my said son in law William Pearte my sole executor of this my laste will and testament and doe give and bequeath unto the said William Pearte all and singular the other motye and halfe of all my said goods cattells and chattells quicke and deade moveable and unmoveable of what kynd quantytye or qualitye soever they be and unbequeathed.

In witness whereof I have hereunto set my hand and seale the day and yeare ffirste above written. These beinge witnesses George Dickons Robt Byshopp George Halton."

This will was proved by the oath of William Pearte on January 16, 1616–17, and probate was granted by the Exchequer Court of York.

CHAPTER II

JOHN ROBINSON'S WIFE

ANOTHER household of Sturton with which our story is concerned is that of the Whites, for it was from this family that John Robinson, the pastor, eventually took his bride, in the person of Bridget White. She made an excellent wife and mother. The White family was settled at Sturton earlier than the Robinsons. While we can point with probability to the grandfather of John Robinson, we can do so with certainty to the grandfather of his wife, who was Thomas White, sometime bailiff for the manor of Sturton. He made his will, October 14, 1579, directing that he was to be buried " in the churche or churche yeard of Sturton." He was then a widower, and his will gives no indication of his wife's name or family. The main bequests are as follows—

" I will and bequeath to Alexander Whyt my eldest sonne all my Glass and paile aboute the nowe dwellingehouse of me the abovesaid Thomas White his ffaither and also my best gowne."

To his son " John Whyte " he left his " ffurred gowne "; to his son William " a Satten dublet and a sleveles damaske coote and a Jackett of marble and a pair of my best slivinge hoise "; to each of his three daughters, Elizabeth, Mary and Jane, " two kyne "; to Jane Davis, his servant, he bequeathed " a yonge waill headed white cowe and xl[s] for her two yeares waiges and four quarters of barlye and the bedd which I lye in and all the furnyture thereunto belonging." Other of his servants were suitably remembered with gifts of cattle or "freese cootes." Then, after a bequest of xiij^{s} iiij^{d} "to the poore people" of Sturton, "to be distributed among them the day of my funerall," the residue of his goods he gives "unto Alexander Whyte John White and William Whyte my three sonnes to be equallie divided amongst them," and with a schedule of debts[1] owing and due, and instructions to Alexander to "maike John Bowles lease according to the articles before drawn for xxi yeares," and to let "Willm Davis have his house for the terme of his lyfe payinge for the same xx^{s} by the yeare," the document ends. It reveals an estate of a value rather higher than those of the average yeomen in the district.

Soon after his father's death, Alexander White married Eleanor Smith and brought her to his home in Sturton. It was a good match. Eleanor Smith was the daughter of William and Katherine Smith of Honington, in the county of Lincoln. If you visit the pleasantly-situated church of St. Wilfrid at Honington, standing on the hill behind the vicarage, you can see the tomb erected to the memory of her father, with a full-length brass representing William Smith in his long robe, "guarded" with fur or velvet trimming and graced with a collarette. A monogram is on each side of his head, one combining the initial letters of the Christian names of himself and his wife, the other his own.

The inscription tells us something of the family.

HERE LIETH WILLIAM SMITH ESQIER WHO DECESED . Y^{E} . X OF . FEBRVARY . AN . DO . MDLI . HE MARIED [KATHERINE DAVGHTER OF] AVGVSTINE PORTER OF BELTON ESQVIER AND HAD ISSVE BY HER THRE SONES . Y^{T} . IS . TO . SAYE AVGVSTINE . WILLIAM . AND EDMONDE AND THRE DAVGHTERS ELIZABETH . ELENOR . et . M$\overset{R}{A}$G$\overset{R}{A}$ET

[1] "*Itm* I owe unto John Curnell for a horse lvs," gives us an idea of the current value of horses.

Something, I say, but not all, for Katherine Porter was a forceful woman, and after the death of William Smith, she married Thomas Disney of Carlton-le-Moorland, who sat in the Parliament of 1563 as member for Boroughbridge. She had borne six children to her first husband, and now had another family of equal number, five sons and a daughter, by her second. The Disneys played a prominent part in Lincolnshire affairs.

By his marriage with Eleanor Smith, Alexander White was brought into touch with several prominent local families. His wife's sister of the full blood, Elizabeth Smith, married Edward Saltmarshe of Strubby, in the adjacent county of Lincoln; while her sister of the half-blood was married, at St. Margaret's, Lincoln, in 1577, to William Monson, a clergyman, a poorish member of a powerful county family, who, perhaps owing to his large number of children, or a reckless habit of spending, does not seem to have made much of things, and died early.

Remembering the hospitable customs of the time, it will be realized that there were plenty of good homes in the counties of Notts. and Lincoln open to the visitation of the Whites. But the energies of the young couple would soon be absorbed in the affairs of their own household, for year by year it increased in number. First came a daughter, who was named Catherine, after her grandmother. She was destined to cross the Atlantic in the *Mayflower* on its memorable voyage. Then came a son, who was christened Charles; a daughter, Bridget, followed, in whom we are specially interested, then three younger sons, Thomas and Roger (of whom we shall hear again in Holland), and Edward, and the family closed with daughters, Jane and Frances, both of whom went to Leyden with the Pilgrim Church. In spite of the increased charges and responsibilities which his growing family brought, Alexander White and his wife prospered and ventured to take on lease properties at some distance from Sturton, amongst them

Beauvale Abbey, in the parish of Greasley. When John Thornhagh, the elder, bought eight acres of land on October 26, 1591, from George Eaton and Francis Eaton, of Fenton, for £30, Alexander White, together with John Thornhagh, junior, witnessed the deed.

In March 1594–5 Alexander White drew up his will, and must have died soon after, as it was proved by his widow in May of the following year. An abstract of the document will give us an idea of the standing of the family and the piety of the household.

I have identified the residence of the Whites as the house and farm known as Wybornedale. The form now used in the parish terrier is Wyberton, and in going through the old "Town's Book" the variants Wybendale, Wibaldon, and Warbendale can he traced.[1] Fields to the west of the village, bounded by Freeman's Lane on the north and Wood Lane on the east, still perpetuate the name.

The Will of John Robinson's Father-in-Law

"In the name of God Amen the xvth day of Mche in the yeare of or lord 1594 I Alexander White of Sturton in the County of Notts beinge holl in health and perfect memory praised be God therefore, do ordaine constitute and make this my last will and testament in mannr and forme followinge. First I comend my soule into the hands of the liveinge god my Creatr and maker most humbly beseechinge him for his deare Sonn Jesus Christ his sake my Redeemer to accept the same by whose death and passion I stedfastly believe my sinnes shalbe remitted and pardoned and the wrath of God his father against me for the same appeased and by whose resurrection and assention I likewise stedfastly trust before his matie both in soule and body at the last day to be justified in the meantime my body to be buried in the earth when and where it shall please God to appoint and for such porcon of these vaine transitory and earthly goods as it hath pleased the lord in his goodness to make me Steward of for the stablishinge of my conscience and quietinge of my wyfe and children so farr as the same shall extend I will shall be divided and bequeathed in such sorte as in this my pnte will shalbe declared and appointed First I will that all my

[1] Letter dated September 15, 1916, from Mr. S. Ingham, of Sturton-le-Steeple.

debtes be dewly and truly paied at such dayes and tymes as the same is or shalbe dew Item I give to the poore people of Sturton xx^{s} to my sister Palliley xx^{s} and every one of her and my Sister pooles children one ewe lamb To Thomas Laicock over and besides his child parte in my handes xx^{s} Item I give unto the Children of my brother John White and Willm̃ White foure pounds yearely of the com̃oditie of my lease at Wragby equally to be devided amongst them dureinge the continuance of the said lease. Item I give unto my sonn Charles White all my seelinge stuffe timber stone troughes glass pale and Rale about my house Item I give unto every one of my Daughters Katherin Bridget Jane and Frances one hundred marks of lawful English money to be paid them when they shall accomplish the age of xxj^{tie} years and if any of them dye before that age then the parte of that dead one to be devided amongst the rest of my Children Item I give to every one of my young^{r} Sonnes Thomas, Roger, and Edward White Two yeares profitt of my lease at Muskhm̃ and Carleton and to every one of them one annutie or yearely Rent of five poundes of lawfull English money to be taken out of my lands and tenem^{ts} in Sturtonne to have and to hold severally unto every one of them and their assigns after such tymes as he or they shall accomplish the age of xxj^{tie} yeares the said Annāll rent of v^{li} yearly to every one of them for and during their naturall lives provided alwaies that my meaninge is that the survivo^{rs} of them shall have but his or their onely rent of v^{li} yearly and the particular v^{li} to sease at the death of every one of them. The Residew of all my landes Messuages tenem^{ts} and other hereditaments whatsoever in Sturton and Littlebrough and also of all my Goods and cattells moveable and immovable I give and bequeath unto Ellene^{r} my loveinge wife whome I make sole Executrix of this my last will and Testament and tutor and garden of all my said Children towards her maintenn̄ce and bringing up of my said Children and dureinge her naturall life yielding & paying unto my said sonne Charles and if he die unto my next heir twentie marks yearly at the Feast of St Michael the Archangell and annunciation of the blessed Virgin Ste Marie after such tyme as he or they shall accomplish the age of xxi years and also the said annuities of v^{li} yearly to my young^{r} sonnes as is aforesaid and if it please God my wyfe be married after my said sonne and heir shall accomplish his said [age] of xxj^{tie} yeares then my will is that my said sonne and heir shall have and hold all my said lands messuages and tenements in Sturton and Littlebrough if he will and pay therefore unto my said Wyfe dureinge her naturall life xx^{li}

yearely of lawfull English money and also the said annuities of vli yearly unto my said Younger children and if the said annuities of vli yearly be not payd unto my said Youngr sonne[s] yearely as I have appointed at the Feast of St Michael and thannunciation of the Blessed Virgin St Marie or wthin xv dayes after either of the said Feastes by even porcons then my finall will is that my said Youngr Sonnes Thomas Roger and Edward shall have and hould all that my Messuage in nethr Sturton and all lande meadows and pastures thereto belonging untill they be satisfied of the said yearly rent and the arrerages thereof if any be.

Witnesses Robert Poole Charles White.

On the 6th day of Maij 1596 the Will of Alexander White late of Sturton in the County of Notts was proved by the Oath of Ellenore White widow the Relict and sole Executrix."

Soon after her father's death Catherine White was married to George Leggatt, a member of a yeoman family long settled at Sturton, and soon the widowed Eleanor White attained the dignity of " grandmother " by the advent of a daughter to the home of the Leggatts, who was named Marie. Before many years had passed Catherine Leggatt lost her husband, and in course of time she married John Carver. It was a happy choice. Carver I take to have belonged to a family represented in the Sturton district in the time of Henry VIII, at which period the name occurs in the Rolls. I do not think the Carvers held land. But Carver was skilled in farm management, and Catherine found him of the greatest possible service in the management of the estate which her first husband left her. Carver, quiet and dependable, had sound common sense, and made her a good husband. He won the affection and regard of John Robinson, and it was on account of his solid merit that he was chosen as the first governor of the Plymouth Colony.

With the marriage of her eldest sister a great deal of responsibility would be thrown upon Bridget, the second daughter in the White family. There were many mouths to provide for, many limbs to clothe, and a large house, for those days, to be kept in order. Bridget received a thorough drilling in all household arts under her mother's careful guidance, much to the advantage of the future home of the pastor of the Pilgrim Church, where the cares of the house were lifted from the master's shoulders, and his mind left free for his pastoral work.

But the health of Eleanor White was failing under the strain of caring for so large a family, and, like the wise woman that she was, she sought to set her affairs in order and make what provision she could for the welfare of her infant children. On April 7, 1599, she made her will, and died within the next few months. The document, with its concern for details of the house and its furnishing, bears the woman's touch, and gives us a good idea of the plenishing and equipment of the home in which John Robinson was, no doubt, a frequent visitor.

Eleanor White here describes herself as " late wife of Alexander White of Sturton." The preamble follows the same form as that in her husband's will. We may note the following bequests—

" I give to my daughter Janie[1] White over and besides the porcon given her by her father xxxiij^{li} vj^{s} viij^{d} " and a like amount in like terms " to my daughter ffrancis White."

To " my sonne Charles White fowerr standing bedsteades, fower covred stooles of one sorte, fower cushens sutable, one cupbord in the best chamber and another cupbord in the great chamber two tables wth there frames and two joyned chaires there; one great chist in my owne chamber . . All the tables cupboarde stooles and formes in the Hall a Vallence of needlework five silk curtaines two of my best fether-bedds two bolsters two payre of fustian pillowes two good mattresses two pair of my best blankitts my best counterpoint wth three of my best covrlets six paire of lynnen sheets and six paire of pillow beares marked with a C two dozen of table napkins two broad table clothes two cupbord clothes my maryage Ringe, my silver salte, one bowl one pott p'cell guilt and six silver spoones, all his fathers bookes, all my

[1] The mother's affectionate diminutive for her daughter in place of the father's plain Jane.

brasse and my pewther wth dishbricke [1] and all boords and cupbords in the kitchen and buttry, all my housells Imple-m[en]ts of husbandrie, ymplements belonging to the stable to the brewhouse to the backhouse kilnehouse, oxehouse and cowhouse and evrye of them.

Itm all the rest of the benefitt and yearly profitt of my lease at Muskham [2] not given by my husband I give and bequeath to my three sonnes Thomas, Roger and Edward whereof my will is that as ev'ry of my said sonnes shall accomplish the aige of xiiij yeares xxli shalbe bestowed towards the binding of them apprentices at London in sure good places . . . . if my Executors and Supervisors shall think them fitt to be put for prentices and if not then the said money to be bestowed for there best advantage . . . . till they come to xxjtie yeares of aige.

Itm I give to my said three sonnes Thomas, Roger, and Edward besides all the benefitt of my lease of Muskħm evrye one of them xxli to be put furth by my exors . . to there best p'fitt and advantage as they shall accomplish there sevrall aiges of fifteene yeares.

Itm I give to my sonne Legatt and his wife [Catherine] tenne pounde betwixt them and to theire daughter Marie Legatt xli wch I will shalbe putt furth for her best advantage when shee shall come to her aige of tenne years . . . . . . to my five youngest children Thomas, Roger, Edward, Janie, and ffrancis xijli xs a yeare out of my lease at Beavall for seven yeares after my deathe.

To my daughter Legatt two paire of lynnen sheets one longe needleworke cushen and two paire of pillowbeares [3] in full satisfaccon of her childes porcon.

Itm I give to my daughter Bridgett fiftie pounde in money ij paire of lynnen sheets ij paire of pillowbeeres two table-clothes one longe needleworke cushen a dozen of napkins two lynnen towells and my newe silvr bowle . . . . to my daughter Janie one silvr spoone two paire of lynnen sheetes and two paire of pillowbeeres . . . to my daughter Francis one silvr spoone guilt, ij paire of lynnen sheets and two paire of pillowbeeres.

Itm I will that the porcon given to my daughter Janie by her father's will and myne shalbe paid within one yeare after my death and put furth . . . to her best profitt and

[1] Earthenware or crockery.

[2] There are two Muskhams, North and South, parishes of Notts., near Newark.

[3] Pillow-cases in modern English.

advantage till her maryage or full aige of xxi yeares . . . of the profitt I do allott v^{li} yearlie for her maintenance and the rest to go forward to the increase of her porcon.

Francis her full porcon shalbe paid within one yeare next after my death to my sonne Leggatt to her use if his wife be then livinge unto whom I committ the bringinge upp of my said daughter [I allot] v^{li} yearlie for her bringing up and mayntenance [the balance was to go forward]

I bequeath to my brother [1] Willm̄ Smith vj^{li} xiij^{s} iiij^{d} to be paid within one yeare after my deathe if he depart this life before receipt thereof then I will it shalbe equallie divided amongst his children.

Itm I give to my sister [2] Saltmarshe one hooped gold ringe . . . to my nephew Thomas Dysney [3] xx^{s} in money . . . to every one of my sister Mounsons children v^{s} a peice . . . . at their severall aiges of xxi^{te} yeares . . . to my servante Anthony xl^{s} in money . . . every one of my other servants ij^{s} vj^{d} apeice to the poore of Sturton x^{s} . . . every one of my god children ij^{s} vj^{d} . . . to my cosen Robert Poole my best gelding or ells in money vj^{li} xiij^{s} iiij^{d} . . . my cosen Thomas Laycocke [4] x^{s}."

Eleanor White left all the residue to her son, Charles White, and makes him sole executor, committing—

" the tuicon custody and bringing upp of all my five youngest children unto him and I appoint my brother Edward Saltmarshe, my brother Thomas Dysney [5] and my cosen Robert Poole sup'visors thereof to whom I committ my said sonne Charles and the execucon of my Will untill by lawe my said sonne Charles may . . . execute the same And I give to either of my said brethren two Aungells of gold.

[Signed] In the presence of Bridgett White, George Legatt, Anthony Greenesmith."

1 This was William Smith of Honington, Co. Lincoln, her old home.

2 Her sister Elizabeth.

3 This was Thomas Disney (bap. September 8, 1579), a much married man: (1) to Ursula Peterson of Deptford, (2) Elizabeth Denman of Notts., (3) Bridget, daughter of Anthony Nevile, of Mattersey Abbey.

4 The Lacocks possessed land in Sturton in the time of Henry VIII and served under him in France. Their motto was " Verus Honor Honestas."

5 Thomas Disney, half-brother of Eleanor White, fourth son of her mother Katherine (Porter) (Smith). He settled at Newark, and was buried there May 31, 1623.

Probate of the will was granted August 2, 1599, by Dr. George Ormerod, Dean of Retford, to Charles White.

Nothing could give us a better idea, in the same compass, than this document, of the type of home from which John Robinson took his bride. Later on we shall see how some of the money here bequeathed was eventually invested in the purchase of the house at Leyden, which became the dwelling-place of John and Bridget Robinson and the home of the Pilgrim Church.

CHAPTER III

JOHN ROBINSON'S BOYHOOD

We have said enough about the locality in which John Robinson was brought up, and the families of Sturton and the district, to enable us to picture him in his boyhood. There was plenty to interest a bright lad in the life of the district. We can picture him running round to John Halton, the shoemaker, with his sister's shoes to be mended, or watching Richard Smyth, the painter, at his work. When the perambulation of the parish boundaries took place he would be there, tramping along with John Quipp and his parish officers "to the middle of Stafford Bridge." He would help to drive stray cattle and horses to the Sturton pound with the pinder, and accompany his father at times to Gainsborough market to sell the corn, or to Retford to sell their kine. Above all, we think of him on the quiet Sunday mornings accompanying his father and mother to the fine old parish church, where the child's sense of awe and wonder would be drawn out into reverence as his thoughts were turned to the sacred mysteries and awful responsibilities of life.

He, with other village children, was there when weddings were afoot, and when the bells tolled for a funeral [1] he went hushed yet curious to the graveyard to see the last burial rites, and then turned with his playmates to catch the minnows in the Oswald Beck. That stream has run on from Saxon times to these in the same channel and under the same name, a type

[1] "Four shillings to them that helpe to ringe the bells for me the day of my buriall." Will of Wm. Flower of Sturton, June 29, 1602.

of the children of our race—ever changing yet ever the same, ever passing yet always renewed.

If you want to know how the people talked in Sturton in those days, here are two illustrative bits of conversation straight from the time—

"*Memorandum*, 22 Jan. 1608, William Hopkinson of North Leverton husbandman being weak in body but of sane memory did by word of mouth declare his last will . . in this wise, *vidz* Edmund Greene first and then John Roydhous moving him to make his will (quod hee the said Willm.) I will make no scribble scrabble I geve to my son and my daughter either of them two shillings and my blessinge in satisfaction of their portions and so god speed them well and I give to Christopher Bomby one bushell of wheate when god sends it of the ground.

"And being then minded of his wife he answered and said she knoweth my debts I know not hers she shall have the rest of my goods and be my executor." *Act Book*, Southwell Peculiar, vol. B. f. 685.

"*Memorandum* that upon the 18th day of January 1609 Robert Shacklock, Jenat Webster and Katherine Murre beinge att the house of one Willm. Smyth of Sturton whoe then lyinge under the visitacon of the Allmighty the said Jannatt Webster being sister to the said Willm. asked him how he felte himselfe he answered 'sister I sente for you that I mighte take my leave of you for I felte my paines soe great that I am not in hope to recover.' Then she willed him to remember his daughters he aunswered againe and saide as for my daughter Harrison I have remembered her alreadye. Then his wief standing by said unto him 'husband whatsoever you will give them I will p'forme yt' who answeringe againe said 'Doll I found the[e] lyke a woeman and I will leave the lyke one therefore I leave all and give all unto the to dispose of all as thou shalte think good. And I make the my executor." [1]

It is not known what school John Robinson attended. There were schools at Retford, Gainsborough and Lincoln of some standing, where a preparation for the University and a grounding in Latin could be got,

[1] The Court took this as a good will, and granted probate to Dorothy Smyth accordingly. York Probate Registry, *Register Book, Wills*, vol. xxxi. f. 317.

and I have thought that the references to Robinson as from Lincolnshire may have arisen from his attendance at the Gainsborough or Lincoln schools, but the Admission Registers of these grammar schools do not go back sufficiently far to decide the point. He refers in his works to the "posing of schoolboys" as though it were something familiar in his experience. We may take it that his progress in school-learning, whether at Sturton or elsewhere, led his parents to feel that he was fitted to take advantage of a further course of study. If the Smiths could send their boy to college, surely the Robinsons could do the same. So when the time came to decide on young John Robinson's course after his schooldays, his parents resolved to send him to Cambridge. His father was still in the prime of life and well established in Sturton, so he would have less desire to retain the young lad to help him on his land. There must have been consultations with his schoolmaster and probably with the vicar of the parish as to the boy's capacities and future career. His bent for books and love of learning pointed to a college course as promising good results. When once that was determined on, the choice of Cambridge would naturally follow, for the tradition and custom of the district had brought it into closer touch with that University than with Oxford. The Neviles of South Leverton had gone up to Cambridge and were doing well. Antony Hickman of Gainsborough was there, and young John Smith of Sturton had by this time taken his degree of Bachelor of Arts and was well on the way to a fellowship. Moreover Roger (*b.*1576) and Francis Manners (*b.* 1578), sons of the late Earl of Rutland, were both at Cambridge. Roger had been at Queen's College under John Jegon, and moved with him when he became Master of Corpus Christi in 1590, and there Francis joined him. Thither it was decided John Robinson should go. We can picture the excitement in the Robinson household at Sturton when the arrangements for young John's journey to Cambridge were complete and the day of his departure drew near. His mother's distress at parting from him would be tempered by a feeling of pride at his becoming a collegian and by her hopes for his future. In all likelihood she pictured him already in the pulpit. There were leave-takings with companions in the village, and presents of money from old John Thornhagh of Fenton Hall and other of his father's friends to help him on his way. And as he left bright and early in the fresh spring morning to join other hopeful scholars on the great North Road bound for the University, I think it likely that little Bridget White, seeing but unseen, would watch him out of sight.

The students in those days arranged to travel up together, both for the sake of company and for safety. They often carried with them their allowance for the term, and highway robbers were well aware of the fact. Journeying southward through Newark, Grantham, Stamford and Peterborough by easy stages they would at last strike the old Roman Road, the Via Devana, which ran across country from Chester to Colchester. Following this ancient line of traffic, they soon reached Huntingdon, and continued on the road thence towards Cambridge. As they came over the hill by Cambridge Castle, the town on the far side of the river, with its noble buildings, was spread out before them. No young lad coming up to the University could fail to be impressed by his first view of the town. Young Robinson, it is true, would know the magnificent cathedral of Lincoln and the fine parish churches of the district in which he was reared, but this wonderful assemblage of collegiate buildings, hostels, and churches was bound to arrest his attention. How eagerly he would look about him as he and his new friends came down the Castle Hill and through Monks' Place to the Great Bridge! Crossing the river he would pass along to St. Sepulchre's Church, where he probably turned to the right into what was then the High Street, leading to the heart of the town. Then, passing round by the old church of St. Benedict, familiarly known as Benet Church, into Luthburne Lane, he would find the approach to the College of Corpus Christi on his right. It passed beneath a gallery leading from the college to an oratory connected with the church. Turning up this somewhat narrow approach, he came to an arched entrance on his left hand, which led him into the courtyard of the college which was to be for him a second home for many years to come.

NOTE.—From evidence given in a dispute as to a " close " of land on the borders of Sturton and South Wheatley in 1638 we have a glimpse of Sturton life in Robinson's boyhood. The close known as "Woodhouse Field," "Woodhouse Waste," or " Beck Close," was claimed by Sir Francis Thornhagh as parcel of his manor of Oswaldbeck. Richard Smyth of Sturton, " paynter," aged about seventy-two, testified that in or about 1578 it was unenclosed, and he had known " John Toppin and after him Willm Midleton, heardsmen of Stourton, staffe-heard and keepe swine in the saide p'cell of ground in the fallowe yeares and in the open time of the yeare." And Richard Spencer of North Leverton, " laborer," aged sixty, said that about 1591 he had seen " the swine-heard of Stourton keepe the Town swine in the place now in question, and that he did so long agoe kepet a flocke of sheepe in the same ground without interupcon of any." [1] We may be sure that John Robinson, as a boy, would be in at the pig-killings, and be ready to lend a hand in driving the swine and sheep to and from the waste.

In another case, of the year 1636, Laurence Smith of Sturton, husbandman, sixty-six years and more, deposed that about 1603 he had been bailiff of the " Manor of Oswaldbecke." He mentioned the " common pound in Stourton " reputed to be within the Manor of Oswaldbec Soke. It was always repaired by the tenants of that Manor. He declared " the said Com̃on Pounde hath stood in the place where it now is for aboue fiftie yeares to this deponent['s] remembrance." [2] The pound was there, then, in Robinson's youth.

[1] Exchequer Depositions, Notts. 13, Charles I. Mich. The evidence was taken at East Retford, Sept. 28, 1638.

[2] *Ibid.*, Notts., Mich. 5, xi. Charles I.

CHAPTER IV

LIFE AT CAMBRIDGE

"THE House of Scholars of Corpus Christi and Blessed Mary" was already a venerable institution in Robinson's day. It could boast of no royal or lordly founder, for the initial impulse which led to its foundation came from the brethren and members of the Guild of Corpus Christi. The idea of forming a college seems to have been broached about the year 1342, when preparatory steps for securing and clearing a site were taken by members of this guild living in the parishes of St. Benedict and St. Botolph. They were soon joined in the scheme by the members of another Cambridge guild—the Guild of St. Mary the Virgin. Their joint efforts were successful in securing letters patent from Edward III in 1352 establishing the college. Formal recognition by the Chancellor and Masters of the University and by the Bishop and Prior of Ely followed three years later. It was not long before the collegiate buildings of Corpus Christi were put up in the form of a quadrangle—a style that became prevalent in later colleges—much on the lines of the larger manorial houses of the period. If the visitor penetrates to the "Old Court" of the college, he will see around him to-day substantially the same set of buildings as those originally put up, and on which the eyes of Robinson also rested. The southern range of buildings held the kitchen, buttery, Hall, and Master's Lodge, which communicated both with the library at the junction with the eastern range and also with the common parlour below. The chambers of the

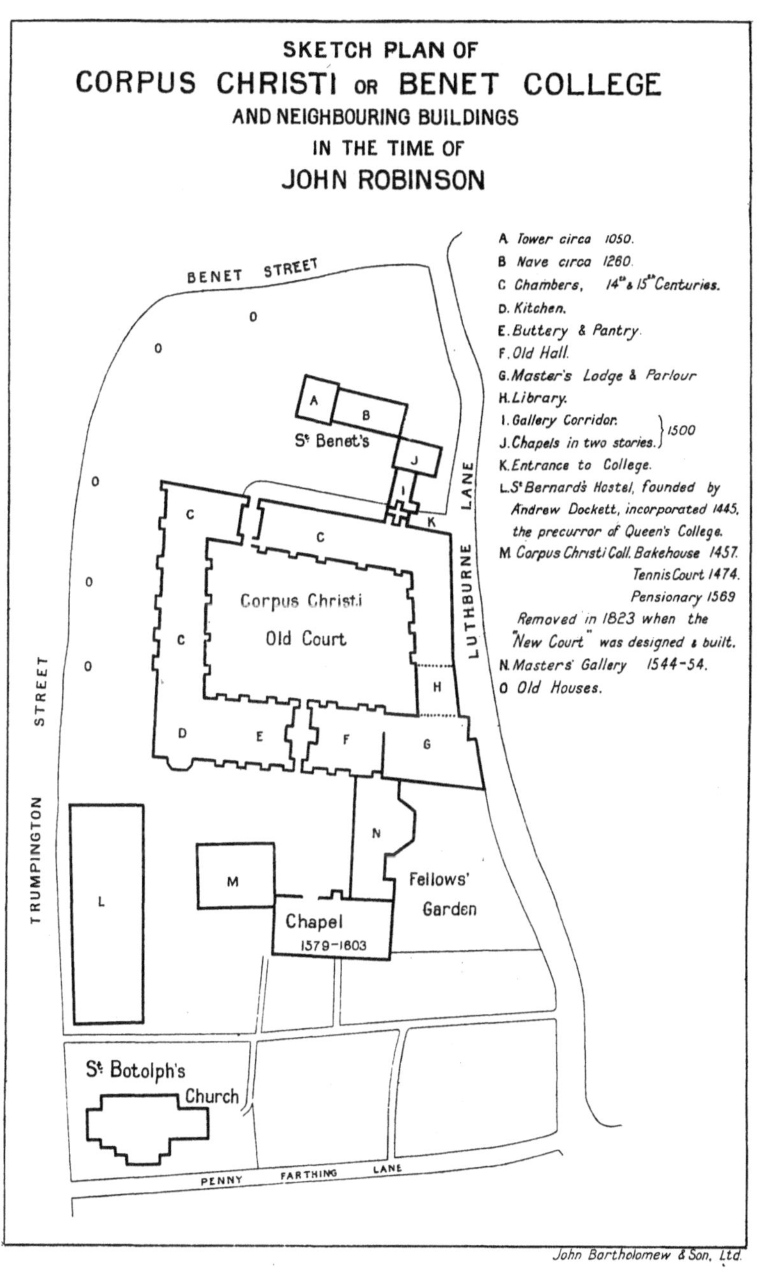
SKETCH PLAN OF
CORPUS CHRISTI OR BENET COLLEGE
AND NEIGHBOURING BUILDINGS
IN THE TIME OF
JOHN ROBINSON
A. Tower circa 1050.
B. Nave circa 1260.
C. Chambers, 14th & 15th Centuries.
D. Kitchen.
E. Buttery & Pantry.
F. Old Hall.
G. Master's Lodge & Parlour
H. Library.
I. Gallery Corridor.
J. Chapels in two stories. 1500
K. Entrance to College.
L. St Bernard's Hostel, founded by Andrew Dockett, incorporated 1445, the precurror of Queen's College.
M. Corpus Christi Coll. Bakehouse 1457. Tennis Court 1474. Pensionary 1569 Removed in 1823 when the "New Court" was designed & built.
N. Masters' Gallery 1544-54.
O. Old Houses.
BENET STREET
LUTHBURNE LANE
TRUMPINGTON STREET
PENNY FARTHING LANE
St Benet's
Corpus Christi Old Court
Fellows' Garden
Chapel 1579-1803
St Botolph's Church
John Bartholomew & Son, Ltd.

other members of the college ran round the other sides of the "quad." There was no elaborate gateway or tower, but a simple arched entrance in the northern range of building giving on to Benet churchyard. Though the work is said to have been finished "in the days of Richard Treton, the second Master," the walls were bare, the windows imperfectly glazed, and mother earth served as the floor for the ground storey until the mastership of Matthew Parker, 1544–53, when much was done to add to the comfort and homeliness of the college. A bequest by Henry Aldrich of Norwich in 1593 seems to point to the remembrance of cheerless and shivery days in Hall: "out of his great regard for his old college of Corpus Christi, he left £40 to provide charcoal for the Hall fire from Candlemas till thirty days after." The college was small, but had been greatly helped by the benefactions of Archbishop Matthew Parker and Sir Nicholas Bacon, and had the promise of a good training-ground for such a youth as John Robinson.

The church of St. Benedict was closely associated with the college, and was used in place of a college chapel for over a hundred years, but some time between 1487 and 1515 two chapels, one above the other, were built for the use of the collegians, adjoining the south wall of its chancel. By special licence in 1578 St. Benet's was appropriated to Corpus Christi College, on condition that the college authorities maintained the services and kept the church in repair. Thenceforward the services were taken, for the most part, by the fellows, while the parishioners supplemented the small stipend by voluntary contributions. Here, no doubt, Robinson would take his turn in preaching after his election to a fellowship. In St. Benet's tower—the most ancient building in Cambridgeshire—still hangs one of the bells (1558) used by the University before the tower of St. Mary's was built. Its tones, as well as those of the mediæval ring of four in St. Botolph's tower, must often have fallen upon young Robinson's ears, calling him to study or to prayer, or to some University Act.

The "Admission Book" of Corpus Christi College, under the heading "Sizatores" and the date April 9, 1592, has the entry—

"Johannes Robinson Eboracensis admissus est. Tutore Mro Jegon."

Either the young student in his nervousness mumbled the name of his county indistinctly, or else, as looks more likely, the person making the entry, having to write Eboracensis just below in admitting a lad from Yorkshire, carelessly gave the term through inadvertence in the entry relating to Robinson. He probably asked the next man his county before completing the entry of the particulars about our man. The first part of the word has been corrected rather roughly in a later hand, so as to read Nottingacensis, which we must take in good faith for Nottinghamiensis.

Robinson, then, entered the college as a "sizar," that is to say, he was one of that large class of students who secured the advantages of a college education in return for the services he rendered in Hall and to the college community to which he belonged. His tutor was Thomas Jegon, a younger brother of John Jegon, the Master. While the tutor exercised oversight over the sizar and directed his studies, the sizar waited on him at table, attended to his lodgings, cleaned his boots, wakened him in time for morning chapels, accompanied him on request when he went out into the countryside, or with his permission ran on errands for the college into the town. This was all honourable service, and the "sizar" had a well-recognized place in the college society, with good opportunities of rising to a post of greater consideration if he had diligence and ability.

They kept early hours in the Cambridge of those days. Morning chapel was at five; lectures in Hall began at six. Here Robinson's knowledge of "grammar" attained at school would be tested and enlarged, and he would be initiated into the arts of logic and rhetoric. Extraordinary attention was paid to the work of setting out in logical form the laws of reasoning which are implicit in human speech. A breath of new life had come into the study of logic at this period owing to the boldness of the new line taken by Peter Ramus, who disengaged himself to some extent from the scholastic Aristotelian methods which had been in vogue in mediæval times. The system of Ramus won a ready acceptance in Protestant centres of learning, and attracted much notice in Cambridge. It was an age of discussion, and hence great importance was attached to the work of securing a sound method of argumentation and a ready aptitude for detecting all defective, misleading and inconclusive statements.

Robinson probably found the lectures on this subject rather stiff and dry. They were given, like the other instruction in the University, in the Latin tongue, and involved a lot of strange terminology. But as he attended day after day, the meaning of the conventional phrases would gradually dawn upon him, and after a while the gist and drift of the whole business would become clear to him. I think he took a greater interest in the lectures on the books of the Old and New Testaments, which were made the subject of special and continued study. He took some pains to acquaint himself with the original Hebrew, and in course of time gained a considerable knowledge in New Testament Greek.

There were two regular meals in the course of the day, but these were supplemented by "bevers" in the early morning and other snacks. After the morning lectures dinner was served in Hall at ten o'clock, the sizars taking their share after waiting on the fellows, fellow-commoners, tutors and pensioners. Then came formal disputations on set subjects, in which the freshmen would play the part of listeners while the "sophisters" exercised themselves in the art of discussion; or it might be an afternoon for further lectures on rhetoric, geography and philosophy, or it might be a free afternoon, on which the sizar would attend his tutor at a game of quoits or field out for him at tennis.

The members met again in chapel for Evensong as the afternoon wore on. Then came the evening meal at five o'clock, and when that was over the sizar would withdraw to con the passages his tutor had set, prepare himself for the work of the morrow, and enjoy the opportunity of the evening hours for intercourse and sky-larking with his fellow-sizars. But the rule was early to bed—at nine in winter and ten o'clock in summer he had to retire. It would be a matter of interest to young Robinson that his tutor, Thomas Jegon, was elected " proctor " in the long vacation of his first year, through the influence of Dr. John Jegon, the Master of his college.

We do not get many personal glimpses of Robinson during his college career. He followed the course of most other students of his station. After his first year as freshman he would become a " junior sophister " and put in attendances as a listener at the disputations in the " Schools." The " Regent Walk," by which the " Schools " were approached, had been made by a former Master of " Corpus," Matthew Parker. The old Regent House and Divinity School still stand, and are incorporated with the University library buildings. The ancient ceiling exhibits the arms of Jegon in the western bay. Through diligent attendance at the " Schools," Robinson would qualify in his fourth year as a " senior sophister," and prepare to become a " questionist." His ability and steadiness gained recognition. When he had nearly completed his fourth year as sizar, he was elected to the rank of a " scholar " on the foundation. The " Order Book " of his college has the entry—

" Johannes Robinson Nottingh. electus in Scholarem, Jan. 23, admissus Febr. 16, 1595 " (*i. e.* 1596 in modern reckoning).

The " scholar " received an allowance from the college chest for his commons, and also free quarters in the college buildings. The entry of his admission to the standing of "scholar" in the Register of his college, however, shows some slight variations from that in the "Order Book." It runs, dated a week later, in this way—

"Johannes Robinson, Lincolniensis, admissus est in Scholarem, Februarii 23°."

There was evidently an impression in some minds that he came from Lincolnshire. But then the Register a little further on gives his county correctly in noting that "Dns. Robinson Nottinghamiensis" was approved for his Bachelor's degree, "approbatus pro gradu Bacchal. Februarii 25°, 1595" (*i. e.* 1596).

The proceedings for securing this degree took place at the beginning of Lent, when Robinson would present himself in the "Schools" prepared to "respond" to such propositions as might be put to him. The "bedell" of the University led the procession of aspiring candidates into the presence of the Vice-Chancellor on Ash-Wednesday. They were in due course presented to him as to a "father," and kneeling down were received by him and admitted (*incepit*) to the degree. Then through Lent the "incepting bachelors" acted as "determiners" in respect to the questions raised in the "Schools," leaving to the senior sophisters the work of "responding."

After passing through these ceremonies Robinson would discard the "round cap" of the undergraduate, and be entitled to wear the square cap and lined hood of his degree.

The next stage in his college career was the course of studies leading up to his Master's degree.

As a scholar and Bachelor of Arts, Robinson would enjoy a good deal more freedom than he had been allowed as a sizar. He would be in a position to take advantage of the lectures by the different University professors, and pursue the study of themes which specially attracted him. The old foundation of the "trivium"—grammar, logic and rhetoric—was now supposed to be securely laid as a solid basis for further studies. After three more years of University training Robinson duly "commenced Master of Arts." But before that time arrived he had been chosen fellow of his college. In the "Order Book," under date 1597, his name stands first among those elected to vacant fellowships—

"Joh. Robinson, Lincolniensis, admissus et juratus, Martii 27."

Was it needful to pass a year's probation before entering on the full privileges of the post? The entry in the Register of the college exactly a year later points in this direction: "Martii 27°, ano Dni. 1598, Johannes Robinson, Notinghamiensis in artibus Bacchalaureus admissus est in socium Coll^{ii}.," *i. e.* John Robinson of Nottinghamshire is admitted into a fellowship of the college. It was quite usual for those elected to fellowships to be Bachelors of Arts. Next year, 1599, on "Martii 28," "Mr. Robinson, Nottingham,"[1] took his Master's degree. It would be a memorable day for him. The ceremony of "the Great Commencement," as it was called, usually took place in Great St. Mary's Church, where, after disputations in divinity and philosophy, the candidates in those subjects received their degrees. The company then crossed over to the Regent House, where Robinson, with other Bachelors of Arts, would kneel[2] before the Vice-Chancellor and be graduated, and so "commence Master of Arts."

In the oath taken by the candidates for this degree they undertook to remain in Cambridge for two years to take their part in tuition and the work of the University. Robinson was now ranked as a "regent master." As a junior graduate it was his duty to give instruction in the subjects in which he himself had been taught. The "Order Book" of Corpus Christi College shows that he fulfilled the duty. It notes that he was

[1] Corpus Christi Register, *sub dato*. See also letter, *penes me*, March 16, 1911, from Mr. A. J. Wallis, Bursar of the College, whose help for this period I gratefully acknowledge.

[2] Joseph Hall knew John Robinson's University status. He refers to this: "You have twice kneeled to our Vice-Chancellor when you were admitted to your degree."—*A Common Apologie for the Church of England*, 1610, p. 90.

elected "Prælector Græcus," or Reader in Greek, in 1599, and in 1600 "Decanus," that is, "Dean," an office involving some special oversight over the students. His name does not occur in the lists of college officers for 1601–3, though we find it duly entered fifth in the list of fellows given in the college Register under the date 4th February 1602 (*i.e.* 1603)—

"Johannes Robinson Nottinghamiensis Artium Mag^r Sacerdos."

The description "sacerdos" is interesting. Robinson no doubt took orders on election to his fellowship according to the rule.[1] He would take his part in the services of the college chapel and his turn in supplying the pulpit of Benet Church. He may also have given occasional help in other churches where the living was in the gift of his college. But this definite description of him as "sacerdos"—priest—points to his having by this time taken up some regular duty in the Church of England while still holding his fellowship.

Affairs at Corpus Christi College were coming to a period. The Master, John Jegon, had been appointed Dean of Norwich, July 22, 1601, and seemed marked out for higher honours, which would take him away from Cambridge. The call of the outside world began to appeal to Robinson with increasing strength. He desired to make a home and carve out a career for himself.

Towards the close of the year 1602, the news leaked out that Jegon was likely to be appointed Bishop of Norwich. The fellows lost no time in addressing the following letter to Sir Robert Cecil. It is signed, among others, by John Robinson, and gives us the names and standing of some of his fellow-collegians—

"Right Honorable. o^r dutie most humblie remembred. wee beseech yor Honor [give] us leave to become humble suitors to you in a cause wch we hope will to yor Ho^ble wisedome appeare reasonable. we the fellowes of Corp^s Christi Colledge in Camb. have gotten knowledge that by yor Ho^ble

[1] Edmund Gurnay (*d.* 1648), one of the Fellows of Corpus Christi College in Robinson's time, was suspended from his Fellowship in 1607 for not being in "Orders." See *Dict. Nat. Biog.* under Gurney.

suite and mediacon to her Matie our worthie Mr. [Master], Dr. Jegon is like to be advaunced to the sea of Norwych, and so thereby his place in governement of vs like thereby to become voyde: wee and this or poore Coll. have received much good by his wisedome and p'vident care over vs and it, in that he hath restored it, wch was neere fullie ruined by some needie and careles Mrs. before him. From whence havinge taken a dew consideracon (as is behovefull for vs) we are desirous and well advised to make choyce of such a one to succeede him, as is for his learninge & degrees, experience, gravitie, and wisedome verie meete and sufficient to guide vs and or little comon wealth; and in his owne estate so well settled as he shall not neede to pray vppon vs, butt wilbe able and carefull to vphold or howse in the p'sent flourishinge estate.

"Now therefore this is or must humble suite, that it would please Yor Honor (as or noble Chauncelor, to whose will we humbly submitt orselves) to vowchsafe yor allowance, that accordinge to or oathes and the statutes of or howse, we may be p'mitted (when or Master shall leave this place) to proceede freelie to a new election. wherein we wilbe so carefull, as we doubte not, but that Yor Honor shalbe fullie satisfied; both in or generall respect to this howse and the good government thereof; and also in or pticuler to yor Honor, when you shall see, that both he and wee have or myndes bente to doe yor Honor all services.

"And so prayinge pdon for this or boldnes, and humbly beseechinge two lynes from yow to allow or free election, (as in that case you have most honourably done to others) we recomend you to the Almightie, who graunte you longe life and continuall encrease of honor and happines.

"At Cambrydge December the 22th, 1602.

"Yor Honors most humblie at comaundement.

"Anthonius Watson, *Propræses.* George Hall.

"Henry Buttes. *Decanus.* / Marlian Higden. *p'lector grec*[*i*].

"William Starkey. *p'lector Rhet.*

"Edward Gent. *p'lector.* /

"Edmund Gurnay. *p'l: top.*

"John Robinson."[1]

[1] MSS. at Hatfield House, 136, *108*. By the courtesy of the Most. Hon. the Marquis of Salisbury we are enabled to give a facsimile of this document with Robinson's signature.

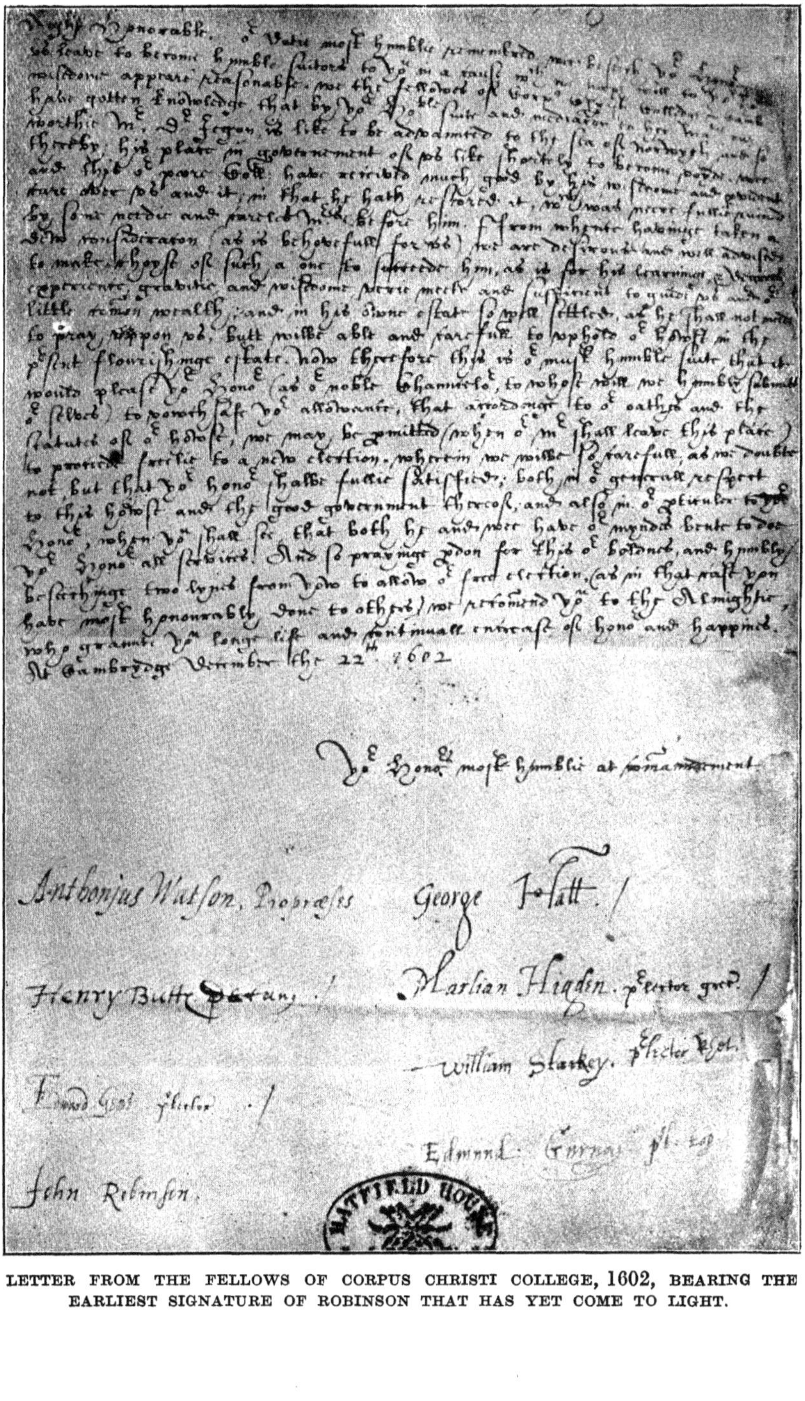

Anthonius Watson, Propraeses

George Platt

Henry Butts

Marlian Higdin

William Starkey

Edmund Gost

Edmund Gurney

John Robinson

LETTER FROM THE FELLOWS OF CORPUS CHRISTI COLLEGE, 1602, BEARING THE EARLIEST SIGNATURE OF ROBINSON THAT HAS YET COME TO LIGHT.

In the following month John Jegon was elected (January 18, 1602–3) Bishop of Norwich. He so managed affairs as to secure the election of his brother Thomas, the former tutor of Robinson, to succeed him as Master of the college. Whitgift was greatly nettled at this, as he wished the post to be conferred on his chaplain, Dr. Carrier, in whose interest he was bestirring himself when he found himself forestalled. Jegon's mastership at Corpus had been a success. He retrieved the financial position of the college by his careful and businesslike administration. He brought several students with him from Queen's College when he took up the post. Thrice he held the office of Vice-Chancellor, and he made the influence of Corpus felt in University affairs. In person he was short and stout, and his appearance, to judge from his picture, not very engaging. Such was the Master under whose oversight Robinson ran the whole of his college career. Jegon was a married man, and the presence of his wife, Lilia, with her little girl and two boys, gave the one domestic touch to the college society.

CHAPTER V

RELIGION IN ENGLAND IN THE DAYS OF ELIZABETH AND JAMES

THE position with regard to matters of religion in England at the opening of the seventeenth century was full of interest. The situation was felt to be charged with important possibilities. Queen Elizabeth was drawing to the close of her life, and men could not help wondering what would happen in the Church after her death. A long and brilliant chapter in the national history was coming to an end, and it was a matter for speculation as to how the story would be continued. For over forty years Elizabeth had pursued a policy with regard to religion largely based upon that of her father, and of all her work this has left the most lasting impress upon the life of our land. Her position as " Supreme Governor of the Church " was secured by the Act of Supremacy, 1559, and the Church government and worship to be followed throughout the land were determined with equal promptitude by the Act of Uniformity, passed in April of the same year. The title of the Act gives us one key to Elizabeth's policy. She bent her energies with remarkable pertinacity upon securing a uniform practice in worship throughout her dominions. In this she was seconded by the firm administration of John Whitgift, whom she appointed Primate in 1583. She did not concern herself much with men's private convictions, but insisted at the least upon an outward conformity with the established plan of worship. Any attempts to express antagonistic opinions, either by means of the Press or by organizing meetings for worship apart from the established and legal form, were rigidly put down.

Roman Catholics, on the one hand, and Puritans on the other, were alike restrained; while Separatists met with drastic treatment, and were, by the law of 1593, banished the realm when found to be irreconcilable to the Anglican Church. The Puritans had struggled manfully for a further reformation of religion. They had looked to Parliament for redress of what they considered flagrant evils in the constitution of the Church and for the removal of "popish" elements in her worship. Elizabeth in her masterful way peremptorily forbade Parliament to meddle with matters of religion, and proceeded to manage ecclesiastical affairs by means of Royal Commissions. For a time the struggle had been severe, but with the closing years of the reign and the opening of the new century there came a lull in the storm. It almost looked as though the policy of enforcing outward assent to the established worship was at length going to secure an inward assent. To some extent this was the case. By use and wont the very words of the Book of Common Prayer became dear to the ears of Englishmen. But the Puritan movement was really far from being crushed. The principles involved in it were bound to find expression. There were those also who felt that the English Common Law and the power of Parliament must be secured in a position of supremacy as against the absolutist tendencies of the Crown and the Church, and these saw most hope in the Puritan movement. If that movement could not be accommodated within the borders of the Anglican Church, then it must find some other means of organizing itself.

The Puritans were quiet at the opening of the century, because they hoped for much from James of Scotland. Whitgift and the Bishops also were less stringent for the time, because they too had an eye on Scotland, and did not quite know what would come out of "the Scotch mist." In the last Parliament of Elizabeth (October 27, 1601, to December 19,

1601) a note of greater independence of the Crown was heard. With the accession of a new monarch a fresh Parliament would be summoned. Who could say what it might not accomplish in the way of reform in religion? So there was a period of hushed expectancy.

Early in the morning of March 24, 1603, Elizabeth died. Whitgift at once sent off Dr. Neville, Dean of Canterbury, to wait upon James, and recommend the Church of England to his protection and favour. Both parties in the Church were busy. The Puritans were active in promoting petitions for reformation and in issuing treatises, and strenuous efforts were made to secure capable party representation in the new Parliament. The Humble Petition of the thousand ministers, known as the Millenary Petition, expressed the Puritan demands in moderate terms. The King summoned a Conference to meet at Hampton Court to consider matters concerning the Church and worship, but the issue of that gathering clearly indicated that the Puritans had nothing to hope for from James. The democratic tendencies inherent in the Puritan movement were instinctively recognized by James and magnified by Bancroft. A pliant Episcopacy was precisely the type of Church government that suited the ideas of the King. The Puritans of England appeared to him to be too much like the Presbyterians of Scotland, of whom he had had bitter experience, and he saw in the episcopate a bulwark for the monarchy. Whitgift died February 29, 1604, and when Richard Bancroft was appointed Archbishop, the hopelessness of effecting any immediate change in the form of worship must have been apparent to all observers. Bancroft had been the strenuous opponent of the Puritans throughout his career. His labours in that direction had been the very ground of his promotion to episcopal rank. An extraordinary document was drawn up by Whitgift, after the death of Aylmer, Bishop of London, for presentation to the Court as a recommendation of

Bancroft for the vacant See. It is for the most part a statement of Bancroft's work in opposition to the movement for a further reformation in religion. His qualification for a seat on the Bishops' Bench was not so much his eloquence or learning, or a spiritual frame of mind and Christian temper of heart, but this : " that since he had professed divinity he had ever opposed himself against all sects and innovations." Thus did Bancroft win his mitre. As Bishop of London he had backed up Whitgift, and now (1604), on promotion to the Primacy, assured of the support of King James, he tightened the cords of subscription and worked for a stricter uniformity.

Bancroft had presided at the Convocation called at the opening of the reign, as the Primacy was vacant. Here, too, he was active against the Puritans. Licence was secured from the King to make canons, and Bancroft introduced a Book of Canons to the Lower House on May 2, 1603, to which he sought to give the force of law, and by which he hoped to keep the clergy of his Church in bounds. It became evident that the terms of conformity were going to be more rigidly enforced, and all variation from the established order in Church affairs repressed. A requisition was sent out to the masters and heads of colleges in Cambridge requiring them to certify as to the conformity of fellows, scholars and students in regard to the regulation dress and " due observation of the Communion Book," and the authority upon which any of their fellows engaged in preaching. The reply from Corpus Christi is extant, but, as Robinson was not in residence, it gives no particulars as to him—

"Corps Christi Coll: in Camb Jan 8 1604. This Chrmas time or fellows are mostle abroade. / Onely fower now in the Colledge vidz.

"Mr. Watson who { was made minister by ye B. of Lincolne / preacheth by or University licence.

"Mr. Walsall who { was made minister by ye B. of Lincoln preacheth by or University licence.

"Mr. Butts who { was made minister by ye B. of Carlile preacheth by licence from ye late B. of London.

"Mr. Higden { was ordeyned Deacon by ye B. of Lincolne / preacheth not as yett.

"We have 8 fellows more abroade and 3 pensionars that bee M^rs^ of Arts of all wch number there bee 6 ministers more, where ordered (*sic*) or how licenced I know not yett till they come and shew; but I see they doo all approve themselves very formall and forward to good order established.

T. JEGON M^r^. Coll^ii^."

This tightening up of the strings of conformity in Cambridge may have influenced Robinson in his decision to resign his fellowship, but a more potent reason was his desire to marry, settle down to regular ministerial work and form a home of his own. A fellowship could not be held by a married man.[1] Matrimony meant resignation. Hence the entry in the Corpus Christi Register under date February 10, 1603–4—

"*Thomas Knolles, Norfolc., electus et admissus est in Socium Collegii unanimi consensu M^ri^ et* 9 *Sociorum, cessante et in scripto resignante M^ro^. Robinson.*"

That is to say, "on the withdrawal and resignation in writing of Master Robinson, Thomas Knolles, of Norfolk, was elected and admitted to a fellowship of the college, by the unanimous consent of the Master and nine fellows." Five days later Robinson was married at the parish church of St. Mary at Greasley, Nottinghamshire, to Bridget White, who was then living at Beauvale in that parish. Beauvale was a Carthusian Priory dedicated to the Holy Trinity, founded by Nicholas de Cantelupe in 1343. In 1540 the Priory was dissolved, the monks pensioned off and the lands leased out. When the mother of Bridget White died she was in possession of a lease of Beauvale. It would be from the farmhouse

[1] Robinson refers to this, he says the Church forbids "marriage to fellows in colleges." *Justification of Separation, Works,* ii. p. 399.

ST. MARY'S CHURCH, GREASLEY, IN WHICH JOHN ROBINSON WAS MARRIED.

adjoining the ruins of the Priory, perhaps from the Prior's house itself, the shell of which is still standing, that the wedding party would set out. May is the month in which to visit this " beautiful valley," but this was a winter wedding, and the young couple would be lucky if the day was brightened by a gleam of sunshine.

The entry in the Register is of: " Mr. John Robynson and Mistress Bridget Whyte," February 15, 1603–4. Both the " Mr." and the " Mistress " are distinctive in the entry, and indicate that the parties were considered, in local esteem, to be of importance. The entries of the weddings of ordinary parishioners give the bare names. Not till 1608 does this formula occur again at Greasley, when " Mr. John Trymmington and Mistress Ann Poole " were married.

Robinson took his bride off with him to Norwich, and in that city a son and daughter were born to them, and named John and Ann after the grandparents.

This meant good-bye to Cambridge and the opening of a new chapter in Robinson's life, but before leaving this period behind it will be well to glance at two of the men of the Cambridge of Robinson's day who exerted an influence upon him and moulded to some extent his thought. The religious problems which were under discussion at Cambridge in his time will be dealt with in the next chapter.

Among the outstanding men on the Puritan side at Cambridge was Laurence Chaderton or Chadderton (1537–1640), who came of a Lancashire family. He was selected by Sir Walter Mildmay to be the first Master of Emmanuel College, in 1584, a post which he held for thirty-eight years. Chaderton opposed any variation from the Calvinism embodied in the Anglican Articles, but, being a man of moderate temper and some caution, he retained his post with honour, and only resigned it (1622) to let in Dr. John Preston, " lest he should be succeeded by a person of Arminian principles." Throughout the whole of Robinson's

Cambridge career Chaderton was active in the affairs of the University, and was looked up to by the young men of Puritan sympathies as a leader and guide. From the press which members of the Pilgrim Church controlled in after years in Leyden, an edition of Chaderton's sermon on Romans xii. 3–8 was issued in 1618, and Robinson refers to it on more than one occasion in his *Works*.

But the man by whom Robinson was most profoundly influenced was William Perkins (1558–1602), a Warwickshire man, educated at Christ's College, and appointed lecturer in the church of Great St. Andrews. His preaching was marvellously effective, and left a permanent mark upon the life of many a young man who attended on his ministry during the impressionable days at college. Townsmen and collegians alike were attracted and stirred by the preaching of Perkins. His well-balanced mind and fervent spirit appealed with power to the average Englishman of the time. He expounded Calvinism in a form which they could grip and make available for life. What other English preacher of the time had his sermons translated by enthusiastic followers into Welsh and Irish? Robinson was deeply indebted to Perkins for the general structure of his scheme of religious thought and his interpretation of Christianity. The fact that Arminius had assailed Perkins "with some acrimony"[1] would act as a spur to Robinson in his chivalrous championship of the Calvinistic cause against the Arminians in the University of Leyden in later years.

[1] In his *Examen*, 1612, *vide* Perkins in *Dict. Nat. Biog.*, by J. Bass Mullinger.

CHAPTER VI

DISPUTATIONS ON RELIGION AT CAMBRIDGE AND LEYDEN

ONE may well ask what were the questions in divinity which interested the minds of men in Cambridge in Robinson's day? They were questions concerning election and justification and points in controversy between the Protestant and Roman Churches. While Whitgift was strong for the episcopacy and the established order in the Anglican Church, he was at the same time an advocate for the Calvinistic theology embodied in its Articles, indeed in his "Lambeth Articles" he presented the Calvinistic positions in an uncompromising form. But a reaction had set in against the extreme Calvinism which had marked the lectures and sermons of many eminent divines in the University. The case of Peter Baro has been frequently brought forward by writers on the period to illustrate this reaction.

In 1595 William Barrett of Gonville and Caius College preached a sermon *ad clerum* in St. Mary's which was judged unsound. In the action taken against Barrett by the University, Dr. Soame and Peter Baro fell out, and all Cambridge became involved in a wordy dispute over abstruse points of Calvinistic doctrine. The Heads of the Colleges appealed to Whitgift. It seemed needful to define the position with authority and lay down what must be believed and taught. Accordingly Whitgift framed the Lambeth Articles, and sent them down to Cambridge with precise instructions that "nothing should be publicly taught to the contrary." The question became a matter of public interest, and the Court got wind of it. Elizabeth quickly let Whitgift know who had the final authority in determining the doctrine of her Church. She sent him word (December 5, 1595) that she "misliked much that any allowance had been given by his Grace and the rest of any such points to be disputed, being a matter tender and dangerous to weak, ignorant minds."

In nervous haste the Archbishop sent down a warning note to the University; but his new Articles were now spread abroad; the most he could do was to try to stop discussion upon them. This was difficult, as Roger Goade, the Vice-Chancellor, was determined to deal with the lapses of Baro on the points concerned, and Cambridge was given up to a carnival of theological disputation. A less familiar case exhibiting this tendency to break away from Calvinism, and one moreover in which Robinson would be specially interested from the actors concerned in it, was that of Dr. John Overall. It will give an insight into the discussions of the times if we describe this case in some detail.

John Overall (1560–1619)[1] was appointed to the Regius Professorship of Theology in 1596, in succession to Dr. William Whitaker, and became Master of Catharine Hall in 1598. He thus held a prominent position in the University. Early in June 1599, some of his auditors were alarmed at opinions expressed by him "upon certain points of doctrine publicly delivered in the Schools in his Divinity lectures and determinations." There are always those keen to scent any departure from the beaten track. Complaint was made to Dr. Jegon, the Master of Benet College, who was Vice-Chancellor of the University for that year. He thought it well to refer the points in dispute to a conference. Accordingly on June 20, 1599, Dr. Roger Goade (1538–1610) and Mr. Laurence Chaderton were appointed to confer with Overall on three main heads of doctrine—

[1] For Overall consult the excellent article by Rev. Alexander Gordon in *Dict. Nat. Biog.*

(1) Concerning justification and faith.
(2) Concerning Anti-Christ.
(3) Concerning the descent into hell.

Sixteen subordinate propositions under these main heads were drawn up. The ground for discussion was thus thoroughly mapped out, and the way prepared for testing Overall's " soundness " according to the preconceived notions of the Calvinists. A meeting was held on August 31, 1599, and the upshot was that after discussing these sixteen propositions they agreed in eight and disagreed in the other eight, out of which eight wherein they differed were then set down by common consent the state, words, and sense of these five questions to be conferred upon—

1. An elect justified man fallen into grave sin lacks imputed justification until he repents.

He becomes condemned or liable to eternal punishment until through repentance and faith he is restored.

2. An elect justified man fallen into grave sins loses for the time being justifying faith.

3. It is likely that Mahomet or the Turk and the Pope equally constitute that Anti-Christ foretold in Scripture.

4. Nothing in the Scriptures hinders the view that the soul of Christ departed as well to the assembly of the damned as to that of the blessed.

5. It is certain that the souls of the fathers before Christ's Ascension, although they were in the bosom of Abraham and a place of bliss, yet were not in heaven properly so called.[1]

Dr. Overall held the affirmative of these propositions, Dr. Goade and Mr. Chaderton the negative. They agreed to put down in writing brief reasons

[1] 1. Homo electus justificatus lapsus in gravia peccata justificatione imputata caret, donec resipiscat. Fit reus sive obligatus ad pœnam æternum donec per penitentiam et fidem restauratur.

2. Homo electus justificatus lapsus in gravia peccata amittit ad tempus fidem justificantem.

3. Mahometem sive Turcam et Papam simul constituere Antichristum illum in Scripturis prædictum, est verisimile.

4. Animam Christi tam ad Cœtum damnatorum quam beatorum concessisse, nihil in scripturis impedit.

5. Animas patrum ante Christi ascensionem, etsi fueriut in linu Abrahæ et loco beatudinis, non tamen fuisse in cœlo proprie dicto, constat.

for their contention by September 6, 1599, and several meetings to discuss the points at issue followed. Dr. Goade and Mr. Chaderton state in their report of the affair—

"Finally, on October 20, we delivered up in writing in the Consistory to Mr. Vice-Chancellor and his assistants (being then present with him) Drs Goade, Soame, Barwell, Clayton, Overall, Montague and Mr. Chaderton, our reasons and brief answers according to his [Overall's] brief marginal answer, then signifying that we intended a larger answer by the end of that Michaelmas term. Both which were then publicly read, and Dr. Overall then openly acknowledged that he had consented to the words and state of the five questions as they were set down and there read, albeit (as he then said) 'they were not by him alone so conceived'; to which we answer that neither were they conceived by us [alone], but jointly agreed upon by us all. At which meeting he seemed only offended at our reference of [to] Amandus Polanus, his answer to Bellarmine's arguments terming him 'a scarecrow not meet to be accounted among divines and a shame to have such alleged.' . . . About the end of Michaelmas term we delivered to Mr. Vice-Chancellor the whole conference in writing, together with our larger answer, praying him to acquaint the Heads therewith by his discretion, that it might in time convenient be brought to the first intended issue. Signed: ROGER GOADE
LAUR. CHADERTON." [1]

After the presentation of this report the matter simmered for awhile. Jegon did not find any "time convenient" for settling the dispute. He left it for his successor in the office of Vice-Chancellor, Dr. Soame, to deal with. It was a knotty problem. The case came up in the summer of the next year, as we learn from "A note what was done at the meeting in the Regent House the 4th June, 1600, by Mr. Dr. Soame, Vice-Chanr., and his assistants, Dors. Goade, Tyndall, Barwell, Jegon, Clayton, Overall and Mr. Chaderton, touching the end of the conference with Dor. Overall." At this meeting the Vice-Chancellor read out "the five questions," stated this time in the

[1] *Calendar of Salisbury Papers*, 139, 120.

negative form, in order that those present might give their opinions. All save Overall "joined in one opinion that the propositions were true, and rightly defended." The report, under the hands of Goade and Chaderton, giving an account of their conferences with Overall, was handed in. Then we read—

> "Mr. Vice-Chancellor earnestly desired Dr. Overall to join with him and the rest in the acknowledgment of the same truth, whereof all present would be most glad. To which he answered 'he was not so persuaded in his conscience, and therefore could not.' Then Mr. Vice-Chancellor, first wishing that God would enlighten his mind, did, both in regard of the common peace of the University and also of a precedent in like case occasioned by a letter from the Lord Grace of Canterbury [Whitgift] then read, require Dr. Overall to forbear impugning the said points of doctrine in any his public exercises, considering that thereby, not only ourselves then present, but many others of that University could not be but greatly offended and excited to a needless and dangerous contention." [1]

The dispute still smouldered, and broke out again into flame at the "Commencement," in the year 1600, of which an interesting account has survived. At this ceremony, in which in all likelihood John Robinson was an active participant, Dr. Soame, the Vice-Chancellor, was "Moderator of the Divinity Disputation on the Commencement Even," June 30, 1600. The Latin speech he then delivered is still extant. "In his moderating," we are told, "he preserved the truth and good order of the disputation soundly, briefly and perspicuously. When the disputation was ended the Vice-Chancellor determined of the last question [*Animæ piorum fuerunt in cœlo ante Christi ascensum.*] against the Popish sort, soundly and perspicuously. . . . When the Vice-Chancellor had ended, Dr. Overall was called by the Beadle, as the manner is, *ad commendationem.*" The opportunity thus presented for wiping off old scores was one he could not pass by. "Forgetting himself," he

[1] *Salisbury Papers*, 139, 123.

" entered into a refutation of the Vice-Chancellor's determination, which action of his was very offensive to the auditory, in regard both of matter and manner. Of matter, for he dealt against truth. Of manner, for the like was never done before, and is flat against all order of disputation."

" The Vice-Chancellor, seeing Dr. Overall (which had been required before the Heads of Colleges to forbear public opposition) to carry himself as he did, commanded him silence, adding that God's book and the ancient writers were flat against him, and that the Lords Archbishops of both the Provinces, and the rest of the learned Bishops of our Church, were of another judgment than he was, and that all such as know and love the religion in the University and abroad and the Reformed Churches dissented from him."

The conclusion of the Vice-Chancellor's speech was that "he wished with all his heart that Dr. Overall had not nourished any errors, at the least that he had forborne the publishing of any in that excellent assembly, which assembly did justly and generally condemn Dr. Overall's action."

Thus, at the outset of the " Commencement proceedings," a good deal of heat was engendered over this abstruse point in divinity. It was felt necessary by the dominant party of reformers to put Overall in his place, and check any tendencies to countenance an opinion which leaned towards the position held by Rome. They asserted themselves on the next day, as we gather from the following account—

" On the Commencement Day, Dr. Playfere, one of the Divinity Readers, was moderator of the disputation. He entered into a defence of the Vice-Chancellor's reasons, and discovered and refuted Dr. Overall's dealing the day before, with such soundness, learning and perspicuity as did greatly content and satisfy the assembly. If some of his speeches were somewhat sharp in regard of the manner, they which love truth will bear a little with him, because he dealt against him [Overall] which had faulted both in matter and manner, and whose public oppositions against the truth are most notorious. Dr. Overall's unsoundness and obscurity in his lectures and 'determinations' have grieved the hearts and opened the mouths of very many against him."

The fact of the matter was that, with the growing sense of security in regard to the settlement in Church and State, after the collapse of the Spanish Armada and the failure of the papal plots against England, it was felt to be less necessary to accentuate points of difference between the Anglican and Roman Churches. There was a shrinking from the extreme logical conclusions of a strong Calvinism. Indications appeared of an incipient Arminianism. This puzzled and alarmed men of the old guard like Dr. Soame, Dr. Goade and Laurence Chaderton, who had borne the brunt of the battle against the plotting Catholics, and had been bred in the atmosphere of the Thirty-nine Articles. The independence of judgment shown by Overall by no means prejudiced his future. He was made Dean of St. Paul's in 1602, received the See of Coventry and Lichfield in 1614, and finished up as Bishop of Norwich.

The fact that Robinson was at Cambridge when these questions of predestination, election, reprobation and justifying faith were so eagerly debated was not without effect upon his mind. The influence of this period is strongly marked in his writings. He was unmoved by the wave of Arminian opinion which now began to set in. He held to the general scheme of theology in which he had been instructed, and which he had learned to defend in the schools. It seemed to him to have ample scriptural warrant in the Pauline epistles, and that was enough for him.

If we bear in mind how thoroughly John Robinson had been steeped in the discussions on the leading points in the Calvinistic theology during his course at Cambridge, we shall be better able to understand an incident during his residence at Leyden related of him in after days. By strange fortune both the University and the city of Leyden were deeply stirred by keen disputations over these very same questions in theology during the period in which the "Pilgrim Church" found refuge there. Here also, just as at Cambridge, the dispute was complicated by political and personal cross-currents, which tended to make it exceedingly keen. Robinson in the course of his ministry at Leyden had not forgotten his old love. He had entered himself in 1615 as a "student in theology" at Leyden University, and interested himself in the controversies which then agitated its members. Edward Winslow, looking back to that time, says—

"Our Pastor, Master Robinson, in the time when Arminianism prevailed so much, at the request of the most orthodox Divines, as Polyander, Festus Hommius, etc., disputed daily in the Academy at Leyden against Episcopius and others the grand champions of that error; and had as good respect amongst them as any of their own Divines. Insomuch as when God took him away from them and us by death . . . some of the chief of them sadly affirmed, 'that *all* the Churches of Christ sustained a loss by the death of that worthy Instrument of the Gospel.'"[1]

William Bradford gives us a more detailed description of these encounters—

"In these Times" [that is, during the stay of their Church in Leyden], he says, "were the great troubles raised by the Arminians, who, as they greatly molested the whole State, so this city in particular, in which was the chief University; so as there were daily and hot disputes in the Schools thereabout. And as the students and other learned were divided in their opinions herein, so were the two Professors or Divinity Readers themselves, the one daily teaching for it, the other against it, which grew to that pass that few of the disciples of the one would hear the other teach.

"But Master Robinson, though he taught [*i. e.* preached] thrice a week himself, and writ sundry books, besides his manifold pains otherwise, yet he went constantly to hear their Readings [lectures], and heard the one as well as the other. By which means he was so well grounded in the controversy, and saw the force of all their arguments, and knew the shifts of the adversary.

"And being himself very able, none was fitter to buckle

[1] Winslow, *Hypocrisy Vnmasked*, p. 94 (1646).

with them than himself; as appeared by sundry disputes, so as he began to be terrible to the Arminians. Which made Episcopius, the Arminian Professor, to put forth his best strength and set forth sundry *Theses*, which by public dispute he would defend against all men.

"Now Polyander, the other [Calvinist] Professor, and the chief Preachers of the city, desired Master Robinson to dispute against him. But he was loath, being a stranger. Yet the other did importune him, and told him, 'that such was the ability and nimbleness of the adversary that the truth would suffer if he did not help them.' So as he condescended and prepared himself against the time."

It was just here, we may suppose, that the notes and memories of his University days at Cambridge helped him.

"When the day came," continues Bradford, "the Lord did so help him to defend the truth and foil this adversary, as he put him to an apparent *non plus*, in this great and public audience. And the like he did a second or third time, upon such-like occasions. The which, as it caused many to praise God that the truth had so famous victory, so it procured him much honour and respect from those learned men and others which loved the truth." [1]

Some students of Robinson's life have been inclined to regard the account of these disputations as somewhat apocryphal, on the ground that the pastor of an obscure refugee church was hardly likely to be called upon to champion the cause of orthodoxy in this way. But the identification of John Robinson with the fellow of that name of Corpus Christi College, and a consideration of the topics that came to the front for discussion in the Cambridge of his day, removes the difficulty. He would be excellently fitted for the task. We may, I think, take the account of this affair given by Bradford as being substantially correct. The discussion, after the manner of the time, would be in Latin, and Robinson, being familiar with that tongue from its use in Cambridge, would find his English birth no bar to participation in the debate on a level with the Dutch members of the University.

[1] Bradford's *Plimouth Plantation*.

CHAPTER VII

JOHN ROBINSON AT NORWICH

When John Robinson settled at Norwich he would find himself in an atmosphere of busy, practical life. It was the chief manufacturing centre of provincial England. There was a large population, a thriving industry and a keen interest in both politics and religion. The commerce of the place brought it into close touch with Holland and Flanders, and there were many foreign workmen settled in the city, some of whom were religious refugees. It was a stimulating experience to step from the academic life at Cambridge into the strenuous existence which Norwich then afforded.

The Reformation was accepted wholeheartedly by the leading townsfolk and the commercial community in Norwich. Under the guidance of John More (*d.* 1592), vicar of St. Andrews, and Thomas Roberts (*d.* 1576), rector of St. Clements, the Puritan party gained a strong hold upon the city. The clergy advocated a further reformation of the Church, and projected a plan for its discipline and governance by deans and superintendents instead of Bishops. They objected to the " imposition of ceremonies " and everything savouring of " popery." [1]

Norwich was a city of many churches, but the provision for the maintenance of its clergy was poor in the extreme. A petition [2] from " the poor and painful ministers of the City of Norwich," presented to Burghley about the year 1592, throws light upon this

[1] " Humble Supplication against the Imposition of Ceremonies," September 25, 1576.

[2] *Hist. MSS. Com. Report on the Salisbury Papers*, Pt. 13, p. 461.

matter. The petitioners point out that there are forty parishes, but the income was ill provided and uncertain, consequently "we that serve at the altar live on the basket, and our people that should maintain us cannot agree about our maintenance; the rich will give little, the meaner sort less and the rest nothing at all." They asked for some scheme to be devised to give a reasonable certainty of income.

There was not much prospect of worldly advantage then in Robinson's move to Norwich, and one may speculate as to the influences which induced him to turn his face thither. For one thing, Norwich was closely associated with Cambridge. Those who framed the petition to Burghley just cited, say, "We are all of us of your University of Cambridge." Many Norwich men had been trained in Robinson's college, and the knowledge that he would find a circle of sympathetic friends there might be a factor in determining him to fix his home in that city. I rather think, however, that it was his close acquaintance with Thomas Newhouse and the opportunity of what promised to be congenial work in fellowship with him that led him thither. Newhouse[1] was one of the circle of earnest Cambridge men profoundly influenced by the teaching of William Perkins, and to that circle John Robinson also belonged. He was some five or six years Robinson's senior at the University, graduating from "Christ's" about 1590, and securing a fellowship in that college a few years later. The parishioners of St. Andrew's, Norwich, invited him to become their minister in 1602. His known Puritan leanings would be a recommendation in their eyes. They had been indoctrinated with similar opinions by John More, who refused to wear the surplice, and took his own line in ecclesiastical matters. The people of the parish bought the advowson of the church in

[1] A letter from Newhouse, dated "Norw^ch feb. 15, 1610," directed to his "approved good freind the L[ady] Knyvett," is in the British Museum. He was very ill. He says: "I have used your Electuarie, wch I hold to be verie soveraigne against a cōsumption." He died 1611.

order to secure the right of presenting a man of their own choice to the living. They seem to have given attention to a stricter discipline in their parish than was customary, and arranged for the maintenance of assistant ministers to help the incumbent in the preaching and pastoral work. It is quite possible that Newhouse, from his personal knowledge of Robinson, invited him to come over to Norwich and help in the work.

A few particulars of Robinson's life at Norwich may be gathered from the manuscript copy[1] of a controversy in which a clerical friend engaged him soon after he had definitely separated from the Anglican Church and migrated to Holland. To the main points in this controversy we shall refer on a later page. We only note here that Robinson's antagonist in this argument refers to him as "sometime a preacher in Norwich."[2] He incidentally lets us know that it was St. Andrew's Church to which Robinson was there attached. In order to give definiteness to their discussion, this friend charged Robinson with schism in leaving St. Andrew's Church, and Robinson for his part undertook to justify his action in so doing. They agreed to discuss this special case of the larger problem of the lawfulness of separation from the Church of the Realm. In expressing his agreement as to the scope of the discussion, Robinson gives us a glint of light upon his Norwich days—

> "The instance you propound," he says, "for the specyall subiect of the question in hand I agree to, which is St. Andrewes in Norwich, wherof indeed I was sometymes a minister (as you saie), but never anie member, having my house-standyng (which is the infallible determinacion of members) within another parish, and my children baptized there."

From this we gather that though minister of St. Andrew's, Robinson lived in another parish in Norwich,

[1] Jones, MS. 30, Bodleian Library.
[2] An advertisement, etc., prefixed to the MS.

and was so far observant of the recognized custom of the Anglican Church that he had his children baptized in the church of the parish in which his house stood, though he himself was officially connected with another parish church in the same city. We also note that Robinson mentions his "children"; more than one child, therefore, was born to cheer the Norwich home of his good wife Bridget. Here was a change from the cloistered academic life of Cambridge. To all appearances Robinson was now well started on the useful and respectable career of the diligent parish minister.

Changes, however, were pending. On the one hand, there was a general screwing up of ecclesiastical affairs to the standard indicated in the Book of Common Prayer. A proclamation was issued in July 1604 requiring all ministers to conform to the new Book of Canons before the end of the following November. The Bishops were stirred to action, and were now less ready to overlook neglect or defiance of the rubrics. John Jegon, the Bishop of Norwich, sought to bring all the refractory clergy in his diocese into line. The fact that Robinson had known him so well in Cambridge may have made him less ready to bow to his authority in Norwich. He was led to question the scriptural authority for diocesan Bishops in the Christian Church. When it came to the point as to whether he should obey his Bishop or his conscience, and the plain injunctions of the New Testament in regard to Church organization and discipline, Robinson did not hesitate. This brought him into conflict with his Bishop. We do not know the details of the case. We only know, on the authority of Joseph Hall,[1] that he was suspended from the exercise of his ministry by episcopal authority. Denied the liberty of preaching, he gathered friends about him more privately for prayer and conference. But those who thus resorted to him

[1] *A Common Apologie*, 1610, p. 114. Compare also Jones MS. 30 p. 50, where the author, addressing Robinson, says: "You and I and others, because we could not obserue all other things required, were put from preaching."

were promptly excommunicated. Henry Ainsworth referred a few years later to these incidents—

> "If any among you not medling with the publik estate of your Church, but feeling or fearing his own particular soul-sicknes, doe resort to a physician (whose receipts are not after the common sort) for advise about his health, or of freindship and acquaintance to see him, he is subject to the censure and thunderbolt of your Church. Witnes the late practice in Norwich, where certeyn citizens were excommunicated for resorting vnto and praying with Mr. Rob[inson], a man worthily reverenced of all the city for the graces of God in him (as your self [Richard Bernard] also, I suppose, wil acknowledge) and to whom the cure and charge of their sowles was ere while committed." [1]

On the other hand, along with this screwing up of episcopal authority there was a development going on in Robinson's own thought in regard to the right ordering of the Church and the nature of Church ceremonies according to the terms of the New Testament. He was no willing deserter from his old Church. He was inclined to regard "the ceremonies" as matters "indifferent." Hall says that on his suspension Robinson "submitted to the prelates' spirituall jurisdiction." He was not contumacious, but the ban upon his ministerial activities—his chosen life-work—led him to review the whole position. Nor did he hastily come to a decision to separate from the Church of England. The Bishops insisted that the "ceremonies" of their Church were not matters of indifference, but matters of necessity. Robinson, as a result of three months' consideration of the question, also came to the conclusion that they were not matters of indifference, but that they were wrong. That being so, to participate in them was evil.

The question of his future career, as well as his position in relation to the Church, would demand his attention at this period. His growing family had to be provided for. The mastership of a hospital offered some attractions to a man of his tastes. He would be

[1] *Counterpoyson*, 1608, p. 246.

less directly under the eye of the Bishop, and have greater freedom and security in such a position than as an ordinary parish priest. Norwich had more than one "hospital"[1] of ancient foundation, where the aged poor found an asylum from the cares of the world. There was St. Stephen's Hospital, which stood without St. Stephen's Gate; there was St. Giles's Hospital, currently known as "The Old Men's Hospital," to the mastership of which the Mayor and Aldermen of the city had the right of election; there was "the Hospital or Spittel hous of St. Mary Magdalene, near Norwich." Robinson, however, if he sought such an appointment did not secure it. It was a scandal of the time that these ancient charities were too often perverted from their intended uses and the offices connected with them put into the

[1] The *State Papers* contain the report of an inquiry into the abuse of the funds of such a Norwich hospital at this period. The Corporation had failed in its trust. "The Master of the house of they' appoyntment hath only a bare pension. The manors and revenues are graunted privily among them selves. All fines of the land come to theyr owne purses without regard of the poore or the King's foundation." *State Papers, Domestic,* James I, vol. v. p. 57. On February 5, 1603–4, the "keeping and governorship of St. Stephen's Hospital, Norwich," was granted to Matthew Barber. Then, on April 11, 1604, there was a grant to Thomas Oglethorp of "the guidership" of St. Stephen's Hospital, Norwich, for life, and a similar grant to "John Palmore" on April 14; while on January 27, 1605, there was again a "grant to John Palmer of the guidership of St. Stephen's Hospital, Norwich, for life." See the *State Papers, Domestic.* These entries suggest a scramble for the post. Perhaps some local antiquary will look into the matter.

The following document illustrates the kind of post Robinson may have sought—

Petition, dated April 1604, to "The Master of ye Roles."

"Good sir where the berer here of Oliver Lloyd Doctor of the civill lawe is a suter unto you for yor meanes unto his Matye for a dispensacon to enable him to hould an hospitall prebend or other promotion spirituall havinge not cure of Souls yf heareafter hee happen to obtayne anie such. I have thought good to signifie unto you that I understand by Sr Richard Swayle, Judge of the faculties, that his suite is convenient and honest and that hee and manie other Doctors have the like and that in regard of the necessarie use the publique estate hath of men of that profession and the small pferremts incident unto them. It is fittinge to give them that incouragement. And so recomending him and his desire unto you I comitte you to thalmightie ffrom Courte Aprilis xiiij 1604."—*State Papers, Domestic,* James I, vol. vii. p. 28.

The Hospital of St. Paul in Norwich, called "Norman's Spital," had been leased to the Corporation in 1575 by the Dean and Chapter of Norwich for 500 years, at a rent of one penny per annum. The Corporation sublet the lands attached to it.

hands of place hunters or of those who made traffic of them.

It is also hinted that Robinson applied to the Corporation at this time for "a lease," which would probably have secured his material necessities, by sub-letting the property which it covered. Joseph Hall makes the gratuitous and ungenerous suggestion that had either of these applications been granted Robinson would never have "separated" from the Anglican Church. He launches it as a Parthian shot at the close of his controversy with Robinson in the concluding words of his *Common Apologie*—

"... neither doubt we to say that the Mastership of the Hospital at Norwich, or a lease from that City (sued for, with repulse), might have procured that this separation from the communion, government, and worship of the Church of England should not have been made by John Robinson."

Clerical Subscription discussed at Norwich

Bancroft's energetic demand for submission to the Canons, and his insistence upon subscription, threw the Puritan clergy into dismay. Pamphlets upon the question of conformity came from the press in quick succession. It was made the theme of many sermons. The constitutional aspect of the matter was closely debated. "We know no kind of law, whereby we may be required to subscribe unto the three articles,"[1] said certain ministers of Devon and Cornwall, for the Canons had not received Parliamentary sanction. They were told for answer that they were required to subscribe "by virtue of a Canon, which is to us a law, being ratified as it is under the King's Majesties hand and seal."[2] The one party was content with the exercise of "the royal prerogative," the other party looked for definite Parliamentary enactment. The whole subject was thoroughly discussed

[1] "Reasons for Refvsal of Svbscription to the booke of Common praier ... with an Ansvvere by Thomas Hvtten, 1605, p. 18.

[2] *Ibid.*, p. 38. "I take it I am not compellable by any law to subscribe," said another minister, *ibid.*, p. 43.

at Norwich, where resistance to subscription was marked. Francis Mason handled the matter in a sermon delivered in the "Greene Yard" there on the third Sunday after Trinity, June 1605. He published it "in sundrie points by him enlarged," in 1607, under the title "The Authoritie of the Church in making Canons and Constitutions concerning things indifferent, and the obedience thereto required, with particular application to the present estate of the Church of England." [1]

It is quite possible that Robinson was present at this discourse—

"The principall marke I shoote at," says Mason, "is to doe my endevour to settle the tender and trembling consciences of those which are not wedded to their owne conceits, but have been carried away rather of weaknesse than of wilfulnesse, that such of them as it shall please the Lord may be reduced to the Tabernacles of peace and follow the trueth in love." [2]

He felt that these internal disputes in the Church of England gave an opening to the Roman Catholics on the one hand, and to Brownists on the other, but he had no proposals to make to remove the difficulties which stood in the way of the Puritans' conformity. Peace in the Church was desirable, but there was no meeting of the Puritans half-way to secure it. Their absolute submission was demanded. The absence of all recognition of the unreasonableness of this attitude on the part of the prelatical party is remarkable. Mason writes in a moderate strain, but gives not the slightest hint of any possible concession to the demands of the Puritan party. He felt that those demands, carried to their logical conclusion, would lead to Brownism, of which the people in Norwich had some practical experience.

"As you reioice the Papists, so you encourage the Brownists, who builde their conclusions vpon your premises and put your speculations in practice. For haue not your ring-

[1] Dr. Williams' Library, *Pamphlets*, 9. 4. 8.
[2] The Epistle Dedicatorie.

leaders proclaimed that our gouernment by Bishops is popish, our liturgie popish, our ministring of baptisme with the crosse popish, our kneeling at the Communion popish; our garments for publike administration, popish; our holidaies, popish and almost euerie thing popish? Wherefore the Brownists, hauing learned that the Pope is Antichrist and the present Church of Rome Babylon; and hearing a voice from heauen crying, '*Goe out of her, my people, that you be not partakers in her sinnes, and that yee taste not of her plagues,*' haue, vpon your former premises, gathered a practicall conclusion and made an actuall separation and rent from the Church of England. And surely, my brethren, as they had their original from your positions, so now they are strengthened by your practices: for they may well thinke that such learned and vertuous men, so famous and renowned Preachers, knowing a *Woe pronounced against them if they preach not the Gospell,* would neuer suffer themselues to be silenced for matters which they iudged indifferent, and therefore they will take it as granted that the things you sticke at are in your opinion simplie vnlawfull. Vpon this dangerous position they will builde an other, for if the Liturgie of the Church of England as it is inioined at this day to be performed, be such as a Minister cannot execute his function with a good conscience: then they conclude that neither may the people heare it with a good conscience because their presence were an approbation of it. Thus the vnquiet wit of man will still be working euen till it runne it selfe vpon the rocke of his owne destruction. Wherefore (my deare brethren) I beseech you, as you tender the good of the Church, to lay aside all contentious humors. Let there not be found in you a spirit of contradiction and singularitie: but follow those things which concerne peace and wherewith one may edifie an other" (pp. 67–68).

Robinson was not convinced by this appeal, and stood firm, suffering suspension from preaching rather than give way contrary to his convictions. It does not appear that he consulted at this time with the obscure Brownist congregation in Norwich, to which Robert Browne and Richard Harrison, and after them Clement Hunt, had ministered. As yet he was not prepared to separate from Anglicanism.

CHAPTER VIII

SEPARATION FROM THE CHURCH OF ENGLAND—ROBINSON AND BERNARD—GERVASE NEVILLE—WILLIAM BREWSTER

As the avenues for useful work or for securing a livelihood at Norwich were now closed to him, Robinson settled up his affairs there and left the city. Where did he go? Hall says: "You went from Norwich to Lincolnshire after your suspension." I think he went home to Sturton-le-Steeple, just across the border from Lincolnshire, in the county of Nottingham. What more natural than that he and his wife should take their children to the grandparents at Sturton till the way should open for fresh work? It would be a refreshing change for them all to get into the restful quiet of the country, after the turmoil of Norwich.

But Robinson's mind was too full of the problems of Church reform according to Scriptural methods to allow him to rest long here. He visited places "where," says he, "I hoped most to fynde satisfaction to my troubled heart." He talked over the difficulties which were weighing upon his mind with clerical friends and neighbours, and especially with those who had a real concern for a further reformation in the Church. Now, as it happened, in the immediate neighbourhood of his old home at Sturton there were those whose thoughts were occupied by the same problems, and who were faced by similar difficulties to those which beset his mind. At Gainsborough John Smith had been checked in his efforts to minister helpfully to the parishioners in the absence of their vicar; at Scrooby William Brewster had organized house-meetings for religious conference and worship in the Manor House, which he occupied; at Babworth Richard Clifton was bringing trouble on himself by refusal to observe the ceremonies of the Church; at Worksop there was agitation against episcopal requirements, and a prospect of independent action on the part of the pious and energetic vicar, Richard Bernard. The Puritan clergy were restive under the demand made upon them to acknowledge the lawfulness of the ceremonies and the requirement to observe them to the letter. The whole question of the nature and constitution of the Christian Church according to the Scriptural teaching was being passed in review.

During this period of freedom from definite ministerial duties Robinson took the opportunity of revisiting Cambridge, and he is reported[1] to have told "one of his acquaintance" on the occasion of this visit "that he had been amongest some company of the seperation before his comming to Camb., and, exercising amongst them, had renounced his former ministery." Robinson, in noticing this report, denies that he had at that time renounced his orders or finally severed his connexion with Anglicanism, but he does not deny his "exercising," that is to say, preaching, praying and exhorting amongst the Separatists at their meetings. He admits he had "made question" of "seperation" at that time, or, as we should say, had made it a subject of discussion and had "disputed for it," but had not "otherwise professed it." Though he might then have been pretty well convinced of the need and obligation of separation from a corrupt Church, he had not as yet acted fully upon that conviction. What he heard at Cambridge only served to strengthen his growing resolution on this point. Twice does he refer to it as a sort of providential message. As he relates the incident in some detail, we may give his account in full. It gives us a picture of what, so far as we know, was his last Sunday in Cambridge—

[1] *A Second Manvdvction*, by Wm. Ames, 1615, p. 29.

"Coming to Cambridge [1] (as to other places, where I hoped most to find satisfaction to my troubled heart), I went the forenoon to Mr. Cha: [*i. e.* Laurence Chaderton] his exercise, who upon the relation which Mary made to the disciples of the resurrection of Christ, delivered in effect this doctrine —that the things which concerned the whole Church were to be declared publicly to the whole Church and not to some part only; bringing for instance and proof the words of Christ, Matt. 18. 17: 'Tell it to the Church'; confirming therein one main ground of our difference from the Church of England, which is, that Christ hath given his power for excommunication to the *whole Church* gathered together in his name, as 1 Cor. 5, the officers as the governors, and the people as the governed in the use thereof; unto which Church his servants are commanded to bring their necessary complaints.

"And I would desire mine opposite [*i. e.* his opponent, the Puritan, William Ames] either to shew me how and where this Church is (having this power) in the parish assemblies; or else, by what warrant of God's word I (knowing what Christ the Lord commanded herein) may with good conscience remain a member of a Church without this power (much less where the contrary is advanced), and so go on in the known transgression of that his commandment: *Tell the Church?*

"In the afternoon I went to hear Mr. B., the successor of Mr. Perkins [*i. e.* Paul Baynes], who, from Ephes. 5 and verse 7 or 11, shewed the unlawfulness of familiar conversation between the servants of God and the wicked, upon these grounds or the most of them—

"(1) That the former are *light* and the other *darkness between which God hath separated.*[2]

"(2) That *the godly hereby are endangered to be leavened with the other's wickedness.*

"(3) That *the wicked are hereby hardened in receiving such approbation from the godly.*

"(4) That *others are thereby offended, and occasioned to think them all alike, and as birds of a feather which so flock together.*

"Whom afterwards privately I desired, as I do also others, to consider whether these very reasons make not as effectually and much more, against the *spiritual communion* of God's people (especially where there wants the means of reformation) with the apparently wicked, to whom they are as *light* to *darkness.*"

[1] *A Manumission to a Manuduction*, 1615, p. 20.

[2] Robinson took the text here alluded to as a motto for the title page of his *Justification of Separation*, 1610: "God separated between the light and between the darkness," Gen. i. 4.

Robinson was alert enough to see that the arguments of Laurence Chaderton and Paul Baynes told with greater force for the Separatist position than for that of the Puritans. The fact that he sought out Baynes after his sermon and privately pressed this point upon him is testimony to his earnestness.

I take it that, on his return from this Cambridge visit, Robinson threw in his lot whole-heartedly with the little group of devout folk in the neighbourhood of his old home who had by this time separated from the Church of England on grounds of conscientious conviction. John Smith led them into the way of separation. When once Robinson had taken the decisive step he did not look back, but shared in all the tribulation which befell his fellow-members on account of their fidelity. According to William Bradford's narrative " these people became two distinct bodies or churches in regard of distance of place, and did congregate severally, for they were of several towns and villages, some in Nottinghamshire, some in Lincolnshire and some of Yorkshire, where they bordered nearest together."

Geographically it was more convenient for Robinson to go over to Scrooby than to Gainsborough. On the latter journey, though the mileage was less, the Trent had to be crossed. The friends at Gainsborough enjoyed the resolute guidance of Smith; there was less need then for Robinson's help in that centre, and he gravitated to the Scrooby group. This was fortunate, for it drew him into close touch with Brewster and Bradford, men of good sense and sound judgment, with whom he maintained a lifelong friendship.

Moreover, there were differences of accent between Smith and Robinson which, in spite of their general agreement as to the necessity and obligation of separation from the Anglican Church, might have led to friction if the two men had been called to labour in close conjunction. Smith, with the downrightness of the pioneer, forswore all communion in religious matters with any members of a Church which he now deemed to be false in its constitution. Robinson, though he would not participate in the public worship of such a Church, was ready to join privately in prayer and religious conference with any sincere and godly member of it.

I think it quite likely that he held meetings for religious worship and conference in Sturton itself. Several relations of his wife, including her brother-in-law, John Carver, accompanied Robinson to Amsterdam from the Sturton district. It is reasonable to suppose that they had already formed the habit of worshipping together.

The actual separation of John Smith and John Robinson from the Church of England, and the renunciation of their "orders" as priests of that Church, created some stir in the locality, especially in clerical circles, but they did not draw into the new movement so many of the local clergy as they had hoped to do. Richard Clifton, the earnest rector of Babworth, was convinced by Smith, and joined them. Hugh Bromehead, the curate of North Wheatley, threw in his lot with them, but Richard Bernard, the vicar of Worksop, of whom they had great expectations, and who went with them up to a point, drew back, and soon became a strenuous opponent of the aims and policy of the Separatists. Some of Bernard's parishioners, however, were led by the earnestness and eloquence of Smith to follow the new path. It is possible that this new religious movement would have made headway in England if it had been given a free field, for it was full of force and vitality, and could boast of capable leaders. It was a movement that could not be ignored. The Archbishop of York and the Bishop of Lincoln would know that if these meetings for worship apart from the Established Church, led by men who had deliberately renounced their orders, were overlooked, their own authority would be seriously weakened. In those days neither the law of the land nor the law of the Church allowed any place for such meetings or such "churches."

The machinery of the Ecclesiastical Commission was set in motion to crush the movement. As Bradford puts it—

"They could not long continue in any peaceable condition; but were hunted and persecuted on every side; so as their former afflictions were but as flea-bitings in comparison of these which now came upon them. For some were taken and clapt up in prison. Others had their houses beset and watched, night and day, and hardly escaped their hands; and the most were fain to fly and leave their houses and habitations, and the means of their livelihood. Yet these, and many other sharper things which afterwards befell them, were no other than they looked for; and therefore were the better prepared to bear them by the assistance of GOD's grace and SPIRIT." [1]

Gervase Neville

The records of the Court of the Ecclesiastical Commission for the Northern Province of England, of which the Archbishop of York was a chief member, give one or two flashes of light upon the story of the "Pilgrim Church" at this period from the official side. One of those cited to appear before it was Gervase Neville.[2] He was a man of some standing in the locality, and as his case is dealt with more fully than usual in the "Act Books" of the Court, we may as well give the record. Preceding writers have not identified this Gervase Neville. He was the Neville of that name who held a considerable extent of land in Ragnell, Dunham, South Leverton and adjacent parts.

Being a son of Robert Neville, he came of a good

[1] Bradford's *History of Plimouth Plantation*, f. 31.

[2] An early reference to Neville I find in the will of Augustine Pickhaver, dated December 27, 1598—

"I give and bequeath unto my verie good frende Mr. Gervase Nevell one frenche crowne trustinge hee wilbee a guide and staye in givinge advise and counsell to my wife and children from time to time." He nominates his brother, Richard Pickhaver, and William Hawkesmore as supervisors of his will, and continues: "I also ordaine and appointe my verie good frende Mr. Gervase Nevell umper over my said sup'visors . . . to advise and directe them from time to time in and about this my will or testament."—"Act Book" of the Southwell Peculiar Court in Notts. Probate Registry, B., f. 284.

family. His grandfather, George Neville, was High Sheriff of Nottinghamshire in 1581.[1] In the Subsidy Roll for 1599[2] I find the entry under "Ragnel": "Gervasius Nevill in terris xl^s–$viij^s$," indicating that he was already assessed on lands there. His title to the house and lands which he occupied in Ragnell was disputed early in the reign of James I, and this gave rise to much irritating litigation. The question appears to have been as to whether the land he held was "Auncient demeasin as of his Ma^{ts} royall Crown of England," or was dependent on the Manor of Dunham. Commissioners were appointed on February 12, 1606, to inquire into the matter, and on the following 26th of March John Thornhagh of Fenton and Edward North sat at East Retford to examine witnesses about it. Some of the depositions give us fresh information in regard to Neville and his family. One of the interrogatories was as to whether the messuage, lands and tenements "in the holding of Jervase Nevill" were "lyable to all paies and layes to Church and kinge wth the towne of Ragnell or wth the towne of Dunham, and whether hath the said Jervase Nevill or his ancestors served as constable and churchwarden for the said Messuage for the towne of Ragnell or for the town of Dunham." Apparently Neville would have been subjected to a stiff fine to quiet his title to the property he had inherited if it were proved to be Crown land. One of his witnesses, "Pawle Taylor of Darlton," deposed that the lands in dispute were "holden of the mannor and soke of Dunham," and further, "he knoweth that the said Gervase Nevill did, after the death of his ffather, paye to this deponent to the use of Sir John Munson, then Lord of the Mannor of Dunham, for the foresaid lands a Relief of fortie nine shillings and fowre pence, wch was a whole yeres rent.

"The said Gervas Nevill doeth paie and his An-

[1] Cf. Letter from the Queen to George Nevill, Brit. Mus. Add. MS., 33, 594, f. 8.

[2] Lay Subsidies, Bassetlaw, Notts., 39 Eliz. $\frac{160}{251}$, Record Office.

cestors dureinge the space of eighteen yeres or thereabout have used to paye tofte penies, otherwise called com̃on ffyne, and that the same hath been yerelie gathered at mychaellmas by the ffreeborrowes and payed to this deponent, bailiffe to the lord of the mannor of Dunham." He said the lands of Gervase Neville were not subject to the annual "king's rent" of £5 12*s*., paid from Ragnell to the sheriff of the county at Retford Sessions.

Henry Howett of Dunham, husbandman, of the age of fourscore years, or thereabouts, sworn and examined sayeth: "that he knoweth the messuage that Gervase Nevill holdeth and occupieth in Ragnell, and saieth that the said Gervase did build that messuage wherein he dwelleth and that the sayd messuages did discend to the said Gervase Nevill from his father and his grandfather."

Another witness, "Richard Unwine of Ragnell, laborer," sixty years of age, deposed that Gervase Neville "is heire vnto another messuage in Ragnell w[ch] his mother in lawe nowe hath for her lyef." And that "he hath knowne the sayd Gervis by the space of Thirtie yeres or more." This shows us that Gervase Neville was in the prime of life, and already married, and distinguishes him from his cousin of the same name who became Rector of Grove in 1611.

We have to remember, then, that Gervase Neville had this trouble with the civil courts on his hands when he was cited before the ecclesiastical authorities on account of his religious opinions. I find from the will of Robert Wood of Dunham, Notts., gentleman, dated September 6, 1607, that Neville had by that time disposed of some of his property. But the fact that he was appointed "overseer" of this will by the testator, and also signed it as a witness, seems to indicate that as yet there was no settled determination to leave for Holland. Robert Wood says in his will—

"Whereas it hath pleased god not to blesse me with anie children of my bodie lawfully begotten, except my wief bee

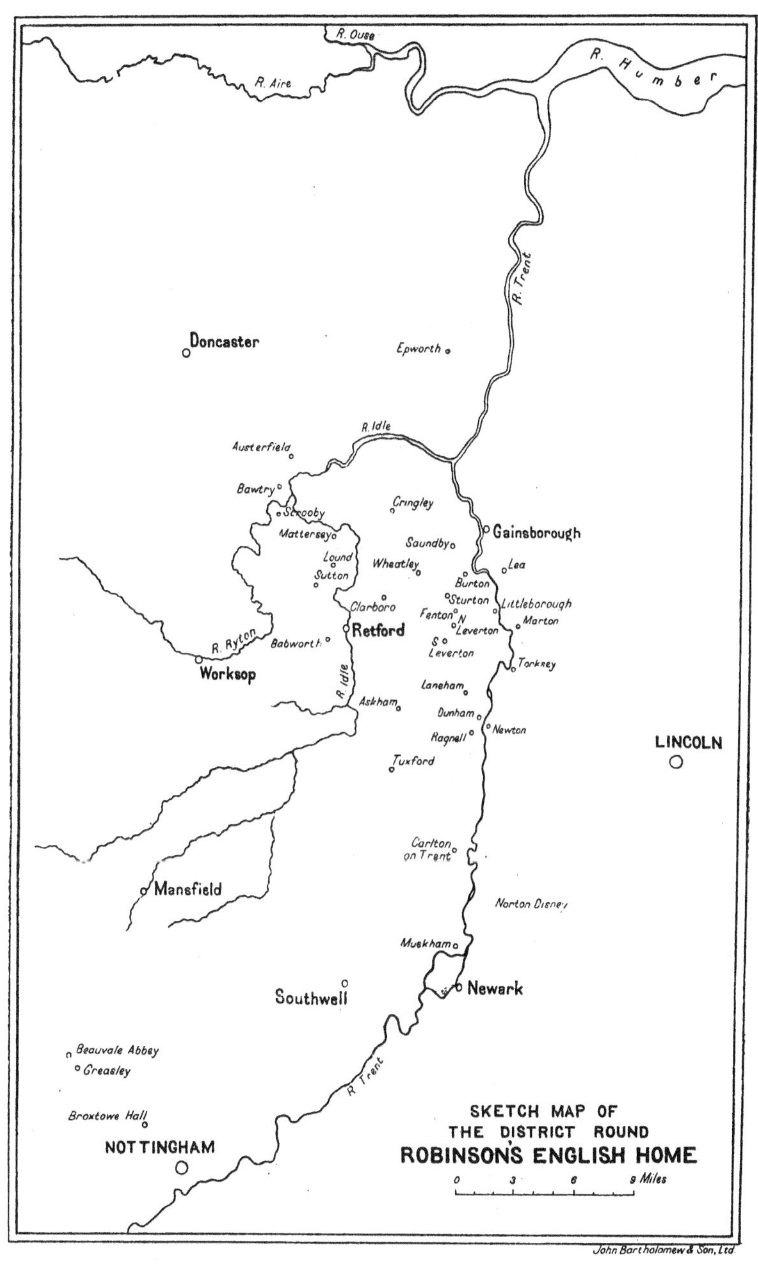

R. Ouse
R. Aire
R. Humber
R. Trent
Doncaster
Epworth
R. Idle
Austerfield
Bawtry
Scrooby
Mattersey
Cringley
Gainsborough
Saundby
Lound
Sutton
Wheatley
Lea
Burton
Sturton
Littleborough
Clarboro
Fenton
N Leverton
Marton
Retford
R. Ryton
Babworth
S Leverton
Torksey
Worksop
R. Idle
Laneham
Askham
Dunham
Newton
Ragnell
LINCOLN
Tuxford
Carlton on Trent
Mansfield
Norton Disney
Muskham
Newark
Southwell
Beauvale Abbey
Greasley
R Trent
Broxtowe Hall
NOTTINGHAM
SKETCH MAP OF THE DISTRICT ROUND ROBINSON'S ENGLISH HOME
0 3 6 9 Miles
John Bartholomew & Son, Ltd

now with childe, which is uncertaine . . . I geve unto Elizabeth my wife one messuage or tenement . . . with the appurtenances therto belonginge which was lately purchased of Gervase Nevile of Ragnell gent. . . . I make and ordaine Gervase Nevile of Ragnell gent., and Hugh ffoxe of ffenton yoman overseers or supervisours of my will." [1]

Soon after this, information was laid against Neville in the Court of the Ecclesiastical Commission for the Northern Province at York. From the Record it is clear that he had already identified himself closely with those in his locality who met separately from the Anglican Church for worship and the discussion of religious matters, renouncing the authority of the Bishops and Archbishops. He was evidently in touch with the Scrooby, Sturton and Gainsborough groups of Separatists. His characterization of the episcopal order of Church government as an "Antichristian Hierarchie," reminds us of the decisive language of John Smith. The fact that the Record describes him as of "Scrooby," points to that little town as a recognized centre for this religious movement. I do not think Neville had any permanent connexion with that parish. He had probably taken up temporary residence in Scrooby in order to be in closer touch with Smith, Clifton, Robinson, Brewster, Helwys and the friends who there foregathered. Neville would know that if he did not conform in three months after conviction he would have to abjure the realm. Here is the record of his case—

"Nov. 10, 1607. Office of the Court *v.* Gervase Nevyle of Scrooby.

"Information hath been given and presentment made that the said Gervase Nevyle is one of the sect of Barrowists or Brownists, holding and maintaining erroneous opinions, and doctrine repugnant to the Holy Scriptures and Word of God, for which his disobedience and schismatical obstinacy

[1] "Act Book" of the Southwell Peculiar Court, in the Nottingham Probate Registry. This will was proved April 20, 1612, by which date the widow Elizabeth Wood, had re-married and was Elizabeth Worsley.

an attachment was awarded to William Blanchard messenger . . . to apprehend him: by virtue whereof being by him brought before His Grace [the Archbishop of York] and said Associates [the Court of Ecclesiastical Commissioners for the Northern Province] and charged with his errors and dangerous opinions and disobedience, his Grace in the name of himself having charged him therewith, as also with certain contemptuous speeches and frequenting of conventicles and company of others of his profession, he required him to take an oath to make answer (so far as he ought and was bound by law) to certain interrogatories or questions by them conceived and set down in writing to be propounded and ministered unto him, and others of his brethren of the separation and sect aforesaid, which he obstinately and utterly refused, denying to give his Grace answer, and protesting very presumptuously and insolently in the presence of God against his authority and (as he termed it) his Antichristian Hierarchy; but yet yielded to answer to the rest of the said Commissioners [the laymen] (excepting his Grace only), although it was by them shewed unto him that his Grace was chief of the Ecclesiastical Commission by virtue whereof he was convented and they all did then and there sit.

"And then, after divers godly exhortations and speeches to him, they did propound and read the said interrogatories unto him and presently set down his answers unto the same in their presences under his hand.

"And forsomuch as thereby, as also by his unreverent, contemptuous, and scandalous speeches, it appeared that he is a very dangerous schismatical Separatist Brownist and irreligious subject, holding and maintaining divers erroneous opinions, the said lord Archbishop with his colleagues have by their strait warrant committed him, the said Gervase, to the custody of William Blanchard, by him to be therewith delivered to the hands, ward and safe custody of the keeper or his deputy keeper of his Highness's Castle of York, not permitting him to have any liberty or conference with any, without special licence from three at least of the said Commissioners, whereof one to be of the Quorum." [1]

On his release from York Castle Neville must have made his way almost at once to Amsterdam, where he attached himself to the Church which had John Smith, Hugh Bromehead and Thomas Helwys as its prominent leaders. We have one or two glimpses

[1] Dexter's *England and Holland of the Pilgrims*, p. 392.

of him in Holland, and it will be simplest to refer to them here, while his case is under our consideration.

When John Smith arrived at the conviction that he and his companions were in error in constituting themselves into a Church by a "covenant," and that the right procedure was by means of baptism, after repentance and profession of faith, he carried Neville with him, and baptized him with the rest of the company, after the manner of the Dutch Anabaptists, by affusion. Closer acquaintance with the Amsterdam Mennonites soon led Smith and his company to question whether they had done the right thing in reviving the practice of baptism for themselves, when there was here a Church already in existence constituted by the baptism of believers after the New Testament method. The point was carefully discussed, and the majority, with Smith, resolved to disavow their action in this matter, dissolve their Church and apply for admission to the Mennonite Church in Amsterdam, under the pastoral care of Hans de Ries.

Though Thomas Helwys and a handful of members dissented from this step, and maintained the validity of the Church position at which they had arrived, and their right to recover the ordinance of baptism for themselves, Smith again carried Neville with him. His name, "Jervase Nevill," is included by Smith in the list of those who petitioned for union with the Mennonites and acknowledged their error in taking into their own hands the task of constituting themselves into a Church by baptism when a Church of that type was already accessible. Nor was Neville daunted by Smith's advance towards the doctrinal position of the Mennonites and his desertion of the Calvinism which marked the Puritan preachers of England in that day. His signature, "Garvase Neuile," heads the second column[1] of the names of those in John Smith's Church who subscribed to the articles contained in *A Short Confession of Faith*, which had been drawn up to serve as a general indication of the belief

[1] Burrage, *Early English Dissenters*, vol. ii. p. 200.

of the Mennonite churches.[1] But his name is struck out by a stroke of the pen. This indicates that he had either died or withdrawn from the society at the time the roll was revised. I think in his case it was an early withdrawal, for we have an intimation in a book published in 1611 by Thomas Helwys that Neville had by that time fallen away. His difficulty was on the point of "Succession." Smith argued that they had no right to constitute the Church anew if a true Church was already in being to which they could affiliate, and from which, in some sense, they could derive authority. Such a Church he held the Mennonite Church to be. Well, then, what about the origin of the Mennonite Church itself? How did that derive? Could it trace a clear succession from Apostolic times and the primitive Church? It seems a singular crotchet to worry the minds of these Anabaptists, but we find another group in London a few years later discussing the same point. Helwys lets us see pretty plainly that Neville was not satisfied on the matter. The passage will bear quoting, as it testifies to Neville's intrepid opposition to the ecclesiastical authorities in England, and on this point Helwys had access to first-hand information, for his own brave wife, Joan Helwys, was a prisoner at York for conscience' sake at the period when Neville was imprisoned there.

"Mr. Jarvase Nevile, having witnessed not only this, but divers other truths for the which he hath been long imprisoned and condemned to perpetual imprisonment, yea, expecting death for the same, yet notwithstanding all his former fidelity and constancy whereby his bonds were famous through the whole land falling with Mr. Smyth upon this your blind succession (forsaking the rock whereon he stood) is now returned beyond his vomit, exclaiming against your Succession, and strives to build up the Succession of Rome which he hath

[1] Helwys, writing to the Mennonites, shows that Neville once accepted their position that magistrates are unfit for Church membership, and quotes him as saying that "Magistrates are no otherwise the ministers of God, but as the devils are." This, he says, "one of our own countrymen, the forenamed Mr. Jervase Nevile (falling upon this and other your errors), most blasphemously hath affirmed." *Advt. unto the New Fryesers*, 1611, p. 73.

formerly with all zeal and holiness pulled down, and so is become a hissing of men and a reproach unto all the godly, and is made a scorn of the wicked, a just reproach for all that fall away." [1]

The following reference also pictures Neville as a backslider from the Separatist cause, which he first espoused with ardour.

On July 8, 1611, new style, Matthew Saunders and Cuthbert Hutten wrote a letter [2] to their Pastor, Francis Johnson, and the elders of his church at Amsterdam, renouncing their separation from the Church of England. In the course of this letter, in pointing to the many varieties of separation, they say: "The ground of Master Nevil's errors was also separation, though now he be further run backward than ever he was forward." Thus he disappears from our story.

William Brewster

Action was also taken against Richard Jackson and William Brewster of Scrooby. They had been served with a "process" to appear before the Court on December 1, 1607, and gave their word to attend, but they did not put in an appearance, consequently they were each fined £20 and their arrest ordered. The next reference to their case is significant—

"Dec. 15th, 1607. Office *v.* Richard Jackson & Wm. Bruester of Scrowbie. For Brownisme. An attachment was awarded to W. Blanchard to apprehend them, but he certifieth that he can not finde them, nor understand where they are."

The fines, however, were duly levied, for in the following spring the Archbishop returned into the Exchequer fines of £20 apiece which had been taken

[1] *An Advertisement or Admonition unto the Congregations which Men call the New Fryesers,* by Thomas Helwys (1611), p. 35.

[2] Lawne, *Prophane Schism,* pp. 55–57.

from "Richard Jackson, William Brewster and Robert Rochester of Scrooby, in the county of Nottingham, Brownists or Separatists," for non-appearance "upon lawful summons at the Collegiate Church of Southwell."[1]

Brewster (*c.* 1567–1644) was one of the leading spirits in the Separatist movement, and closely associated with the Pilgrim Church from its inception. He stood at Robinson's right hand in many a time of difficulty, and gave the Church the benefit of his experience and wise counsel in the office of ruling elder. Brewster's father was of the same name, and I think the conjecture that he was connected with the family of Brewsters, long seated at Wrentham, in Suffolk, and with Henry Brewster, the vicar of Sutton-cum-Lound from 1565 to 1598, and the James Brewster who then succeeded to that benefice, has great probability. William Brewster senior held the office of postmaster at Scrooby, and the responsible position of Receiver and Bailiff to the Archbishop of York for his "Lordship and Manor of Scrooby, and all the liberties of the same in the County of Nottingham." He had power to distrain for any arrears of customary dues and payments that might accrue in the Archbishop's manors in Askham and Laneham. He was a well-known man in the district. When Thomas Wentworth of "Scrowbie Manor" died (will dated March 27, 1574), Brewster took on the tenancy of the Manor House, as its roomy outbuildings were suited for the stabling of the post horses. His gifted son was sent to Cambridge, and matriculated at Peterhouse December 3, 1580, but did not stay at the University long enough to graduate. Entering the service of William Davison, one of Her Majesty's Secretaries of State, young Brewster gained an insight into public affairs and saw something of foreign parts. When Davison lost favour with the Queen, and was deprived of his office, Brewster was free to go home to Scrooby and assist his father in his declining years. The old man

[1] Hunter's *Collections concerning Founders of New Plymouth*, p. 131.

died in the summer of 1590,[1] leaving his wife Prudence to the care of his son. Young William Brewster succeeded him in the office of "Post of Scrooby," though he was nearly ousted through not taking pains to get his appointment confirmed at once.[2] The fact that no mention is made of brothers or sisters in the Grant of Administration does not necessarily imply, as American writers have imagined, that there were none. It is not at all unlikely that James Brewster, Vicar of Sutton, was a brother.

We must not linger here over the interesting details of Brewster's career. Suffice it to say that he showed a marked interest in matters of religion, and gave of his substance to secure effective preachers for the locality. He married as soon as his position was assured, and had children at Scrooby, Jonathan, Patience and Fear, all of whom accompanied him and their mother, Mary Brewster,[3] to Holland, and in due course went on to New England—the girls following their parents and brother thither in the good ship *Anne* in 1623. Such was the man who gathered friends and neighbours in his house for religious meetings and entertained them with generous hospitality. He was now compelled to look abroad for the liberty denied at home, and in his next venture he went hand in hand with John Robinson.

[1] I have examined the "Act Book" of the Deanery of Retford-cum-Laneham, where the Note of Administration, July 24, 1590, to William Brewster is given. The old man had not made a will.

[2] The position of postmaster became a sort of family possession if the duties were faithfully attended to. Fosters held the position for years at Tuxford, the stage south of Scrooby, and Hayfords at Doncaster, the stage to the north. I find in the will of "John Nelson of Scrooby, in the County of Notts., postmaster," dated April 25, 1617, the following bequest: "to my eldest son, Willm Nelson xs and the revercon of my office in full satisfaction of his child's porcon." And the bequest held good, for, turning to the accounts of the Postmaster-General, I find that William Nelson received the salary for Scrooby from July 1, 1617 to Sept. 2, 1630.

[3] The maiden name of Mary Brewster has not been handed down. I suggest Mary Wentworth of Scrooby.

CHAPTER IX

"AN ADVENTURE ALMOST DESPERATE"

William Bradford

THE little company of fellow-believers had managed to continue together in England about a year, and "kept their meetings every Sabbath in one place or another, exercising the worship of God amongst themselves," but now, finding there was no hope of liberty for their separate worship at home, they discussed the possibility of emigrating to Holland. "By a joint consent," says Bradford, "they resolved to go into the Low Countries, where, they heard, was freedom of religion for all men, as also how sundry, from London and other parts of the land, had been exiled and persecuted for the same cause, and were gone thither, and lived at Amsterdam and in other places of the land." Preparations were at once made to act upon this resolution. Brewster gave up his office as "Post" of Scrooby at the end of September in 1607; arrangements were made with reliable friends to take charge of property that could not be realized immediately. Thomas Helwys was specially active and useful in furthering this passage into a strange country. "If any brought oars, he brought sails," was the picturesque phrase with which Robinson described his eager help. But there was great difficulty in getting away, "for though they could not stay, yet they were not suffered to go; but the ports and havens were shut against them, so as they were fain to seek secret means of conveyance, and to bribe and fee the mariners, and give extraordinary rates for their passages. And yet were they oftentimes betrayed, many of them, and both they and their goods intercepted and surprised, and thereby put to great trouble and charge."

Bradford gives an instance or two of these difficulties. In one case "a large company" of them were betrayed after they had got on board a ship near Boston, in Lincolnshire. This led to their imprisonment for a month at Boston, and even when the main body were released and sent to their homes, seven of the leading members were kept in prison and bound over to the Assizes, amongst the number being William Brewster. In the following spring another concerted attempt to embark between Grimsby and Hull in a Dutch ship was foiled by the authorities, who swooped down on the party after the first boat-load of men had got on board. The Dutch ship-master sailed away with those who had reached his vessel, while the rest of the men on shore, and the women and children stranded on the mud-bank in a small bark, waiting for the rising tide, were left behind. Hence arose more anxiety and delay. "Notwithstanding all these storms of opposition, they all gat over at length, some at one time and some at another, and some in one place and some in another, and met together again, according to their desires, with no small rejoicing." Two of those who went over in the summer of 1608 from Sutton-cum-Lound, where James Brewster was vicar, were married in Amsterdam soon after their arrival. Here is the record—

"1608, July 5.—Henry Cullandt of Nottinghamshire, bombazine worker, 20 years old,—producing certificate under the hand of Richard Clyfton, preacher at Sutton, that his banns had been published there,—and Margarete Grymsdiche of Sutton, 30 years old."

They had evidently prepared for marriage in England, but, owing to persecution or to an opportune chance of a safe passage, they hasted away.

It was only after much trouble and with greatly diminished resources that the Pilgrims reached their haven of refuge in Holland. We have no account of Robinson's crossing. A memorandum in the Clifton family Bible tells us that "Richard Clifton, with his wife and children, came into Amsterdam, in Holland, August 1608." Probably Robinson got over about the same time, for Bradford tells us "Master Robinson, Master Brewster, and other principal members . . . were of the last, and stayed to help the weakest over before them."[1] After the harassing months of the preceding winter and spring, the re-united friends now had a breathing space. They were at last free to give attention to the better ordering of their Church affairs. Already they had "joined themselves, by a covenant of the Lord, into a Church estate in the fellowship of the Gospel to walk in all his ways made known or to be made known." John Murton, referring to Robinson, says: "Do we not know the beginning of his Church, that there was first one stood up and made a covenant and then another, and these two joined together and so a third, and these became a Church say they."[2] The indications are that this group of refugees now became more closely organized, and definitely chose John Robinson as pastor and John Carver as deacon. Not until they got to Leyden, however, was Brewster appointed "ruling elder." They were content with Robinson's ministrations and did not elect any "teacher" as colleague.

[1] *History of Plimouth Plantation*, fo. 41.

[2] *John Smith the Sebaptist, Thomas Helwys and the first Baptist Church in England, etc.*, Burgess, 1911, p. 84.

STURTON-LE-STEEPLE CHURCH (PRIOR TO THE RESTORATION OF 1870), SHOWING ITS FORM AS ROBINSON KNEW IT. A DISASTROUS FIRE ON SUNDAY, FEBRUARY 24, 1901, DESTROYED THE NAVE OF THE RESTORED EDIFICE.

CHAPTER X

RELIGIOUS REFUGEES AT AMSTERDAM

THE stay of Robinson and his company at Amsterdam was of short duration. The religious refugees from Nottinghamshire, Lincolnshire and Norfolk who gathered round him found other groups of English religionists already settled in this thriving city. There was the Church under the pastoral care of Francis Johnson, with Henry Ainsworth serving it as doctor or teacher. This was the Separatist Church, constituted in London under the leadership of Henry Barrow, John Greenwood and John Penry, whose members found a refuge in Amsterdam when persecution made it impossible for them to meet in peace at home. Representing the first body of English religious refugees, it took the name of the "Ancient Church," to distinguish it from other and more recent societies. There had been another early group of Separatists, described in 1597 as "that poore English Congregation in Amstelredam to whome H[enoch] C[lapham] for the present administreth the Ghospel." [1] Yet another group had come from the west of England under the leadership of Thomas White. These west-countrymen first joined in fellowship with Johnson's Church, but differences arising, they soon parted company, and set up a meeting among themselves. The story of the Ancient Church has been fully and frequently told, but that of the Separatist Church in the western parts of England has received less attention. A few fresh details con-

[1] *Theologicall Axioms,* by Henoch Clapham, 1597.

cerning it, throwing a sidelight on our story, will not be out of place.

This western Church was active in the district where the counties of Wilts, Gloucester and Somerset meet together, and from that neighbourhood there were some who in later years joined the Pilgrim Church at Leyden. This congregation in the west paved the way for the sturdy nonconformity which marked the locality in after years. A hostile writer, referring to the Separatists as early as the year 1588, says—

> "Though their full swarm and store be (as it is most likely) in London and the parts near adjoining, yet have they sparsed of their companies into several parts of the Realm and namely into the West almost to the uttermost borders thereof."

Then again, in 1593, when John Penry was under sentence of condemnation, and standing in the shadow of death, he wrote to his fellow-believers in these terms—

> "I would wish you earnestly to write, yea, to send, if you may, to comfort the brethren in the West and North countries, that they faint not in these troubles, and that also you may have of their advice and they of yours what to do in these desolate times."

The question naturally arises as to whether we can learn anything of the leaders and members of this early Congregational Church in the west. From recent investigations I have been able to recover something of its history.

The course of development of this western Church runs parallel with that of Separatist Churches in other parts. There was a feeling that the Reformation had stopped half-way. People desired to see the Church order brought into closer accord with that indicated in the New Testament as instituted in the Primitive and Apostolic Churches of Christ. They considered that the ceremonies retained in the State Church savoured too much of papal practices. For example, Thomas Baslyn, a schoolmaster of Wiltshire, and his wife got into trouble with the authorities in 1588, because they declined to have the sign of the cross used in the baptism of their daughter. Baslyn's parish minister would not undertake to " baptyze his child accordyng to Christe's institution onlie," so he arranged for the baptism to take place " at his dwelling-house, by Mr. Thomas Hickman, a minister . . . in the presence of divers other faithful people." From opposition to the ceremonies of the Established Church the more earnest of the reformers passed on to a deliberate separation and a refusal to recognize the authority of the Bishops to prescribe their religious belief and practice. Christ alone was the Head of His Church. Those holding such views began to meet together for conference and worship, and thus we have a nascent Congregational Church coming into being. The references to this western Church in contemporary literature are given in general terms. Names and places are seldom mentioned. To give precise details would only bring the brethren under the clutches of the ecclesiastical courts.

Still, a few names may be recovered. One of the leaders in this western movement was undoubtedly William Smith. He was born about 1563, and entered the ministry of the Church of England. He received " orders " from the Bishop of Coventry and Lichfield. Subsequently he secured a licence to preach from the Bishop of Salisbury, and then settled at Bradford-on-Avon in Wiltshire. But he was uneasy in his mind. He desired the further reformation of the Anglican Church. Somehow he heard of the Separatist Church in London, and he came up in 1593 for the express purpose of conferring with its leaders, John Greenwood and Francis Johnson. While he was attending a meeting of this religious society at the house of Nicholas Lee, in Smithfield, " to see and hear their order," the assembly was disturbed and he suffered arrest. Smith was thrown into prison. Refusing to conform, he was banished. He seems to have withdrawn to

Holland, where he exercised some oversight of the exiled congregation during the incarceration of its pastor, Francis Johnson, in the Fleet prison. Some writers have confused him with John Smith the se-baptist, but William Smith was an older man, and threw in his lot with the Separatists while John Smith was still at Christ's College in Cambridge. There is reason to think that William Smith afterwards conformed, while John Smith never returned to the Church of England after he renounced his "orders."

The next glimpse we have of this western Church is in the district of Wiltshire within easy reach of Bradford-on-Avon. Here a group of clergy and laymen were actively interested in the religious questions which were pressing upon the consciences of earnest-minded men of the day. What was a true Church of Christ? What constituted a true ministry? Which was of higher authority, the word of the Prelates, or the Divine Word of the New Testament? These questions were discussed in conferences and debated in many a home.

One of the most strenuous advocates of religious reform in the west was a young minister, Thomas White, curate of Slaughterford, a tiny village on the north-western confines of Wiltshire. He advanced to the conclusion that the ministry of the Church of England had no valid standing. Consequently, early in the year 1603, he gave up his cure. He then joined himself to that Church in the west parts of England which held the same faith with the English Separatists of London and Amsterdam. White was opposed by John Awdrey, vicar of Melksham, who went over to Slaughterford and delivered a special lecture in the church there to refute the position taken up by White and his friends. Some of White's leading parishioners adopted his views, and his successor in the cure of St. Nicholas at Slaughterford, Thomas Powell by name, also became his follower, and would have replied to Awdrey from the Slaughterford pulpit had he not been prevented.

At this juncture, "about the time of the new King's coming into England," Francis Johnson took the daring step of coming over from Amsterdam to England, with a view to presenting a petition to James for toleration on behalf of the exiled Church, and to see what prospect of liberty there might be at home under the new condition of things. He took the opportunity of going down into the west to confer with fellow-believers there, and actually ventured to hold religious meetings at the jeopardy of his life. The renewed activity of the western Separatists at this period stirred up the authorities to action, and led to the migration of a small company from this part of Wiltshire to Amsterdam in 1604.

One of the places of meeting at Slaughterford was at the house of Thomas Cullimer, a member of a good old local yeoman family. He, with his wife Ann, were ardent supporters of the cause, and at their house Francis Johnson preached. Another place of meeting in the same parish was at the house of William Hore, a fuller by trade. Here a memorable meeting was held on Sunday, February 26, 1604, at which Thomas White preached. "There were assembled about three score persons to hear him." He preached with effect, and at this gathering received Thomas Powell, his successor in the cure of Slaughterford, into the fellowship of his new Church. One present at the gathering described the incident a few days later in these terms—

> "Thomas Powell, late preacher at Slatenford, was at the preaching of White upon the XXVIth of Feb.: and there made a public confession that he had heretofore spoken against their courses, but that from that time he would manifest love and fellowship with them by defending and maintaining of their doctrine. And he was admitted by White into the society of their Church. . . . When Powell was so admitted he promised to leave the fellowship and communion of this Church of England." [1]

[1] *Sessions Roll* for Wiltshire, Easter Term, *sub dato.* I consulted this at Devizes.

One of the lay members of this congregation, Silvester Butler by name, a weaver of Castle Combe, was examined by the Bishop of Salisbury. He was firm and resolute in his convictions. The note of his examination tells us "he professeth that he will continue one of the same Church while he liveth, and will not conform himself to come to any other Church." Another weaver, John Harford of Eaton, was equally brave. He was brought before the Bishop and—

"being demanded when he was at the parish church where he dwelleth, or at any other parish church to hear divine service, saith he resorteth to the 'Church of God,' but for the temple made with hands he alloweth it not for a church."

Fleeing from persecution at home, White and Powell, with a handful of companions, arrived safely at Amsterdam, and joined the exiled Church already settled there. Francis Johnson entertained White in his own house for nine or ten weeks, but the two did not get on well together. The Wiltshire men did not feel quite at home with the older Separatists. On a closer acquaintance the discipline and order of the exiled Church did not impress them favourably.

With Thomas White himself matters moved swiftly. He quickly fell in love with a young English widow, Rose Philips, who was under sentence of excommunication by the Church of Johnson for trivial reasons. This will account in some measure for White's subsequent bitterness against the English exiled Church at Amsterdam. In April 1604 they published the intention of their marriage at Amsterdam. The Dutch clerk was puzzled by the word Slaughterford, and he entered it as Sachtenfort. White gave his age as twenty-six years, and the maiden name of his betrothed is set down as Rose Grimbrye, or Grempre, and her place of origin as London, while her description is "widow of John Philips."

Johnson tells us that White—

"coming over to Amsterdam and desiring to be partaker of the Lord's Supper with us, did in our public meeting before us all, with his own mouth testify his consent with us in the same faith we profess."

But this union did not last long, for White and Powell soon organized their little company as a distinct Church. They sent word to England of their doings in a letter addressed to their " brethren, the Church in the west, partakers of the same heavenly vocation," in which they say that, though their hope of forming a distinct body in their own country was frustrated, yet it was now accomplished in a strange land. White's Church soon collapsed. The difficulties of his position led him to reconsider his action. He determined to return to the Anglican fold. One of the easiest ways of regaining favour with the prelates would be to write against his Separatist associates. It was this mean course that Thomas White took. He issued, in 1605, with the encouragement and connivance of the prelatical party, an ill-natured and slanderous little book entitled, *A Discoverie of Brownisme*, in which he presented in the worst possible light any story he could gather to the detriment of Johnson's Church and its members. His work naturally raised a storm of protest against him amongst his old friends, and he was glad to get away from their midst to England. Eventually he secured preferment in the Anglican Church, and became rector of St. Mary Woolnoth in Lombard Street, London, on November 14, 1609. He did not long enjoy his benefice. His health was broken, and he died on November 20, 1611. " When he had gotten a benefice," says Richard Clifton, " in such sort as he did, the Lord soon ended his days."

His defection from the cause, though disappointing to his new friends, did not mean the extinction of that Church of Christ in the west which he had first joined on giving up his country cure. The points in question between the Separatists and the adherents of the Episcopal Church were still eagerly discussed in Wiltshire. Johnson indicates that John Jesop, incumbent of Maningford Bruce in that county, "and other his fellows there have bestowed much labour in reading our writings." Joseph Hall, afterwards Bishop of Norwich, refers scornfully to this religious society as a Church meeting in a "parlour in the west." It was small, and it was persecuted, but it persisted, and, to some extent, leavened the religious thought of the district. When liberty was secured and the power of the prelacy for the time being broken Congregational and Baptist pioneers found Wiltshire, Gloucestershire and Somersetshire fruitful fields for their labours. The obscure "Church in the western parts" of an earlier day had prepared the ground.

The story of the little company of refugees led by White, from the western parts of England, and their relations with the "Ancient Church" under Francis Johnson, will help us to understand the position and feeling of the group under Robinson's leadership. They wanted freedom to work out their position in their own way. To some extent the movement was still experimental. They did not wish to be absolutely tied to Johnson's conclusions. Though they had come to a settled conviction on the main points of separation, there were related matters which they desired to consider together at leisure and explore more thoroughly in the light of Holy Scripture.

Differences between John Smith and the leaders of the Ancient Church had already become apparent, and there were threatenings of discord and contention in the Ancient Church itself. It was partly to avoid entanglement in these actual and potential controversies that Robinson and his friends decided to leave Amsterdam. Already Smith had come to the conclusion that, as the Church of England was wrongly and falsely constituted, it had no more power to bestow valid baptism than it had to bestow valid "orders" on the ministry. Just as they had renounced their "orders," they ought also to renounce their baptism and start afresh. He discussed the matter with Richard Clifton, and was eager to talk it over with other leaders among the Separatists, but they were chary, and he "had neither conference with them by speeches nor writing about these matters, save only with Mr. Robinson." [1] The Pilgrim Pastor recognized the disintegrating and explosive forces latent in the ideas which now claimed the attention of John Smith's active mind. Amsterdam was likely to become a storm centre. He felt he would be more able to hold his flock together if they moved out of its range.

[1] Clifton's *Plea for Infants*, 1610, Epistle to Reader.

CHAPTER XI

ROBINSON'S CONTROVERSIES WITH JOSEPH HALL AND JOHN BURGESS

THE number of religious refugees who fled from England and gathered round John Smith and John Robinson in Amsterdam was but small—a " handful," as Joseph Hall put it—and consequently many considered the movement too insignificant for serious notice. " Many laugh at it," said Bernard, and " some account it a matter scarce worthy thinking upon." [1] But those who knew the standing of the leaders recognized its importance. Smith and Robinson were soon called upon to justify their separation and defend their new position. Their old friend and neighbour, Richard Bernard, vicar of Worksop, quickly issued a little book deprecating what he called the " Separatists' schism." News of this breach with the Anglican Church came through to Joseph Hall (1574–1656), then rector of Halstead in Essex. He would know something of the leaders in the movement from his acquaintance with them in Cambridge, and he lost no time in sending them what he described as a " loving monitory letter," in which the monition is more conspicuous than the love. Hall had accompanied Sir Edmund Bacon on a journey to Spa in 1605, and on the way back he apparently fell in with one whom he calls a " harbinger " of the nonconformists—some one who was arranging a refuge in Holland for those clergy in England who were harassed and troubled about the ceremonies enforced by the Bishops. Hall connected this incident

[1] *Christian Advertisements,* 1608, Epistle Dedicatorie.

with the "separation" of which he now heard. So long as the Separatist movement was made up, in the main, of craftsmen and tradesmen, the Anglican priesthood could affect to ignore it, but when men who had held fellowships and were well known in University circles led a Separatist exodus it called for remark. Hall's letter was addressed "to Mr. Smyth and Mr. Rob[inson], ringleaders of the late separation at Amsterdam." It was written in vigorous style, "setting forth their injury done to the Church, the Injustice of their Cause and Fearfulness of their Offence: censuring and advising them." They were reported to him not as "parties in this evil, but authors." If they had gone over quietly to Holland by themselves it would not have excited much remark. Many Puritan clergy had taken that course. It was an ominous point that they had led companies of fellow-believers with them. "Your flight," he says, "is not so much as your misguidance."[1] That curious tone of airy superiority peculiar to the controversial writings of those who hold clerical offices protected by the State, runs through the whole of this forceful letter. Not without reason did Robinson call it a "censorious epistle." The intense aversion amongst the Anglican clergy from anything in the nature of "separation" from the Church of England is reflected in Hall's parting warning to his two "brethren" and former "companions," in which he says, "Your souls shall find too late that it had been a thousand times better to swallow a ceremony than to rend a Church; yea, that even whoredoms and murders shall abide an easier answer than separation."[2]

Robinson soon penned a reply to this singular letter. He declared that Hall had been too forward in censuring a cause of which his discourse showed him to be "utterly ignorant." For it was not merely a distaste for the ceremonies that had led to his separation, but a conviction that the Anglican Church, from

[1] *Works*, vol. iii. p. 401. [2] *Ibid.*, p. 404.

the Scriptural point of view, was radically wrong in its make-up and constitution. Hall had not appreciated the point that it was something more vital than the ceremonies that was in question. Robinson freely and thankfully acknowledged the graces and good things in the Anglican Church, of which he had partaken when he was in communion with it, just as Hall acknowledged the good things in the Church of Rome, from which, nevertheless, he also separated! He had not entered the way of separation lightly; he "durst never set foot into this way, but upon a most sound and unresistible conviction of conscience by the Word of God."[1] If he and his friends had to answer for their separation in "the Consistory Courts" or before "the Ecclesiastical Judges" in the Church of England, then they might find Hall's threat, that it would be easier to answer for murder and unclean living, perfectly justified. "But," says Robinson in conclusion, "because we know that not Anti-Christ, but Christ, shall be our Judge, we are bold upon the warrant of his Word and Testament . . . to proclaim to all the world separation from whatsoever riseth up rebelliously against the sceptre of his Kingdom; as we are undoubtedly persuaded the communion, government, ministry, and worship of the Church of England do!"

Robinson expressed the wish that his answer might "come to the hands of him that occasioned it." His wish was satisfied. On receipt of it Joseph Hall took up his pen again and set to work on an elaborate reply to the general position of the Separatists. This time he took pains to make himself more thoroughly acquainted with their arguments by reading the published works of Francis Johnson, Henry Ainsworth, John Smith, and other leaders in the movement. The result was his book entitled *A Common Apologie of the Chvrch of England Against the Vnjust Challenges of the overjvst Sect commonly called Brownists.* It represents the attitude of those in the

[1] *Works*, vol. iii. p. 406.

"central line" in the Anglican Church towards Separatists and thorough-going reformers, and gives a fair view of the state of the controversy in 1610.

Meanwhile Robinson was engaged in a discussion with another old acquaintance, a minister of Puritan leanings who, though an advocate for further reform in the Anglican Church, was startled by Robinson's definite act of separation. The record of this controversy remains in manuscript in the Bodleian Library at Oxford.[1] My own conjecture was that Robinson's friendly antagonist in this discussion was John Burgess (1563–1635), who had been educated at St. John's College, Cambridge, and then made rector of St. Peter Hungate in Norwich. He refused to subscribe to the new Book of Canons in 1604, was silenced, withdrew to Leyden, and there studied medicine. Returning to England he received in due course the degree of Doctor of Physic from the University of Cambridge. Eventually he conformed and accepted the benefice of Sutton Coldfield. Burgess seemed to me to fit the conditions which the identification of this anonymous opponent of Robinson demanded. The conjecture was justified and turned into a certainty on a comparison of the handwriting of the author with that of Burgess. John Burgess, though serving in Holland as chaplain to Sir Horace Vere, the governor of Brill, was kept informed of Norwich affairs. He was much upset by the news of Robinson's "falling of[f] from the Churche of England." In conversation with Matthew Slade (an English schoolmaster, formerly in fellowship with the Church of Francis Johnson), he expressed his feeling in regard to Robinson's "rupture," or act of separation, and his wish to "speake with him" on the subject. Slade passed the word on to Robinson, who soon sent a letter to his worthy friend, setting out the grounds for his action. John Burgess replied,

[1] Jones, MS. 30. Attention was directed to this MS. by Mr. Champlin Burrage, who published extracts from it in *New Facts Concerning John Robinson*, Oxford, 1910. I have studied the document independently.

indicating that it was not a question of Robinson's faith, but his "rupture from the Churche" that he was concerned about. Could he justify his separation? Let them discuss the particular case of his separation from "that churche or parishe of St. Andrewes in Norwich of which he had lately beene a minister." Robinson willingly accepted the challenge: "The instance you propound for the specyall subiect of the questyon in hand I agree to, which is St. Andrewes in Norwich." His antagonist argued that "St. Andrewes parish in Norwich is a trewe church of Christe with which a christian man maie lawfullye communicate in the worship of God." Robinson argued that it was a false Church, because it was not rightly constituted, and was involved in all the defects and corruptions inherent in the Church of England as a whole, of which it was part and parcel. Burgess at this stage left for a brief visit to England, and had no opportunity of answering Robinson's arguments till his return. He then drew up a reply, incorporating, after the manner of the time, the main part of Robinson's statement of his case. A copy of this reply he arranged to be carefully written out, as though for the Press, and after adding a prefatory "advertisement" and a few marginal notes, it was sent on to some friend at Reading, possibly William Burton, for his consideration and perusal. Thence it passed through various hands to its present resting-place in Oxford. The preface will put us at the right angle of vision—

"AN ADVERTISEMENT OF THE ANSWEARER SERVINGE FOR INTRODUCTION

"Mr. Robinson sometimes a preacher in Norwich fell to Brownisme and became a pastor to those of the seperation at Leyden. I bewayled to Mr. Slade of Amsterdam this his fallinge of from the churche of England wishinge that I mighte speak wth him. Uppon notice hereof Mr. Robinson wrote to me and propounded certayne reasons for his seperation. I returned a letter, praying him to interpret my

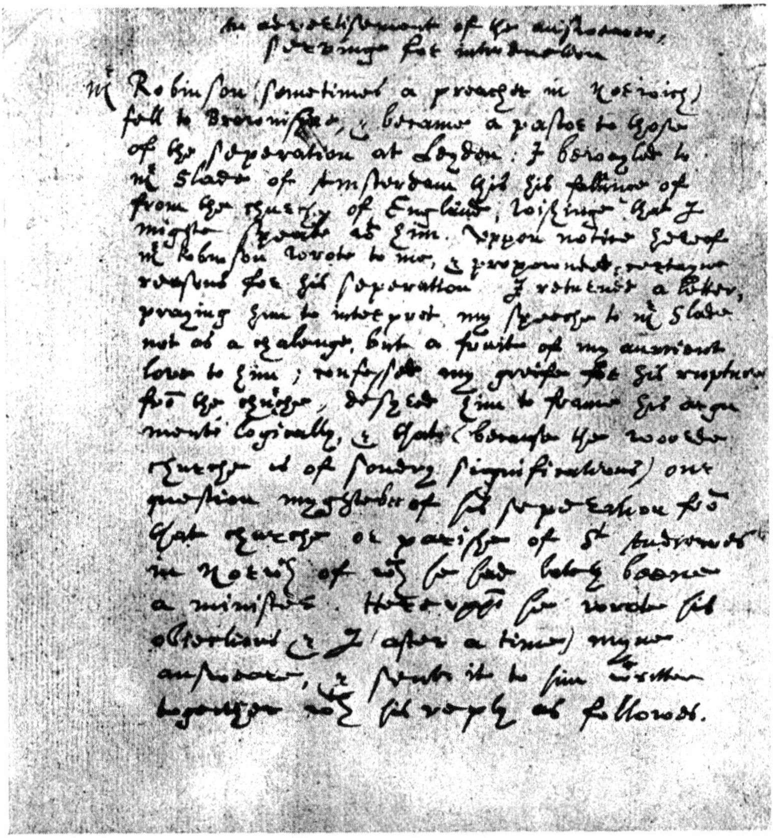

PREFATORY "ADVERTISEMENT" TO THE ANONYMOUS MANUSCRIPT IN THE BODLEIAN LIBRARY, WHICH TELLS THAT ROBINSON "HAD LATELY BEENE A MINISTER" OF "ST. ANDREWES IN NORWICH." COMPARE THE WRITING WITH THE ACKNOWLEDGED HAND OF JOHN BURGESS REPRODUCED AT PAGE 408.

speeche to mr. Slade not as a chalenge, but a fruit of my auncient love to him; confessed my greife at his rupture frō the churche, desyred him to frame his argument logically & that (because the woorde church is of sondry significations) our question myghte bee of his seperation frō that churche or parishe of St. Andrewes in Norwch of wch he had lately beene a minister. Herevppō he wrote his objections & I, after a time, myne answear and sente it to him written together wth his reply as followes."

Then comes the little treatise in which the author endeavours to counter Robinson's arguments. He concludes it in these friendly terms—

"I heartily commend you to the Lord God of mercy and truth and beseech him to open your eyes that you may see your errors made and to give you a true humble spirit that you may not be ashamed to become wise and [may come to] a worthy resolution to give God glory in returning [to the Church of England] and causing those poor souls that depend upon your lips to return, that you may find peace in the end which in this course [of separation] I am persuaded you cannot. And thus praying you to pass by any escapes of the writer with love and to believe that I love your person for the Lord Christ his sake, whose wandering servant I still esteem you, I end and rest your fellow-servant and loving friend desirous to embrace you in the fellowship of the Church of Christ."

Burgess then added a postscript, indicating that after he had penned his answer he was in two minds about sending it on, but hearing "on every side of great braggs cast out" to the effect that he could not meet Robinson's reasoned argument for separation, he decided to forward it to him, "that I might not," says he, "be guiltie of hardening them in their sinne whose error I so much bewayle: farewell."

By the time that this reply was forwarded to Robinson he and his company of adherents had left Amsterdam for Leyden. In the next chapter we shall follow them and trace their fortunes in that fair city.

CHAPTER XII

THE PILGRIMS AT LEYDEN

NOT many months had passed after their arrival in Amsterdam before this Pilgrim company under Robinson's leadership came to the decision to settle in Leyden, if the way were clear and permission to do so could be secured. They weighed up the advantages and disadvantages of the move. On the one hand, Leyden "wanting that traffic by sea which Amsterdam enjoys, it was not so beneficial for their outward means of living and estates," on the other hand, the University at Leyden was an attraction to Robinson and Brewster, and moving thither, their Church would be more likely to escape the contentions which marred the harmony of the other English refugees at Amsterdam. Early in 1609 the decision to make the move was arrived at, and steps were taken to prepare the way. A formal petition was presented to the authorities, of which the Registrar made the following note in the Court "Day-book" on February 12, 1609—

"TO THE HONOURABLE THE BURGOMASTERS AND COURT OF THE CITY OF LEYDEN:

"With due submission and respect Jan Robarthse[n], Minister of the Divine Word, and some of the members of the Christian Reformed Religion, born in the Kingdom of Great Britain, to the number of one hundred persons or thereabouts, men and women, represent that they desire to come to live in this City by the first day of May next, and to have the freedom thereof in carrying on their trades, without being a burden in the least to any one. They therefore address themselves to your Honors, humbly praying that your Honors will be pleased to grant them free consent to betake themselves as aforesaid.

"This doing, etc."

The decision of the Burgomasters upon this petition is inserted by the Registrar in the margin against the entry—

"The Court in disposing of this present Memorial declare that they refuse no honest persons free ingress to come and have their residence in this City, provided that such persons behave themselves and submit to the laws and ordinances. And, therefore, the coming of the Memorialists will be agreeable and welcome.

"This done by the Burgomasters in their sitting at the Council House the 12th day of February 1609.

"In my presence,
"J. VAN HOUT,
"*Secretary.*"

So far so good. The question about freedom to exercise their crafts was important. In English corporate towns at this period there were all sorts of irritating restrictions imposed by the "guilds" upon strangers coming into their bounds to work. If anything of the same kind existed in Leyden it was well they should know it before moving. They would be reassured by the friendly response to their petition, and emboldened to push on with their preparations for removal. Late in April, when all the countryside was showing promise of new life, and the fields were decked in the beauty of spring, the Pilgrims made their way by road and quiet waterways to the new city of their abode. It was an auspicious time, for in that very month (April 9) a truce between Holland and Spain was signed which gave good hope of peace and security.

It is not yet known where Robinson first had his dwelling in Leyden. Probably he rented some roomy building in which his flock could meet for worship and the transaction of their Church affairs. Not many weeks passed, however, before entries concerning members of the Pilgrim company began to be made in ordinary course in the various record books of the city in relation to the civil side of their life. Thus, in the large "Procuratie Book," which recorded grants of "powers of attorney," under date June 12, 1609, is an entry of the grant by "Ann Pecke,[1] born at Launde, Notts." [*i. e.* Lound, near Retford], and her guardian, William Brewster, to Thomas Simkinson, a merchant of Hull, of power to receive on their behalf seven pounds sterling, which she had left with "Mr. Watkin," pastor of Clarborough, when she left England.

Clarborough is the next parish over the hill to the west of Sturton, where Robinson lived. Nicholas Watkins [2] had been instituted as vicar there May 21, 1577, and held that benefice till his death in 1617. He was well known to the leaders in the Pilgrim company. Ann Peck, on December 24, 1616, became the second wife of John Spooner, a ribbon weaver at Leyden.

The Registers of St. Pancras, Leyden, record the burial, on Saturday, June 20, 1609, of a child of William Brewster. A few days later his name occurs in another record. It appears that Bernard Rosse, an English cloth merchant of Amsterdam, had taken a bale containing five pieces of cloth to Brewster's house in St. Ursula's Lane. When the bale was opened, one piece of cloth was found to be damaged. The damaged portion had to be jobbed off at a reduced

[1] Thomas Pecke of Hayton, by will April 15, 1602, bequeathed £20 to Anne Pecke, his third daughter. His four daughters were then "under age." Thomas Southworth was a supervisor of this will. "Richard Pecke, my younger son," is mentioned, but no Robert Pecke.

[2] There are frequent references to Watkins in the wills of his parishioners. Take one instance from the will of Thomas Southworth of Wellam in Clarborough, dated 1612: "*Item* I give and bequeath to Nicholas Watkins, vicar of Clarebrough, for tyethes forgotten vj^{s} viij^{d} I will and doe give towarde the repaire of the North Cawsey in Clarebrough meadowe and the way over Clarebrough more leadinge from Clarebroughe Church to Moregate xx^{s} which I will shalbe paid to the surveyors of the wayes and the vicar of Clarebroughe . . . to be imployed by them to the use aforesaid."—York Probate Registry, vol. xxxii. f. 278.

price. Rosse claimed against those who supplied the cloth to him, and he needed the evidence of Brewster's family in support of his claim. He got the bailiff to summon them before the court to testify to the facts. Accordingly on June 25, 1609, there appeared before the Aldermen Jaspar van Vesanevelt and P. van de Werff, " William Brewster, Englishman, aged about forty-two years; Mary Brewster, his wife, aged about forty years, and Jonathan Brewster, his son, aged about sixteen years," who confirmed on oath the statements set out in Rosse's claim. This gives us a clue to Brewster's age. In the autumn, Robert Peck, brother of Brewster's ward, Ann Peck, having got a job in Leyden as a fustian worker, decided to venture on marriage. On October 1, 1609, he and Jane Merritt, with friends as witnesses, went before the proper official to record their betrothal. They were married on the following November 21. Robinson and his Church were in hearty agreement with the form of civil marriage in vogue in Holland, in accordance with which many couples of their society were united in wedlock during their stay in Leyden. Robinson, in common with other Separatists of the time, held that marriage was not a function of the pastoral office. The only recorded instance even of his witnessing to a betrothal amongst his flock is in the case of his sister-in-law, Jane White. It was one ground of his objection against the Anglican Church that marriage was there " made a ministerial duty and part of God's worship without warrant." [1] In Holland this was not required, but the parties, appearing before the magistrates in due form, gave their faith and fealty to one another, pledging themselves never to desert one another, but to live peaceably, lovingly and in concord together as true children of God and in awe of Him, following His ordinance until death should them part. In testimony of their pledge they called upon Almighty God to bless their marriage, grant them His Holy Spirit and crown

[1] *Works*, vol. iii. p. 413.

their union with His grace and favour, and then they signed the book.

The Pilgrims carried with them to New England the form and custom of marriage before the magistrate with which they had become familiar in Holland. It scandalized Archbishop William Laud in after years when he found that Edward Winslow, a mere layman, in his position as magistrate, had celebrated marriage in the Plymouth Colony.

Among other weddings in the early years at Leyden was that of William Pontus with Wybra Hanson, whose betrothal took place November 13, 1610. Three weeks later comes the record of their marriage. Their good faith and intentions were vouched for by William Brewster, Edward Southworth, Roger Wilson, Mary Butler, Anna Fuller and Jane White. Pontus eked out a poor but respectable living in Leyden, first as a weaver of fustian, and then as a wool-carder, subsequently following the Pilgrims to Plymouth, New England.

Another marriage, on December 31, 1610, was that of John Jennings, who hailed from the Colchester district, and Elizabeth Pettinger, who I take to have come from the northern part of Nottinghamshire, where the name was familiar. Edward Southworth, Roger Wilson, Jane Peck and Anna Ross attended as their witnesses. In the next year, 1611, there were no less than five weddings of members of this Church, indicating that they were beginning to feel their feet in Leyden and were prepared to settle down there for some time. London, Suffolk and Kent were represented by the parties to these marriages, as well as Sturton and Scrooby. The original company was quickly being leavened by recruits from other parts of England.

Occupations and Trades

One of the first problems of those who were led by Robinson and Brewster to Leyden was how to win a decent livelihood. There was a considerable demand for labour in the various trades of the town, particularly in that of weaving and dressing cloth, and there were plenty of openings for unskilled labour. The lower-paid classes of labour were open to those who had physical strength. The crafts involving more skill were regulated by "guilds," and it was necessary before one opened a shop or engaged in trade on one's own account to become enrolled as a citizen. The candidate for citizenship had to find two or more citizens as sureties, and pay the admission fee. He took an oath to be loyal to the country of Holland, and to stand up for the rights and privileges of Leyden and his fellow-citizens. He was not eligible till he had attained the age of twenty-five. There were Englishmen already settled in Leyden who would put these new-comers in the way of things. Roger Wilson, from Sandwich, attached himself to the Pilgrim company, and on becoming twenty-five (he was baptized at St. Clement's, Sandwich, in 1584), he took up his citizenship. He was a baker by trade, and was guaranteed by Matys Ians (Matthias Jones) and Pieter Boey (Peter Bowie), paying his fee of three florins and twenty stivers on December 7, 1609.

In the course of the next year, six members of this Church became full citizens, for five of whom Roger Wilson stood in turn as one of the guarantors—

1610.	April 2.	Bernard Ross, cloth and leather merchant.
	June 21.	William Lisle, from Yarmouth.
	June 25.	Abraham Gray, from London, cobbler.
	Sept. 27.	John Turner, merchant.
	Dec. 3.	William Robertson, leather-dresser.
	Dec. 10.	Henry Wood, draper.

Every succeeding year till the year of the departure of the *Mayflower* saw one or more members of Robinson's Church qualifying for citizenship in Leyden. The uncertainty of their affairs in 1620 will account for the blank in that year. From that time down to the year of Robinson's death the names of fourteen more members of his company appear as citizens. They displayed the English instinct and capacity for trading and handicraft work.

The House of the Green Door

As the members of this little company of religious refugees in Leyden became more accustomed to their surroundings, and gained confidence in their power to win a living in their new home, they began to look round for more suitable quarters for the worship and activities of their Church than the temporary premises or the houses of various members in which they had hitherto been content to hold their meetings. After consideration they decided to buy a house fronting on the Kloksteeg, or Bell Alley, over against the cathedral church of St. Peter. The house had a fair-sized plot of ground at the end of its garden, opening out behind the adjoining properties, and bounded on the west by a covered canal (Donckeregracht), on the east by grounds of the Commandery, and on the south by the grounds and tenements of the Veiled Nuns. This plot of ground at the rear presented possibilities for the erection of small dwellings in which members of the Church might make their homes. In many an English country town in the old days you could find at the rear of buildings fronting the main street a court of tiny cottages, built on what had been the garden or orchard, and approached by a passage. It was not fresh air so much as cosy companionship that people sought, and a rent within their scanty means. The property on the Kloksteeg, viewed by the experienced eye of William Jepson, a house-carpenter by trade, seemed suited for such an arrangement. There must have been a good deal of discussion of ways and means, for, after all the expenses of the enforced removal to Amsterdam and the voluntary migration to Leyden, it was necessary to husband their resources. Probably both Robinson and his wife were able to raise something towards the expense. His wife's sister, Jane White, was entitled under the will of her mother to a certain sum either on her marriage or her coming of age. Jepson and Henry Wood, the draper, were men of some substance. These four clubbed together to buy the property. The contract to purchase was made on January 27, 1611, between John Robinson, minister of God's Word of the English congregation, William Jepson, Henry Wood and Jane White—not married at this time, but assisted by Nicholas White, jeweller, of the one part, and Johann de Lalaing of the other part. The entry in the Register noting the conveyance of the property and completion of purchase, subject to a mortgage of three-fourths of the agreed price, was not made till May 5. In the meantime, Jane White had married Randall Thickins, a looking-glass maker, who hailed from London. They were betrothed on April 1, with an intimate group of relations and friends as witnesses—William Brewster, Robinson and his wife, and Rosamund Jepson—and wedded on April 21, on the expiration of the customary three weeks. Consequently the name of Thickins was entered as the fourth party to the purchase: "Raynulph Tickens who has married Jane White." The property was subject to an annual rent charge of eleven stivers and twelve pence to the manorial lord of Polgeest, a village a few miles out of Leyden. The price was 8000 gilders, 2000 paid down on the spot, and 500 to be paid on May Day 1612, and a like amount annually till the whole was paid off. De Lalaing reserved for his own use a small room over the door of the house. From this latter feature the house had long been known as the Green Door [Groene Port]. It was probably the door giving access not directly to the house, but to the passage or entry leading to the premises behind. On those premises twenty-one little tenement houses were in due course built, and there various members of the Pilgrim company had their dwelling. Robinson occupied the main building, and looking back in memory Winslow pictured it as roomy.

There the Pilgrims took their parting meal before leaving for their venturesome voyage to the shores of New England. Eventually Jepson, on December 13, 1629, bought out the shares of the other three purchasers. Thickins, on June 1, 1621, then living at Amsterdam, and being about to return to England, had given Robinson authority to deal with the part of this property he owned in right of his wife. On February 2, 1622, Henry Wood gave Henry Jepson, the brother of William, power of attorney to sell his portion, but the matter was not settled up till four years after Robinson's death, when Jepson came to terms with his widow, Bridget Robinson, and secured all rights in the Groene Port property. After Jepson's death, another Englishman, Christopher Ellis, bought the portion of this estate which he left from the guardians of his only surviving child, Martha Jepson, June 25, 1637. For nearly sixty years this property was in the hands of those of English birth.

This little colony of houses down the entry through the Green Gate was the home of some of the leading members of the Pilgrim company. Isaac Allerton, from London, lived there 1620. John Allerton also, 1616. Thomas Blossom, from Cambridge, 1617; Jonathan Brewster, son of Elder Wm. Brewster, 1619; Samuel Fuller, from London, 1615; Edmond Jessop, 1618, and Wm. White in the same year.

The census of October 15, 1622, refers to several English households as living in Zevenhuysen Ward, without any mention of the particular lane, street or "hof" in which their dwelling was situated. Probably some of them were residents in the Pieterskerkhof, at the rear of Robinson's house of the Green Gate. There was Zechariah Barrow, the wool-carder, and Joan his wife; Roger Chandler, from Colchester, a say weaver, and his wife Isabella (Chilton), from Canterbury, with their children Samuel and Sarah; Joseph and Christina Crips, from Chichester, with their children Anna and Jeremiah; he was a card-maker. In this ward also lived Daniel and Rebecca Fairfield, with their children, Daniel, Rebecca and John; he was a say weaver from Colchester. Another of the same trade was Stephen Tracy, living in the same quarter, with his wife Tryphosa. They crossed to New England with their daughter Sarah along with the company which went by the *Anne* and the *Little James*. Then there was Thomas Willet, from Norwich, and his daughter Hester, and Roger Wilkins, a wool-carder, with his wife Margaret (Barrow) and their daughter Sarah. He is noted in the census as "too poor to be taxed." Besides these, we hear of the widow Josephine Brown and her four children; Albert and Susanna Garretson, with their five boys and girls; Susanna, the widow of Clement Halton, and her two children, and John Smith, from Yarmouth, a say weaver, all living in the Zevenhuysen Ward.

Next door but one to Robinson Thomas Brewer had his dwelling, with his wife and six children. We see, therefore, that a good number of the Pilgrim Church lived close at hand to their place of meeting.

CHAPTER XIII

ROBINSON'S "JUSTIFICATION OF SEPARATION"

IN his first year at Leyden Robinson was busied in preparing and seeing through the Press his longest literary work, which was at once a defence of the Separatist position on the matter of Church order and a rejoinder to the criticisms directed against it by his old University friend, Richard Bernard, the vicar of Worksop. It is a solid quarto, bearing the title "A IVSTIFICATION OF SEPARATION from the Church of England, against M^r. Richard Bernard his invective INTITVLED 'The Separatists' Schisme.'" This book finds its place in a long and wordy controversy in which several writers took a hand. It does not appeal to the modern reader, but at the time it was issued the topics it dealt with were of living interest, and further editions were called for in 1639 and 1644. To understand the circumstances of its composition and publication, in 1610, we must turn for a minute to Bernard's book, against which it was expressly directed. Bernard had leaned in the direction of separation from the Church of England on account of its corruptions and need of further reformation. He eagerly discussed the questions at issue with John Smith, Robert Southworth, John Robinson, Richard Clifton and other clergy and laity of the Puritan party in his locality. They exchanged papers in which the arguments for and against the order of Bishops were set out and the nature of a true Church, according to the Biblical evidence, was depicted. But Bernard drew back from the absolute and uncompromising position which Smith took up, and on suspension from his vicarage he thought the matter over again and yielded to the authority and jurisdiction of his diocesan. He did not think the corruptions and admitted defects in his Church justified the extreme step of separation from her. As Robinson put it, he was "loth to leave that Church and to join us when he thought we had the truth." [1]

The fact that Bernard had in his hands certain documents which John Smith had sent him describing the form and nature of a true Church of "saints," gave him an advantage in writing against his old associates. Moreover, some of Bernard's parishioners, baptized long before he saw their faces, "some twenty, some thirty, some forty years," [2] had been captured by the forceful eloquence of Smith and the influence of Robinson, and drawn into the Separatist Churches. This induced Bernard to raise a "hue and crie" after them in his *Christian Advertisements and Counsels of Peace.* Of this "breach" and separation he says, "To me hath it been just cause of sorrow, and therefore could I not lightly passe it by, but in love to such as yet abide with us, and in desire to doe my best to recover againe mine owne whom God once gave me, I have published these things." [3] His little book was a composite volume. After the opening "counsels of peace" there came "Disswasions from the way of the Separatists," or, as the title page phrased it, "Dissuasions from the Separatist's Schism, commonly called Brownisme," This formed the bulk of the book. The whole was rounded off by "Certaine Positions held and maintained by some godlie Ministers of the Gospell against

[1] *Works*, vol. ii. p. 294. Bernard's Puritan leanings are shown by the fact that he was indicted at the Notts. County Sessions, July 11, 1611, "for refusing to use reverence in administering baptism," *i. e.* he objected to making the sign of the Cross. *Notts. County Records*, by H. H. Copnall, p. 139.

[2] *Ibid.*, p. 10.

[3] *Christian Advertisements*, Epistle Dedicatorie, dated from Worksop, June 18 [1608].

those of the separation and namely against Barrow and Greenwood."

To the leaders in the Churches which had found refuge in Holland this book seemed to demand instant reply. Henry Ainsworth was first in the field with an answer. He was engaged in bringing out a volume when Bernard's book came to his hands, and he seized the opportunity of incorporating with it a refutation of Bernard's arguments and a survey of his objections.[1]

Next we find John Smith tackling the subject and giving a reasoned reply to Bernard's onslaught. He felt specially called to the task, inasmuch as Bernard had taxed him by name and used some of his writings (including a long letter written hurriedly in the closing months of 1607) as the target for his criticisms. Smith, speaking of his reply to Bernard, says—

> " I have attempted it vppon two private groundes wherein I am especially interessed to this busines. One is certayne aspersions by you personally cast vppon mee : Another is certayne particular oppositions directed against some of my writings." [2]

Accordingly, in 1609, Smith issued his—

> " PARALLELES, CENSVRES, OBSERVATIONS aperteyning to three several WRITINGES—
>
> "1. A Lettre written to Mr. Ric. Bernard by Iohn Smyth.
>
> "2. A Book intituled, The Separatists' Schisme published by Mr Bernard.
>
> "3. An Answer made to that book called the Sep. Schisme by Mr. H. Ainsworth."

Smith says he added his observations on this last writing because there were " some particulars wherein Mr. Ainsworth hath left me and the truth in the open playne field to shift for our selves."

1 "*Counterpoison* . . . Mr. Bernard's Book intituled 'The Separatists' Schisme' . . . examined and answered by H. A.," 1608.

2 Smith, *Paralleles*, § 1, 1609.

I think Smith was aware that Robinson also intended to reply to Bernard's book, yet he felt it laid upon him especially to enter the lists, " although it be once answered," he says, " by another: and happily may receave a third answer [Robinson's] yet I cannot overpasse it least [I] seme to betray the truth who am by name singled out to the cōbat." In due course, then, he published his book with some of the primary documents in the controversy.

We may take it that Robinson was engaged on his reply to Bernard in 1609, and we find that news of it reached Worksop in the following year. This we gather from the preface to Bernard's rejoinder to Ainsworth and Smith, in his *Plaine Evidences: The Church of England is Apostolicall the seperation Schismaticall directed against Mr. Ainsworth the Separatist and Mr. Smith the Sebaptist; Both of them severally opposing the Booke called the Separatists' Schisme. . . . Set out by Authoritie Anno* 1610. " I heare," says Bernard, " of Mr. Robinson's answere also; if it had come in hee should also have been replyed vpon. Though I be a weake man and my weapons be against these three Captaines of three Companies and but a stone in a sling yet shall Israel prevaile." [1]

While Robinson's *Justification of Separation* was passing through the press a copy of Bernard's rejoinder to Smith (the *Plaine Evidences* of 1610) came to his hands. He accordingly took the opportunity of giving an answer to " all the particulars which are of weight " in that " second treatise." In a note to the " Christian reader " at the end of his volume [2] Robinson explains the circumstances and adds, " For that I have been occasioned by the one and other book to handle all the points in difference, I intreat thee to compare with this my defence, such other oppositions especially as respect myself, whether in print or writing, till more particular answer be given." This " defence against Mr. Ber[nard's] Invective "

[1] *Plaine Evidences*, 1610, preface, p. iii.
[2] In edition of 1639, p. 388.

would serve, then, in addition, as a sufficient answer to such opponents as William Ames, Robert Parker, John Paget, John Burgess and other forward Puritan preachers.

We can now see pretty well the place in order of time which this work occupies in the controversy between the Anglican and the Free Churchman. What about its matter and form? Robinson follows Bernard with remarkable pertinacity and calm insistence from beginning to end of his book. He enters upon "an examination of the particulars, one by one, that so in all points the salve might be answerable to the sore."[1] He aimed at producing "a familiar and popular kind of defence" in the style adopted by Bernard for his attack. But Robinson had not the swiftness and lightness of touch which his opponent had at command. The questions at issue were too near to his heart for him to treat them in anything but a sober and serious strain. Still, keeping in view his intention of writing a "popular" defence of his position, he avoided the syllogistic style of argumentation in vogue amongst scholars of his day, and produced a book, lit up with many a homely touch and proverbial saying, which would appeal to the plain man interested in the matters handled. Put shortly, the main difference[2] between Bernard and Robinson was about the nature and constitution of a true Church according to the teaching of the New Testament. Robinson maintained that the authority for constituting a genuine Christian Church, and the pattern which such a Church was to take in perpetuity, were to be sought for in the Bible. He declared that the Church of England was not framed according to the model of the New Testament Churches; consequently it was a duty to separate from it. The true Church was constituted of those who made a voluntary profession of faith and separ-

[1] *Works*, vol. ii. p. 1.
[2] "The gathering and governing of the Church . . . are the main heads controverted betwixt you and us."—*Justification of Separation*, p. 49.

ated themselves from the world "into the fellowship of the gospel and the covenant of Abraham."[1] Robinson poured scorn upon the legal conditions for membership in the Anglican Church. "A man," he says, "may go out of these countries [Holland] where I now live, as many do, and hire a house in any parish of the land," and then become "by the right of his house or farm, a member of the parish church where he dwells, yea, though he have been nursled up all his life long in Popery or Atheism, and though he were formerly neither of any Church or religion. Yea, though he should profess that he did not look to be saved by Christ only and alone, but by his good meanings and well doings; yet if he will come and hear divine service he is matter true as steel for your Church; yea, be he of the King's natural subjects he shall, by order of law, be made true matter of the Church, whether he will or no." To Robinson this seemed to be putting the conditions of Church membership upon an entirely wrong footing. In his judgment membership of a Christian Church involved definite personal responsibility in regard to matters of faith and conduct. Only those who made a voluntary profession of Christian faith and undertook to follow the Christian way of life were fitted for the high privilege of membership in a Church of Christ. Any two or three making sincere professions of religion in this way could join together and so constitute a true Church.

"This we hold and affirm," says Robinson, "that a company consisting though but of two or three, separated from the world . . . and gathered into the name of Christ by a covenant made to walk in all the ways of God known unto them, is a Church, and so hath the whole power of Christ."[2] Judged by this standard the "parish assemblies" in England were not Churches at all.

The most fruitful point about the conception of

[1] *Works*, vol. ii. pp. 232, 288.
[2] *Ibid.*, p. 132.

the Church which Smith and Robinson brought into prominence was that the authority for Church government, for electing officers and for exercising discipline, rested with the members themselves. The seat of authority was to be found in the whole body of members, acting under the governance and rule of Christ. It did not rest with Archbishops or Bishops; it did not reside in a college of presbyters or elders, but was vested in the corporate society of Church members. "This opinion," said Bernard, "is indeede the first A.B.C. of Brownisme whereupon they build al the rest of their untrueths. . . . This is the ground of their outbreaking from al the Churches in the world." [1] The assertion of this democratic principle of Church government struck the hesitating Puritans with amazement, and they at once pointed out the dangers of this "popularity." Smith manfully stood to his position, and in this particular was followed by Robinson. They both upheld the privileges and rights of the humblest and meanest Church member. Every member was interested in the work of the Church—in its choice of pastor and officers and in its exercise of discipline. Every male member also had the right of speaking in an orderly way in the Church meeting. The Pauline prohibition closed the mouths of women members in the full meeting, but they were free to assemble by themselves for religious discussion and prayer. Robinson put the matter in this way—

"The Lord Jesus is the king of his church alone, upon whose shoulders the government is, and unto whom all power is given in heaven and earth; yet hath he not received this power for himself alone, but doth communicate the same with his church as the husband with the wife. And as he is 'anointed by God with the oil of gladness above his fellows' so doth he communicate this anointing . . . to every member of the body and so makes every one of them severally kings and priests and all jointly a kingly priesthood or communion of kings, priests and prophets. And in this

[1] Bernard's *Separatists' Schisme*, 1608, p. 90.

holy fellowship by virtue of this plenteous anointment every one is made a king, priest and prophet not only to himself but to every other, yea, to the whole—a prophet to teach, exhort, reprove and comfort himself and the rest; a priest, to offer up spiritual sacrifices of prayer, praises and thanksgiving for himself and the rest; a king to guide and govern in the ways of godliness himself and the rest. . . . And as there is not the meanest member of the body but hath received his drop or dram of this anointing, so is not the same to be despised either by any other or by the whole to which it is of use daily in some of the things before set down and may be in all. . . . So that not only the eye, a special member, cannot say to the hand, a special member, I have no need of thee; but not the head, the principal member of all, unto the feet, the meanest members, I have no need of you." [1]

Smith and Robinson went together in this assertion of the high privileges and responsibilities of membership in the Christian Church—

" You are to remēber that Christ's Church in several respects is a Monarchie, an Aristocraty, a Democratie. In respect of Christ the King it is a Monarchy, of the Eldership an Aristocratie, of the brethren joyntly a Democratic or Popular government. . . . Wee say that the body of the Church hath all powre immediately from Christ: and the Elders have al their powre from the body of the Church. . . . Wee say that the definitive sentence, the determining powre, the negative voice is in the body of the Church, not in the Elders."—Smith, *Paralleles*, 1609, pp. 416–7, Whitley's edition.

" Wise men having written of this subject have approved as good and lawful three kinds of polities: monarchical where supreme authority is in the hands of one; aristocratical when it is in the hands of some few select persons; and democratical in the whole body, or multitude. And all these three forms have their places in the Church of Christ. In respect of him the head it is a Monarchy, in respect of the eldership an Aristocracy, in respect of the body a popular state."—Robinson, *Justification of Separation*, 1610, *Works*, vol. ii. p. 140.

[1] *Works*, vol. ii. p. 141.

This clear conviction of the democratic nature of Christ's Church and the feeling that authority was vested in the whole body of its members by divine sanction had an effect in moulding the civil polity of the Pilgrim company in later years.

The call to face danger and take risks in the effort to build up on earth the ideal Church according to the New Testament pattern made a strong appeal to men and women of earnest religious temper. It rang with a deeper note of sincerity than the " rhyming rhetoric " in which Bernard urged his readers to tread the beaten path of conformity—

" Goe even
Be no Atheistical Securitane
Nor Anabaptisticall Puritane;
Bee no carlesse Conformitant
Nor yet preposterous Reformitant:
Be no neuterall Lutheran
Nor Hereticall popish Antichristian:
Be not a schismaticall Brownist
Nor fond and foolish Familist:
Be not a new Novelist,
Nor yet any proud and arrogant Sectarie
To draw disciples after thee.
Be no follower of any such
Beware of them all carefully." [1]

Bernard, in the course of his argument, gives us a reminiscence of one remark made by John Robinson before the time of his separation, and though it was misapplied and misreported, we get a glimpse through it of Robinson's feeling at the period when he was meditating a severance from the Anglican Church. Robinson observed how men of sincere religious conviction were attracted to the Separatist cause in those parishes where it was discussed, and remarked upon the fact. Bernard gave his version of the remark at the close of his list of " likelihoods " that the way of separation was not a good way.

[1] Bernard's *Christian Advertisements*, etc., 1608, p. 2.

Here we print the thrust and parry side by side—

"To conclude they [the Separatists] leave rather a curse than a blessing where they come, so as good things little prosper after them. They are like a scorching flame swinging where it cometh [so] that the growth of things are hindered by it. So said one (that is now amongst them) before hee went that way: thus can men so observe and discerne before and be blind afterwards."—Bernard, *Separatists' Schisme*, p. 43.

"Mr. B. concludeth his likelihoods with 'a cursed farewell, which,' said he, 'we leave in all places like a scorching flame singeing where it comes, so as the growth of all things are hindered by it.'

"And this observation he fathers upon me, though in truth it be his own bastard. I affirmed indeed that where this truth [concerning the need of gathering the Church by a covenanting together of faithful people to walk in all God's ways] came, it left the places barren of good things, in taking away the best sort of people. But this I spake to no such purpose as is here insinuated. The scorching flame which hinders all things in the Church of England is the prelacy, to which by universal and infallible observation no man applies himself, no, nor inclines but with a sensible decay of the former graces which he seemed to have. He that but once enters into the high priest's hall to warm himself at the fire there, shall scarce return without a scorched conscience."—Robinson, *Justification of Separation*, *Works*, vol. ii. pp. 67–68.

No one was in a better position than Bernard to make the application implied in the retort of his old friend.

Before Robinson's *Justification* saw the light John Smith had moved on along a line of theological development where Robinson could not follow him. "His instability and wantonness of wit," said Robinson, "is his sin and our cross."[1] Some of his arguments against Bernard were expressly disavowed by Robinson. For example, in countering the objection that his definition of a Church would exclude the heroes of the Old Testament who "committed and suffered knowne sinne," Smith asserted that the Church of the Old Testament was merely "typical and ceremonial,"[2] "the worship of the old testament a ceremonial worship; the ministry a typical ministry; the government a typical government; the people a typical people; the land or country a ceremonial country and so forth of the rest by proportion." And he went on to frame a fearful and wonderful syllogism, so that on this point Bernard should "never be able to reply or once to mutter against the truth any more." Bernard, however, was equal to the occasion. He picked out this choice example of wordy argumentation and made fun of it in his own way—

"But to stop my mouth, that I shall not once mutter, as he saith (oh the admirabilitie of the man!), he reads me as he thinks a riddle to the amazement of all his intoxicated Disciples and frames his argument both against the truth and me thus. 'If in the Old Testament their visible typicall communion was typically polluted by typicall and ceremoniall uncleannesse uncleansed: then in the new Testament our spirituall visible communion is really polluted by morall uncleannesse uncleansed; that is, sinne unrepented of. But in the Old Testament their visible typicall communion *was* typically polluted by the typicall and ceremoniall uncleannesse uncleansed: Ergo.' . . . Surely, such as of his as were blinded with his Heresie and affected with his folly were too-tooly moued with a merry conceit at this riddlement as not to be answered; through the obscure profunditie of his reason over reaching our poore apprehensions: which made him say he would stop my mouth for muttering. But let vs see how I can mutter against it.

Mr. Smith's Riddlement

[1] *Works*, vol. ii. p. 62.

[2] Smith, *Paralleles*, p. 376.

What! a Goliath? Then see the strength of a pibble stone in a sling. Have at a Goliath. Let him save his head; for by his contrarying so daily himselfe it seemes his braines be already crackt. But ere I answere, I read him againe this riddle. 'If in his last old yeares, their Separatisticall communion was Brownistically polluted, by a Schismaticall rending of themselves from the Church of England for some supposed ceremoniall and Antichristian uncleannesse uncleansed: then in this his new yeare their Anabaptisticall Communion is Smithically polluted by their but halfe Anabaptistrie, new unheard of Heresies, even spirituall and morall uncleannesse uncleansed, that is, their sinne not yet repented of. But in his last old yeares, their Separatisticall Communion *was* Brownistically polluted, by a Schismaticall rending of themselves from the Church of England for some supposed ceremoniall and Antichristian uncleannesse uncleansed: Ergo.' And now to his argument. . . . Observe reader that the proofe stands vpon his owne coyned Analogie and proportion."—*Plaine Evidences*, p. 170.

Robinson characterized this argument of Smith as "erroneous and Anabaptistical,"[1] and for his part kept nearer to general opinion in regard to the historical value of the Old Testament. Nor did he follow Smith in his renunciation of the baptism received in the Anglican Church, and his contention that the true Church was to be constituted by baptism and confession of faith, and that consequently the rite of baptism was not to be administered to infants. In another point there was an early divergence between the two men. The question arose as to whether a Church—a company of faithful people covenanted together—since it had the "power of Christ," had not, therefore, authority to administer the sacraments of baptism and the Lord's Supper even though it had not a pastor, elder or teacher. To this Robinson said no. He held to the policy indicated in the Confession of the earlier Separatists, that "no sacraments are to be administered until pastors or teachers be ordained in their office."[2] Bernard, he declared, knew as well

[1] *Works*, vol. ii. p. 111.
[2] See Sec. 34 of *A True Confession of the Faith*, 1596, p. xix.

as themselves that they had not "practised otherwise." [1] To this position the Pilgrim Church adhered years afterwards in America.

But Smith took a more independent line, and would not bar the liberty of the Church as a spiritual corporation even in this matter—

> "It may be questioned," he says, "whether the Church may not as well administer the Seals of the Covenant [*i. e.* baptize and celebrate the Lord's Supper] before they have Officers as Pray, Prophecy, Elect Officers and the rest; seeing that to put the Seals to the Covenant is not a greater work than publishing the Covenant, or Election of Officers, or Excommunication." [2]

The companies of Anabaptists which arose here and there in England through the influence of Smith took advantage of the liberty he thus allowed, and did not hesitate to administer baptism and celebrate the Lord's Supper among themselves even at times when they had no pastor.

[1] *Works*, vol. ii. p. 130. [2] Smith, *Paralleles*, pp. 419–20.

CHAPTER XIV

ROBINSON'S INTERCOURSE WITH AMES, PARKER AND JACOB

HOLLAND was a place of refuge, not only for English Separatists, but also for many Puritan clergy who were unable to conform to the ceremonies of the Anglican Church, yet still counted themselves as members thereof, and shrank from separation from it. Amongst these was William Ames (1576–1633). He had some discussion with Robinson upon a point which he felt contained " the very bitterness of separation." The rigid Separatists in their rebound from the older Church organizations laid it down that it was wrong to have religious communion with those they did not consider to be in a true Church fellowship, even though they might be recognized as personally devout Christians. This struck Ames as harsh. It hurt. Apparently Robinson had written to Ames urging him to pass in review his position in relation to the Anglican Church, and consider whether he ought not to throw in his lot with the Separatists. In his reply, February 25 [1610–11], Ames, omitting criticism of Robinson's contention that his separation was similar to that of the first reformed Churches in Holland and France, " for you have irons enough in the fire about that question," concentrated upon this one point: he argued that if you recognized any people to have inward communion with Jesus Christ, it was permissible to have external communion with them in religious matters, though they were not in due Church order. Had not the members of Robinson's own Church, when they came together for their "covenant making," joined together "in prayer for direction, assistance and blessing"? Yet they were not a Church until they had entered into covenant, "which you hold to be the form of a Church," therefore, argued Ames, "it is not only lawful, but necessary also that there be a communion out of a visible Church." Robinson did not agree with this. In his rejoinder, dated "Leyden, this second of the week" (names of the days of pagan origin were avoided), he declared that visible Churches "have not only internal communion with Christ, but external also in the order which he hath set; for which we stand and for the want of which alone, we withdraw ourselves, as we do in this case, not daring to break Christ's order for men's disorder." As for prayer together by those who intend to join by covenant into a Church, it was not on all fours with the case of one in true Church order engaging in religious acts with any one out of that order. "And when men are so met with a purpose to unite, and do begin prayer for the sanctification of it, they are in the door coming into the house and not without."[1]

It looked as though the efforts of Ames to modify Robinson's attachment to the rigid position of the Separatists on this point were to be fruitless. Yet such was not the case. We are frequently influenced by after-reflection upon points brought up in an inconclusive discussion. It was so in this instance. Not many months passed before Robinson modified his opinion, and returned to a more charitable view in regard to religious intercourse between members of such Churches as his own and the godly members of the parish assemblies in England. He is perfectly frank about the change. The unauthorized publication of his correspondence with Ames gave him an opportunity of explaining his new position.

The letters appeared in a scurrilous book put forth under the names of "Christopher Lawne, Clement Saunders and Robert Bulward," who left the Church

[1] *Works*, vol. iii. pp. 87–89.

under Francis Johnson, and issued this work, entitled *The Prophane Schisme of the Brownists*, to justify their defection. It was entered at Stationers' Hall July 6, 1612. Robinson naturally objected to his name and Church being associated in any way with charges against the Amsterdam society, with which they had nothing to do. He thought Ames himself was responsible for the publication of his correspondence. He "hath published to the world," says Robinson, "in the body of that book, without my consent, privity, or least suspicion of such dealing, certain private letters passing between him and me about private communion betwixt the members of the true visible Church and others." [1]

I am inclined to think that John Paget had a hand in the matter. William Best, writing in after years, exclaimed, "What consent had hee [Paget] of Mr. Robinson when hee printed certain letters of his sent privately to Dr. Ames?" [2] However that may be, Robinson made it the occasion for a fuller explanation of his position, in a book issued in 1614, entitled, *Of Religious Communion Private and Public.* The preface to this volume indicates the change in his point of view, and has in itself an autobiographical value, as the following extensive extracts will show—

"Great offence hath been taken by many at our extreme straitness in respect of the order wherein we walk: and more especially for refusing communion in the private and personal exercises of religion with the better sort in the assemblies [*i. e.* the English parish churches] as wherein we have not only made a separation from the wicked and from the godly also in things unlawful or unlawfully performed, but even in their lawful actions. This Mr. Ames calls the bitterness of separation: and for it, as it seems, thinks it lawful to cast upon me the reproach of the sins of other churches and persons. . . . Whether or no there were in the assemblies faithful and godly persons, and the same so appearing unto men, I never called in question, nor could without sinning greatly against mine own conscience: the

[1] *Works*, vol. iii. p. 96.
[2] Best, *The Churches Plea for her Right*, 1635, p. 10.

thing I feared, was the violation and breach of order in the communion between the members of the true visible church [a church constituted on New Testament lines like Robinson's] and others out of that order, or in the contrary. . . . Here was use of a distinction of religious actions into personal and church actions: which if either Mr. Ames had observed unto me, or I myself then conceived of, would have cleared the question to my conscience: and with which I did wholly satisfy myself in this matter when God gave me once to observe it."

When this distinction between personal religious acts and Church actions became clear to Robinson's mind it eased his position, and he felt it was legitimate to join in private prayer with those who were "joint members of the mystical body of Christ by faith," even though they were not duly constituted in the true Church order. He went thoroughly into the matter in this book—

"The thing I aim at in this whole discourse," he says, "is that we who profess a separation from the English national, provincial, diocesan and parochial church and churches, in the whole formal state and order thereof, may notwithstanding lawfully communicate in private prayer and other the like holy exercises (not performed in their church communion nor by their church power and ministry) with the godly amongst them, though remaining, of infirmity, members of the same church or churches." [1]

This intercommunion in personal religious acts they might practise, so Robinson now argued, "except some other extraordinary bar come in the way between them and us."

"My judgment therein," he says, "and the reasons of it I have set down in the first part of the book: unto which I bind no man further to assent, than he sees ground from the Scriptures. . . . I myself, and the people with me generally, did separate from the formal state of the parish assemblies in this persuasion, and so practised all the while we abode in England, as some there continuing have done to this day: there having been sundry passages between Mr. Smith, and

[1] *Of Religious Communion Private and Public, Works,* vol. iii. p. 105.

me about it; with whom I also refused to join, because I would use my liberty in this point; and for which I was by some of the people with him excepted against when I was chosen into office in this Church. Indeed afterwards finding them of other churches [Johnson, and Ainsworth, and Smith] with whom I was most nearly joined, otherwise minded for the most part, I did through my vehement desire of peace, and weakness withal, remit and lose of my former resolution and did (to speak as the truth is) forget some of my former grounds; and so have passed out upon occasion, some Arguments against this practice. Which yet notwithstanding I have, in the same place, so set down as all may see I was therein far from that certainty of persuasion, which I had and have of the common grounds of our separation of which I think this no part at all. But had my persuasion in it been fuller than ever it was, I profess myself always one of them, who still desire to learn further, or better, what the good will of God is. And I beseech the Lord from mine heart that there may be in other men (towards whom I desire in all things lawful to enlarge myself) the like readiness of mind to forsake every evil way, and faithfully to embrace and walk in the truth they do or may see as by the mercy of God, there is in me; which as I trust it shall be mine, so do I wish it may be their comfort also in the day of the Lord Jesus.

"[Signed] JOHN ROBINSON."[1]

The moderation of Robinson in comparison with some of the other zealous leaders in the way of separation was well recognized. Bernard referred to him as early as 1610 as "one yet nearest the truth unto us, as I heare, and not so Schismaticall as the rest."[2] His readiness to fraternize with the devout members of other religious societies in private religious acts brought him into collision, on the one hand, with the hard-shell zealots of the separation, both in his own Church and at Amsterdam, and, on the other hand, encouraged his Puritan friends to endeavour to convince him of the lawfulness of joining with them in public religious actions. John Paget refers to both these results in his *Arrow against*

[1] Closing sentences of the Preface *Of Religious Communion*, pp. v. and vi., edition of 1614.
[2] *Plain Evidences*, p. 73.

the Separation of the Brownists, published in 1618. Addressing Henry Ainsworth, he says, "You have been openly, in your own congregation, by your own people, desired and urged to answer Mr. Robinson," [1] on this point of the legitimacy of religious communion with those out of due Church order. He refers to the Puritan effort also in these terms—

"Do you not consider that upon the coming forth of this book [Robinson's *Religious Communion*] there was presently published a *Manuduction* for Mr. Robinson to lead him unto *public communion* and this by the same person that had convinced his private separation to be unlawful?" [2]

The reference is to a little tractate appended to Bradshaw's *Vnreasonablenesse of the Separation*, which came out in 1614. It appears that a correspondent at Dort wrote to Ames asking his opinion "touching that partition wall which M. Robinson hath lately reared up for to make a separation with betwixt privat and publick communion." Accordingly Ames penned a criticism of Robinson's position, and sent it on to his correspondent with a letter concluding in these terms—

"Wishing to M. R[obinson] from the god of all grace, the same light and enlargement of heart for *this*, which hee hath received for the *other* part of communion, I commend my epistle to your friendly censure and myself to your accustomed love. November 23 [1614]."

The tract reached Dort in time to be issued with Bradshaw's treatise against Johnson: [3] "A MANVDICTION [error for Manuduction] for MR. ROBINSON and Such as consent with him in privat communion, to lead them on to publick. Briefly comprized in a letter to Mr. R. W., At Dort. Printed by George Waters And are to be sould at his shop at the signe of the Snuffers on the fish market. 1614."

The argument in this letter appeared to Robinson

[1] Paget, *Arrow against the Separation of the Brownists*, p. 60. [2] *Ibid.*
[3] Neither treatise is paged, but the signatures of the two are continuous.

weak and unconvincing. He considered that "this manuducent" or "hand-leader" would have done better

> "to guide men by the plain and open way of the Scriptures . . . beaten by the feet of the apostolical churches and not by subtle *quaeries* and doubtful suppositions and such underhand conveyances as may lead the unwary into a maze and there lose him."

So he soon issued "A MANVMISSION TO A MANVDVCTION or answer to a letter inferring publique communion in the parish assemblies upon private with godly persons there. Stand fast in the liberty wherewith Christ hath made you free. Gal. 5. 1. Be not partaker of other men's sinns: keep thyself pure. 1 Tim. 5. 22. By Iohn Robinson. Anno Domini 1615."[1]

Robinson argued that to remain in fellowship with the Church of England or to exercise one's ministry in virtue of the prelate's licence was to uphold a system of Church government and order not sanctioned by the New Testament, and opposed to the order there laid down. "All the parochial ministers," so he had contended in his book on *Religious Communion*, "are subject unto the jurisdiction of prelates spiritually." But Ames rejoins with a supposition which reminds us of his own position. Suppose if a deprived minister "now rejected by the prelate and witnessing against his corruptions shall, without seeking any new licence, find place to preach the Gospel in occasionally elsewhere, why should any refuse to hear him?"

"Mine answer is," says Robinson, "that this man, remaining by the prelate's ordination a minister of the Church of England, and as he was before his institution or licence and so preaching by that calling, communion cannot be had with him therein without submission unto and upholding of the prelate's anti-Christian authority which in that way he exerciseth."

[1] Only two copies of this tract by Robinson have come to light. I have consulted the copy procured for the British Museum by the late R. W. Dale. It formerly belonged to Nicholas Munt (*d.* February 2, 1803) of Harwich.

To evade the difficulty in regard to the authority and rule of the prelacy, Ames pleaded that—

"the greatest part of this jurisdiction being external and coactive or forcing is from the King derived unto those that doe exercise the same and therefore must of necessitie bee a civill power. . . . Now though some corrupt vsurpations and abuses bee mingled with that civill power, yet that doeth not make all subjection to it unlawfull much less perniciously infecting by contagion, as M. Robinson will have it, especially in those that refuse to execute vnlawfull commaunds." [1]

To this Robinson could not assent. He had no regrets about the renunciation of his "orders," and with a reminiscence of his Norwich experience he rejoined—

"The Bishops may and do exercise all and every part of their episcopal authority where they have not the least civil authority, *viz.* in the cities and corporations within their provinces and dioceses; as for example the Bishop of Norwich in the city of Norwich where his civil authority is no more than mine."

Again he says—

"The prelates' power in their provinces and dioceses is not civil, but a kind of external spiritual power which I have also in my former book proved antichristian as usurping upon Christ's royal prerogatives, subverting the order of true Church government and swallowing up, as with full mouth, both the people's liberty and elders' government wherewith Christ the Lord hath invested the true Church."

The *Manumission* is a forceful little tract, written with spirit. Robinson evidently felt pretty strongly on some of the points in question. His opponent penned "A Second Manvdvction for M^R. Robinson or a confirmation of the former in an answer to his Manumission. Anno Domini MDCXV"; but it added little that was fresh to the discussion.

[1] *Manuduction*, Sig. Q. 3.

Lawfulness of Hearing Ministers in the Church of England

This controversy led up to a further modification in Robinson's opinion in regard to the fitting relationship between members of such Churches as his own and the faithful in the Church of England. He would not go so far as to countenance participation with them in the service of the Common Prayer-Book or the sacraments, but he advanced to the conclusion that it was lawful on occasion to resort to the parish assemblies to listen to the sermons of godly and helpful preachers of the Anglican Church. Though it carries us out of the chronological sequence of Robinson's works, it will be as well to touch on his *Treatise of the Lawfulness of Hearing of the Ministers in the Church of England* in this place, in order to complete our survey of the development of his opinion on this point.

The very buildings which had been devoted to Roman Catholic worship were regarded by the more rigid Separatists with aversion, and it was regarded as a sin to resort to such " idol houses." Robinson himself had used strong language against them, but by 1617 he had come to a more reasonable and kindly judgment. As Paget tells us—

> " Mr. Robinson though he have written in such high words against these temples . . . yet hath he for this long time tolerated Mr. Br[ewster] to hear the word of God in such places," and " now of late this last month [*i. e.* July 1617] as is witnessed unto me he . . . begins openly in the midst of his congregation to plead for the lawful use of these temples." [1]

He also came to the conclusion that it was allowable to resort to such churches or temples to listen to the sermons of godly and faithful ministers. His views on the point were set out in the Treatise " printed according to the copie that was found in his studie

[1] Paget's *Arrow against the Separation of the Brownists*, pp. 28, 29.

after his dec[e]ase." The fact that it was held back from publication for nine years, and did not appear till 1634, possibly indicates that some in the Leyden Church were not altogether satisfied on the point, though when Robinson was with them he secured "the whole consent of the Church" to the sending of a letter, drawn up by himself and dated Leyden, April 5, 1624, to the ancient Separatist Church in London, wherein judgment in a case of this nature is given in accordance with the more liberal principles embodied in this posthumous treatise. There is no reason to question the authenticity of this work or the good faith of those who put it to the press "for the common good." It reveals Robinson in a pleasant light, and is valuable as giving us a clear view of his feeling and conviction on a much-controverted point. He professes himself both a companion and guide of such as "seek how and where they may finde any lawfull dore of entry into accord and agreement with others."

"I have still opposed," he says, "in others and repressed in myne own (to my power) all sowre zeal against, and peremptory rejection of, such as whose holy graces chalenged better use and respect from all christians.

"And in testimony of my affection this way and for ye freeing of mine owne conscience, and information of other men's, I have penned this discourse, tending to prove the hearing of the word of God preached by the ministers of the Church of England (*able to open and apply the doctrine of faith by that Church professed*) *both lawfull and in cases necessary for all of all sects or sorts of christians havinge opportunitie or occasion of so doing,—though sequestring themselves from all communion with the formall and hierarchicall order there established*." [1]

In the course of his argument Robinson refers to some of the works we have already touched on, and gives us his estimate of them—

"There is in the hands of many," he says, "a Treatise published by a man of note, containing 'certain reasons to

[1] MS. copy, *Of the Lawfulness of Hearing the Ministers of the Church of England*, British Museum, Add. MSS. 24,666.

prove it unlawful to hear, or have spiritual communion with the present ministry of the Church of England.' This hath been answered, but indeed sophistically and in passion. Neither hath the answerer much regarded what he said, or unsaid, so he might gainsay his adversary. With that answer was joined another, directed to myself and the same doubled, pretending to prove public communion upon private, but not pressing at all, in the body of the discourse that consequence, but proceeding upon other grounds, and in truth consisting of a continued equivocation in the terms 'public licence,' 'government,' 'ministry,' and the like, drawn to another sense than either I intended them, or than the matter in question will permit. Whereas he that will refute another, should religiously take and hold to his adversary's meaning, and if, in any particular, it be not so plainly set down, should spell it, as it were, out of his words. But it is no new thing even for learned and godly men to take more than lawful liberty in dealing with them, against whom they have the advantage of the times favouring them like the wind on their backs; but God forbid I should follow them therein! I will on the contrary use all plainness and simplicity as in the sight of God that so I may make the naked truth appear as it is to the Christian reader's eye what in me lieth."[1]

He goes on to show that Francis Johnson, in the treatise mentioned, had confounded "hearing of" and "having spiritual communion with" the ministry of the Church of England as though they were one and the same thing. The mere hearing a clergyman preach, Robinson contended, was no act of spiritual communion for those who were neither "members of, nor in ecclesiastical union or combination with, the said Church"—

". . . hearing simply, is not appointed of God to be a mark and note, either of union in the same faith or order amongst all that hear; or of differencing of Christians from no Christians, or of members from no members of the church: as the sacraments are notes of both [*i. e.* notes of union in both faith and order] in the participants. The hearing of the Word of God is not so inclosed by any hedge or ditch,

[1] *Works*, vol. iii. p. 361.

divine or human, made about it, but lies in common for all, for the good of all."[1]

Sixteen objections to such hearing of the sermons of Anglican ministers are carefully considered and met by Robinson, who then entreats—

"the differently minded one way or other that they would exercise mutually that christian charity one toward another, and compassion one of another's infirmities, which become all that will be in truth and deed followers of Christ Jesus; and which is most needful, specially in things of this kind, for the preserving of the unity of the spirit in the bond of peace. Which bond of peace whilst men are not careful to keep inviolated, by brotherly forbearance in matters of this nature, they miserably dissipate and scatter themselves and one another, even as the ears in a sheaf are scattered when the bond breaketh."[2]

With a warning against making "a hearing course" a substitute for entering into true church-order this treatise draws to a close—

"This hearing is only a work of natural liberty in itself. . . . It is lawful to use it upon occasion, as it is to borrow of other men; but to make it our course, is to live by borrowing, which no honest man that can do otherwise possibly, would do. Yea, what differs it from a kind of spiritual vagabondry in him that can mend it, though with some difficulty, to live in no certain church-state and under no church order and government?"

One of the most arresting parts in this tract is Robinson's penetrating analysis of the various classes of opponents to the practice he here vindicates. He hits them off to the life. Their characters are vividly presented. Have we not all met with those of whom it may be said, it is not "their manner to read or willingly to hear that which crosseth their prejudices," and those "who think it half heresy to call in question" any of the practices of those whom they look back upon with veneration as religious leaders?

[1] *Works*, vol. iii. p. 363. [2] *Ibid.*, p. 375.

"We must not think that only the Pharisees of old and Papists of later times are superstitiously addicted to the traditions of the elders and authority of the church. In all sects there are divers . . . that rather choose to follow the troad[1] of blind tradition, if beaten by some such foregoers as they admire, than the right way of God's word by others to be shown them afterwards.

"Some again are as much addicted to themselves as the former to others, conceiving in effect . . . the same of their own heads which the Papists do of their head—the Pope—*viz.* that they cannot err or be deceived and this especially in such matters, as for which they have suffered trouble and affliction formerly and so having bought them dear they value them highly."

These, also, we know, as well as another sort—

"highly advancing a kind of privative goodness and religion, and who bend their force rather to the weakening of other men in their courses than to the building up of themselves in their own . . . half imagining that they draw near enough to God, if they can withdraw far enough from other men."

And those too—

"so soured with moodings and discontentment as that they become unsociable. . . . If they see nothing lamentable, they are ready to lament. If they take contentment in any, it is in them alone whom they find discontented. If they read any books they are only invectives especially against public states and their governors. All things tending to accord and union any manner of way are unwelcome unto them."[2]

Men and women of the temper indicated in these character sketches were an abomination to Robinson, and a vexation to his spirit.

John Robinson and Robert Parker

Another Puritan minister with whom Robinson came into touch in Leyden was Robert Parker (*c.* 1564–1614). He had been a student at Magdalen College, Oxford, where he got into trouble in 1588 for not donning the surplice. He was beneficed at Patney, in

[1] Troad = the trodden path, the track. [2] *Works*, vol. iii. pp. 356–7.

Wiltshire, in 1591. In 1607 he published *A Scholasticall Discourse against Symbolizing with Antichrist in Ceremonies, especially the Signe of the Crosse.* He wished to differentiate the Anglican Church more sharply from the Roman Catholic Church, and to avoid all appearance of participation in what he deemed to be her erroneous practices. This work brought him into disfavour with Bancroft, and the King was persuaded to issue a proclamation offering a reward for his arrest. Parker accordingly withdrew to Holland after an exciting period of hiding in London. Nethenus, the biographer of Ames, says that some wealthy merchants sent Parker and Ames to Leyden for the purpose of engaging in controversy with the supporters of the English Church. We may take it that some assistance was given in this way for their support while they were preparing and printing books upon the Puritan side. Parker busied himself in Leyden in a controversy (which excited much attention at the time) about the bodily descent of Christ to Hell. Bilson, Bishop of Winchester, pleaded in 1598 for the reality of this descent as stated in the Apostles' Creed. Amongst those opposed to him on this point was Hugh Samford, who, however, died before he could finish his reply. The work of Samford was put into Parker's hands for completion, and he spent four years in the task. During that time it is probable he enjoyed much friendly intercourse with Robinson. In 1611 he brought out his work "De Descensu Domini Christi . . . ad inferos." He then passed on from Leyden to Amsterdam. There he joined John Paget, who gives us a picture of him. It is clear that at his coming from Leyden he was under the influence of Robinson's ideas concerning the independency and self-sufficiency of each rightly ordered Church of Christ—

"When he came from Leyden, where he and Mr. Jacob had sojourned together for some time, he professed at his first coming to Amsterdam, that the use of synods was for counsel and advice only, but had no authority to give a definitive sentence. After much conference with him when he had more seriously and maturely considered this question, he plainly changed his opinion, as he professed, not only to me, but to others: so that some of Mr. Jacob's opinion were offended at him and expostulated, not only with him, but also with me for having occasioned the alteration of his judgment. I had the means of understanding his mind aright, and better than those who pervert his meaning, since he was not only a member of the same church, but a member of the same family and lived with me under the same roof; where we had daily conversation of these things, even at the time when Mr. Jacob published his unsound writing upon this question. He was afterwards a member of the same eldership, and, by office, sat with us daily to hear and judge the causes of our church, and so became a member of our classical combination; yet did he never testify against the 'undue power' of the classis, or complain that we were not a 'free people' though the classis exercised the same authority then as it doth now. He was also for a time the scribe of our consistory, and the acts of our eldership and church were recorded by his own hand."[1]

There was a prospect of Parker being chosen into ministerial office in Amsterdam, but the burgomasters vetoed the plan in order to avoid offending King James, who frowned upon any favour shown to refugee Puritans. Consequently he moved in 1613 to Doesburg, to serve as preacher to the English troops, and there died in 1614.

He left behind an incomplete work in Latin, on "The Ecclesiastical Polity of Christ and the opposed Hierarchical Polity." I am inclined to think the manuscript of this work was entrusted to John Robinson for editing. It appeared from the press of Godfrey Basson at Frankfort in 1616, with an admonition to the reader prefixed from John Robinson in the name of himself and his Church. Parker had mapped out a work of six books to cover the ground, but when he had finished three "he was translated to that purer Church in heaven, whose image he was seeking so diligently on earth." The book assumes the ultimate authority of the Scriptures for a fixed Church order

[1] Paget's *Defence of Church Government.*

and polity. It expounds the Presbyterian system against the advocates of episcopacy. But Robinson considered that in his occasional references to Brownists and Separatists, Parker had spoken too sharply, and as though they were guilty of an unrighteous schism from the Anglican Church. He points out that Parker's description of the Church government adopted by the Separatists as democratical needs some qualification. He denies that their separation is so absolute as Parker insinuates, or that their secession is principally based upon those grounds which Parker imagines. Robinson and his Church acknowledge the existence of many excellent doctrines and persons in the so-called Churches of England—

" In short," says he, " we do not separate ourselves in the proper sense or especially because ' the discipline of Christ is rejected or corrupted in the Anglican Church ' (as it seems to Mr. Parker, Book I, chapters 13 and 14) but because the discipline and rule of Antichrist is received and sanctioned by royal statutes and ecclesiastical canons. And it is a matter of conscience with us not to submit ourselves in any way to him. And seeing that Parker himself (like others in other books) in this most learned treatise of his asserts in many words and argues that this Hierarchical Government obtaining in these Churches is unlawful, papal and Antichristian, how can our submission to the same be lawful and Christian, or how can there be any communion in ecclesiastical ordinances (to each and all of which the government of the Church necessarily extends) without this unlawful submission. With the best will in the world we cannot really see how the latter contention is consistent with the former. We seek enlightenment on the point from others who, as is quite possible, see further into the matter, for we are always prepared (by the grace of God) to give way modestly to those who teach better things. Farewell." [1]

[1] "Denique non nos propriè, aut præcipuè nosmet sejungimus, propter *Christi disciplinam repudiatam* aut *corruptam* (sicuti illi videtur lib. 1, cap. 13 et 14) sed propter disciplinam et regimen Antichristi receptum et sancitum statutis regijs et canonibus Ecclesiasticis : cui nos nosmet ullo modo subjicere religio est. Et quandoquidem Regimen hoc Hierarchicum in hisce Ecclesijs obtinens (ut alibi alij) PARKERVS ipse, vel in hoc doctissimo scripto et multis verbis asserat et doceat argumentis, illegitimum, papale, et Antichristianum esse, quæ nostra eidem subjectio legitima et Christiana; aut quæ

Thomas Drakes of Harwich, an old associate of John Smith at Cambridge, was quick to seize upon Robinson's admissions, as the following passage from his *Ten Counterdemaunds propounded to those of the Separation* reveals. We may place the extracts in parallel columns. Drakes sings the praises of the Churches of England as a set-off to the criticisms of Separatists, and continues—

"In which Churches (as one of the princi[p]all Separatists I[ohn] R[obinson] in his admonition ad lectorem in his owne name and in the name of his faction, lately prefixed before the third booke [three books] of M. Robert Parke[r] *de politia ecclesi[æ]* confesseth that[)] the grace of God by the Gospell in respect of the chiefe heads of true Christian faith by diuers of the faithfull preached, doth so abound, that there are very many godly and holy men in these assemblies both of Reformitants and Conformitants which they acknowledge for brethren in Christ etc."—Drakes' *Ten Counterdemaunds*, 1618, Sig. A 3.	"Verum quidem est nos separationem instituere ab Ecclesiarum (vti appellant) Provincialium, Diocœsanarum, cathedralium & parrochialium formali statu; vtpote quæ & conflatæ sunt ex omnibus & singulis regni subditis sine vllo discrimine, vi pœnarum legalium in easdem coactis. . . . In qua tamen et rerum & personarum confusione, Dei Gratia, per Evangelium (quo ad capita summa veræ fidei Christianæ à nonnullis fideliter annunciatum) ita exuberare, & firmiter credimus, & libenter profitemur ut plurimi in istis cœtibus pij & sancti viri existant, cum reformistæ tum conformistæ (uti vocant) quos & pro fratribus in Christo habemus & quibuscum communionem in omnibus licitis (nostro saltem judicio) piè colimus."—Robinson's *Admonitio.*

communio in institutis Ecclesiasticis (in quæ omnia et singula Regimen Ecclesiæ se necessario diffundit) sine hac illicita submissione esse poterit?

Nobis certe videre non est, licet maximè velimus, quomodo posterius priori conveniat; ab alijs audire cupimus, qui (quod facilè fieri potest) plus vident: semper paratī meliora docentibus (per Dei gratiam) submissè cedere. Vale."—Robinson's *Admonitio ad Lectorem*, prefixed to Parker's *De Politeia*, closing sentences.

John Robinson and Henry Jacob

Intercourse with such men as Ames and Parker kept the mind of Robinson fresh and alert, and helped him in hammering out his own position. A third Puritan clergyman over whom he exercised considerable influence was Henry Jacob (1563–1624), a refugee in Holland on account of religion, who issued at Leyden, in 1610, a little treatise on *The Divine beginning and institution of Christ's true, visible and material Church.* Jacob had turned his attention to the questions at issue between the Church of England and the Separatists as early as 1599, when he defended the Anglican Church and ministry against Francis Johnson, who contended that neither Church nor ministry was true. Jacob at that time hoped for a further reformation in the Anglican Church and earnestly laboured to that end. Years went by, and reform seemed more remote than ever, so in 1616 he came over to London and gathered an "independent" congregation. It is clear that in this action he was guided by the example of Robinson. The covenant of this new society was based on the covenant which Robinson and his company had derived from John Smith.

Jacob ignored the older Separatist Church in London, formed in 1592, the remnants of which, even after the migration of the major part to Amsterdam, kept up its meetings. The members of that older society condemned the Anglican Church as a false Church, and had no fellowship with its adherents. Jacob would not go to those lengths, and, as we have seen, Robinson had returned to a more genial view, and permitted private communion with its members and occasional hearing of its pious ministers. From different directions Jacob and Robinson had moved to the same position. When Sabine Staresmore and his wife went over to Leyden, Robinson received them into fellowship in virtue of the covenant they had taken in the Church of Jacob. And when the rigid Separatists of the older

London Church put the question "whether Mr. Jacob's congregation be a true Church or no?" Robinson replied, "We have so judged . . . and so do we judge still."[1] This was no hasty conclusion, but a considered judgment. He enclosed with this letter to the Londoners from himself and his Church at Leyden "certain papers in which that matter is handled."

The memory of Robinson's association with these Puritan ministers remained fresh in the minds of the members of his Church in after days, and from their lips John Cotton of Boston obtained first-hand information of their intercourse and the modification that ensued in their views. "We some of us knew Mr. Parker, Doctor Ames, and Mr. Jacob in Holland, when they sojourned for a time at Leyden," says Bradford, looking back in 1648 to that earlier period, and he tells us that "Doctor Ames was estranged from and opposed Master Robinson, and yet afterwards there was loving compliance and near agreement between them."[2]

When that sturdy and zealous Scots Presbyterian, Robert Baillie, in his *Dissuasive from the Errors* of his times, identified in Robinson's doctrine of the Church "the womb and seed of that lamentable Independency in Old and New England which hath been the fountain of many evils already," it gave John Cotton an opportunity of stating Robinson's position more exactly.

This is how Cotton put the matter. It is a very fair summary—

> "As a fruit of his [Robinson's] studious inquisition after the Truth hee resorted (as I have understood) to many judicious Divines in England for the clearing of his Scruples which inclined him to separation; and when hee came into Holland hee addressed himselfe to Doctor Ames and Mr. Parker; rather preventing [*i. e.* anticipating] them with seeking counsell and satisfaction then (*sic*) waiting for their compassion. But as they excelled in learning and godlinesse

[1] "Letter to our Beloved in the Lord the Church of Christ in London," dated Leyden, April 5, 1624.

[2] Young's *Chronicles of the Pilgrims, Dialogues*, pp. 435, 439.

so in compassion and brotherly love also, and therefore as they discerned his weanednesse from selfe-fulnesse so did they more freely communicate light to him and received also some things from him.

"The fruit of which was (through the Grace of Christ) that the Disswader himselfe confesseth '*hee* [Robinson] *came backe indeed the one halfe of the way: acknowledging the lawfulnesse of communicating with the Church of England in the Word and Prayer but not in the Sacraments and Discipline, which was* (*saith hee*) *a faire Bridge, at least a faire Arch of a Bridge for union.*' But when hee [Baillie] saith '*hee came on to communicate with the Church of England in the Word and Prayer,*' it must not bee understood of the Common-Prayer-Book, but of the Prayers conceived by the Preacher before and after Sermon. And yet in comming on so far as he did, he came more then halfe way of any just distance.

. . . .

"It is true Mr. Robinson did not acknowledge a Nationall Church governed by the Episcopacy to be a Church of Divine Institution. But though he acknowledged the stile and privilege of a Church in the New Testament to belong to a particular Congregation of visible Saints; yet such Nationall Churches French or Dutch, as were governed by Presbyters and separate from the world at the Lord's Table he did not disclaime Communion with them. I have been given to understand that when a Reverend and godly Scottish Minister came that way (it seemeth to have been Mr. Iohn Forbes) he offered him Communion at the Lord's Table, though the other for feare of offence to the Scottish Churches at home excused himselfe.

"Yea, when some Englishmen that offered themselves to become Members of his Church, would sometimes in their confessions professe their Separation from the Church of England Mr. Robinson would beare witnesse against such profession avouching they required no such professions of Separation from this or that or any Church but onely from the world. All which doe argue that his comming on to Protestant Churches was more then the half way." [1]

[1] Cotton's *Way of the Congregational Churches Cleared*, 1648, pp. 7–9. This work was put to the press for Cotton by Nathaniel Homes, who signs the "Epistle Pacificatory." It was printed by Matthew Simmons for John Bellamie. The "Imprimatur," dated January 1, 1647, by "John Bachiler" is phrased in cordial terms.

CHAPTER XV

ROBINSON DISCUSSES QUESTIONS OF INFANT BAPTISM, FLIGHT IN PERSECUTION AND THE MAGISTRATE'S OFFICE

WHILE Robinson sustained a controversy with representative Puritan ministers on the one hand, he was also engaged in a disputation with old associates on the other. John Smith, through a fresh study of the Gospels, had disengaged himself from the Augustinian and Calvinistic theology in which he had been reared. He gave up the practice of baptizing infants. The New Testament, it seemed to him, pointed to the constitution of Churches not by means of a covenant, but by the assumption of baptism after repentance and profession of faith. He and his followers accordingly dissolved their Church estate entered into by covenant at Gainsborough. He "dispastored" himself and made a fresh start. His company being gathered together for the purpose in their place of meeting, Smith first baptized himself, and then baptized Thomas Helwys, and so John Murton and the rest, each "making their particular confessions."[1] The method of the baptism was undoubtedly that in vogue amongst the Anabaptists, *viz.* by affusion, not by immersion. The candidate knelt down, and the administrator, taking a handful of pure water from the basin, applied it to his head, baptizing him into the name of the Lord Jesus.

Criticism was at once directed against Smith's act of self-baptism. "Why," said John Hetherington, "would you not receive your baptism first from some

[1] *Works*, vol. iii. p. 168.

one of the Elders of the Dutch Anabaptists ?" Smith pondered the question, and becoming convinced that the Mennonites were indeed a true Church, he felt that he and his friends ought to have applied to them for baptism, and not resuscitated the rite for themselves. It is testimony to the force and charm of Smith's personality that he was able to lead the majority of those still associated with him to join him in a declaration of regret that they had taken their baptism into their own hands, and in applying for admission to membership with the Mennonites. The Dutch took time—plenty of time—for consideration. Before the application was granted, John Smith had died. His death must have raised feelings of affectionate regret in Robinson and those at Leyden who had known him so well in the old days in England. Smith left behind a remarkable "Confession of Faith" and a short tract reviewing the controversies in which he had been engaged. These were published in a tiny volume "by the remaynders of Mr. Smithe's company," and Robinson felt it necessary to take some notice of the publication.

He also entered into controversy with Thomas Helwys on the subject of baptism and the question of flight in time of persecution. Helwys went a long way with Smith in his religious progress, but parted company with him when he entered into negotiation with the Dutch Anabaptists. He and Murton, with a few others, were satisfied that their recovery of baptism for themselves was quite permissible. They were content with the Church order into which they had thus entered. Instead of disavowing it, they justified it. Nay, they carried the war into the enemy's camp, pleading with the Mennonites to reject Smith's petition for union, and at the same time pointing out to Brownists and Separatists the inconsistency of their attitude about baptism. The Separatists stigmatized the Anglican Church as a false Church, yet they retained its baptism as true. How could the baptism of a false Church be true?

Or, if the baptism were true, how could the Church which bestowed it be false? It took all Robinson's skill in making " distinctions " to parry this attack.

The practice of Robinson's Church in regard to those admissible to baptism can be briefly stated in his own words: " We profess withal," he says to Helwys, " that no infant . . . of any parents, the one whereof is not faithful, is to be baptized; and practise accordingly, as he knew well." [1] Either the father or mother, if not both, were required to be in Church fellowship before the child was accepted for baptism. To this position Robinson's Church consistently adhered, both in Holland and in New England. Helwys characterized it as an absurd notion that Christians beget Christians by generation. It is this idea, he said, " which hath brought in such madnes amongst men as the Brownists hold and profess, that no infants that die are under the Covenant of grace and salvation but such as they beget. Thus do *they only* beget infants that are heirs of salvation." [2] In his book, issued in 1612, entitled *A Short Declaration of the Mistery of Iniquity*, Helwys devotes a section to laying open " some particular errors in Mr. Robinson's book of *Justification of Separation*."

Robinson argued that in its " essential causes " the baptism received in the Anglican Church was all right, though it was administered in a false Church. The spiritual grace it conferred was made effective for believers by their after-repentance. He compared it with the vessels of the Temple which, " carried into Babylon, remained still, both in nature and right, the vessels of the Lord's house; though in respect of their use, or rather abuse, they became Belshazzar's quaffing bowls." [3] Helwys sliced through this analogy. " It is evident that it was moulded and made," he said, " in the Church of England, which you confess is Babylon; Mr. Rob[inson], had not you and all your

[1] *Of Religious Communion, Works*, vol. iii. p. 197.
[2] Helwys, *A Short Declaration of the Mistery of Iniquity*, 1612, p. 172.
[3] *Justification of Separation, Works*, vol. ii. p. 299.

congregation the true matter (as you call it) and true form of your baptism in England, and was it not administered upon you all in the assemblies of England? Then was your vessel of baptism made *there*. See your deceit herein, if there be any grace or understanding in you."[1] Helwys hits out gamely, and presses Robinson with a dilemma which Joseph Hall had put to him two years before—

"This strait are you now driven unto either to confess that before your separation you were infidels or unbelievers, and then you must believe and be baptized, or else that you were believers and faithful and then have you Separated from a faithful and believing people and not from the world, and you must return to your vomit with the false prophet[2] [Robert Browne] your first and chief shepherd that hath misled you upon these false grounds, who not being able (through his infidelity) to keep his face towards Ierusalem and the Land of Canaan hath fainted in the way and rebelled in the wilderness and is returned to his so much formerly detested Babylon and Egypt."[3]

Helwys acknowledged that he had "written in some things sharply," but it was wholesome medicine, and should be taken in good part.

"There are divers of you both near and dear unto us whom we require in love (as we do all) to apply the sharpest reproofs to themselves for they had need. And touching you Mr Rob[inson] remember that you have a letter of most loving respect in your hands concerning these things to which you have not made answer whereby to prevent the publishing of this that especially concern[s] you."[4]

This book of Helwys closed with a postscript[5] of some eight pages, in which the question of "flight

[1] *Mistery of Iniquity*, p. 145.

[2] The reference is to Robert Browne (*c.* 1550–*d.* 1633) who had been educated at Corpus Christi, Robinson's old college, and subsequently gathered a religious society denominated by outsiders as "Brownists." He published at "Middelbvrgh," in 1582, a treatise on *Reformation without tarying for anie*. In 1591, however, he conformed, received orders, and was presented first to the living of Little Casterton, in Rutland, and then to that of Achurch in Northamptonshire. He held the latter till his death. Browne was twice married: (*a*) to Alice Allen, (*b*) to Elizabeth Warrener, a widow.

[3] *Mistery of Iniquity*, p. 126. [4] *Ibid.*, p. 156. [5] *Ibid.*, pp. 204–12.

in persecution" is handled. He there deals with "the perverting of those words of our Saviour Christ, 'when they persecute you in one city flee into another,' contrary to all the meaning of Christ." He had come to the conclusion that it was wrong to flee in the face of persecution. Christ did not intend by that precept that they were "to flee to save themselves, but to flee or go to another City to preach the gospel. . . . But when will these men according to this rule of Christ shake off the dust of their feet for a witness against Amsterdam and Leyden which Cities neither receive them nor the word they bring otherwise than they receive Turks and Jews and all sorts who come only to seek safety and profit? . . . How much better had it been that they had given their lives for that truth they profess in their own Countries."

Helwys had the courage of his convictions. He crossed over to London with Murton and a few faithful associates apparently in the winter of 1612–13. Bonds and imprisonment awaited him. By the spring of 1616 he was dead. The copy of his book which he had the daring to present to the King remains in the Bodleian Library, with an inscription in brave terms on its flyleaf, in his own hand, to testify to his intrepid spirit.

The advance of Smith to the Anabaptist position, the approximation of his views to the Mennonite doctrines, and the attack by Helwys, seemed, in the opinion of Robinson, to demand some attention. "Divers weak persons," he says, "have been troubled and abused" by some things in Helwys's book, and "two or three simple people" were affrighted by his "loud and licentious clamours" from their baptism received in the "assemblies" in England.

Accordingly he issued, along with his treatise on *Religious Communion,* four additional chapters, which are really separate tracts, one dealing with "flight in persecution," the next asserting that "the outward baptism received in England is lawfully retained," another treating the general question " of the baptism of infants " at large, and lastly " a survey of the confession of faith published in certain conclusions by the remainders of M$^{r.}$ Smith's company after his death," which rounds off the volume. These tracts take up far more space in the book than the one on " Religious Communion," which gives the leading title.

In regard to flight in persecution, Helwys had referred to the commendation given to the Churches of Thessalonica and Pergamos for their patience in affliction, and set them up as an example. Robinson rejoined[1]—

> " As those churches knew not, haply, whither to go to be better in those days, so neither was their persecution such, but that they might enjoy their mutual fellowship and ministers, and bring up their children and families in the information of the Lord and his truth . . . which in England all men know, we could not possibly do."

And he concludes—

> " For flight then thus much. As we read that Christ our Lord, the prophets, and apostles did at some times and ordinarily avoid and flee persecution and at other times not; so are we to know that there are times and occasions seasonable for both. . . . As we, then, shall perceive either our flying or abiding to be most for God's glory and the good of men, especially of our family and those nearest unto us, and for our own furtherance in holiness; and as we have strength to wade through the dangers of persecution, so are we with good conscience to use the one or other. Which (our hope and comfort also is) we have done in these our days of sorrow; some of us coming over [to Holland] by banishment and others otherwise." [2]

Though this conclusion may not reach the heroic level, it certainly contains much sound common sense.

With regard to the nature of the rite of baptism and the distinctions about it which justified to Robinson's mind the retention of the " outward

[1] *Works*, vol. iii. p. 163. [2] *Ibid.*, pp. 162, 164.

baptism " received in the national Church, we may give his own words [1]—

" I conclude," he says, " that there is an outward baptism by water, and an inward baptism by the Spirit : which though they ought not to be severed in their time by God's appointment, yet many times are [so severed] by men's default : that the outward baptism in the name of the Father, Son, and Holy Ghost, administered in an apostate Church is false baptism in the administration, and yet in itself and [its] own nature a spiritual ordinance, though abused : and whose spiritual uses cannot be had without repentance; by which repentance and the after-baptism of the Spirit it is sanctified and not to be repeated."

This " double consideration " of baptism saved the situation for Robinson and his associates, but it struck laymen like Helwys as somewhat sophistical.

In his reply to Helwys on the general question of the baptism of infants, " a point of both great difference between us and weight in itself," Robinson makes the admission that he had drawn out the thread of his answer further than he intended. He does indeed make various digressions in the course of his answer, " for the better clearing of things thereabout " (notably an excursion in respect to the nature of the covenant with Abraham, which he identifies with the covenant of the Gospel), but the upshot of his argument was, that the children of believing parents were proper subjects for baptism. There was difficulty in finding plain Scriptural support for the practice. It was difficult to parry the argument that baptism, according to the New Testament, was to be administered to those who had been brought into discipleship to Christ by instruction, and had made a voluntary repentance and profession of faith, of which infants were incapable.

" Whereas some marvel," says Robinson, " why the Holy Ghost speaks not more plainly and expressly of the admission of infants into the Church and baptism thereof. They must remember—

" (1) That none must presume to teach the Lord how to

[1] *Works*, vol. iii. p. 185.

speak but that all are with reverence to search out his meaning.

"(2) That they may with as much reason marvel, why there is no express mention made of the casting out of the Jewish infants with their unbelieving parents."[1]

He concluded that "God ordinarily includeth in the parents the infants, as branches in the root either for blessings or judgments." He ran an elaborate parallel between baptism and circumcision, the one coming in the place of the other, but though this might serve his argument in respect to the boys, the retort was quickly made, "What about the girls?" The fact of the matter is that the renunciation of infant baptism was such a violent break with long-established Christian usage, that very few reformers were prepared to make it. The shock would be too great. Moreover, for social, political and doctrinal reasons, there was a strong prejudice against the Anabaptists. The average man made no discrimination amongst them. As Robinson rejected the denomination "Brownist," he might well shrink from any practice by which he would be associated with a name in deeper disfavour. It was too much to expect Robinson to base his retention of infant baptism on the natural grounds of fitness and the desire of the parents, when a fresh young life has been entrusted to them, to publicly express their thanks and their vow to do their best for the child. He comes nearest to an appeal to common sense in the matter when he says it is "absurd" to exclude infants "from the Church or state of grace because they cannot themselves make profession of faith and repentance."[2] According to the method of his time, he was mainly concerned about finding Scriptural authority for his practice.

The closing tract included in this volume is a "survey" by Robinson of the remarkable "Confession of Faith" drawn up in a hundred "propositions" by his old companion, John Smith, and published soon

[1] *Works*, vol. iii. p. 216. [2] *Ibid.*, p. 235.

after his death by the remainder of his company, under the editorship of Thomas Piggot. This survey is penned in a calm and even tone, with a studied absence of all invective, and with some approach to the recognition that all who are sincere seekers after God's truth are worthy of brotherly regard and stand within the compass of God's love. The serene Christian temper which marked the last writings of Smith was not without effect upon the tone of his critic. It goes without saying that Robinson defended the Calvinistic doctrines of predestination and election. He is not afraid to face some of the repellent consequences which flow from an extreme application of those doctrines. He is jealous of any teaching which would derogate from the absolute sovereignty and majesty of God. The old-world problem of how the presence of evil and sin is to be reconciled with the existence of an Almighty and Loving God is still with us, as it was with our fathers.

"This[1] sin he doth also suffer," says Robinson, "not as men oft suffer things to come to pass, without care or consideration of it, but of purpose and with infinite wisdom, as knowing how to bring light out of darkness, and by the creature's sin, to effect his most holy work according to his unsearchable counsel: the depth whereof may swallow up the mind, but cannot be sounded by it, and in meditation whereof, the best bound and bottom is for man to consider and confess that God is both more wise and holy than he."

Holding fast to the Calvinistic theology of the Anglican Articles, in which he had been exercised and instructed from youth, Robinson opposed Smith's contentions—

"That original sin is an idle term and that there is no such thing as men intend by the word, because God threatened death only to Adam, not to his posterity, and because God created the soul; . . . that as there is in all the creatures a natural inclination to their young ones, to do them good, so there is in the Lord toward man; for every spark of goodness

[1] *Works*, vol. iii. p. 241.

in the creature is infinitely good in God:—that as no man begetteth his child to the gallows, nor no potter maketh a pot to break it, so God doth not create or predestinate any man to destruction, . . . that although the sacrifice of Christ's body and blood offered up unto God his Father upon the Cross be a sacrifice of a sweet-smelling savour and that God in him is well pleased, yet it doth not reconcile God unto us, which did never hate us nor was our enemy, but reconcileth us unto God and slayeth the enmity which is in us against God."

This last contention, which reminds us of the teaching of Socinus as to the efficacy of Christ's death on the Cross, is characterized by Robinson as "most untrue, and indeed a very pernicious doctrine, destroying the main fruit of Christ's sacrifice and death."

Both Robinson and Smith back up their respective opinions by abundant references to Scripture, and this "survey" shows us very well how sincere men may frequently draw opposite conclusions and different meanings from the same texts, according to the different standpoint from which they are viewed.

The Soul and Religious Liberty

Before we leave this book, we may touch on two minor points in this section on which Robinson gives his opinion.

First, in regard to the nature of the soul. The Mennonites and Anabaptists, in order to evade the doctrine of the fall of man, asserted that God created the soul, and that "the soul, coming from God, must needs be good and therefore without sin until it be joined to the body."[1] Robinson considered the point, and came to the conclusion that God had given virtue and power unto mankind to beget and generate both soul and body. This he thought Adam had done "after a manner convenient to either nature." He goes on to say—

"If these two positions cannot stand together that God createth the soul immediately and that there is original sin:

[1] John Murton, quoted by John Wilkinson in 1613.

where these men [the followers of Smith and Helwys] conclude that there is therefore no original sin, *I* conclude contrariwise, that, therefore, the soul is not immediately created." [1]

Second, in the section criticizing Smith's propositions relating to the magistracy and the taking of oaths, Robinson gives us his views as to the duty and powers of the magistrate or civil ruler in regard to religion. John Smith and Thomas Helwys had come to the conclusion that Kings and magistrates were going beyond their function in meddling with matters of religion and coercing men in spiritual things by means of civil penalties. Both of them pleaded for full religious liberty for all peaceable citizens. Their plea bore fruit in after days. Smith contended—

"That the magistrate is not by virtue of his office to meddle with religion or matters of conscience to force and compel men to this or that form of religion or doctrine; but to leave Christian religion free to every man's conscience and to handle only civil transgressions . . . for Christ only is the King and lawgiver of the Church and conscience." [2]

Robinson was not prepared to uphold that position. Like the Puritans, he was still disposed to look to the civil power for assistance in promoting a further reformation of religion. The text (James iv. 12) brought by Smith to support his position does not prove, in the judgment of Robinson, that the magistrate may not use—

"his lawful power [3] lawfully for the furtherance of Christ's kingdom and laws. . . . It is true they [the magistrates] have no power *against* the laws, doctrines and religion of Christ: but *for* the same, if their power be of God they may use it lawfully, and against the contrary."

Robinson was apparently unconscious that in writing thus he was justifying the action of the Bishops in persecuting those holding similar opinions to his own.

[1] *Works*, vol. iii. p. 248.
[2] *John Smith the Se-baptist*, etc., p. 255, Proposition 84.
[3] *Works*, vol. iii. p. 277.

Murton and the followers of Helwys were not slow in pointing this out. In a forceful argument issued in 1615, "that no man ought to be persecuted for his religion," they refer to "some that make more show of religion" than the Anglicans, but "although themselves be now persecuted . . . maintain the same thing." And "if Kings were of their mind" they would be as cruel as the Anglican prelates.[1] The reference is to Robinson and those Separatists who agreed with his opinion on this matter.

While John Robinson was engaged in writing the collection of tracts which ends with his review of Smith's *Confession of Faith*, he received a paper from another Anabaptist of Amsterdam. It came from Mark Leonard Busher, citizen of London, a man who held some peculiar millenary views and published a forceful *Plea for Liberty of Conscience* in 1614. We do not know the nature of the inquiry he put, but Robinson did not think it worth while to reply. He was probably too busy, or felt that a sufficient answer would be found in the tracts he was about to issue. Busher was rather nettled at his silence. He refers to the matter in connection with a suggestion that none should be allowed to "confirm their religion and doctrine by the Fathers and by prisons, burning and banishing, etc., but by the holy scriptures; then error will not be written or disputed." This prohibition would happily reduce the number of books.

"Yea, I know by experience among the people called Brownists, that a man shall not draw them to write, though they be desired; for one of their preachers called Master Rob[inson], hath had a writing of mine in his hands above six months [*Note in margin:* "Now above twelve months"] and as yet I can get no answer. It seems he knoweth not how better to hide his errors than by silence. And this will be the case of all false bishops and ministers who had rather be mute and dumb than to be drawn into the light with their errors."[2]

[1] *Objections Answered by Way of Dialogue*, 1615, reprinted in *Tracts on Liberty of Conscience*, Hanserd Knollys Society.
[2] *Religions Peace, a Plea for Liberty*, etc., p. 52.

The Brownists were in general ready enough with their pens, and we may well forgive Robinson for his self-restraint in respect to Busher's paper of inquiry. We come, indeed, now to a period in which for some four years Robinson published no fresh books of his own beyond his brief "Manumission" already noticed. It gives us an opportunity of turning again to a consideration of the life of himself and his friends in Leyden.

CHAPTER XVI

THE PILGRIM CHURCH AND THE CIVIC AND UNIVERSITY LIFE OF LEYDEN

THE year of the publication of Robinson's tracts on *Religious Communion* saw the election of a new Parliament in England. Men's hearts were full of hope that the evils in Church and State would be swept away. There was great excitement at the polls, and the election saw the birth of a popular party, led by men of high principle, prepared to vindicate the liberties of the nation and oppose the arbitrary policy of the Court and the Prelacy. Petitions for the redress of grievances poured in from all sides; amongst them was presented the *Plea for Liberty of Conscience*, which Mark Leonard Busher had penned. James was alarmed at the spirit displayed in the new House against his policy. He was not the man to deal with opposition, nor had he the gift of gauging popular feeling which marked the statesmanship of Elizabeth. As soon as a pretext presented itself he dissolved Parliament. It had only sat for two months. The fact that it had shown its teeth was enough for King James, and for seven long years, from 1614 to 1621, he ruled as an absolute and despotic monarch. In that interval no Parliament was summoned.

The expectation of Robinson and his Church that through the initiation of a new policy by the Parliament they might soon be allowed to return to their beloved Motherland was dashed. It became clear that they must continue to abide in Holland for a while longer.

Fresh members came dropping over from England to fill the gaps caused by deaths and removals. The strength of the Church was thus well maintained. Men like Joseph Crips from Chichester, Robert Cushman and John Keble from Canterbury, Thomas Blossom of Cambridge, Richard Masterson of Sandwich, Alexander Price, the camlet merchant, Edward Pickering of London, Degory Priest, the hatter, of the same place, Stephen Butterfield from Norwich, Samuel Lee, a hatter, James Kingsland, a clothier, John Jennings and Roger Chandler from the Colchester district, and George Morton, the merchant, from York, all added fresh experience to the religious society under Robinson's pastoral care and gave it stability. One or two members came to them from Amsterdam. Of such were Alexander Carpenter and his family, originally from Wrington in Somersetshire, and Thomas Smith, a cloth merchant from Colchester, who had been a deacon in the English Church at Amsterdam. Particulars relating to all these and many others connected with the Pilgrim Church have been lovingly gathered from the town records of Leyden by Dr. H. M. Dexter and his son, Morton Dexter, enabling us to form a clear view of their trades and occupations, their marriages, their bereavements, and, in some cases, their purchase of houses and cottage homes.

In the year 1615 we come upon the name of a member of rather higher social standing than those mentioned. This was Thomas Brewer, who belonged to a land-holding family of the county of Kent. He was keenly interested in religion and theology. Though he was then thirty-five years of age and the father of a family, he matriculated as a student in "Letters" at Leyden University on February 17, 1615. He evidently felt there would be no chance of a safe return to England for some time, for on June 17, 1617, he bought the residence known as the "Green House" (Groenehuis), next door but one to Pastor John Robinson's, for 3,200 guilders from Johann de Lalaing. When the census of 1622 was taken he was described as an English nobleman (Engelsch Edelman). He became one of the Merchant Adventurers, and so had a direct business interest, as well as a personal concern, in the project for colonizing New England. He sold his house in Leyden July 15, 1630, when presumably he returned to England. We shall hear of him again. The registrar of the University entered his name on the record as "Thomas Braeber." Robinson soon followed the example of Brewer in matriculating in the University. Robert Durie, minister of the Scots Church in Leyden, had matriculated at the age of fifty-five in the spring of 1610, being described in the record as "Anglicanæ Ecclesiæ Min[ister]." To become a member of the University gave admission to the academic circles of the city and conferred certain privileges. It exempted one from service in the civic guard, and permitted the purchase of certain quantities of wine and beer free from duty.

Robinson applied for permission to matriculate to the Burgomasters. Apparently no objection was raised, and on August 5, 1615, they gave their consent. In due course Robinson's name was enrolled on the list of University students. The entry of matriculation runs as follows—

"1615	Joannes Robintsonus, Anglus
Sept. 5°	Ann. xxxix
Coss. permissu.	Stud. Theol. alit Familiam."

It will be seen that the permission of the magistrates is noted, as well as the fact that Robinson supported a family and was in his thirty-ninth year. This is the only direct testimony we have to his age.

Robinson attended some of the Divinity lectures, notably those of John Polyander, who had come from Dort in 1610 to be Professor of Sacred Theology at Leyden, and with whom he was familiar, and those of Simon Biscop, better known by his Latin name of

Episcopius, who championed the Arminian system of doctrine. These lectures would remind Robinson of his old days at Cambridge, and be of service to him both in his pulpit work and his controversial writings.

The points at issue between the rival Dutch factions of Arminians and Gomarists were discussed with extraordinary passion in the towns and Universities of Holland. Political feeling was drawn in to reinforce religious zeal. Calvinism became a badge of the supporters of Prince Maurice and Arminianism a token of sympathy with the political aims and aspirations of Barneveldt. Leyden was a storm centre in the bitter disputes that resulted.

There, in the year that the Pilgrims settled in the city, Arminius,[1] the gifted leader of the liberal theologians, had died. In July 1610 the Curators of the University elected Conrad Vorstius as his successor, but the appointment roused a violent opposition, and King James of England actually took a hand in the resultant controversy. Robinson and the leaders of his Church must have been interested in the religious disputations taking place at their doors.

Conrad Vorstius, born at Cologne July 19, 1569, had a distinguished career as a student. He gave courses of lectures in the Academy of Geneva at the request of Theodore Beza. In 1605 he was appointed Professor of Theology at Steinfurt, in spite of some suspicions of Socinianism, which had been aroused by his volume of *Theses on Various Points of Dogmatic Theology*, printed in 1596. He had issued at Steinfurt in 1602 a treatise on *The Nature and Attributes of God*. It was a subject upon which he had deeply meditated. In the year of his appointment to Leyden he published an enlarged edition of this work, with copious notes. The title is *Tractatus Theologicus de Deo*. Editions appeared

[1] James Harmensen, better known as Arminius, born at Oudewater, 1560, died 1609.

at Steinfurt and Hanover in 1610. His opponents at Leyden seized on this book with avidity. They drew from it matter for their attack on the new professor. He was charged in May 1611 by six ministers with publishing heretical doctrine, and a regular storm of opposition broke upon the poor man's devoted head. It must have been something of a surprise to Vorstius, " a lover of peace and moderation," to find what a stir his book created, and to learn that a royal antagonist had entered the lists against him. King James was not content with writing a *Confutation of Vorstius* and ordering his treatise *De Deo* to be burnt at St. Paul's Cross and at Oxford and Cambridge; but brought pressure to bear on the States of Holland, through Winwood, his ambassador, to prevent the preferment of Vorstius. Winwood was to let them know " how infinitely " His Majesty would be displeased " if such a Monster receive advancement in the Church." The act was unspeakably petty and unkingly. The States and University authorities thought it wisest to bar Vorstius from lecturing, and sent him honourably to Gouda for a year to prepare an answer to the accusations brought against him. The malignity of James pursued him even here, and we find the English deputies at the Synod of Dort putting in extracts from his famous book, on May 3, 1619, and demanding that it should be solemnly burnt. The next day the Synod of Dort passed sentence on Vorstius in his absence. It charged him with calling in question " most of the fundamental doctrines of the Reformed Religion . . . as the Most Potent King of Great Britain and several Divines had shewn." He was accordingly deprived of his professorship and banished from the United Provinces. He withdrew at length into Holstein, and there died, September 29, 1622.

Amongst those who joined in the hue and cry against Vorstius was Matthew Slade, sometime an elder in Johnson's Church at Amsterdam, but now in fellowship with the Dutch Church. Slade was well known to Robinson, who would probably hear of his *Disputation on the Blasphemies, Heresies and Atheisms distinguished with a Black Mark by James, King of England, in Vorstius's Treatise concerning God.* It was something great for a religious refugee at Amsterdam to endorse the judgment of his King.

On the withdrawal of Vorstius from Leyden in 1612 the Curators of the University elected Simon Episcopius (1583–1643) to lecture in theology. He gave his inaugural address on February 23, 1612, on *How best the Kingdom of God may be built up among Men.* It was hardly to be expected that a young man of liberal outlook, such as he was, would in those days escape the charge of heresy. He inherited some of the troubles of his predecessors. Festus Hommius, pastor of the Walloon Church in Leyden, and later on one of the two secretaries of the Synod of Dort, a great stickler for orthodoxy, brought a charge of Socinianism against him in 1615, but was unable to substantiate it before the Curators of the University and Burgomasters of the city.

We may assign to this period the incident of Robinson's disputation in the University of Leyden against the Arminians.[1]

When in later years a slanderous report was circulated by opponents of the Pilgrim Fathers to the effect that they had been driven out of Leyden by the civic authorities and had not left of " their own free choice and motion," Bradford referred to this disputation in rebutting the slander, and gave it as an example of the regard in which Robinson was held in Leyden. The Pastor's successful advocacy of the Calvinistic scheme of theology, says Bradford, procured him much honour and respect amongst lovers of truth in Leyden.

" Yea, so far were they from being weary of him and his people or desiring his absence; as it was said by some of no mean note ' that were it not for giving offence to the State

[1] See above, p. 57.

of England they would have preferred him otherwise if he would: and allowed them [*i. e.* his religious society or Church] some public favour.' Yea, when there was speech of their removal into these parts [New England] sundry of note and eminence of that nation would have had them come under them [colonize under the Dutch flag], and for that end made them large offers."

This, amongst other instances, Bradford thought would suffice "to show the untruth and unlikelihood of this slander" against the pioneer Pilgrims.

It is clear from this account that Polyander and the Calvinistic party were pleased with the assistance that Robinson had afforded them, and that the members of the little Church, meeting in Robinson's house, were proud of the part he had taken in the controversy. Some of the honour their pastor had deservedly won was reflected upon themselves. It is possible the authorities might have granted them the use of some convenient public building for their worship as a mark of their favour, as they had done in the case of the Scots Church under Robert Durie; but they had to keep an eye on England. They knew well how James had interfered to bar William Ames from preferment in their University. They knew of his deep displeasure against Vorstius. They knew of his annoyance that Puritan clergy found a refuge in Holland. If they gave any official encouragement to this company of Englishmen and their pastor, who had renounced their allegiance to the Anglican Church, it would be likely to breed trouble. They had to show their regard in other ways. When Sir Dudley Carleton succeeded Winwood as English Ambassador at the Hague, in March 1616, he received special instructions from his Royal master, who reminded him of "the violent and sharp contestations" among the towns of Holland in regard to religion. "If," he says, "they should be unhappily revived during your time, you shall not forget that you are the minister of that master whom God hath made the sole protector of his religion." Carleton's dispatches make reference to the differences at Leyden " betwixt the orthodox and Arminian factions," so there was real ground for the caution of the city authorities about extending any official recognition to Robinson's Church.

CHAPTER XVII

THE PILGRIM PRESS AT LEYDEN

William Bradford, in giving an account of Brewster and his life at Leyden, tells us that during the latter part of his time there, in addition to teaching English to the sons of Danes and Germans, " he also had means to set up printing by the help of some friends; and so had imployment enough: and by reason of many books which would not be allowed to be printed in England they might have had more than they could do." The Separatists at Amsterdam had already run a press for some years, under the direction of Giles Thorpe, who turned out some very good work. Men who hold opinions which they deem to be of importance to the world always desire to spread them. It was natural that the company under Robinson should avail themselves of the first opportunity to control a press of their own. I think it is quite possible that Robinson added to his income in Leyden by reading and correcting for the press before Brewster embarked on his venture. Thomas Brewer found the bulk of the capital for the new press, and the attic of his house seems to have been used for part of the work. They got John Reynolds, a printer by trade, over from London to help in the work, and he felt sufficiently secure in his job to betroth himself to Prudence Grindon (also from London) on July 28, 1617, and to marry on August 18. Jonathan Brewster and Mary Allerton, with Mary Brewster, the wife of his master, came along to witness his betrothal. After the " Pilgrim Press " was broken up Reynolds moved on to Amsterdam. It was probably in the autumn of 1616 that Brewster began this venture, for on October 22, 1619, Carleton says that Brewer "for the space of these three years hath printed prohibited books and pamphlets." A good, clear fount of type was bought, similar to some that Thorpe had used at Amsterdam, with some distinctive ornamental "rules," initials and "tail-pieces." English books had already come out at Leyden, in the production of which the Pilgrims probably had some hand. Amongst the volumes left by William Brewster, for example, was a copy of "*The Revelation of S. John Illustrated* . . . by Thomas Brightman. Imprinted at Leiden by John Claesson van Dorpe," in this very year of 1616. Now, however, they were to command a press of their own for a few years, till the printing of a book obnoxious to King James brought them into trouble.[1] Two of the books issued were in Latin and bear Brewster's imprint; those printed by him in English give no direct indication of the press from which they came. Among the first of his productions was an unexceptionable volume of Cartwright's *Commentaries on the Book of Proverbs*, to which John Polyander, Professor of Sacred Theology in the University of Leyden, supplied a preface, dated December 31, 1616. This was followed by a controversial work, from the pen of William Ames, entitled *Guilielmi Amesii ad Responsum Nicolai Grevinchovii Rescriptio contracta*, 1617. Both of these indicate the printer thus: "Apud Guilielmum Brewsterum. In vico Chorali." That is to say, "at William Brewster's office in Choir Alley."

There seems to have been a demand for reprints of some of the earlier Puritan controversial literature, and these were supplied from Brewster's press in handy form and sent over to England. In 1618 he took in hand a larger work from a manuscript left by Thomas Cartwright, entitled *A Confutation of the*

[1] The Hon. Henry C. Murphy, *Historical Magazine*, vol. iv., Boston and New York, 1860, and Professor Edward Arber, *The Story of the Pilgrim Fathers*, 1897, p. 195, have unravelled this narrative for us.

Rhemists' Translation, Glosses and Annotations on the New Testament, a bulky book of folio size.

The next year a Scotsman appeared in Leyden with some manuscripts he wished to get quietly printed. Brewer and Brewster undertook the work, and this proved their undoing. How did this come about? What were the books in question?

We must remember that King James was at this time bent upon breaking the spirit of the Scottish Presbyterians and enforcing episcopacy upon the Church of Scotland. He pressed his plans with vigour at the General Assembly of the Kirk at Perth in August 1618. David Calderwood voiced the resentment of the militant Presbyterians in a tract entitled *Perth Assembly*, in which "he demonstrated the utter nullity of that meeting and all its proceedings." He also penned a Latin treatise giving an exposition of the form of government in the Scottish Church, *De regimine Ecclesiæ Scoticanæ, brevis relatio*. He sent these writings over to Holland by a trusty friend, who got Brewster to print them. The copies of *Perth Assembly* "were smuggled over into Scotland in April 1619 with great risk and difficulty—in short, the pamphlets were packed up in vats as if they had been a mercantile consignment of French wines or strong waters." [1] They were landed at Burntisland, and in June passed into general circulation. The style of the book revealed its authorship, and Calderwood, after remaining in hiding for a time, fled in August 1619 to Holland. James was furious; he spoke of him as "that knave who is now loupen over sea, with his purse well filled by the wives of Edinburgh." The King thought James Cathkin, the Edinburgh bookseller, might have had a hand in printing the obnoxious tract, and the poor man, being in London on business, was arrested in June 1619, and brought before His Majesty. An extraordinary cross-examination followed. Cathkin denied

[1] "Life of Calderwood," by Thomson, in Calderwood's *History of the Church of Scotland*.

all share in the publishing of *Perth Assembly*, but, questioned as to whether Calderwood had been at his house, Cathkin confessed that he had slept there occasionally, "and that he had spoken with him within these fifteen days."

"We have found the taed!" exclaimed the King, and Cathkin was remanded to prison for further examination. He cleared himself of the imputation of issuing *Perth Assembly*, and in three weeks was at liberty.

King James, soon after this, heard of the real source of this annoying pamphlet. Sir Dudley Carleton, his Ambassador at the Hague, was shown a copy of *Perth Assembly* about the middle of July 1619, and was informed that it was "printed by a certain English Brownist of Leyden." As the "States General" of the Netherlands had issued an Edict or "Placaat" in the preceding December against unlicensed printing, Carleton thought he had just ground to complain to them about this issue. On July 17, 1619, he sent a copy of the book in question over to Sir Robert Naunton, the Secretary of State, with a covering letter explaining what he proposed to do in the matter when he had obtained "more particular knowledge of the printer." He lost no time in making further inquiry. On July 22 he sent a despatch from the Hague in which he says—

"I sent your Honour a book intituled *Perth Assembly*, of which, finding many copies dispersed at Leyden and from thence some sent into England, I had reason to suspect it was printed in that town; but upon more particular inquiry do rest somewhat doubtful. Yet in search after that book I believe I have discovered the Printer of another, *De regimine Ecclesiæ Scoticanæ;* which His Majesty was informed to be done at Middelburg; and that is one William Brewster, a Brownist, who hath been for some years an inhabitant and printer at Leyden: but is now within these three weeks removed from thence and gone back to dwell in London; where he may be found out, and examined, not only of this book *De regimine Ecclesiæ Scoticanæ*, but likewise of *Perth Assembly;* of which, if he was not the printer himself, he assuredly knows both the Printer and the Author. For, as I am informed, he hath had, whilst he remained here, his hand in all such books, as have been sent over into England and Scotland. As particularly a book in folio intituled *A Confutation of the Rhemists' Translation, Glosses and Annotations on the New Testament,* anno 1618, was printed by him.

"So was another in decimo sexto, *De vera et genuina Jesu Christi Domini et Salvatoris nostri Religione;* of which I send your Honour herewith the Title Page. And if you will compare that which is underlined therein with the other *De regimine Ecclesiæ Scoticanæ* of which I send your Honour the Title Page likewise; you will find it is the same character. And the one being confessed as that, *De vera et genuina Jesu Christi, etc., Religione,* Brewster doth openly avow; the other cannot well be denied."

With regard to Carleton's assertion that Brewster had gone back to London at some time in the early weeks of July, we know from other sources that he was there in May of this year, along with Robert Cushman, negotiating with a view to forming a colony for the "Pilgrim Church" in America. When Cushman wrote to the Leyden friends on May 8, he reported "M^r. B[rewster]" to be "not well at this time; whether he will come back to you or go into the North I yet know not." It is possible that he visited his old friends about Scrooby, and then had crossed to Leyden to report, and returned to London early in July. But when Sir Robert Naunton, acting on Carleton's suggestion, sought for him in London at the end of that month, he could not be found. "I am told," he says, writing on August 3, "William Brewster is come again for Leyden; where I doubt not but your Lordship will lay for him if he come thither; as I will likewise do here; where I have already committed some of his complices and am commanded to make search for the rest."

On both sides of the North Sea, therefore, a sharp watch was kept for Brewster. By this time I think he was aware that the authorities were on his track, and that it would be the safest course to remain quiet for a time. His name disappears for the present from the list of those actively promoting the plan for emigration. Carver, Cushman and Christopher Martin were left to attend to the public business which that plan entailed.

The Leyden friends would naturally do what they could to put Carleton off the scent. On Friday, August 20, 1619, he reports " after good enquiry " that he had been assured that Brewster had not returned to Leyden and was not likely to, because he had removed his family and goods thence.

King James was eager to mark down his victim. A despatch sent from Whitehall on Monday, August 23, 1619, by the Secretary of State to Carleton, informed him how much annoyed the King was by the underhand printing of Puritan pamphlets abroad and " the practices of Brewster and his complices in those parts." Information had come to hand that several of Brewster's accomplices had " very lately " made an escape and slipped over to Holland with him. His Majesty desired his Ambassador " to deal roundly " with the Dutch States-General in pressing for the arrest of Brewster as they tendered His Majesty's friendship.

The information as to Brewster's withdrawal from London was probably correct, for on Saturday, August 28, Carleton writes from the Hague : " Touching Brewster I am now informed that he is on this side the seas and was seen yesterday at Leyden, but as yet is not there settled." On the following Friday he writes again, reporting that Brewster " keeps most at Amsterdam, but, being *incerti laris*, he is not yet to be lighted upon," and adds, " I understand he prepares to settle himself at a village called Leerdorp [Leiderdorp] not far from Leyden, thinking there to be able to print prohibited books without discovery : but I shall lay wait for him both there and in other places, so as I doubt not but either he must leave this country; or I shall, sooner or later, find him out."

The Ambassador did not let the grass grow under his feet. He went to work to effect his Royal master's will through the instrumentality of Jacob von Brouckhoven, the representative for the city of Leyden in the Council of the provincial State of Holland, who lived at the Hague. Brouckhoven brought the matter to the notice of the Leyden authorities, who summoned Thomas Brewer before them, September 9, 1619, to be examined in reference to the King's complaint. Brewster was the man wanted, but it is Brewer who is examined. It looks as though Brewer came forward to shelter the Elder of his Church. He told the magistrates that his business heretofore had been printing or having printing done, but he had stopped the printing office in consequence of the Proclamation about the printing of books. At the time of the issue of the Proclamation or "Placaat" the business was mostly his own. His partner, William Brewster, was then in town, but sick.

As Brewer was a matriculated member of the Leyden University, the aldermen and magistrates of the city decided to hand him over to the University authorities.

The Council resolved, Thursday, September 9, 1619, "in regard to William Brewster to bring him, inasmuch as he is sick, into the Debtor's Chamber provisionally, where he went voluntarily." This was clearly no arrest. It appears to me that the Council merely took this course to save their face, and were quite lukewarm in this action against Brewster. He evidently was not detained, and had an opportunity of getting away before Sunday. Carleton, however, on Brouckhoven's report to him, jumped to the conclusion that Brewster had actually been arrested, and was inclined to take the credit for that to himself.

"Fri. 10 Sep. I have at length found out Brewster at Leyden whom the magistrates of that town at my instance apprehended yesternight though he was sick in bed." Brouckhoven went over to Leyden on this

Friday, and on his return would report the true state of affairs to the Ambassador, or, at any rate, tell him that Brewster was not really under arrest.

So on Sunday, September 12, Carleton forwarded a correction to England—

> "In my last [10 Sep.] I advertised your Honour that Brewster was taken at Leyden: which proved an error in that the Scout [bailiff] who was employed by the Magistrates for his apprehension being a dull, drunken fellow took one man for another."

Well, that story was good enough for Carleton and King James.

Meanwhile, when Carleton heard of the action of the Leyden City Council in the case of Brewer and Brewster, he had at once sent Brouckhoven over from the Hague to Leyden to secure the seizure of their books and type, and to press for their examination about all the books, Latin or English, printed by them in the past "eighteen months or two years." No time was lost. On the following day, Saturday, September 11, Loth Huyghenszoon Gael, bailiff of the University, applied to have an assessor and a magistrate associated with him for seizing Brewer's type, and any books "printed or caused to be printed by him within a year and a half or thereabouts," and examining him on the matter. It will be observed that the authorities took the shortest period suggested by Carleton for this investigation and ignored his "two years." Take this in conjunction with the fact that they appointed Dr. John Polyander, who had written a preface for one of the first books printed by Brewster, as "assessor," and its significance will be seen. Dr. William Bontius was joined with Polyander in the business.

In pursuance with the power granted to them, they visited Brewer's house. "The types found in the garret were seized: the garret door nailed in two places and the seal of the Officer impressed in green wax over paper is placed upon the lock and nails, a catalogue is made of the books, and the chamber where the same were found is sealed with the aforesaid seal upon the lock and nails."

All this was promptly reported to Carleton, who, though nettled at the escape of Brewster, was gratified at the detention of Thomas Brewer, and was now inclined to think the latter was the more responsible of the two, for he, "being a man of means, bare the charge of his printing." "I intend," he says, writing on Sunday, September 12, "to send one expressly to visit his books and papers; and to examine him particularly touching *Perth Assembly*, the discourse *De regimine Ecclesiæ Scoticanæ*, and other Puritan pamphlets which I have newly recovered.

The next day, Monday, September 13, the University appointed Dr. Cornelius Swanenburg in the place of Polyander to join with Bontius in the examination of Brewer, and further, they ordered his type "to be brought for better keeping from his house to the University Rooms." Jacob V. Vervey noted on the records that this was accordingly done on that very day.

In the course of the same week, in fulfilment of his intention, Carleton drew up a list of interrogatories to be put to Brewer in his examination, and sent them over to Leyden, with one of his staff and a Dutch Advocate of the Hague who understood English. He was not pleased with Brewer's replies, "which," says he, "are so indirect that they give no man satisfaction that sees them." He reports this in a long despatch, written on Saturday, September 18, 1619, in which, after remarking on the unsatisfactory nature of Brewer's answers, he goes on to say—

"Therefore I have now used the Prince of Orange's authority: who hath spoken himself to the Rector of the University not to give the prisoner any liberty until His Majesty's pleasure be known concerning him: which the Rector doth promise shall be fulfilled notwithstanding that the whole Company of Brownists doth offer caution [to go bail] for Brewer. And he being a University man the scholars are likewise stirred up by the Brownists to plead Privilege in that kind when caution is offered.

"Wherefore I am requested by the Rector and by the Deputy of the town of Leyden, Monsieur Brouckhoven, residing here, in the Council of Holland (whose serious care in this business I cannot but commend to His Majesty), to know His Majesty's pleasure with the soonest, whereby to prevent some disorder which may happen upon this occasion.

"Meantime I intend to have him further examined, which Monsieur Brouckhoven will give order for on Monday next when he goeth to Leyden for two or three days: And if there be any things more particular in his Confession I will send the same speedily to your Honour; as with these [papers] which go herewith, I thought it my duty to despatch this bearer expressly.

"Amongst the books touching which I have caused him to be examined I have inserted some as that *Amesii in Grevinchovium* which as he cannot deny so he may and doth confess it without difficulty; but by that character [style of type] he is condemned of the rest. And certain experienced printers which have viewed the letters affirm that all and every one of the books with which he is charged, particularly those *De regimine Ecclesiæ Scoticanæ* and *Perth Assembly* were printed by them. And it appears that this Brewer, and Brewster whom this man set on work, having kept no open shop nor printed many books fit for public sale in these Provinces, their practice was to print prohibited books to be vented underhand in His Majesty's Kingdoms.

"And if hereupon, His Majesty will be pleased that I move the States General to take some strict order therein, through all their Provinces; either by further explanation of their late Placaat concerning printing of Books and Libels, [*i. e.* pamphlets] or some other way; as I believe they will do it very willingly, so will it serve for preventing of the like inconvenience hereafter.

"What this Brewer is, and what fantastical courses he hath run heretofore, your Honour will see by an 'Information' which hath been given me concerning him.

"Thus I humbly take my leave

"From the Hague the 18th of September 1619.

"Postscript. Upon some just ground of suspicion that Master Ames hath his hand in many of these books, which your Honour will find specified in these 'Interrogatories.' I have desired the Curators of the University of Leyden not to admit him to a place of Public Professor, to which he doth pretend and [for which he] hath many strong recommendations, until he hath given His Majesty full satisfaction; which they do very willingly yield unto: and I am very well assured his preferment will here stay, unless His Majesty give way unto it.

"Thus I rest your Honour's, etc.

"Dudley Carleton."

Where Brewster remained in hiding all this time does not appear. His friends and fellow-members kept a discreet silence and loyally screened him. We may be sure that on the next day after the above despatch, being Sunday, fervent prayers would be offered up in the meeting in Robinson's house for the safety and welfare of both these members of the Church who were now in peril.

In the meantime Carleton had made inquiry for Brewster at Amsterdam, and on Saturday, September 18, Matthew Slade addressed a note to him in these terms—

"Right Honourable. My duty remembered unto your good Lordship.

"May it please the same to understand that I have made the best enquiry that I could, concerning William Brewster, among them that know him well. But cannot hear otherwise than that he is yet dwelling and resident at Leyden.

"Neither is it likely that he will remove his dwelling hither, there being another English printer named William [Giles] Thorp also a Brownist, settled here; and for that there is also variance about religion between the Separatists at Amsterdam and them of Leyden.

"If he lurk here for fear of apprehension, it will be hard to find him. But I will speak with our Burgomaster about that business, at his return; who is not yet in two or three days expected."

At Amsterdam, therefore, Carleton drew a blank, and he now waited instructions from England as to procedure against Thomas Brewer. These were soon forthcoming in a despatch dated at Hampton Court on Tuesday, September 28, 1619, from Sir Robert Naunton, as follows—

"Sir: For answer to your last of the 18th of September, it is His Majesty's pleasure that you present his princely thanks to that noble Prince [Maurice] also to Monsieur Brouckhoven and the Rector [of the University] for their serious care and respect, shewed in the apprehension and examination of Brewer. From whom His Majesty hopes well that you will draw more particularities in his after [*i. e.* later] Confessions than yet he sees in those you have sent over, which meanwhile he takes in good part as a fair beginning and introduction to the rest.

"When you shall have discovered all you can there, His Majesty would have you move the States earnestly in his name, that he [Brewer] may be remanded hither. Which he promiseth himself, that they will not take it for an unreasonable request since he is his own native subject: they having formerly remanded some of their own hither upon His Majesty's like motion.

"But if any fond scruple or difficulty should be made herein in respect of the scholars there pleading their privilege in that tumultuous town, especially in these troubled times, or otherwise; His Majesty will have you (rather than you should fail in his design) to descend thus much further as to promise them—that if they [the members of the University] shall so require, he will return him back again, after he shall have informed himself from him of divers things merely concerning his own personal service: His Majesty having no intention to touch him, either in body or goods, or to punish him further than with a free confession of his own misdemeanours and those of his complices.

"And for the time to come you are required to move the States to take some strict order through all their Provinces, for the preventing of the like abuses and licentiousness in publishing, printing and venting underhand such scandalous and libellous pamphlets.

"For Ames his preferment, His Majesty doth utterly distaste it; as if a new Vorstius were reviving in him, and would in no sort have any way given unto it."

On receipt of these instructions Carleton made a request for the extradition of Thomas Brewer, but the University and town of Leyden, being jealous for their privileges, were loth to surrender a prisoner at the request of King James. "An extraordinary meeting" of the Curators of the University and Burgomasters of the city was held on October 11,

1619, according to English reckoning, to consider the question, and the following resolutions were arrived at—

(*a*) To offer Brewer, as before, for further examination in the presence of any one whom the Ambassador might appoint;
(*b*) Or to cause him to go for examination before the Ambassador himself.
(*c*) If neither of these suggestions was accepted as sufficient, then before giving up Brewer a formal bond should be demanded from His Excellency the Ambassador that he should be restored in safety to Leyden again within two months.

If Carleton did not consent to this, the matter would have to be referred to their High Mightinesses the States of Holland and West Friesland, as founders and patrons of the University. The Ambassador saw that he would have to walk warily if his Royal master was not to be baulked in his desire to have Brewer sent over to England. From his next despatch, dated October 13, it is clear he saw which way the wind was blowing, though he does not seem to have yet heard the result of the " extraordinary meeting " at Leyden. In this despatch he reports—

(1) In regard to further examination of Brewer that he finds it lost labour, he persisting in his former answers. The only fresh point was that Brewer had written him a long, impertinent [irrelevant] letter which he encloses.

(2) With regard to Brewer's extradition, " I know," says he, " it will be a matter of much difficulty to effect His Majesty's desire, in regard of the scrupulosity of the Town and University of Leyden in point of Privilege, both which are interested herein as a mixed cause; he being apprehended by the Public Escoutete [City Bailiff] and kept in the University Prison."

Carleton had thought it best to begin the matter

in Leyden rather than in the assembly of the States-General of Holland. He had "prepared" the Curators of the University, and got Brouckhoven to do the same with the magistrates of the town. He had also spoken to the Prince of Orange on the matter. "The Curators," he goes on to say, "are now at this present at Leyden, upon the admission of some of their new Professors, and have promised me their endeavours to give His Majesty satisfaction."

(3) When he knew the decision of the Curators he could then make proposals to the States-General for the prevention of this unlicensed printing in all the provinces of the Netherlands.

After making this report, and before sending his next despatch, dated October 22, 1619, Carleton was waited on by two deputations from Leyden, who made known to him the decisions of the authorities there. The first deputation consisted of two of the Curators of the University, who talked over with the Ambassador a possible means of getting round the difficulties which the surrender of Brewer presented. They asked if he "would give them an act in writing in manner of a Safe Conduct for Brewer's return in case they should send him into England." He replied that His Majesty's word given by any of his Ministers should be sufficient. The second was a deputation of five from the town and University, consisting of the Rector and one of the Curators of the University, with two Assessors and a deputy from Leyden.

"They alleged unto me," says Carleton, "these difficulties—

"First—the Privilege of the University which any man that is matriculated, as this Brewer is, may plead, upon any accusation, for his trial upon the place without having his cause or person removed elsewhere contrary to his own mind.

"Secondly—the nature of their University: consisting chiefly of strangers, to whom if they should not carefully preserve their privileges in a matter of this consequence, they would all fly their University.

"Thirdly—the condition of the time there being now newly

a Reformation made [*i. e.* the Arminians having been purged out after the decisions of the Synod of Dort], and if they should neglect the preservation of their privileges they should expose themselves unto the scandal of such as are deported.

"Lastly—the example of one Cluverus a German, who having printed a book against the Emperor Rodolph and thereupon being required of the States to be sent to Prague there to be punished, the University made an absolute refusal, as that which could not be granted without breach of their privileges."

Carleton replied to all these objections with much astuteness, pointing out, among other things, that, though Brewer "were a matriculate man, his printing-house, where he for the space of these three years hath printed prohibited books and pamphlets (not for the use of the University of Leyden, or these Provinces; but for His Majesty's disservice and the trouble of his Kingdoms) was in the town," and not in the University precincts.

"I asked them if some busy or factious Arminian, a subject of these Provinces, should matriculate himself in one of the Universities of Oxford or Cambridge; and there print and send over hither, books of that argument; of which *their* Ambassador should complain and desire to have him remanded [back to his own country] how they would take it, if they should be answered by a plea of Privilege?"

The members of the deputation seemed to be impressed by Carleton's arguments, but desired him "to forbear pressing this matter any further" till the assembly of the "States" or Provincial Council of Holland, which was due in two or three weeks. He agreed, but told them, had they readily consented to Brewer's extradition, he "made no doubt but that Brewer might be in England and returned again before the meeting of the "States" of Holland.

At the close of this despatch Carleton indicates the course which the authorities at Leyden were now taking in the matter—

"I understand they have privately appointed Polyander and Walæus to deal with Brewer of his own accord to desire to go into England whereby to satisfy His Majesty and preserve their privileges, which I do not mislike. For if he yield thereunto His Majesty hath what he requires. If he make difficulty I have the more just subject to press his remanding which at the time of the assembly of the States of Holland I will not fail to do."

It was well for Carleton that he got this despatch off when he did, for on the very next day, Saturday, October 23, Sir Robert Naunton sent him a line from Whitehall to hurry matters up—

"His Majesty hath charged me, once more, to require you, as from himself, that you press with all earnestness, the matter of Brewer in all three points I recommended to you from Hampton Court 28° Septembris."

Before this reminder reached him Carleton forwarded to England a letter[1] from Polyander, with this covering note—

"What is done about Brewer at Leyden; your Honour will see by a letter I have even now received from Polyander.

"Thus I humbly take my leave.

"From the Hague, this 25th of October, 1619."

A week later (Monday, November 1, 1619) another deputation came over expressly from Leyden University to the Hague to let Carleton know "their resolution to send Brewer into England." It consisted of one of the Curators and the Rector of the University, with John Polyander and Daniel Heinsius. They brought a document in Brewer's handwriting, in which he stated his own desire to go into England "as a dutiful subject to His Majesty." This safeguarded the privileges of the University, which could not be said to have given up a prisoner at the demand of the King of England if the man went of his own free will. But Brewer was not prepared to blindly

[1] The Secretary of State, in a despatch of November 20, reported His Majesty's assent to the course proposed in Polyander's letter, but by that date Carleton had arranged matters.

play the "fly" to King James's "spider." The memory of the burning fate of Bartholomew Legate and the imprisonment of John Murton and others was too fresh for that. So he expressed his readiness to go—upon conditions.

Let Carleton tell us about the stipulations and how the matter was eventually arranged. Brewer, he tells us, required, "in the said Writing" to be assured by the University on the following points—

"(*a*) [That] it is His Majesty's own pleasure to have him sent.
(*b*) Next, that he may go as a free man under caution of his lands and goods; not as a prisoner.
(*c*) Then that he may not be punished during his abode in England either in body or goods.
(*d*) And that he may be suffered to return hither in a competent time.
(*e*) And lastly, that his journey be without his own charge.

"These things were requested of me by the Curator, the Rector, and the rest in his behalf.

"Wherein I made them this verbal promise, without being further moved by any of them, as I was formerly, to give them my act in writing—

(*a*) That for the first: it was His Majesty's express will and pleasure: which I might the better assure them having the same now a second time reiterated unto me by your Honour's letter of the 23rd of October; which at that instant I received.

(*b*) Next, that if they would take caution of him of his lands and goods for his rendering himself to His Majesty in England, I left it to their discretions. But to send him as a free man could not well be, as long as he remained *in reatu* [in the position of one charged with an offence].

(*c*) Then—that for his body and goods during his abode in England. I undertook he should not be touched, being so warranted by your Honour's former letter of the 21st of September.

(*d*) And for his return,—that it should be within the space of three months at the furthest, and sooner if he dealt ingenuously and freely in his Confessions.

(*e*) Touching the charge of his journey I made no difficulty to free both him and them thereof: not doubting but His Majesty will be pleased to allow it.

"So as there [was] remaining this only point of difference between us, whether he should go as a prisoner or as a free man? In the end we concluded of a middle way betwixt both—that he should go *sub libera custodia*, being attended from Leyden to Rotterdam by one of the Beadles with another Officer of the University, and be there delivered to some such person as I should appoint for his safe convoy into England; where I have undertaken for him, he shall not be cast into any common prison, nor be ill used. Though for his liberty, I let them know, he must not expect it, but according as he shall merit it by the satisfaction he shall give His Majesty. Wherein if he fail of what he now seems willing to perform, the fear of being returned back and thither again to the place where he hath lain ever since his first apprehension; (and where he may lie long enough unless he be delivered by His Majesty's grace and favour) will be a sufficient torture.

"But on the other side, if he carry himself well and dutifully, I beseech your Honour to be a means to His Majesty that he may be well treated and sent back with contentment: the rather because he hath taken his resolution of presenting himself unto His Majesty, against the minds of some stiff-necked men in Leyden, who endeavoured to dissuade him.

"And it will give all inferior persons encouragement by his example according to the like occasions, willingly to submit themselves; he being a Gentleman of a good house, both of land and living which none of his profession [in religion] in these parts are—though through the reveries of his religion (he being, as I advertised your Honour, a professed Brownist) he hath mortgaged and consumed a great part of his Estate.

"This noble Gentleman Sir William Zouche, being to go into England upon his own affairs, hath, upon my intreaty, willingly undertaken the charge of conducting Brewer to your Honour. For which purpose, he hath stayed his journey until this time when I am promised Brewer shall meet him at Rotterdam. And he being a Gentleman of His Majesty's Privy Chamber, as well as a servant to this State, His Majesty may be pleased to take notice of his readiness to do His Majesty service.

"Thus I humbly take leave. From the Hague, the 3rd of November, 1619."

An interesting letter of Sir William Zouche to Carleton, dated November 13, 1619, shows that, even after the plan was adopted, Brewer was in no hurry to leave Leyden.

"Right Honourable. I did purpose to have advertised your Lordship of our proceedings. I was last night almost out of hope of having my expected company, but about ten of the clock Master Brewer arrived, conveyed hither by the Beadle of the University, Master Robinson and Master Kebel, accompanied by two other of his friends, their names I think are not worth the asking.[1]

"We go forward about two or three of the clock, and if we find not a boat of Terveer ready to go away we intend to lie at Dort this night.

"The Gentleman seems very ready and willing to go with me, and hath good hope of his despatch and happy issue, if he be not referred to the judgment of the Bishops; concerning which he says he made caution before his departure, and if you have not written so much already he desires you will do so much when you write next to Master Secretary. He excuses his long stay by reason of the sudden warning to provide him [for the passage into England]. He demanded of me if I had order to defray him? I have told him 'Yes.' He says he is contented; but says it was not his desire nor mentioned by him. I assure your Lordship I will make no delay; but take the speediest opportunities to be rid of this employment.

"My best service humbly remembered to your Honour and my honourable Lady. I take my leave and rest,

"Ready to observe and serve you,

"W. Zouche.

"*Rotterdam, the* 13*th of November*, 1619."

Zouche and Brewer journeyed by Middleburg, where they were entertained at a dinner arranged by Brewer's friends on Monday, November 15. Here Zouche met the Treasurer-General and his two brothers, and one "Master Vosberghe, Chief Reckon-Master [accountant], who was on the way towards Holland to speak to His Excellency [the Prince] in Master Brewer's behalf, and to have advised him to

[1] "Yet I will inquire of them by the way," is a note that Carleton makes here. Zouche supplied the names in his letter of November 26: "The names of the other two that came with Master Brewer to Rotterdam are Jenkins and Lile."

have challenged the privileges of the University and of the town by which he should have had his trial there."

"They did expostulate the business," says Zouche, who found them "exceedingly earnest" in Brewer's cause and concerned at the great power the English King had in their land, "to have a prisoner, after he had been kept in prison longer than the law of the land doth allow, to be sent to him." All this Zouche reported to Carleton from Flushing on November 26, where they had been delayed for ten days by contrary winds and foul weather.

At length, on November 28, there came a favourable easterly wind, and Carleton writes—

> "I hope it will carry over Sir William Zouche and Master Brewer to your Honour; who have lain long together at Flushing: and his fellow-Brownists at Leyden are somewhat scandalized because they hear Sir William hath taught him to drink healths."

The turn in the wind enabled them to make the crossing, for on December 3 Sir Robert Naunton advised Carleton that Sir William Zouche had at length arrived with his charge, and that he was daily awaiting the King's directions for proceeding in that business.

What was the upshot, now that James had got his man? The King showed a petulant annoyance that Brewer should have come over in the way he had done, protected by pledges for his safe conduct and return. Brewer seems to have enjoyed the situation, and was inclined to ride the high horse. It went against the grain with James to have any one who had annoyed him surrender himself for examination on terms and conditions. Forgetful of the instructions sent to his Ambassador, he sent this message to Carleton—

> "Thurs. 16 Dec. 1619.
>
> "His Majesty's pleasure is and I am commanded to instruct you, that you should take heed of being too forward

hereafter in confounding matters so different and so punctually to be distinguished as are the overtures of treating with a free State and the accepting of capitulations from a subject delinquent."

If the States-General of Holland had sent Brewer "by their own authority, whether he had been willing to have come or not," His Majesty would have given them thanks, but his manner of coming "a little troubled His Majesty." It put him at a disadvantage. As to Brewer, he was put in charge of one of the Messengers of the Chamber, and was to be examined by Sir John Benet and Sir Henry Martin. James was mean enough to try to evade the cost of Brewer's voyage, "for the charge of his journey His Majesty hath no purpose to take it upon him longer than whiles he is within his dominions."

Sir John Benet, one of the examiners of Brewer, had some experience already in examining men of religion with whom the authorities were at loggerheads. In 1599 he was placed on a commission to enforce the Act of Uniformity in the Province of York, and in 1617, when a pamphlet satirizing King James and his Court, entitled *Corona Regis*, appeared, he was sent over to Brussels on a special mission to secure the punishment both of the printer and of Henri Dupuy, the author. His colleague, Sir Henry Martin, was also an expert examiner from his varied experience in the Admiralty Court. But they do not seem to have got much satisfaction out of Brewer, judging from the following despatch—

"Sir Robert Naunton to Sir Dudley Carleton, White Hall, Friday, January 14, 1619–20.

"My Lord Ambassador,

"I have cleared His Majesty's construction the best I can, touching Brewer, who did all that a silly creature could to increase his unsatisfaction: viz. standing upon Terms of Covenant publicly passed by your Lordship, and I know not what, as he saith Heinsius, Polyander and I know not who assevered it unto him. But I have beaten him from his asse and drawn something from him that hath in part contented his Majesty: who bade me tell you that he gives no credit to this fool's confident and improbable assertions; and that he will be very good friends with you, if you can procure Brewster to be taken, wherein he makes no doubt of your careful endeavour."

Naunton added a postscript—

"I thought fit to let you know by this Postcript that I have discharged Brewer; who hath hitherto been defrayed by His Majesty, but offered to return upon his own charge. I doubt he will advise Brewster to conceal himself and therefore have thus forewarned your Lordship. He [Brewer] will be known of no privity or so much as conjecture that he can make, how their pamphlets have been vented: which I presume will be better learned from him there upon the place [University of Leyden] before he shall be discharged by perusing his papers and other examinations."

James appears to have been effectually baffled here, but he had the satisfaction of learning from his Ambassador, in a despatch dated January 13, 1619–20, that the States-General had "finally published a Placaat against licentious printing of libels and pamphlets, either in strange languages or their own, which doth concern strangers in amity with this State as well as themselves."

It does not appear that Brewer returned at once to Leyden, where the authorities were still keeping his type and papers. John Polyander, writing from Leyden, January 12/22, 1620, to Sir D. Carleton, says—

"Monseigneur. Les charactéres de Thomas Brewer sont bien gardés en la chambre de Messieurs les Curateurs; et ses livres et papiers en sa propre maison."

Carleton reported from the Hague, January 29, 1620, as follows—

"I have acquainted the Curators of the University of Leyden with the good treatment which hath been given unto Brewer far beyond his deserving and with his delivery. For which they render His Majesty their humble thanks. And, at his return hither, unless he undertake to them to do his uttermost in finding out of Brewster—wherein I will not fail likewise of all other endeavours—he is not like to be at liberty. The suspicion whereof, I believe, keeps him from hence, for as yet he appears not in these parts."

As late as April 29, 1620, a memorial from Carleton was read at a University meeting, that the types and papers of Brewer might remain in the keeping of the University, upon which it was resolved "to keep the said types as hitherto." Nothing is said of the "papers"; these being at Brewer's house, he may have already resumed possession.

All this time Brewster keeps silence. He may have been in England quietly furthering the preparations for the Pilgrims' colonial enterprise, or may have found refuge for a time with friends in Essex or in Nottinghamshire. We do not know. The next mention of him which I have noted is on June 14, 1620, when John Robinson refers to him in a letter to John Carver, in which he endeavours to account for Thomas Weston suddenly withdrawing his capital from the venture on which the Pilgrims were about to embark. He wonders whether Weston "hath thought by withholding to put us upon straits, thinking that thereby Master Brewster and Master Pickering would be drawn by importunity to do more." Clearly Brewster was at that time making ready to give substantial help to their contemplated enterprise.

ST. WILFRID'S CHURCH, SCROOBY.

CHAPTER XVIII

INTERCOURSE BETWEEN LEYDEN AND AMSTERDAM—RICHARD CLIFTON, FRANCIS JOHNSON, HENRY AINSWORTH

THE responsibility of leadership in the Separatist movement must have come home more forcibly to Robinson as the pioneers were one by one called away by death. John Smith, as already noted, had died in 1612, and now, on May 20, 1616, Richard Clifton passed away at Amsterdam. The news would be received with regret by his old friends and associates at Leyden. He left a fragrant memory with those who had known him. Clifton has frequently been mentioned as " the original pastor or teacher of the Scrooby church."[1] Professor Edward Arber went so far as to say that " the Pilgrim Movement originated in the rectory and church of Babworth," of which Clifton was incumbent.[2] I do not think Clifton was ever in office in the Pilgrim Church. He is, indeed, mentioned in connexion with its early days by Bradford in these terms, after referring to the Church at Gainsborough under John Smith—

" In this other church [the Scrooby group] besides other worthy men, was Master Richard Clifton, a grave and reverend Preacher; who by his pains and diligence had done much good; and under God, had been the means of the conversion of many."

But there is no mention of his call to the pastorship. I take it that when Clifton was deprived of

[1] Dexter's *England and Holland of the Pilgrims*, p. 561.
[2] He was instituted to the living on July 11, 1586.

his "living" at Babworth, on account of his nonconformity, he threw in his lot with the neighbouring group of religiously-minded friends at Scrooby, and gave them the benefit of his help and experience in their meetings for worship, and quietly assisted sympathetic Puritan clergy in the district as occasion offered, among them James Brewster, the vicar of Sutton-cum-Lound.

Clifton was strongly influenced by John Smith, who convinced him that the Separatist Church he had gathered was, indeed, a true Church. They had some friendly conference upon the question of the Church's power of excommunication [1] and other outstanding points of difference between them when in England, apparently to mutual satisfaction, for when Clifton passed over to Holland in the summer of 1608 it was with the intention of joining the Church under the pastoral care of Smith. Owing to the latter's rapid change of views, however, Clifton associated himself with the "Ancient" or first Separatist Church in Amsterdam, and when Henry Ainsworth, the "Teacher" in that Church, withdrew, on account of differences with its "Pastor," Francis Johnson, Clifton was chosen to fill his place, and admitted to exercise the office without re-ordination, which marked a modification in Johnson's practice and the previous requirement of his Church. Ainsworth points to this when, in speaking of the members remaining with Johnson—the Franciscan Brownists, as they were scoffingly called—he says they—

> "have placed over them one that was made Priest by a Lord bishop's ordination, so as because of it they did not ordeyn or impose hands on him when at the same time they ordeyned and imposed hands on others whom togither with him they set over the Church." [2]

All the testimony to Clifton's character points to him being a man of earnest and lovable disposition.

[1] Clifton's *Plea for Infants*, 1610, p. 4.

[2] Ainsworth's *Animadversion to Master Richard Clyfton's Advertisement*, 1613, p. 59.

He had the gift of winning regard alike from young and old. Bernard wrote of him after his separation as one—

"whom I truely and entirely loued in our way [*i. e.* when he was an Anglican minister], as a man deuoted to God and every way worthy of loue for his vn-reprouable life and conuersation." [1]

Christopher Lawne in 1612 contrasted his bearing favourably with the "loftie lookes" of Francis Johnson.

"Master Clifton," he says, "though a Teacher of the Franciscanes, yet is he knowne to be farre from the arrogance of the other; yea, he is pitied as being a bondslaue vnto S. Francis." [2]

Bradford as a youth had enjoyed the advantage of "Master Richard Clyfton's illuminating ministry not far from his abode," [3] and he looked back in veneration to him as one who had strengthened his religious life. His reminiscence gives us a detail as to Clifton's personal appearance—

"He was a grave and fatherly old man," says he, "when he came first into Holland, having a great white beard; and pity it is that such a reverend old man should be forced to leave his country and at those years to go into exile. But it was his lot and he bore it patiently. Much good had he done in the country where he lived and converted many to God by his faithful and painful ministry both in preaching and catechizing." [4]

He issued a "Catechism" for the use of his parishioners. His *Plea for Infants and Elder People concerning their Baptism*, 1610, has already been noticed. In reply to Lawne's venomous book he published in 1612 "*An Advertisement concerning a Book lately published . . . against the English exiled Church at*

[1] Bernard's *Plaine Evidences*, 1610, p. 57.
[2] *The Prophane Schisme*, 1612, p. 64.
[3] Mather's *Magnalia*, Bk. II. p. 3, ed. 1702.
[4] First Dialogue, Young's *Chronicles of the Pilgrims*.

Amsterdam. By Richard Clyfton, Teacher of the same Church." His death was a distinct loss to the cause of the Separatists, and it would stir many memories in the mind of John Robinson.[1]

Francis Johnson survived Clifton by nearly a year and eight months. Matthew Slade attended his funeral and reported his death to Carleton—

" *Amsterdam. Saturday, January* 10, 1617 [1618].

" This day we have buried master Francis Johnson, a man that hath many years been Pastor of the Brownists and (having cast himself and drawn others, into great troubles and miseries for their oppressions and schism) did, a few days before his death, publish a Book, wherein he disclaimed most of his former singularities and refuted them. To which Work he hath also annexed a brief Refutation of the Five Articles."

The book here referred to is made up of three tracts, the second of which contains the refutation of the Five Points of the Arminian doctrinal system to which Slade refers. The volume is entitled " *A Christian Plea conteyning Three Treatises*: (1) Touching the Anabaptists. . . . (2) Touching such Christians as now are here commonly called Remonstrants or Arminians. (3) Touching the Reformed Churches with whom myself agree in the faith of the Gospel of our Lord Jesus Christ. Made by Francis Johnson, pastor of the Ancient English Church now sojourning at Amsterdam, in the Low Countreys . . . 1617." It proves that Johnson, like Robinson, modified some of his previous opinions. In order to counter the conclusions of the Anabaptists he now asserted that the Romish and Anglican Churches were true (though corrupted) Churches, and consequently their baptism was valid. But he did not give way in regard to

[1] An interesting sidelight on Clifton's work in England has recently been drawn from the Sessions Rolls of Notts., from which we learn that " Johes Broome of Babworth " and his wife were presented to the Court October 12, 1617, " for Brownists." Broome was fined 10*s.* vide *Notts. County Records*, p. 140, and Letter *penes me* from H. Hampton Copnall, Clerk of the Peace, July 17, 1919.

the general grounds on which he had separated from the Church of England.

His later views about the place and power of the "eldership" in the Church led to the shipwreck and weakening of his own Church and to acute differences on the point between himself and Robinson, to which we may here briefly refer. It will be remembered that one of the reasons inducing Robinson and his friends to move on to Leyden was that they foresaw the probable outbreak of contention in the Amsterdam Church. They were right. Before many months the brethren at Amsterdam were rent asunder by a fierce dispute about the authority of the "elders" in Church government. Johnson had a most difficult flock to lead. Their practice of bringing cases of discipline before the whole Church for consideration on every Lord's Day gave too many openings for bickering and strife. It needed a charitable temper and a generous spirit of forbearance for such a system to work with success. In the first glow of the new movement the restraining force of religious and brotherly feeling brought out the advantages of this careful watch over one another's conduct, but the disadvantages became more evident as the early fervour waned. Johnson came to feel that the Presbyterian plan of leaving the discipline of the Church in the hands of the Pastor, Teacher and lay elders was the better course. They had resisted the tyranny of the Prelacy in the Church of England; it now seemed to him that the Church of Christ was being subjected to an equally dangerous tyranny—the tyranny of the rank and file in the Church. The people participating in the exercise of discipline might overrule the judgment of the "eldership" in matters of excommunication. "We have lately been taught," says Johnson, referring to Robinson's *Justification of Separation*, "that the people as kings have power one over another, and that the saints, being kings, are superior to their officers." His claims to authority on the part of the college of "elders," the officers, or "the presbytery" of the individual Church, under Christ, "the only King and Lord of His Church" were stoutly resisted by a strong body of the members, headed by Ainsworth, who were jealous for their new-found freedom. Efforts at accommodation were unavailing. If the Church was to have any being at all it must have some government and order; the point at issue was the extent of the members' liberty within that order and how best to secure it. How was a due balance between the power of the eldership and that of the people to be maintained? Happily Robinson's Church solved the question in a practical way for themselves, but the members of Johnson's Church could not adjust the rival claims.

An appeal was made to Robinson and the friends at Leyden for advice and assistance. He and Brewster afterwards furnished an account of their part in the discussions at the request of Ainsworth, "that the ages present and to come may have true information of these matters."[1] It is headed "The Testimonie of the Elders of the Church at Leyden," and signed by Robinson and Brewster.

From this document we learn that a letter subscribed by "some thirty" members of Johnson's Church was sent over to Leyden invoking aid. Some of them had charged as an error Johnson's exposition of Matt. xviii. 17, in which he took the words "Tell the Church" as equivalent to "Tell the elders." They were now called upon to substantiate the charge, and wanted Robinson's "help in that great business." They were the more earnest in this request "because Mr. Ainsworth was so sparing in opposing of Mr. Johnson's new doctrine (though always misliking it) as they scarce knew how he was minded in the things; so loth was he to come to any professed and public opposition with him [Johnson] whom he rather hoped to pacify by moderation than by opposition to stop in his intended course." The Leyden friends did not go over in response to this letter, "but wrote to the

[1] Ainsworth's *Animadversion*, p. 123.

Church and showed them what the substance of the letter was." They said they were unwilling to interpose unless they were called in by the general consent of the Amsterdam Church as a whole, and under conditions giving " best hope of good issue." The Amsterdam friends declined to approve officially of the Leyden elders coming over; they " would only permit it "; and they insistently asked to be furnished with a copy of the letter which the dissidents had sent to Leyden. After some demur and delay this point was conceded, and a copy was forwarded. It had only been withheld from reluctance " to minister matter of further scanning " amongst them.

After further consideration the Leyden friends resolved, even without any official invitation, to send a delegation with a view to composing the differences in a friendly way, and they wrote to Amsterdam conveying news of their intention in these terms—

> " Our purpose therefore is (according to the request of the brethren which have moved us, and our duty), to send or come unto you : not to oppose any person or to maintain any charge of error, but by all other brotherly means to help forward your holy peace (if so the Lord's will be); which how precious it is unto us, we hope to manifest to the consciences of all men; than which we know nothing in this world we have more cause to endeavour both with God and yourselves. Of which our coming we pray you to accept, and to appoint us some such time as seems to you most convenient. Where also we shall satisfy you to the utmost, both touching the letter and other particulars in all equity, yea, so far as we can without apparent sin."

Still the Amsterdam Church, say Robinson and Brewster in their *Testimonie,* " would not approve, but only permit of our coming, as men use to permit of that which is evil and which indeed they could not hinder." Apparently when the Leyden Church had already come to the decision to send a deputation to Amsterdam, Henry Ainsworth came over in person to urge them to come.

"When no means among ourselves," says Ainsworth, "could end the strife they know how I both intreated them to consent [that] they [the pastor and elder of Leyden] might be sent for, and when they would not, my self went and obteyned their coming."[1]

Robinson and Brewster continue their narrative with an account of their interview with Johnson's Church. They acknowledge they spoke with some heat, and give testimony to Johnson's moderation in proposing that the unsatisfied members should be peaceably dismissed to the fellowship of the Church at Leyden—

"And so we came unto them; first of ourselves and afterwards at the request of M^r^. Ainsworth and them with him, being sent by the Church whereof we are: and so enforcing ourselves upon them for the delivering of the Church's message did reprove what we judged evil in them, and that, we confess, with some vehemency. And in that regard it was that (upon the motion made by Mr. Johnson for the free dismission of such members with them, unto us, as could not there walk with peace of conscience, there lying no other cause against them, which should also be mutually performed on our part) we signified, as he writeth, that '*We little thought they had been so inclinable to peace, and that if we had so thought we would have carried ourselves otherwise towards them than we did.*'

"And good cause had we so to speak. For neither is the same carriage to be used towards men prosecuting their purposes and persuasions with all violence and extremity, and towards them which manifest Christian moderation in the same. Neither had we before, [n]or have we since found the like peaceable inclination in them."

Johnson's proposal was received by the members of his own Church with general assent, but, coming as a surprise to Robinson and Brewster, they felt it necessary to refer the matter for consideration to the members of their Church at Leyden. The proposal was understood at first to involve the transference of the dissatisfied members of Johnson's society to

[1] Ainsworth's *Animadversion*, p. 109. It is possible, however, that this refers to a second visit.

Leyden to live. This would mean the breaking up of homes in Amsterdam, and "that those by them dismissed should remain at Leyden with us notwithstanding their want of means of living." It would cast a burden on the Leyden friends until the new adherents found fresh employment. But, in spite of this, on consideration "the church also at Leyden condescended" to the proposal—

"and so sent back the officers [Robinson and Brewster] for the further ratification of it, and for some other purposes tending to the establishing of peace amongst them. Whereupon it was also the second time by them confirmed, always indeed with submission to the Word of God as was meet, and that if either they or we minded otherwise we should so signify."

The agreement between the two Churches was to cover the case of the friendly dismission from either of them to the other of such members as were not satisfied in conscience in regard to the government and Church discipline in vogue in the respective Churches. Some members were content in cases of difference on such points with making a formal "protestation" and statement of their objection and then continuing in fellowship. The difficulty was with those who could not quiet their consciences in this way.

But when the terms of the agreement were under discussion a fresh point emerged. One[1] amongst Johnson's party said that if this "dismissal" of members took place the Church at Leyden "should not dismiss them back . . . to live a distinct congregation in the same city [Amsterdam] with them." Robinson and Brewster say that Johnson and his elder, Daniel Studley, immediately replied "that that concerned not them but that they would leave it unto us." But the inconveniences of such an arrangement, which some of the members of Johnson's Church evidently now contemplated, became

[1] This person is indicated by the initials I. O., see Ainsworth's *Animadversion*, p. 136. Who was he? Was it John Oldham?

more apparent on further reflection. If it were needful to remain in Amsterdam to earn a livelihood, could they not hold together as one society in two sections? In the case of a charge being brought against a member who accepted their pastor's theory it could be dealt with *in camera* by the eldership; and if a charge were brought against one who accepted the theory of Ainsworth the "teacher," it could be considered by the whole section of members in agreement with him, and the "admonition" be given in public before them. These suggestions were put forward in the following letter—

Letter from the Church at Amsterdam to that of Leyden

"Beloved, touching the things that have now lately been spoken of between the two churches, yours and ours, about the dismission of such, on either part, as are not content with protestation peaceably to walk in their difference of judgment, we have occasion to entreat the continuance of your consideration yet further thereabout.

"First—Because yourselves signified it came suddenly upon your church; and if either you or we minded otherwise by the Word of God we should after signify it. Wherefore we expect to hear whether you continue like-minded as heretofore.

"Second—Because there is with us a new motion [proposal] of walking together thus,—by bearing one with another, so as, for peace, to permit of a double practice among us, that those that are minded either way should keep a like course together, as we would do if we were asunder, according as the persons shall be that have the causes. Which way, if it may be found warrantable by the Word of God, and peaceable unto and among ourselves, we hope all that love peace in holiness will accord.

"These things as *we* are to consider of, so pray we *you* to do the like with us and for us, that we may do that which is most to God's glory and our mutual comfort.

"Thus, etc.,

"*Amsterdam, November* 5, *old style*, 1610."

The friends at Leyden soon replied; they did not encourage this new proposal; they were content to stand by "the agreement" into which they had entered, but they proposed a third course of procedure, based on their own practice, which might solve the difficulties at Amsterdam. Here is their letter—

Reply of the Church at Leyden to that of Amsterdam

"Touching the agreement, brethren, between the churches for our mutual peace and the relief of the consciences of our brethren, we did and do repute the same as full and absolute on both sides, except either some better course can be thought on, or this manifested to be evil, and that it be reversed with the mutual consent of both churches.

And for this last motion, about a double practice, as we are glad of the great and godly desire to continue together, in it manifested, so we do not see how it can stand either with our peace or itself; but [we see] that it will not only nourish, but even necessarily beget endless contentions, when men diversly minded shall have business in the church.

"If therefore it would please the Lord so far to enlarge your hearts on both sides, brethren, as that this middle way be held, namely, that the matter of offence might first be brought for order, preparation, and prevention of unnecessary trouble unto the elders as the church governors (though it is like we for our parts shall not so practice in this particular) and after, if things be not there ended, to the church of elders and brethren, there to be judged on some ordinary known day ordinarily: the admonition being carried according to the alteration practised and agreed upon by all parts, till it shall please the God of wisdom and Father of lights by the further consideration and parties discussing of things, either in word or writing, to manifest otherwise for our joint accord.

"It would surely make much to the glory of God and the stopping of their mouths which are so wide opened upon us in respect of our daily dissipations, and should be to us matter of great rejoicing whose souls do long after peace and abhor the contrary: and that thus walking in peace and holiness we might all beg at God's hands the healing and pardon of all our infirmities, and so be ready to heal and forgive the infirmities of one another in love.

And with this prayer unto God for you and for ourselves we re-salute you in the Lord Jesus.

"*Leyden, November* 14, 1610."

The "middle course" of procedure in Church discipline suggested by Robinson was the course followed in his own Church, though his society did not regard it as fixed and unalterable. Probably now that the question was raised there were some, even in Robinson's company, who were unduly jealous for the kingly rights of the individual Church member, and sought to protect them from all encroachment, and the insertion of the saving clause, "though it is like we for our parts shall not so practice," would, in the event of the Ainsworthian party joining the Leyden Church, leave the way open for a further consideration of the matter, and a settlement of the point more distinctly on the lines favoured by them.

The Amsterdam friends under Ainsworth, however, rejected this proposal. They also rejected the suggestion of following a "double practice" by which both sections should continue together after a sort. Some of the friends under Johnson for their part "became more opposed" to the suggested union of the dissatisfied members with the Leyden Church and their immediate return to live in Amsterdam as a separate religious society. The more they thought about it the less they liked it. Would this second society be a true Church? They might keep up business relations with their old friends, but could they legitimately continue in spiritual communion with them? Their letter speaks for itself—

Reply of the Church of Amsterdam to that of Leyden

"Your letter, brethren, we received and read publicly. Concerning which we have occasion to signify some things unto you thereabout.

"And first, touching the agreement treated of between us; that for such of us as will not come thither to remain with you, but purpose still to live here in this city apart from us. Albeit there be some that could be content notwithstanding, so to dismiss them, yet there are others of us that having more considered of it, think it not lawful to have any hand in consenting thereunto, and mean therefore to reverse our former agreement unto it. Besides that, divers of us say, they never consented hereunto.

"And further, some of us also begin to think that it will be found unlawful to keep spiritual communion with them in such estate, however we may still retain with them civil society.

"The reasons minded, why [we ought] not so to dismiss them, nor to have spiritual fellowship with them in such estate and walking, are these—

1. Because we cannot find warrant for it in the Word of God.

2. Because they refuse, disobey and speak evil of the truth and way of God.

3. Because they refuse to continue and keep communion with us, though they may be suffered to walk with us in peace with protestation in their difference of judgment.

4. Because some of them profess they will not deal in causes (as may fall out between us) by way of protestation neither when they are with us nor when they are from us.

5. Because they go not from one church and pastor to another so to live and remain; but purpose, when they have come and joined unto you, then presently [at once] to return and live here in this town apart from us.

6. Because by such walking of theirs great reproach will come upon us all, with much dishonour to God and hindrance to the truth what in them lieth.

7. Because we think there should alway be somewhat in such cases used, as whereby the Lord may work upon their consciences to consider their estate and to repent and yield to the truth and way of God which they have hitherto refused and oppugned, &c.

"Thus we thought to acquaint you with these things and the reasons thereabout: which yet are so minded of us as, if either among ourselves, or by others we shall hereafter better discern what is according to the will of God herein, we shall, God willing, be ready so to receive and walk.

"As touching the double practice misliked by you, although indeed it may seem somewhat strange and difficult, yet, for the present, some of us could like better of it than of a parting: but the brethren differing from us will not admit of it.

"Neither will they yield to that middle course propounded in your letter. Yet have we left it, with the former things to their further consideration.

"And howsoever it pleaseth the Lord to dispose of us, our trust is, that he will work all in the end to the furtherance of his truth and [the] peace of his church in Christ Jesus. To whose gracious protection and guidance we commend you, &c.

"*Amsterdam, November* 19, 1610."

To the "reasons" in this letter the friends at Leyden made no answer. In a week or two after the despatch of this letter the old Separatist Church at Amsterdam split asunder, the dissidents going off with Ainsworth and finding temporary quarters next door but one to the meeting-house of their old companions. Why was no reply sent from Leyden?

"The causes were," say Robinson and Brewster, in their *Testimonie*—

"First—For that they [the members of Johnson's church] continued not long together after they [the 'reasons'] came to our hands.

"Secondly—We had upon occasion of the motion made for a double practice, propounded another course, both more fit and warrantable, as we thought, than that, for the bringing of things first to the elders as appears in our letter.

"Unto which course, though we do not bind our brethren, yet may we safely say, so far as we remember, that there never came complaint of sin to the church since we were officers, but we took knowledge of it before either by mutual consent on both sides or at least by the party accused; with whose Christian modesty and wisdom we think it well sorteth that being condemned by two or three brethren he should not trouble the church or hazard a public rebuke upon himself, without counseling with them who are set over him and who either are or should be but able to advise him.

"Thirdly and which was the chief course, we were without all hope of doing good when they once misliked the motion which made it [*i. e.* made the proposal to dismiss the Ainsworth party to Leyden]. Whilst they liked it we had hope, though it were with hard measure to the other [the Ainsworthians] and so did further it to the utmost of our power; but when they laid it down, we knew all our labour would be lost in endeavouring their second liking of it."

The intervention of Robinson and his fellow-members was not successful in preventing the breach in the Amsterdam Church. They were evidently in agreement with Ainsworth and his party on the point at issue, and held to the position of the early Separatists that, though the body of Church members delegated power for governing and discipline to their elected officers, yet they did not thereby surrender the ultimate authority in Church matters which under Christ rested in them.

A remarkable letter,[1] dated "The eighth of July 1611, new style," from Matthew Saunders and Cuthbert Hutten, two members of Johnson's Church, gives us the picture of the position of affairs at that date. Referring to "the many sorts of the separation at this day cursing or rejecting one another, others thinking but basely one of another," they proceed in these terms: "To begin with ourselves, whom Master Ainsworth and his followers hath left and rejected as false Christians; master Robinson holding but keycold brotherhood with vs, and master Ainsworth and he and we jarring about ruling Elders."

It was indeed a pitiful dispute. Echoes of it were heard amongst the Separatists in London, who wrote to inquire how matters stood and what was the nature of "the differences that be amongst you."

> "Thos[e] that come over [to London] of M. J[ohnson] his side say they hold no more concerning the Eldership then M. A[insworth] hath written against M[aster] Smyth: others say to the contrary, we doo therefore intreat M. A[insworth] to certifie us of the truth." [2]

There was ground for uncertainty in regard to Ainsworth's opinion. He had shied at the charge of "popularity" when Bernard brought it against the Brownists, and dissociated himself then from the full democratic position which Smith frankly accepted.[3]

The rift between the Ainsworthian and Franciscan Brownists was widened when "two brethren and a widow" among the former instituted a civil suit

[1] Lawne's *Prophane Schism*, pp. 55–57, 1612.
[2] *Animadversion*, 1613, p. 1.
[3] See Ainsworth's *Counterpoison*, p. 159, and Smith's *Paralleles*, p. 67, 1609.

for the possession of the old meeting-house in the Brownists' Alley. This place of worship, put up by the joint efforts of the brethren, with assistance from England, in 1607, seems to have been held on a proprietary basis. The land on which it stood was held in the name of a member adhering to the party of Johnson, and they pleaded "that they which build on another man's ground are by law to lose their building." The three chief shareholders or proprietors of the building disputed this plea, and the matter was referred to the Burgomaster. Suggestions for arbitration were rejected. Ainsworth's party contended that they held the opinions of the original founders, and that the name of the person in whom the land was vested "was but used in trust." They won their suit. Johnson and his friends were dispossessed.

When Robinson and Brewster wrote their *Testimonie* Johnson and his Church were "about to leave" Amsterdam "and to settle their abode elsewhere."[1] They removed to Emden, but appear to have returned before long to Amsterdam again. After Johnson's death the remnants of his broken Church, under their elder, Francis Blackwell, "prepared for to go to Virginia." Blackwell was not the right stamp of man to lead such a venture. Moreover misfortune dogged their steps. Their expedition came to grief, most of them perishing from want, dysentery and sickness on a miserably prolonged voyage. It is to the credit of the members of Robinson's Church that this failure did not daunt them in their preparations for a similar effort to effect a settlement in America upon which they were soon to be engaged.

By the death of Francis Johnson Henry Ainsworth and John Robinson were left as the conspicuous leaders of the Separatist Churches. Ainsworth busied himself in the intervening years till his death in preparing and issuing from the press his "*Annotations vpon the five Bookes of Moses, the booke of the*

[1] *Works*, vol. iii. p. 475.

Psalmes and the Song of Songs or Canticles." These appeared separately at various dates from 1612 to 1623, and collectively in one large folio in 1627. They embody a fresh translation of each chapter, followed by annotations. The difference in tone between Ainsworth's controversial writings and his Biblical annotations is remarkable. In the latter he writes with detachment from current controversies, and restrains himself from taking advantage of the many openings his exposition afforded for pressing his own peculiar views about Church government. Here the party spirit was happily absent.

His excessive application to study brought on bodily weakness, and he suffered much in his last years. In 1619 he speaks of "the extreme infirmity of my body."[1] He died in 1622, as one who knew him well tells us "from that sore perplexing and tedious disease of the stone."[2]

[1] *Annotations upon . . . DEVTERONOMIE*, 1619, ad fin.

[2] "Epistle," by Sabine Staresmore, prefixed to *Notes of M. Henry Aynsworth, His Last Sermon*, printed 1630. His *Song of Songs in English Metre*, published in 1623, is prefaced by a letter to the "Christian Reader" from one who describes him as: "Full of faith and good works, fruitfull in his life, comfortable in his death to all beholders, of which there were many, my selfe being one amongst the rest." We have full particulars of Ainsworth's illness, as details of it were recorded in a contemporary medical text-book as an interesting case. A stupid and wicked story was set afloat in after years that he was poisoned by Jews jealous of his Rabbinical knowledge. It has taken a long time to kill that lying fabrication.

CHAPTER XIX

ROBINSON'S PLEA FOR LAY PREACHING

JOHN ROBINSON was remembered by some of his old flock in Norwich and the neighbourhood long after he had left their midst. His books were circulated and read amongst them and had some influence upon their religious practice. They even ventured to hold meetings at which ordinary members exercised their gifts of preaching and expounding the " Word of God " to the edification of the assembled company. This was regarded as a grave irregularity by the ordained clergy. The Rev. John Yates was then minister of St. Andrew's, where Robinson had formerly laboured, and he undertook the task of reproving those who upheld what he regarded as a dangerous and disorderly practice. One of their number, whose initials only are given, justified their action by an appeal to the arguments in favour of lay preaching by ordinary Church members set out in Robinson's book on the *Justification of Separation*. This appears to have been one William Euring, who, to use his own words, had been brought up not " among the Muses, but Mariners." He subsequently engaged in religious controversy with Thomas Drakes, " preacher of the Word at Harwich and Dovercourt." Euring turned to Robinson's book for support in the practice of " prophesying," of which he was an ardent advocate. He abstracted Robinson's arguments, and the Scripture texts on which they were based, and sent them on to Yates.[1] The matter was not allowed to rest there. Yates promptly laid down ten arguments

[1] *The People's Plea*, 1618, p. 47.

"to prove ordinary prophecy in public out of office unlawful," and appended an answer to the reasons and texts brought forward by Robinson in his book in favour of that practice.[1] It was a weighty and skilful production, and deserved careful consideration. Euring felt this was a case for Robinson himself to handle. He obtained the consent of Yates to the despatch of his manuscript, duly attested before a magistrate, to Leyden for Robinson's perusal. Robinson was stirred up to reply, and soon issued *The People's Plea for the Exercise of Prophesie against Mr. John Yates his Monopolie.* Curiously enough, some have taken the word "Monopolie" as the title of Yates's treatise. Clearly it is used by Robinson in reference to the claim made, on behalf of the clergy and ordained ministry, by Yates to a "monopoly" in the work of preaching or prophesying. The book, "printed in the yeare 1618," was issued from the press of William Brewster. Robinson was evidently in good heart at the time of penning this treatise. He handles his subject with ease and confidence. He writes as one who is sure of his ground and satisfied with the position he holds. He had a sincere respect for John Yates, and speaks of him as "a man of good gifts in himself and [of] note amongst"[2] the friends in Norwich, but he does not spare him when pressing home his refutation of the arguments Yates had brought forward to overthrow the practice of prophesying by ordinary Church members.

In a preface, addressed "to my Christian Friends in Norwich and thereabouts," Robinson declared it was "matter of unfeigned rejoicing" to him "to hear how God hath of late stirred up amongst you divers instruments" in the work of prophesying, whose zealous labours God had blessed. It would be gratifying to Robinson to learn that his Norwich friends had not forgotten him, and that his labours amongst them were bearing fruit so long after he had been forced to leave them.

[1] *Works,* vol. iii. p. 309. [2] *The People's Plea,* 1618, Preface.

The matter of the book need not detain us long. Both Yates and Robinson agreed that the Scripture was the final court of appeal. The question, then, was whether Scripture sanctioned the exercise of prophecy or preaching by men out of office. Yates alleged that Christ had granted the power of prophecy in public " to none but such as he sends and ordains thereunto." Robinson had no difficulty in bringing forward numerous Scriptural cases of ordinary people out of office exercising the gift of prophecy. Yates rejoined that all these cases were extraordinary and, in his opinion, were specially warranted " by the secret motion of the Spirit," consequently they were not to be made the example for ordinary practice. Robinson, for his part, took them in the plain sense as cases of ordinary men exercising the gift of exhortation or prophecy in the public assembly, and accordingly affording ample warrant for the practice he advocated.

In the course of his argument he gives a picture, for Mr. Yates' benefit, of the course followed in this matter in his own Church at Leyden—

> " Thus we practise. After the exercise of the public ministry [is] ended, the rulers in the Church do publicly exhort and require that such of their own or other Church as have a gift to speak to the edification of the hearers should use the same; and this, according to that which is written Acts xiii. 14, etc., where Paul and Barnabas coming into the synagogue, the rulers, after the work of the ordinary ministry was ended (considering them not as apostles, which they acknowledged not, but only as men having gifts), sent unto them, that if they had any word of exhortation to the people they should say on." [1]

Throughout the controversy Yates has his eye fixed on the ministerial office. Robinson looks first to the man : " The gift of prophecy comes not by the office," he says, " but, being found in persons before, makes them capable of the office by due means." [2]

The discussion of various texts and arguments bearing on the subject is carried on at considerable

[1] *Works*, vol. iii. p. 292. [2] *Ibid.*, p. 293.

length, and the modern reader will be tempted to say of the whole controversy, as Robinson himself said in reference to the second argument of Mr. Yates, "Here is a long harvest for a small crop."[1] The book, however, gave a sound and sensible defence of lay preaching and the layman's right to exercise his gift of exhortation on religious themes. It was in virtue of its argument for lay preaching that a second edition[2] of this work was called for in the year 1641.

WILLIAM EURING AND THOMAS DRAKES

We have referred to the suggestion that William Euring was specially interested in this vindication of the layman's right to speak in the church. He was concerned also in a controversy with Thomas Drakes. Drakes had rejoined to Seven Demands of the Separatists with Ten Counter-Demands, and in 1619 Euring brought out his *Answer to the Ten Counter-Demands propounded by T. Drakes*. In this work we have an interesting reference to Virginia. Drakes, in his last "Demand," suggested that if the Separatists could not see their way to return to the Anglican Church, it might be a good thing for them, "for the avoiding of scandal, and in expectance of some prosperous success, by the permission of our noble King and honourable Council, to remove to Virginia and make a plantation there, in hope to convert infidels to Christianity."

To this Euring replied—

"Not only I myself, but all of us that now are separated from you, would much more willingly and gladly return again, and labour to plant ourselves again in the meanest part of England to enjoy peace with holiness (Heb. xii. 14), and to follow the truth in love, among our kindred and friends in our own native country, than either to continue where now

[1] *Works*, vol. iii. p. 291.

[2] The British Museum Copy, E 1093, has a MS. note on the title page after the author's name thus: "ye Brownist at Leyden." The book is 16mo, pp. vi, 72, A.D. 1641.

many of us as yet live, or to plant ourselves in Virginia, or in any other country in the world, upon any conditions or hope of any thing in this life whatsoever.

"Yet even for Virginia, thus much—When some of ours desired to have planted ourselves there, with His Majesty's leave, upon these three grounds—

"(1) That they might be means of replanting the Gospel amongst the heathen.

"(2) That they might live under the King's government.

"(3) That they might make way for, and unite with, others, what in them lieth, whose consciences are grieved with the state of the Church in England:

"——the Bishops did by all means oppose them and their friends therein."

CHAPTER XX

"THIS WEIGHTY BUSINESS ABOUT VIRGINIA"

John Robinson.
William Robinson.

WE have already referred to the venture at colonizing which the members of John Robinson's Church contemplated. In order to understand the nature of that venture and the inception of the idea of forming a colony in America we must go back a step or two in our story. The notion seems to have presented itself to the mind of Robinson early in 1617, and was discussed by him privately with Brewster and "sundry of the sagest members." There was a great call for colonists to settle in Virginia at this time, and it seemed not unreasonable to think they might be allowed to settle together in those new lands and enjoy there that religious liberty which was denied them at home.

The ten years' truce between Holland and Spain would run out in the spring of 1619, and the indications were that hostilities would then be renewed. The difficulty of securing a decent livelihood in Holland for English refugees deterred many who desired a further reformation in religion from throwing in their lot with Robinson. This was a disappointment to him. He often used to say "that many of those who both wrote and preached now against them; if they were in a place where they might have liberty and live comfortably they would then practise as they did."[1]

Furthermore, it seemed unduly difficult for them in Holland to bring up their children in the nurture and admonition of the Lord, as they desired. They were in danger of losing their name and nation and being merged in the Dutch. "Lastly," says Bradford, "and which was not least, a great hope and inward zeal they had of laying some good foundations, or at least to make some way thereunto, for the propagating and advancing the Gospel of the Kingdom of Christ in those remote parts of the world; yea, though they should be but even as stepping-stones unto others for the performing of so great a work."

This missionary note in their project must never be forgotten; it was a dominant note in all their effort.

After the proposal had been discussed by Robinson and the leaders of the congregation, it was brought before the members of the whole Church, and laid open "to the scanning of all." The difficulties in the way of carrying it out were at once stated by those averse to the scheme. But the plan appealed to the imagination of the bolder spirits. To the objectors it was answered—

> "That all great and honourable actions are accompanied with great difficulties; and must be both enterprised and overcome with answerable courages. It was granted the dangers were great, but not desperate; the difficulties were many but not invincible. For though there were many of them likely, yet they were not certain. It might be sundry of the things feared might never befall; others by provident care and the use of good means might in a great measure be prevented; and all of them through the help of God by fortitude and patience might either be borne or overcome. . . . Their ends were good and honourable; their calling lawful and urgent; and therefore they might expect the blessing of God in their proceeding. Yea, though they should lose their lives in this action, yet might they have comfort in the same, and their endeavours would be honourable. . . . After many other particular things answered and alleged on both sides, it was fully concluded by the major part '*to put this design in execution, and to prosecute it by the best means they could.*'"

Having come to this resolution, the next thing was to decide upon the place for their colony. "Some, and none of the meanest, had thoughts for Guiana . . . others were for some parts of Virginia, where the English had already made entrance and beginning." The voyages of Raleigh had roused much interest in Guiana, and men's eyes were now turned in that direction, because at this very time the veteran explorer was making his last venture to the Orinoco, hoping, if successful, to be reinstated in the Royal favour. Some of the Pilgrim company, too, may have heard at first hand from Captain Charles Leigh of the richness of those sunny lands and the needs of their natives. Leigh had been well known to some of the Separatists at Amsterdam. He had voyaged to Guiana in 1604, and sent home a request to the Privy Council that " able preachers " might be sent out, as " the Indians were anxious for instruction." [1]

The danger from the jealousy of the Spaniards against any successful colony in those parts turned the scale of decision against Guiana.

But suppose they went to Virginia; if they lived under the Government of that colony they would be " in as great danger to be troubled and persecuted for Cause of Religion as if they lived in England, and, it might be, worse," and yet if they lived too far off they could not expect help from that colony when danger threatened.

> " At length," says Bradford, " the conclusion was to live as a distinct body by themselves, under the general Government of Virginia; and by their friends to sue to His Majesty that he would be pleased to grant them Freedom of Religion. And that this might be obtained, they were put in good hope by some Great Persons of good rank and quality that were made their friends."

They little knew what a serious bar to securing official sanction for their venture this claim for " freedom of religion " was destined to be.

The Leyden Church, having thus decided to go and where [2] to go, the next step was to sound the authorities upon the plan, and see if permission to go could

[1] *State Papers, Domestic,* James I, vol. viii. No. 87.

[2] " Our eye," says Winslow, " was upon the most northern parts of Virginia."

be got. The members accordingly chose John Carver and Robert Cushman to act as agents, and sent them over to England at the expense of the Church to further the project. They made application to the First or London Virginia Company, which had jurisdiction over the Jamestown district and adjacent parts. They went to Sir Edward Sandys, with whom William Brewster had an old acquaintance, and met with a friendly reception. In order to overcome possible objections to their plan from those hostile to their religious opinions Carver and Cushman were supplied with a paper of " Seven Articles," subscribed by Robinson and Brewster, in which the position of the Leyden congregation is defined.

The differences between them and the Anglican Church are made to appear as small as possible, and the civil authority of the Bishops, as derived from the Crown, is acknowledged. The document reminds me of views expressed by Henry Jacob, and marks a recession from the position of the earlier Separatists. As we read it the purpose for which it was expressly intended must be kept in view—

" Seven Articles which the church of Leyden sent to the Council of England to be considered of in respect of their judgments occasioned about their going to Virginia, *Anno* 1618.

" 1. To the confession of faith published in the name of the Church of England and to every Article thereof we do, with the Reformed Churches where we live, and also elsewhere, assent wholly.

" 2. As we do acknowledge the doctrine of faith there taught, so do we the fruits and effects of the same doctrine to the begetting of saving faith in thousands in the land (conformists and reformists) as they are called, with whom also, as with our brethren, we do desire to keep spiritual communion in peace, and will practise in our parts all lawful things.

" 3. The King's Majesty we acknowledge for Supreme Governor in his Dominion in all causes and over all persons, and that none may decline or appeal from his authority or judgment in any cause whatsoever, but that in all things obedience is due unto him, either active if the thing commanded be not against God's word, or passive if it be, except pardon can be obtained.

"4. We judge it lawful for his Majesty to appoint Bishops, civil overseers or officers in authority under him in the several provinces, dioceses, congregations or parishes, to oversee the churches and govern them civilly according to the Laws of the Land, unto whom they are in all things to give an account, and by them to be ordered according to godliness.

"5. The authority of the present Bishops in the Land we do acknowledge so far forth as the same is indeed derived from His Majesty unto them, and as they proceed in his name whom we will also therein honour in all things and him in them.

"6. We believe that no Synod, Classes, Convocation or Assembly of Ecclesiastical Officers hath any power or authority at all, but as the same by the magistrate [is] given unto them.

"7. Lastly, we desire to give unto all Superiors due honour, to preserve the unity of the spirit with all that fear God, to have peace with all men what in us lieth, and wherein we err to be instructed by any.

"Subscribed per
"JOHN ROBINSON
and
"WILLYAM BREWSTER."[1]

We catch a glimpse of the course of the negotiations from a letter dated "London, November 12th, *anno* 1617," addressed by Sir Edwin Sandys to "Master John Robinson and Master William Brewster," in the course of which he commends the "good discretion" of Carver and Cushman as doing both themselves and their society credit—

"After my hearty salutations," he says, "the agents of your Congregation, Robert Cushman and John Carver, have been in communication with divers select Gentlemen of His Majesty's Council for Virginia; and by the writing of *Seven Articles* subscribed with your names, have given them that good degree of satisfaction which hath carried them on with a resolution to set forward your desire in the best sort that may be for your own and the public good."

Sandys goes on to say that particulars would be reported to them by their agents, and he concludes a friendly letter by commending them and their

[1] *State Papers, Colonial,* vol. i. p. 43. The document is a copy, not the original, and its spelling is quaint.

design, which he hopes verily is the work of God, "to the gracious protection and blessing of the Highest."

The negotiations had begun hopefully, and the letter of Sandys encouraged the friends at Leyden to press on with the matter. Their reply to Sandys is a memorable document, and brings clearly to his notice various points to prove that they were the right stamp of folk to build up a permanent colony—

Letter to Sir Edwin Sandys

"Right Worshipful,

"Our humble duties remembered in our own, our Messengers', and our Church's name. With all thankful acknowledgment of your singular love expressing itself, as otherwise, so more specially in your great care and earnest endeavour of our good in this weighty business about Virginia, which, the less able we are to requite, we shall think ourselves the more bound to commend in our prayers unto God for recompence: Whom, as for the present, you rightly behold in our endeavours; so shall we not be wanting on our parts, the same God assisting us, to return all answerable fruit and respect unto the labour of your love bestowed upon us.

"We have (with the best speed and consideration withal, that we could) set down our Requests in writing, subscribed, as you willed, with the hands of the greatest part of our Congregation, and have sent the same unto the Council by our Agent and a Deacon of our Church, John Carver, unto whom we have also requested a gentleman of our Company to adjoin himself, to the care and discretion of which two, we do refer the prosecuting of the business.

"Now we persuade ourselves, Right Worshipful, that we need not provoke your godly and loving mind to any further, or more tender care of us; since you have pleased so far to interest yourself in us that, under God, above all persons and things in the world, we rely upon you; expecting the care of your love, counsel of your wisdom, and the help and countenance of your authority.

"Notwithstanding, for your encouragement in the work, so far as probabilities may lead, we will not forbear to mention these instances of Inducement—

"*First*—We verily believe and trust the Lord is with us (unto Whom and Whose service we have given ourselves in many trials), and that He will graciously prosper our endeavour according to the simplicity of our hearts therein.

"*Secondly*—We are well weaned from the delicate milk of our mother country, and inured to the difficulties of a strange and hard land; which yet, in great part, we have by patience overcome.

"*Thirdly*—The people are, for the body of them, [as] industrious and frugal, we think we may safely say, as any company of people in the world.

"*Fourthly*—We are knit together, as a body, in a most strict and sacred Bond and Covenant of the Lord; of the violation whereof we make great conscience, and by virtue whereof we do hold ourselves straitly tied to all care of each other's good and of the whole by every one, and so mutually.

"*Lastly*—It is not with us as with other men whom small things can discourage or small discontentments cause to wish themselves at home again. We know our entertainment in England and in Holland. We shall much prejudice both our arts and means by removal. If we should be driven to return, we should not hope to recover our present helps and comforts: neither, indeed, look ever, for ourselves, to attain unto the like in any other place during *our* lives, which are now drawing towards their periods.

"These Motives we have been bold to tender unto you, which you, in your wisdom, may also impart to any other our worshipful friends of the Council with you: of all whose godly and loving disposition towards our despised persons we are most glad; and shall not fail by all good means to continue [to deserve] and increase the same. We will not be further troublesome; but, with the renewed remembrance of our humble duties to your Worship—and (so far as in modesty we may be bold) to any other of our well-willers of the Council with you—we take our leaves: committing your persons and counsels to the guidance and direction of the Almighty.

"Yours much bounden in all duty,

"JOHN ROBINSON

"WILLIAM BREWSTER.

"Leyden, December 15th, *anno* 1617."

Sandys got Sir Robert Naunton, the Secretary of State, to sound the King about granting protection to these would-be colonists. "By what means will they exist there?" asked His Majesty. When it was answered, "Fishing," he replied with his ordinary asseveration, "So God have my soul! 'tis an honest trade. It was the Apostles' own calling." At first the

King assented to the request, but when he reflected further upon their petition "to enjoy their liberty of conscience under his gracious protection in America," he referred them on this point to the "Bishops of Canterbury and London." There was not much hope of favourable consideration from that quarter, yet Sandys did approach the Archbishop, George Abbot, on the subject. His action was misconstrued. An opponent asserted that he moved the Archbishop to "give leave to the Brownists and Separatists to go to Virginia and designed to make a free popular State there, and himself and his assured friends to be the leaders."

Their suit to the King for liberty of religion failed. Bradford says, "There were divers of good worth laboured with the King to obtain it, amongst whom was Sir Robert Naunton, one of his chief Secretaries, and some others wrought with the Archbishop to give way thereunto, but it proved all in vain." The matter was discussed also in the Privy Council, as we learn from letters sent through Sabine Staresmore to Sir John Wolstenholme.

Here again the stumbling-block was the peculiar views in regard to religious polity held by the Leyden Church. Some of the Council wanted to know the views of the Leyden congregation with regard to the nature of the ministry, the sacraments and the oath acknowledging the King as supreme over the Church. Staresmore stood by and watched the Privy Councillor read the papers on these points which Robinson and Brewster sent over. He pictures the scene for us. Wolstenholme evidently felt that neither of the papers was suitable for helping the business through, and hoped to get the matter settled without making them public.

Here is an extract from Staresmore's vivid letter to the Leyden friends, dated February 14, 1617–8—

"Your Letter to Sir John Wolstenholme I delivered, almost as soon as I had it, to his own hands; and stayed with him the opening and reading.

"There were two Papers inclosed. He read them to himself, as also the Letter; and in the reading he spake to me and said, 'Who shall make them?' *viz.* the Ministers.

"I answered his Worship, 'that the power of making [ministers] was in the Church, to be ordained by the Imposition of Hands by the fittest Instruments they had. It must either be in the Church or from the Pope; and the Pope is Anti-Christ.'

"'Ho!' said Sir John, 'what the Pope holds good, as in the Trinity, that we do well to assent to; but,' said he, 'we will not enter into dispute now.'

"As for your Letters, he would not show them at any hand; lest he should spoil all. He expected you should have been of the Archbishop's mind for the calling of Ministers; but it seems you differed. I could have wished to have known the contents of your two inclosed [notes] at which he stuck so much, especially the larger.

"I asked his Worship 'what good news he had for me to write to-morrow?'

"He told me, 'Very good news, for both the King's Majesty and the Bishops have consented.'

"He said he would go to Master Chancellor, Sir Fulke Greville, as this day [*i. e.* Saturday, Feb. 14], and next week I should know more.

"I met Sir Edwin Sandys on Wednesday night. He wished me to be at the Virginia Court the next Wednesday, where I purpose to be.

"Thus, loath to be troublesome at present, I hope to have somewhat next week, of certain, concerning you. I commit you to the Lord.

"Yours,
"SABINE STARESMORE."

We are more favoured than Staresmore, and can look into the letter and notes which Sir John Wolstenholme thought might endanger rather than help forward the delicate negotiations for securing permission to migrate. Here they are—

The Copy of a Letter sent to Sir John Wolstenholme

"RIGHT WORSHIPFUL,

"With due acknowledgment of our thankfulness for your singular care and pains in the business of Virginia; for our, and, we hope, the common good, we do remember our humble duties to you; and have sent inclosed, as is required, a further explanation of our Judgements in the Three Points specified by some of His Majesty's honourable Privy Council. And though it be grievous unto us, that such unjust insinuations are made against us, yet we are most glad of the occasion of making our just purgation unto so honourable Personages.

"Two Declarations we have sent inclosed; the one more brief and general, which we think the fitter to be presented; the other something more large, and in which we express some small accidental differences; which, if it seem good unto you and others of our worshipful friends, you may send instead of the former.

"Our prayer unto God is that your Worship may see the fruit of your worthy endeavours, which on our parts we shall not fail to further by all good means in us.

"And so praying that you would please, with the convenientest speed that may be, to give us knowledge of the success of the business with His Majesty's Privy Council, and accordingly, what your further pleasure is, either for our direction or furtherance in the same.

So we rest. Your Worship's in all duty

"John Robinson
"William Brewster.

"Leyden, January 27th, anno 1617, old style [*i.e.* Feb. 6 1618]."

The first brief *Note* was this—

"Touching the Ecclesiastical Ministry, namely, of Pastors for Teaching, Elders for Ruling, and Deacons for distributing the Church's contribution : as also for the two Sacraments—Baptism and the Lord's Supper; we do wholly and in all points agree with the French Reformed Churches, according to their public *Confession of Faith.*

"The Oath of Supremacy we shall willingly take, if it be required of us, and that convenient satisfaction be not given by our taking the Oath of Allegiance.

"John Robinson
"William Brewster."

The second was this—

"Touching the Ecclesiastical Ministry, etc. . . . (as in the former) . . . we agree in all things with the French Reformed Churches, according to their public *Confession of Faith,* though some small differences be to be found in our practices, not at all in the substance of things, but only in some accidental circumstances.

"As first—Their Ministers do pray with their heads covered, ours uncovered.

"Secondly—We choose none for Governing Elders but such as are able to teach; which ability they do not require.

"Thirdly—Their Elders and Deacons are annual, or at most for two or three years; ours perpetual.

"Fourthly—Our Elders do administer their Office in Admonitions and Excommunications for public scandals, publicly, and before the Congregation; theirs more privately and in their Consistories.

"Fifthly—We do administer Baptism only to such infants as whereof the one parent at the least is of some Church; which some of their Churches do not observe; though in it our practice accords with their public *Confession* and the judgment of the most learned amongst them.

"Other differences worthy mentioning we know none in these Points. (Then about the Oath as in the former [note].)

"Subscribed,

"JOHN ROBINSON

"WILLIAM BREWSTER."

Though their attempt to gain toleration and allowance by the King's public authority failed, they gathered that "he would connive at them, and not molest them, provided they carried themselves peaceably. . . . This was all the chief of the Virginia Company or any others of their best friends could do in the case."

When the messengers returned to Leyden with this answer, it naturally "made a damp in the business." Though the project was hung up for a time, it was kept alive by frequent discussion amongst the friends, and by interest in the similar venture of the remnants of the Church of Francis Johnson at Amsterdam, who got away for Virginia in the summer of 1618, under the leadership of their elder, Francis Blackwell.

"Some of the chiefest" in the Leyden congregation thought they might proceed on the King's promise of connivance. "If," said they, "there were no security in this promise intimated, there would be no great certainty in a further confirmation of the same. For if, afterwards, there should be a purpose or desire to wrong them, though they had a seal as broad as the house floor, it would not serve the turn, for there would be means enough found to recall or reverse it. And seeing therefore the course was probable, they must rest herein on God's providence, as they had done in other things."

Accordingly, other messengers passed "too and again" about the business between Leyden and London. But when they returned once more to London in the spring of 1619, "to end with the Virginia Company as well as they could, and to procure a Patent with as good and ample conditions as they might by any good means obtain," they found the Virginia Company distracted by disputes, and unable to give immediate attention to them. One of Cushman's letters preserved by Bradford tells us all about it—

Letter from Robert Cushman in London to the Church in Leyden

"To his Loving Friends, etc.,

"I had thought long since to have writ unto you, but could not effect that which I aimed at, neither can yet set things as I wished. Yet, notwithstanding I doubt not but Master B[rewster] hath written to Master Robinson, I think myself bound also to do something, lest I be thought to neglect you.

"The main hindrance of our proceedings in the Virginia business is the dissensions and 'factions,' as they term it, amongst the Council and Company of Virginia; which are such as that ever since we came up,[1] no business could by them be despatched.

"The occasion of this trouble amongst them is, for that a while since, Sir Thomas Smith, repining at his many Offices and Troubles, wished the Company of Virginia to ease him of his Office in being Treasurer and Governor of the Virginia Company. Whereupon the Company took occasion to dismiss him, and chose Sir Edwin Sandys Treasurer and

[1] Cushman and Brewster had evidently been in the country for some time before going up to Town.

Governor of the Company; he having 60 voices, Sir John Wolstenholme 16 voices, and Alderman Johnson 24 voices.

"But Sir Thomas Smith, when he saw some part of his honour lost, was very angry; and raised a faction to cavil and contend about the election, and sought to tax Sir Edwin with many things that might both disgrace him, and also put him by his Office of Governor. In which contentions they yet stick, and are not fit nor ready to intermeddle in any business; and what issue things will come to, we are not yet certain.

"It is most like Sir Edwin will carry it away; and if he do, things will go well in Virginia; if otherwise they will go ill enough. Always we hope in two or three Court Days things will settle.

"Mean space I think to go down into Kent and come up again about fourteen days or three weeks hence, except either by these aforesaid contentions or by the ill tidings from Virginia, we be wholly discouraged. Of which tidings I am now to speak.

"Captain Argall is come home this week. He, upon notice of the intent of the Council, came away before Sir George Yeardley came there; and so there is no small dissension. But his tidings are ill, though his person be welcome.

"He saith, Master Blackwell's ship came not there till March. But going towards winter they had still north-west winds, which carried them to the southward, beyond their course. And the Master of the ship and some six of the Mariners dying, it seemed they could not find the Bay till after long seeking and beating about. Master Blackwell is dead and Master Maggner the Captain, yea, there are dead, he saith, 130 persons one and other in that ship. It is said there were in all 180 persons in the ship, so as they were packed together like herrings. They had amongst them the flux and also want of fresh water; so as it is here rather wondered at that so many are alive, than that so many are dead.

"The Merchants here say, 'It was Master Blackwell's fault to pack so many in the ship.' Yea, and there were great mutterings and repinings amongst them, and upbraiding of Master Blackwell for his dealing and disposing of them when they saw how he had disposed of them, and how he insulted over them. Yea, the streets at Gravesend rang of their extreme quarrellings, crying out one of another, 'Thou hast brought me to this!' and 'I may thank thee for this!' Heavy news it is, and I would be glad to hear how far it will discourage [you]. I see none here discouraged much, but [they] rather desire to learn to beware by other men's harms, and to amend that wherein they have failed.

"As *we* desire to serve one another in love, so [let us] take heed of being enthralled by any imperious person; especially if they be discerned to have an eye to themselves. It doth often trouble me to think that, in this business, we are all to learn and none to teach; but better so, than to depend upon such teachers as Master Blackwell was.

"Such a stratagem he once made for Master Johnson and his people at Emden; which was their subversion. But though he then cleanly, yet unhonestly, plucked his neck out of the collar, yet, at last, his foot is caught.

"Here are no letters come [from the survivors of Blackwell's party]. The ship Captain Argall came in, is yet in the West parts. All that we hear is but his report. It seemeth he came away secretly. The ship that Master Blackwell went in will be here shortly. It is as Master Robinson once said, 'he thought we should hear no good of them.'

"Master B[rewster] is not well at this time. Whether he will come back to you, or go into the North [to Scrooby and Sturton], I yet know not. For myself, I hope to see an end of this business ere I come, though I am sorry to be thus from you. If things had gone roundly forward, I should have been with you within these fourteen days. I pray God direct us, and give us that spirit which is fitting for such a business.

"Thus, having summarily pointed at things, which Master Brewster, I think, hath more largely writ of to Master Robinson, I leave you to the Lord's protection.

"Yours in all readiness, etc.,

"ROBERT CUSHMAN."

May 8th *anno* 1619.

If Cushman kept to his plan he would be up in London again from Kent in time to attend "Master John Wincob" at the meeting of the Virginia Company on May 26, 1619, to secure the endorsement and seal of the Company to their *Patent*, granting permission to settle in New England. By the advice of some friends the *Patent* was not taken out in the name of any member of their own congregation. They sheltered under the name of Wincob, who belonged to the household of the Countess of Lincoln, and who intended to accompany them.

The minutes of the London Virginia Company, under date Wednesday, May 26, 1619, record that—

"One Master Wencop, commended to the Company by the Earl of Lincoln, intending to go in person to Virginia, and there to plant himself and his Associates [Robinson and his congregation] presented his *Patent* now to the Court; which was referred to the Committee that meeteth upon Friday morning at Master Treasurer's house to consider, and if need be to correct the same."

A fortnight later, Wednesday, June 9, 1619, the minutes record—

"By reason it grew late and the Court [being] ready to break up, and as yet Master John Whincop's *Patent* for him and his Associates [remained] to be read; it was ordered, That the seal should be annexed unto it, and have referred the trust thereof to the Auditors to examine that it agree with the original; which if it do not they have promised to bring it into the Court and cancel it."

The Pilgrims had now got some sort of authority for making the settlement they desired, but, in the event, John Wincob, or Whencop, never went with them, nor did they ever make "use of this *Patent* which had cost them so much labour and charge."

I think the main reason which prevented them from taking immediate advantage of this *Patent* of June 1619 was the fact that Brewster was in trouble about printing books distasteful to His Majesty. In a week or two after this *Patent* was signed the authorities in England and Holland were searching for Brewster. Until that cloud had blown over it would be folly to proceed with their project. The angered King, so far from conniving at their scheme, would now be actively hostile. Robinson, despairing of support or allowance from the home authorities, turned to the Dutch.

On February 2, 1619–20, the directors of the New Netherland Company, trading to the parts "in latitude from 40 to 45 degrees between New France and Virginia," presented a petition to the Prince of Orange, in the course of which they say—

"It happens that there is residing at Leyden a certain English Preacher versed in the Dutch language, who is well inclined to proceed thither to live, assuring the Petitioners that he has the means of inducing over four hundred families to accompany him thither, both out of this country and England, provided they might be guarded and preserved from all violence on the part of other Potentates by the authority, and under the protection of, your Princely Excellency and the High and Mighty Lords States-General in the propagation of the true, pure Christian religion, in the instruction of the Indians in that country in true learning, and in converting them to the Christian faith, and thus through the mercy of the Lord, to the greater glory of this country's Government, to plant there a new Commonwealth, all under the order and command of your Princely Excellency and the High and Mighty Lords States-General."

The Petitioners go on to refer to the English efforts to settle in those parts, and they ask that for the preservation of Holland's rights there—

"The aforesaid Minister [John Robinson] and the four hundred families may be taken under the protection of this country, and that two ships of war may be provisionally despatched to secure to the State the aforesaid countries; inasmuch as they would be of much importance whenever the West India Company is established, in respect to the large abundance of timber fit for ship-building."

Bradford, in writing his *History*, slurred over these negotiations with the Dutch, merely noting that, about the time of the Pilgrims' perplexity with the proceedings of the Virginia Company, "some Dutchmen made them fair offers about going with them." Winslow indicates that if they would have stood in with the Dutch they might have been transported to the Hudson River free of charge, and every family provided with cattle[1]—a most important provision for a colony.

The petition of the New Netherland Company directors for the support of two men-of-war was twice rejected. But Robinson and his congregation had by this time broken off the negotiations with the Dutch on the advice of Thomas Weston—

[1] *Hypocrisy Vnmasked*, 1646, p. 91.

"One Master Thomas Weston, a Merchant of London, came to Leyden about the same time, who was well acquainted with some of them and a furtherer of them in their former proceedings. Having much conference with Master Robinson and others of the Chief of them [he] persuaded them to go on as it seems; and not to meddle with the Dutch or too much to depend on the Virginia Company. For if that [Company] failed [them], if they came to resolution, he and such Merchants as were his friends, together with their own means, would set them forth. And they should make ready, and neither fear want of shipping nor money, for what they wanted should be provided.

"And not so much for himself, as for the satisfying of such friends as he should procure to adventure in this business, they were to draw such *Articles of Agreement* and make such *Propositions* as might the better induce his friends to venture.

"Upon which, after the former's conclusion [*i. e.* in accordance with Weston's suggestions], *Articles* were drawn and agreed unto, and were shown unto him and approved by him, and afterwards by their Messenger (Master John Carver) sent into England. Who, together with Robert Cushman, were to receive the monies and make provision both for shipping and other things for the Voyage; with this charge, not to exceed their Commission, but to proceed according to the former *Articles*."

Weston's plan was to form a sort of joint stock company to raise funds to equip the venture and support the projected Plantation. Those who invested in the scheme were called the "Adventurers," those who actually sailed were called the "Planters." The shares in the venture were fixed at £10. Every Planter of sixteen years or upwards was allotted one share without payment, in virtue of his or her personal interest in the matter. A Planter could also take up shares as an Adventurer by investing his cash, either £10 or multiples of £10, in the scheme, or by bringing in approved goods to the value of £10 for the general use of the Plantation. The Plantation was to be run as a joint stock corporation for seven years. As originally arranged, at the end of the seven years the capital and a ccumulated profits were to be divided amongst the shareholders, or Adventurers in proportion to their several holdings of shares, but the houses and the land brought under cultivation (particularly the gardens and home lots) were to be left undivided and in the possession of the Planters. While the Planters were to work in general for the Company, or Corporation of Adventurers, they were to have two days a week for their own private employment.

The alteration of these last two points in the agreement at the instance of Weston, without consultation with the Leyden friends, caused great friction and misgiving. John Robinson especially opposed the change, and promptly sent over a paper of *Reasons* against it. But Cushman, who wanted to get things done, saw that the whole venture would be imperilled unless he agreed to the alteration. The new proposals were, that the houses and lands should be included in the division of assets at the end of the seven years, and that all the labour of the planters should be credited in that time to the common stock. Robert Cushman was a thorough believer in the community idea. He felt that by working for the good of all, the welfare of each would be promoted. He made a spirited defence of his concession to Weston's proposals.

The amended *Articles* and *Conditions* were as follows—

"*Anno* 1620.

"1. The Adventurers and Planters do agree: That every person that goeth being aged sixteen years and upwards, be rated at £10 : and £10 to be accounted a Single Share.

"2. That he that goeth in person and furnisheth himself out with £10 either in money or other provisions, be accounted as having £20 in Stock: and in the Division shall receive a Double Share.

"3. The persons transported and the Adventurers shall continue their Joint Stock and Partnership together the space of Seven Years: except some unexpected impediment do cause the whole Company to agree otherwise: during which time all profits and benefits that are got by trade, traffic, trucking, working, fishing or any other means of any person or persons [are to] remain still in the Common Stock until the Division.

"4. That at their coming there [to America] they choose out such a number of fit persons as may furnish their ships and boats for fishing upon the sea; employing the rest in their several faculties upon the land; as building houses, tilling and planting the ground and making such commodities as shall be most useful for the Colony.

"5. That at the end of the Seven Years the Capital and Profits (*viz.* the houses, lands, goods and chattels) be equally divided betwixt the Adventurers and Planters. Which done, every man shall be free from other of them, of any debt or detriment concerning this Adventure.

"6. Whosoever cometh to the Colony hereafter, or putteth any [goods or money] into the Stock, shall, at the end of the Seven Years, be allowed proportionately to the time of his so doing.

"7. He that shall carry his wife and children or servants shall be allowed for every person now aged sixteen years and upward a Single Share in the Division, or, if he provide them necessaries, a Double Share: or if they be between ten years old and sixteen, then two of them to be reckoned for a person both in Transportation and Division.

"8. That such children as now go, and are under the age of ten years, have no other Share in the Division but fifty acres of unmanured land.

"9. That such persons as die before the Seven Years be expired, their executors to have their part or Share at the Division proportionately to the time of their life in the Colony.

"10. That all such persons as are of this Colony are to have their meat, drink, apparel and all provisions out of the Common Stock and goods of the said Colony."

The clause struck out relating to time for private use was to this effect: "that they should have two days in a week for their own private employment, for the more comfort of themselves and their families; especially such as had families."

The following letter, written on Wednesday, May 31, 1620, from four who had resolved to join the venture, illustrates the feeling on these points—

To their loving friends John Carver and Robert Cushman, these, etc.

"Good Brethren. After salutations, etc. We received divers letters at the coming of Master Nash, and our Pilot, which is a great encouragement unto us, and for whom we hope after times will minister occasion of praising God. And indeed had you not sent him, many would have been ready to faint and go back; partly in respect of the new *Conditions* which have been taken up by you, which all men are against, and partly in regard of our own inability to do any one of those many weighty businesses you refer to us here.

"For the former whereof:—Whereas Robert Cushman desires reasons for our dislike, promising thereupon to alter the same; else saying we should think he hath no brains: we desire him to exercise them therein, referring him to our Pastor's former reasons; and them to the censure of the godly wise. But our desires are that you will not entangle yourselves and us in any such unreasonable courses as these are, *viz.*—

"That the Merchants should have the half of men's houses and lands at the Divident.

"And that persons should be deprived of the two days in a week agreed upon, yea, every moment of time for their own particular [*i. e.* their own private concerns].

"By reason whereof, we cannot conceive why any should carry servants for their own help and comfort; for that [since] we can require no more of them than all men one of another.

"This we have only by relation from Master Nash, and not from any writing of your own; and therefore hope you have not proceeded far in so great a thing without us; but requiring you not to exceed the bounds of your Commission, which was to proceed upon the things or *Conditions* agreed upon, and expressed in writing at your going over [to England] about it. We leave it; not without marvelling that yourself (as you write), knowing how small a thing troubleth our consultations and how few (as you fear) understand the business aright, should trouble with such matters as these are, etc.

"Salute Master Weston from us; in whom we hope we are not deceived. We pray you make known our estate unto him, and, if you think good, show him our letters. At least tell him that under God, we much rely upon him and put our confidence in him. And as yourselves well know, that if he had not been an Adventurer with us we had not taken it in hand, presuming that if he had not seen means to accomplish it, he would not have begun it. So we hope in our extremity he will so far help us as that our expectation be no way made frustrate concerning him.

"Since therefore, Good Brethren, we have plainly opened the state of things with us in this manner, you will, etc.

"Thus beseeching the Almighty, Who is all sufficient to raise us out of this depth of difficulties, to assist us herein, raising such means, by his Providence and fatherly care for us, his poor children and servants, as we may with comfort behold the hand of our God for good towards us in this our business which we undertake in his name and fear, we take leave, and remain,

"Your perplexed, yet hopeful brethren,

"Samuel Fuller.
"Edward Winslow.
"William Bradford.
"Isaac Allerton.

"June 10th, new style, *anno* 1620"
[*i. e.* May 31, in English reckoning.]

I gather that one clause in the *Conditions*—the one relating to the division of houses and lands—was altered; and one clause (that relating to the two days free labour a week) was struck out. This was done to conciliate opposition and induce hesitating investors to venture their money. Cushman felt that the elimination of the latter clause left the question of the free labour for the benefit of one's family open—

"'You may have three days in a week,' he says, 'for me, if you will.' And when I have spoken to the Adventurers of times of working they have said, 'They hope we are men of discretion and conscience, and so fit to be trusted ourselves with that.'"

Robinson, however, was far from satisfied. He was greatly concerned about the change in the agreement. It was objected to the plan accepted by Cushman that all members of the Colony would be placed thereby on the same footing, whereas in fact "all men are not of one condition." His answer to this objection shows his point of view—

"If by condition you mean wealth, you are mistaken. If you mean, by condition, qualities, then I say: He that is not content his neighbour shall have as good a house, fare, means, etc., as himself is not of a good quality.

"Secondly—Such retired [unsocial] persons as have an eye only to themselves are fitter to come where catching is than closing, and are fitter to live alone than in any society either civil or religious."

The reply of Cushman to the brethren at Leyden, written on Sunday, June 11, 1620, tells of the resolve of himself and Thomas Weston to hire a ship for the voyage. They had one in view—the *Mayflower*, I take it—of which they had got the refusal till the next day. She had discharged a cargo of "french wyne" the previous month at London.

"Salutations, etc. I received your letter by John Turner, with another the same day from Amsterdam by Master W. savouring of the place whence it came.

"And indeed the many discouragements I find here together with the demurs and retirings there [amongst those in Holland] had made me to say 'I would give up my accounts to John Carver, and at his coming acquaint him fully with all courses; and so leave it quite, with only the poor clothes on my back.'

"But gathering up myself, by further consideration, I resolved yet to make one trial more: and to acquaint Master Weston with the fainted state of our business. And though he hath been much discontented at something amongst us of late, which hath made him often say 'that save for his promise he would not meddle at all with the business any more,' and yet (considering how far we were plunged into matters; and how it stood both on our credits and undoing) at the last, he gathered up himself a little more; and coming to me, two hours after, he told me, he would not yet leave it.

"And so, advising together, we resolved to hire a ship; and have took liking of one till Monday, about sixty last, [in burden] for a greater we cannot get, except it be too great. But a fine ship it is. And seeing our near friends there [at Amsterdam] are so strait-laced; we hope to assure [to secure this ship] without troubling them any further; and if the ship fall too small, it fitteth well, that such as stumble at straws already, may rest them there awhile, lest worse blocks come in the way ere the Seven Years be ended.

"If you had beaten [discussed] this business so thoroughly a month ago, and writ to us as you now do, we could thus have done [*i. e.* hired shipping] much more conveniently. But it is, as it is.

"I hope our friends there [in Holland], if they be quitted of the ship hire, will be induced to venture the more.

All that I now require is that salt and nets may there be bought; and for all the rest, we will here [in England] provide it. Yet if that will not be, let them but stand for it a month or two, and we will take order to pay it all.

"Let Master Reynolds tarry there and bring the ship [*i. e.* the *Speedwell*] to Southampton. We have hired another Pilot here, one Master Clarke, who went last year to Virginia with a ship of kine.

"You shall hear distinctly by John Turner, who, I think, shall come hence on Tuesday night. I had thought to have come with him, to have answered to my complaints [*i. e.* the complaints against me], but I shall learn to pass little for their censures, and if I had more mind to go and dispute and expostulate with them, than I have care of this weighty business; I were like them who live by clamours and jangling. But neither my mind nor my body is at liberty to do much; for I am fettered with business, and had rather study to be quiet than to make answer to their exceptions. If men be set on it, let them beat the air.

"I hope such as are my sincere friends will not think but I can give some reason of my actions. But of your mistaking about the matter, and other things tending to this business: I shall [in my] next inform you more distinctly. Mean space entreat our friends not to be too busy in answering matters before they know them. If I do such things as I cannot give reasons for, it is like you have set a fool about your business; and so turn the reproof to yourselves and send another, and let me come again to my combs [Cushman was a wool-comber]. But (setting aside my natural infirmities) I refuse not to have my cause judged, both of God and all indifferent [impartial] men; and when we come together I shall give account of my actions here.

"The Lord, who judgeth justly without respect of persons, see unto the equity of my cause, and give us quiet, peaceable, and patient minds in all these turmoils, and sanctify unto us all crosses whatsoever!

"And so I take my leave of you all, in all love and affection,

"Your poor Brother,

"ROBERT CUSHMAN.

"June 11, 1620.

"I hope we shall get all here ready in fourteen days."

Cushman felt that he had done the best he could in difficult circumstances to further their plan. His letter would probably go by John Turner on the following Tuesday night. On the Wednesday John Robinson, with anxious care, was penning the accompanying letter to his quiet and faithful brother-in-law, John Carver, unaware, of course, that the hiring of the *Mayflower* was so imminent—

A Letter of Master Robinson's to John Carver

"My dear Friend and Brother, whom with yours, I always remember in my best affection, and whose welfare I shall never cease to commend to God by my best and most earnest prayers.

"You do thoroughly understand, by our general letters, the estate of things here, which indeed is very pitiful, especially by want of shipping and not seeing means likely, much less certain, of having it provided [free of charge to the colonists] though withal there be great want of money and means to do [other] needful things.

"Master Pickering you know before this will not defray a penny here, though Robert Cushman presumed of I know not how many £100 from him and I know not whom, yet it seems strange we should be put to him to receive both his and his partner's Adventure; and yet Master Weston writ unto him that in regard of it [*i. e.* on account of Pickering's promised investment in the venture] he hath drawn upon him a £100 more. But there is in this some mystery, as indeed it seems there is in the whole course.

"Besides, whereas divers are to pay in some parts of their money yet behind, they refuse to do it till they see shipping provided, or a course taken for it. Neither, do I think, is there a man here would pay anything if he had again his money in his purse.

"You know right well we depended on Master Weston alone; and upon such means as he would procure for this common business; and when we had in hand another course with the Dutchmen broke it off at his motion, and upon the *Conditions* by him shortly after propounded. He did this in his love, I know, but things appear not answerable from him hitherto. That *he* should have first put in his monies is thought by many to have been but fit; but that I can well excuse [*i. e.* I can excuse him for not yet paying his money into the hands of our agents] he being a Merchant and having use of it to his benefit; whereas others, if it had been in their hands, would have consumed it. But that he should not but have had either shipping ready before this time, or at least certain means and course, and the same known to us, for it, or have taken other order otherwise, cannot in my conscience be excused.

"I have heard that when he hath been moved in the business he hath put it off from himself and referred it to the others; and would come to George Morton and inquire news of him about things; as if he had scarce been some accessory unto it. Whether he hath failed of some helps from others which he expected and so be not well able to go through with things; or whether he hath feared lest you should be ready too soon and so increase the charge of shipping above that [which] is meet; or whether he hath thought by withholding [his money] to put us upon straits, thinking that thereby Master Brewster and Master Pickering would be drawn by importunity to do more; or what other mystery is in it we know not. But sure we are, that things are not answerable to such an occasion.

"Master Weston makes himself merry with our endeavours about buying a ship; but we have done nothing in this [purchase of the *Speedwell*] but with good reason, as I am persuaded, nor yet that I know [of] in anything else,—save in those two—

"[1] The one, that we employed Robert Cushman, who is known, though a good man and of special abilities in his kind, yet most unfit to deal for other men, by reason of his singularity and too great indifferency for any conditions, and for (to speak truly) that we have had nothing from him but terms and presumptions.

"[2] The other that we have so much relied, by implicit faith as it were, upon generalities, without seeing the particular course or means for so weighty an affair set down unto us.

"For shipping Master Weston it should seem is set upon hiring, which yet I wish he may presently [immediately] effect. But I see little hope of help [for the ship-hire] from hence if so it be. Of Master Brewer you know what to expect. I do not think Master Pickering will engage, except in the course of buying in former letters specified.

"About the *Conditions* you have our *Reasons* for our judgments of what is agreed. And let this specially be borne in mind—that the greatest part of the Colony is like to be employed constantly not upon dressing their particular land and building houses, but upon fishing, trading, etc.; so as the 'land and house' will be but a trifle for advantage to the Adventurers, and yet the division of it, a great discouragement to the Planters, who would [if land and house were to remain their own] with singular care make it comfortable with borrowed hours from their sleep.

"The same consideration of common employment constantly, by the most, is a good reason not to have the two days in a week denied the few Planters for private use, which yet is subordinate to common good. Consider also how much unfit [it is] that you, and your likes, must serve a new prenticeship of Seven Years, and not a day's freedom from task!

"Send me word what persons are to go; who of useful faculties and how many; and particularly of everything.

"I know you want not a mind. I am sorry you have not been at London all this while but the provisions [the purchasing of stores and necessaries] could not want you. Time will suffer me to write no more. Fare you and yours well, always in the Lord, in whom I rest,

"Yours to use,

"JOHN ROBINSON."

Reading between the lines we can see the anxiety of Robinson for the welfare of his people. He does not like to show distrust of Thomas Weston, whose large and general promises when at Leyden had led the friends there to come to the definite resolution to go forth to colonize in New England, and yet he feels that Weston had not done all that might have been reasonably expected to further their project. Delay was dangerous; a spirit of misgiving was spreading amongst those who had sold up their possessions, invested their money in the common stock and prepared themselves for the voyage. The Pilgrims were dependent on the help of others to set forth their expedition and supply the needs of the Colony in its early years. They were too poor to undertake such a venture alone, and when a merchant like Edward Pickering, one of their own religious fellowship, showed reluctance to help to the limit of his means, we need not wonder that there was difficulty in raising the needful capital from outsiders.

I take it that William Brewster, Thomas Brewer, George Morton, John Carver and his wife, William Bradford, John Turner, William White, Edward Winslow and Isaac Allerton all contributed substantially to the venture. We must not forget the difficulties which Weston and John Peirce would have to overcome in forming the company of Adventurers in England to support the enterprise. Commerical and religious motives intermingled. Some investors were more swayed by the one than the other. Captain John Smith, who was keenly interested in New England, watched the efforts to form this colony with close attention. He describes the "Company of Adventurers" who set the colonists forth, as a body of about seventy, "some Gentlemen; some Merchants; some Handicraftsmen; some adventuring great sums, some small, as their estates and affection served. These," he says, "dwell most about London. They are not a Corporation, but knit together by a voluntary combination, in a Society without constraint or penalty, aiming to do good and to plant Religion."[1] They elected a President and Treasurer annually, to whom the transaction of ordinary business was left, "but in more weighty affairs the assent of the whole Company is required." If the minutes of the proceedings of this company of Adventurers had survived, we should have had the business counterpart to Bradford's *History* of the early years of the colony, but given from the point of view of London. Here and there we get a glimpse of their activities until the Adventurers went into voluntary liquidation and wound up the company by a composition with the colonists on November 15, 1626. By that time some of the Adventurers, like Weston, had unloaded their shares. Only forty-two signed the Composition Deed. One or two of these, such as William Collier and Timothy Hatherley, subsequently crossed to New Plymouth and became useful colonists. Shareholders were ready to dispose of their rights under the Composition Deed for an immediate cash payment. James Sherley, who had faith in the venture, bought many of them out, and in 1627 became "y[e] receiver of most part of y[e] adventurs."

[1] *General History of Virginia*, 1624, p. 247.

CHAPTER XXI

THEY PREPARE FOR THE VOYAGE—THE "MAYFLOWER"

MEANWHILE friends at Leyden were making their preparations for the voyage. On September 19, 1619, Cushman had sold some property in Leyden, held by him since 1611, to John de Later, and on April 1, 1620, Thomas Rogers, who sailed in the *Mayflower*, sold his house in Barbara's Lane for 300 gilders to Mordecai Cohen. To meet the immediate need for money Robinson, Brewster and William Jepson mortgaged property in Leyden in 1620. This tided them over the occasion, and six months later they were able to pay off the mortage.[1] The Leyden friends were keen on buying shipping, and purchased a little vessel of some sixty tons, named the *Speedwell*, intending to use her for trading purposes on the New England coast. Reynolds was sent over from London to navigate her to Southampton. The preparations in England were made under considerable difficulty. In order to act fairly by those Planters who were joining the venture in England, one from their number, Christopher Martin [2] by name, was appointed to act as agent with Carver and Cushman. They did not find him easy to work with. He went his own way, with little regard to their advice, which led Cushman to say of him, "he that is in a Society and yet regards not counsel may better be a king than a consort."

The main preparations were made at Southampton. It does not appear why that port was chosen. My own

[1] Information from Dr. Rendel Harris.

[2] Martin belonged to a church at Billericay, Essex, and was summoned before the Archidiaconal Court for allowing his son to answer "that his father gave him his name." He fled to Leyden and joined Robinson's Church. He died January 8, 1621, on the *Mayflower*. *Transactions* of Congregational Historical Society, vol. vii. p. 243.

conjecture is that they regarded it as less dangerous for the religious refugees than London. They would be less likely to suffer arrest there, and be less under the eye of the ecclesiastical authorities. With Carver at Southampton, Cushman and Weston hiring shipping and getting stores in London, Martin collecting provisions in Kent and the Leyden contingent equipping the *Speedwell* at Delftshaven, there was too little room for concerted action and too much room for misunderstanding.

When, by the report of one of their messengers from England, it seemed that the way was at last clearing for the realization of the plan so long cherished in their minds, Robinson called his flock together to hold a solemn "Meeting and keep a Day of Humiliation, to seek the Lord for his direction." He took for his text the words—

> "And David's men said unto him, See, we be afraid here in Judah: how much more if we come to Keilah against the host of the Philistines? Then David asked counsel of the Lord again" (1 Sam. xxiii. 3, 4).

"From which text," says Bradford, "he taught many things very aptly, and befitting their present occasion and condition, strengthening them against their fears and perplexities and encouraging them in their resolutions."

We may be sure that Robinson laid stress upon the ideal side of their venture, which was ever uppermost in his mind.

After this religious service—

> "they concluded both what number and what persons should prepare themselves to go with the first, for all that were willing to have gone could not get ready . . . in so short a time, neither, if all could have been ready, had there been means to have transported them all together.
>
> "Those that stayed, being the greater number, required the Pastor to stay with them; and, indeed, for other reasons he could not then well go; and so it was the more easily yielded unto.
>
> "The others then desired the Elder, Master Brewster, to go with them; which was also condescended unto."

Bradford does not specify the other reasons preventing John Robinson from joining the Pilgrims. I fancy they arose from hostility to the Pastor's religious views on the part of some of the London merchants who were supporting the venture with their money. We shall see how this religious prejudice blocked Robinson's plan of joining Brewster in New England a year or two later. The Leyden friends thus separating agreed that each part should be considered " an absolute Church of themselves," since " it might come to pass they should for the body of them never meet again in this world." But they were to have a right of membership in either Church, so that if any went to or fro to Leyden or New England they would need no " dismission or testimonial." Winslow records a mutual agreement between them—

> " If the Lord should frown upon our proceedings, then those that went were to return and the brethren that remained still there to assist and be helpful to them.
>
> " But if God should be pleased to favour them that went, then they also should endeavour to help over such as were poor, and ancient and willing to come." [1]

The pledge recorded by Bradford shows the same spirit of comradeship and the same desire to help—

> " It was promised to those that went first, by the body of the rest, *that if the Lord gave them life, and means, and opportunity, they would come to them as soon as they could.*" [2]

Nor were these idle words, as the sequel abundantly shows.

When the news reached Robinson that the good ship *Mayflower* had been hired, and would go round from London to Southampton to await the colonists from Leyden, the preparations for departure were soon completed—

> " So, being ready to depart, they had a day of Solemn Humiliation : their Pastor taking his text from Ezra viii. 21 : ' And there, at the river by Ahava, I proclaimed a Fast that we might humble ourselves before our God; and seek of him

[1] *Hypocrisy Vnmasked*, p. 90. [2] *History*, f. 73.

a right way for us, and for our children, and for all our substance.' Upon which [passage] he spent a good part of the day very profitably and suitable to their present condition. The rest of the time was spent in pouring out prayers to the Lord with great fervency, mixed with abundance of tears. And the time being come that they must depart, they were accompanied with most of their brethren out of the City unto a town sundry miles off, called Delftshaven, where the ship [the *Speedwell*] lay ready to receive them. So they left that goodly and pleasant city, which had been their resting-place near twelve years, but they knew they were Pilgrims, and looked not much on these things, but lift up their eyes to the heavens, their dearest country, and quieted their spirits."

These are the words of William Bradford. On his companion, Edward Winslow, also, the events of that time made an ineffaceable impression. The parting service, the farewell feast, the scenes at the departure on the quay and on the boat were all charged with strong emotion—

"They that stayed at Leyden," he says, "feasted us that were to go at our Pastor's house, being large, where we refreshed ourselves after our tears with singing of Psalms, making joyful melody in our hearts as well as with the voice, there being many of the Congregation very expert in music; and indeed it was the sweetest melody that ever mine ears heard."

It was Winslow also who set down in after years, perhaps from notes taken at the time, his recollections of Robinson's farewell address—

"THE WHOLESOME COUNSEL MASTER ROBINSON GAVE THAT PART OF THE CHURCH WHEREOF HE WAS PASTOR AT THEIR DEPARTURE FROM HIM TO BEGIN THE GREAT WORK OF PLANTATION IN NEW ENGLAND

"Amongst other wholesome instructions and exhortations he used these expressions, or to the same purpose—

"We were now ere long to part asunder; and the Lord knoweth whether ever he should live to see our faces again. But whether the Lord had appointed it or not; he charged us, before God and his blessed angels, to follow him no further than he followed Christ: and if God should reveal anything to us by any other instrument of his, to be as ready to receive it, as ever we were to receive any truth by his Ministry. For he was very confident the Lord had more truth and light yet to break forth out of his holy Word.

"He took occasion also miserably to bewail the state and condition of the Reformed Churches, who were come to a period in religion; and would go no further than the Instruments of their Reformation. As, for example, the Lutherans: they could not be drawn to go beyond what Luther saw, for whatever part of God's will He had further imparted and revealed to Calvin, they will rather die than embrace it. 'And so also,' saith he, 'you see the Calvinists. They stick where he left them, a misery much to be lamented.

"'For though they were precious shining lights in their Times, yet God had not revealed his whole will to them; and were they now living,' saith he, 'they would be as ready and willing to embrace further light, as that they had received.'

"Here, also, he put us in mind of our Church Covenant; at least that part of it whereby 'we promise and covenant with God and one with another to receive whatsoever light or truth shall be made known to us from his written Word;' but withal exhorted us to take heed what we received for truth; and well to examine and compare and weigh it with other Scriptures of truth before we received it. 'For,' saith he, 'it is not possible the Christian World should come so lately out of such thick antichristian darkness; and that full perfection of knowledge should break forth at once.'

"Another thing he commended to us was, that we should use all means to avoid and shake off the name of 'Brownist,' being a mere nickname and brand to make religion odious and the Professors of it, to the Christian world.

"'And to that end,' said he, 'I should be glad if some godly Minister would go over with you before my coming. For,' said he, 'there will be no difference between the unconformable Ministers and you, when they come to the practice of the Ordinances [of religion] out of the kingdom.'

"And so [our Pastor] advised us, by all means, to endeavour to close with the godly party of the Kingdom of England [the Puritans]; and rather to study union than division, *viz.* How near we might possibly, without sin, close with them; than, in the least measure, to affect division or separation from them. 'And be not loath to take another Pastor or Teacher,' saith he, 'for that Flock that hath two Shepherds is not endangered, but secured by it.'

"Many other things there were of great and weighty consequence which he commended to us. But these things

I thought good to relate at the request of some well-willers to the peace and good agreement of the godly—so distracted at present about the settling of Church Government in the Kingdom of England—that so both sides may truly see what this poor despised Church of Christ now at New Plymouth in New England, but formerly at Leyden in Holland, was and is—how far they were and still are, from separation from the Churches of Christ, especially those that are Reformed."

We have to bear in mind, when reading this summary of Robinson's farewell address, that Winslow does not profess to give the Pastor's actual words. It is evident also that he desires to minimize the differences between the Pilgrim Church and the Puritan members of the Church of England, and to emphasize the points of agreement. But I think, allowing for this, he gives us in this report a good representation of the spirit of Robinson's teaching and of his general outlook. Though the Covenant of their Church had a definite reference to the Bible, or the "Word of God," as the ultimate source of religious truth and light, yet it was free from finality. It left the way of advance open. It left room for fresh interpretations and new applications of the Divine Word. Robinson was not without a consciousness of the freshness of their religious venture, and was too clear-sighted to imagine that the Reformers had attained to the whole truth of religion at a bound. Those who have read Robinson's *Works* with attention will notice several points of connexion with his thought in the summary which Winslow gives of his memorable farewell address.

In the very year before this occasion, Robinson had issued in Latin *A Just and Necessary Apology*, or defence of his Church against slanderous reports raised against it by opponents. Those false reports had blocked the negotiations for permission to cross to Virginia, with allowance to exercise their religion according to their convictions. It seemed needful to rebut the charges laid against them. In this book Robinson lays stress upon the points of agreement with the forward members of the Anglican Church and with the published Confession of the "Belgic Reformed Churches," while frankly setting out some of the points of difference in practice. He tells us that some of those in England, "reputed the chief masters and patrons both of religion and truth," had framed against him and his Church "a solemn accusation to them in special authority." Robinson here refers to the charges made against them in the Privy Council, to meet which he and Brewster sent the two written "Papers" to Sir John Wolstenholme by Sabine Staresmore already referred to.

The accusation he tells us was—

"First—that we (lewd Brownists) do refuse and reject one of the sacraments.

"Secondly—that we have amongst us no ecclesiastical ministry, but do give liberty to every mechanical person to preach publicly in the church.

"Thirdly—that we are in error about the very Trinity.

"Fourthly and lastly—that being become so odious to the magistrates here, as that we are by violence to be driven the country, we are now constrained to seek some other and far part of the world to settle in." [1]

In the "Apology" designed to clear himself and his Church from these misreports Robinson says, "Such is our accord in the case of religion with the Dutch Reformed Churches as that we are ready to subscribe to all and every article of faith in the same Church as they are laid down in the *Harmony of Confessions of Faith*, published in their name," with one slight modification in respect to the Apocryphal Books.

Again, in the last chapter of this *Just Apology*, in treating directly of their "secession and separation" from the Church of England, "a great matter of exception against us and the same the fountain well-nigh of all our calamity," Robinson says—

"Our faith is not negative, as papists used to object to the evangelical churches; nor which consists in the condemning of others, and wiping their names out of the bead-roll of

[1] *Works*, vol. iii. p. 8.

churches, but in the edifying of ourselves; neither require we of any of ours in the confession of their faith, that they either renounce, or, in one word, contest with the Church of England, whatsoever the world clamours of us this way. . . . If by the church be understood the Catholic Church dispersed upon the face of the whole earth, we do willingly acknowledge that a singular part thereof, and the same visible and conspicuous, is to be found in the land [of England] and with it do profess and practise, what in us lays, communion in all things, in themselves lawful and done in right order.

. . . .

"If in anything we err, advertise us brotherly, with desire of our information, and not, as our countrymen's manner for the most part is, with a mind of reproaching us or gratifying of others; and whom thou findest in error, thou shalt not leave in obstinacy, nor as having a mind prone to schism."[1]

The spirit and tenor of such statements, in which Robinson seeks to draw as near as possible to godly men in other Churches, are quite in line with Winslow's recollections of the farewell address delivered in the following year.

One point in Winslow's report of Robinson's farewell words of advice to the departing Pilgrims is supported by an incidental remark in one of Cushman's letters. I refer to the passage in which Robinson recommends them to choose a second pastor or teacher to accompany them. His own going was opposed. If one of the Puritan clergy would consent to go with them it might conciliate opponents and disarm the hostility which was manifested against them on religious grounds. Arrived in New England, far from the episcopal eye, Robinson was confident that such a minister would fall in with the method and practice of his own Church.

Now in Cushman's letter of June 10, 1620, to John Carver, we find this passage—

"For Master Crabe of whom you write he hath promised to go with us: yet I tell you, I shall not be without fear till I see him shipped; for he is much opposed. Yet I hope he will not fail."

[1] *Works*, vol. iii. pp. 63, 78.

Bradford notes in the margin of his *History* against this name: "He was a Minister." His sailing with them was evidently contemplated, but the opposition to his going, as Cushman feared, proved to be too strong, and he was prevented.

Note on the "Mayflower"

The *Mayflower* was a staunch little square-rigged vessel (Bradford casually mentions her "topsail halliards"), double-decked, broad in the beam and tubby, with upper works rising rather high at the stern. It was an obligation on the passengers to construct their own cabins between decks. Her tonnage is variously given as "about sixtylast" = 120 tons, "140 tuns," and "about nine score in burden" = 180 tons. She was partly owned [1] by her Master, Christopher Jones, and seems to have been registered at Harwich, where the Jones family were settled as merchants. Christopher Jones was a good seaman. He was not a raw hand at the job. As early as 1606 we find him making a voyage in command of the *Jason* to Bordeaux. Later on he was engaged in the Greenland whale-fishery. He had confidence in his vessel. When the "Pilgrims" were a bit daunted by the Atlantic storms he told them "he knew the ship to be firm and strong under water." Jones was a good shot and a kindly man. Going ashore from the *Mayflower*, on Friday, February 9, 1621, he "killed five geese, which he friendly distributed among the sick people." When the "Pilgrims'" own stock of beer ran out, on Christmas Day, of all days, and they began "to drink water aboard," Bradford says, "at night the Master caused us to have some beer. And so on board we had divers times, now and then, some beer: but on shore none at all." Jones helped the Planters in their work of exploration, and allowed them to use the *Mayflower* as their rendezvous till their humble dwellings were made ready on shore. They held their Sunday

[1] Roland G. Usher thinks she belonged to Thomas Goffe, one of the Adventurers. But it was the *Mayflower* of 1629 in which Goffe was interested. Even if she were the same ship, he had no share in her in 1620.

services on board till Sunday, January 21, 1621, when, they say, "we kept our Meeting on land." The colonists named the first considerable stream they found after the Captain, and it bears his name, "Jones River," to this day.

Of the crew carried by the *Mayflower* we hear of Robert Coppin, "our pilot," and John Clarke a second pilot. These two ranked as "master's mates." I think the third mate was "Master Williamson," who accompanied Miles Standish, March 22, 1621, to meet the Indian "King" "at the brook," on the first approach of the Indians to the infant colony.

We may construct a rough log of the *Mayflower* for her memorable voyage as follows—

"1620. June or July. *Mayflower* chartered.
,, July 19. Arrived at Southampton.
,, July 26. Joined there by the *Speedwell*.
,, Aug. 5. Sailed from Southampton.
,, Aug. 13. Put into Dartmouth.
,, Aug. 23. Left Dartmouth.
,, Sept. 6. Sailed from Plymouth. Wind E.N.E.
,, Nov. 9. Made Cape Cod at daybreak. Shape courseS.S.W. for the Hudson, but owing to shoals and contrary winds put about at night.
,, Nov. 11. Dropped anchor in Cape Cod Bay.
,, Nov. 15–27, Dec. 5. Exploring parties sent out.
,, Dec. 8. Friday, at nightfall an exploring party landed on an island in Plymouth bay. It was named after John Clarke, and is still known as Clark's Island.
,, Dec. 11. Landing of the exploring party on the mainland at Plymouth.
,, Dec. 14. Exploring party returns to the *Mayflower*.
,, Dec. 15. Weighed anchor at Cape Cod and made an abortive attempt to get into Plymouth Bay. Wind N.W. Course West.
,, Dec. 16. *Mayflower* dropped anchor in Plymouth Bay, New England, and there wintered.
"1621. April 5. Sailed for Old England.
,, May 5 or 6. Arrived in London. Refit and sail for Rochelle.
,, Oct. 19. Discharging cargo of Bay Salt in London."

Christopher Jones did not long survive this voyage. He died the next summer, and on August 26, 1622, letters of administration for his estate were granted to his widow, Joan Jones.

The ship's surgeon on the *Mayflower* was one Giles Heale, who, with John Carver and "Christopher Joanes," witnessed the nuncupative will of William Mullins of Dorking, one of the Pilgrims who died on board in the sickness of that first winter. The *Mayflower* was in poor trim when she lay at Rotherhithe in 1624, and was valued, with her "one suit of worn sails" and her fittings, at £138 8*s*. Whether she was made seaworthy again and was the same *Mayflower* which carried other colonists to New England, does not certainly appear.[1] On her voyage in 1620 she carried a Master Gunner and some good ordnance, designed for the defence of the Planters. One of her crew died on the outward voyage. In addition to her ordinary ship's company and the Pilgrim passengers the *Mayflower* carried five hired men, one of whom was John Alden, "hired for a cooper at Southampton . . . a hopeful young man." He elected to stay in the colony, and married Priscilla Mullins. The other four were sailors, John Allerton, "reputed one of the company," and Thomas English, engaged to be the Master of their shallop at New Plymouth for coasting and fishing (these two died in the first sickness), William Trevore and one Ellis, both of whom were "hired to stay a year in the country," but returned when their time was out. Trevore pitched some fine yarns about New England when he got back to London. His reports stimulated interest in the colonization of those parts. These four extra seamen would be a help in working the *Mayflower* on her passage out.

Wherever the Englishman goes there goes his dog, and the *Mayflower* had dogs aboard. There is no mention of goats or swine or poultry. It is possible that a couple of goats were carried, as the Planters had a herd of goats in 1623, when Bradford and Allerton wrote from Plymouth that goats "will

[1] Dr. Rendel Harris thinks she was the same.—*Last of the Mayflower*, 1920, p. 48.

here thrive very well . . . and live at no charge ether wenter or sommer . . . also they are much more easily transported . . . then other kattle, yet tow of those which came last dyed by the way." But I fancy these were not on the *Mayflower*, as the colonists had their minds intent upon fishing at the outset. Not till the spring of 1624 had the Planters any neat cattle. Then Edward Winslow took back with him three heifers and a bull, and Bradford's anticipation that "it might be a good benefite after some encrease that they might be able to spare some to others that should have thoughts this way," [1] was amply verified. The trade in cattle was a main source of wealth to Plymouth Plantation in after days.

Of course the greatest of the assets carried on the *Mayflower* were not the stores for the Plantation, but the intangible cargo. The Planters went out with wives and children. They went to found homes, not to seek fortunes. There were Pilgrim Mothers in the company skilled in all the arts of housewifery. These English folk carried their language, their laws, their traditions, and their native capacity for orderly administration with them. They were deeply religious, and their convictions in matters of religion had been tempered to a fine edge by the experiences through which they had passed and by the wise guidance of John Robinson, their pastor. Nor must we forget the broadening effect which ten years' residence in Leyden had wrought upon the civic and political ideals of their leaders. Narrow in some respects they were, it is true, when judged from the modern standpoint. They were severely Biblical. They had their share of cranky people. But *for their time* they had a remarkable breadth of view. They sought liberty, indeed, for themselves first, but they already had their faces set in the direction which would lead them in time to grant that liberty to others.

[1] Letter of Bradford and Allerton, September 8, 1623, in Public Record Office. For information as to the *Mayflower* see an article by R. G. Marsden in the *English Historical Review*, October 1904.

CHAPTER XXII

THE SAILING—ROBINSON'S LETTER OF ADVICE—ROBERT CUSHMAN'S LETTER—THE "MAYFLOWER'S" VOYAGE

THE time of parting from the Leyden friends at length arrived. It was with a wrench that they said farewell at the waterside in Delftshaven. With tears and choking voices, and many "lively and true expressions of dear and unfeigned love," they separated. Some of the members of Ainsworth's Church at Amsterdam had also come over to wish them Godspeed, and sundry Dutch strangers, who stood on the quay as spectators, were deeply moved by the scene.

> "The tide," says Bradford, "which stays for no man, calling them away that were thus loth to depart, their Reverend Pastor falling down on his knees, and they all with him, with watery cheeks, commended them with most fervent prayers to the Lord and his blessing. And then, with mutual embraces and many tears, they took their leaves one of another, which proved to be the last leave to many of them."

Bradford notes in the margin of his *History* that the date of the sailing of the *Speedwell* was "about 22nd of July." This was a Saturday, and with a favouring wind they made a quick passage to Southampton, "where they found the bigger ship come from London, lying ready, with all the rest of their Company." Thomas Prince tells us the *Mayflower* "had been waiting there with Master Cushman seven days." Cushman, then, for his part, was up to time.

Further delays now followed. For one thing, the

Speedwell was not in fit trim for the Atlantic voyage, and had to be overhauled: for another, it was important to come to some definite understanding with the general body of Adventurers about the *Conditions* on which the Planters or Colonists joined in the venture, and this involved more discussion. They evidently expected the leading Adventurers would come down to Southampton to attend a joint meeting to settle the terms. Apparently only Thomas Weston turned up, and he came not to discuss, but to get their signatures to the altered *Conditions.* I take it that Robinson had advised them on no account to consent to the new terms, for they refused to sign, and told Weston—

"He knew right well that these were not according to the first *Agreement.* Neither could they yield to them without the consent of the rest that were behind, and, indeed, they had special charge when they came away, from the Chief of those that were behind, not to do it. At which he was much offended, and told them, 'they must then look to stand on their own legs,' so he returned in displeasure."

The Pilgrim company wrote a letter from Southampton to the "Merchants and Adventurers," explaining the position of affairs. They did not wish to be thought unreasonable—

August 3rd, *anno* 1620.

"Beloved Friends,

"Sorry we are that there should be occasion of writing at all unto you, partly because we ever expected to see the most of you here, but especially because there should any difference at all be conceived between us. But seeing it falleth out that we cannot confer together, we think it meet, though briefly, to show you the just cause and reason of our differing from those *Articles* last made by Robert Cushman, without our consideration or knowledge. And though he might propound good ends to himself [in so doing] yet it no way justifies his doing it.

"Our main difference is in the Fifth and Ninth Articles concerning the dividing, or holding, of house and lands, the enjoying whereof, some of yourselves well know, was one special motive amongst many others to provoke us to go. This was thought so reasonable, that when the greatest of you in adventure [Thomas Weston], whom we have much cause to respect, when he propounded *Conditions* to us [at Leyden] freely of his own accord, he set this down for one. A copy whereof we have sent unto you, with some additions then added by us, which being liked on both sides, and a day set for the payment of monies, those of Holland paid in theirs.

"After that, Robert Cushman, Master [John] Peirce, and Master Martin brought them into a better form, and writ them in a book now extant and upon Robert's showing them [*i. e.* on Robert Cushman showing them to Mullins] and delivering Master [William] Mullins a copy thereof under his hand, which we have, he paid in his money.

"And we of Holland had never seen other before our coming to Hampton but only as one got, for himself, a private copy of them. Upon sight whereof, we manifested utter dislike, but had put off [sold] our estates, and were ready to come; and therefore it was too late to reject the voyage. Judge, therefore, we beseech you, indifferently [impartially] of things; and if a fault have been committed, lay it where it is, and not upon us, who have more cause to stand for the one [set of *Conditions*] than you have for the other [altered *Conditions*].

"We never gave Robert Cushman commission to make any one Article for us, but only sent him to receive monies upon *Articles* before agreed on, and to further the provisions [preparations] till John Carver came, and to assist him in it.

"Yet, since you conceive yourselves wronged as well as we, we thought meet to add a branch to the end of our Ninth Article, as will almost heal that wound of itself, which you conceive to be in it.

"But that it may appear to all men that we are not lovers of ourselves only, but desire also the good and enriching of [you] our friends, who have adventured your monies with our persons; we have added our [?one] last Article to the rest, promising you again by letters in behalf of the whole Company—

> "That if large profits should not arise within the Seven Years, that we will continue together longer with you, if the Lord give a blessing.

This, we hope, is sufficient to satisfy any in this case, especially friends, since we are assured that if the whole charge were divided into four parts [the Adventurers or Shareholders], of three of them would not stand upon it [the alteration in the *Conditions*], neither do regard it, etc.

"We are in such a strait at present as we are forced to sell away £60 of our provisions to clear the haven, and withal put ourselves upon great extremities, scarce having any butter, no oil, not a sole to mend a shoe, nor every man a sword to his side, wanting many muskets, much armour, etc. And yet we are willing to expose ourselves to such imminent dangers as are like to ensue, and trust to the good providence of God rather than his name and truth should be evil spoken of, for us.

"Thus saluting all of you in love, and beseeching the Lord to give a blessing to our endeavour, and keep all our hearts in the bonds of peace and love, we take leave, and rest,

"Yours, etc."

This letter was "subscribed with many names of the Chiefest of the Company."

Robinson's Parting Counsel

After they had at length despatched all their business and were ready to leave Southampton, the company was called together to listen to a letter from John Robinson, giving them helpful advice as to the manner and spirit it would befit them to show in their great adventure. They were to display a loving forbearance; they were to avoid taking offence at trifles, and were to subordinate their own interests to the general good of the society to which they belonged. Robinson refers to this "large letter" in a short private communication to his brother-in-law, John Carver, which may first be read—

"My dear Brother,

"I received enclosed your last letter and note of information, which I shall carefully keep and make use of, as there shall be occasion. I have a true feeling of your perplexity of mind and toil of body, but I hope that you, having always been able so plentifully to administer comfort unto others in their trials are so well furnished for yourself, as that far greater difficulties than you have yet undergone (though I conceive them to be great enough) cannot oppress you, though they press you as the apostle speaketh. 'The spirit of a man (sustained by the Spirit of God) will sustain his infirmities' (Prov. xviii. 14). I doubt not so will yours, and the better much, when you shall enjoy the presence and help of so many godly and wise brethren for the bearing of part of your burden; who also will not admit into their hearts the least thought of suspicion of any the least negligence, at least, presumption, to have been in you, whatsoever they think of others.

"Now, what shall I say, or write unto you, and your good wife, my loving sister? Even only this, I desire, and always shall, mercy and blessing unto you from the Lord as unto my own soul, and assure yourself that my heart is with you and that I will not foreslow my bodily coming at the first opportunity.

"I have written a large letter to the whole, and am sorry I shall not rather speak than write to them, and the more considering the want of a preacher, which I shall also make some spur to my hastening towards you.

"I do ever commend my best affection unto you, which, if I thought you made any doubt of, I would express in more and the same more ample and full words.

"And the Lord, in whom you trust, and whom you serve, ever in this business and journey, guide you with his hand, protect you with his wing, and show you and us his salvation in the end, and bring us in the meanwhile together in the place desired (if such be his good will), for his Christ's sake. Amen.

"Yours,
"JOHN ROBINSON.

"July 27, 1620."[1]

Of the "large letter" we have three versions, one printed in what is known as *Mourt's Relation* in 1622, one given in Bradford's *History* and a third in Nathaniel Morton's *New England's Memorial*, based on Bradford. The first gives the best text. Doubtless it would be read to the assembled company by William Brewster. It shows us incidentally that the

[1] I take this date to be new style. If this is so the letter was probably written in view of the departure of the *Speedwell* and sent by her. Catherine Carver was very likely already in England with her husband.

form of government under which they were to order themselves had been carefully discussed. The democratic principles familiar in their Church order were to be applied to their civil government, and the voice of the majority was to regulate their public affairs. They were to initiate a bold experiment for which their close association in Church life had prepared them. The introduction of a contingent from London and Essex into the society, however, called for all the more care in ordering their estate, so that the new elements might be safely and securely absorbed into the general body. In *Mourt's Relation* the authorship of this letter is not stated. Initials only, "I. R.," are given. The prejudice against Robinson on the part of bigoted religionists was too strong to be stirred up without good warrant.

"Certain USEFUL ADVERTISEMENTS sent in a LETTER written by a discreet FRIEND unto the PLANTERS in New England, at their first setting sail from Southampton, who earnestly desireth the Prosperity of that, their new, PLANTATION

"LOVING AND CHRISTIAN FRIENDS,

"I do heartily, and in the Lord, salute you all: as being they with whom I am present in my best affection, and most earnest longings after you, though I be constrained, for a while, to be bodily absent from you. I say, constrained: God knowing how willingly much rather than otherwise, I would have borne my part with you in this first brunt, were I not, by strong necessity, held back for the present. Make account of me in the mean while, as of a man divided in myself, with great pain, and as, natural bonds set aside, having my better part with you.

"And though I doubt not but, in your godly wisdoms, you both foresee, and resolve upon, that which concerneth your present state and condition, both severally and jointly; yet have I thought [it] but my duty, to add some further spur of provocation unto them who run already, if not because you need it, yet because I owe it in love and duty.

"[1] And first, as we are daily to renew our repentance with our God, special, for our sins known, and general, for our unknown trespasses: so doth the Lord call us, in a singular manner, upon occasions of such difficulty and danger as lieth upon you, to a both more narrow search, and careful reformation, of our ways in his sight, lest he (calling to remembrance our sins forgotten by us, or unrepented of) take advantage against us; and, in judgment, leave us for the same to be swallowed up in one danger or other. Whereas, on the contrary, sin being taken away by earnest repentance, and pardon thereof from the Lord sealed up unto a man's conscience by his Spirit, great shall be his security and peace in all dangers, sweet his comforts in all distresses, with happy deliverance from all evil, whether in life or in death.

"[2] Now next after this heavenly peace with God and our own consciences, we are carefully to provide for peace with all men, what in us lieth, especially with our associates: and, for that end, watchfulness must be had, that we neither at all in ourselves do give, no, nor easily take offence being given by others. Woe be unto the World for offences! For though it be necessary (considering the malice of Satan, and man's corruption) that offences come; yet woe unto the man, or woman either, by whom the offence cometh! said Christ (Matt. xviii. 7). And if offences, in the unseasonable use of things in themselves indifferent, be more to be feared than death itself, as the Apostle teacheth (1 Cor. ix. 15), how much more in things simply evil, in which neither honour of God, nor love of man, is thought worthy to be regarded.

"Neither yet is it sufficient that we keep ourselves, by the grace of God, from giving offence; except withal, we be armed against the taking of them, when they are given by others. For how unperfect and lame is the work of grace in that person who wants charity to cover a multitude of offences, as the Scriptures speak.

"Neither are you to be exhorted to this grace, only upon the common grounds of Christianity, which are, That persons ready to take offence, either want charity to cover offences, or wisdom duly to weigh human frailty; or lastly, are gross, though close, hypocrites, as Christ our Lord teacheth (Matt. vii. 1, 2, 3). As indeed, in mine own experience, few or none have been found, which sooner give offence, than such as easily take it; neither have they ever proved sound and profitable members in societies, which have nourished in themselves that touchy humour.

"[3] But, besides these, there are divers special motives provoking you, above others, to great care and conscience this way.

"As, first, you are, many of you, strangers as to the

persons so to the infirmities one of another, and so stand in need of more watchfulness this way, lest when such things fall out in men and women as you suspected not, you be inordinately affected with them, which doth require at your hands much wisdom and charity for the covering and preventing of incident offences that way.

"And, lastly, your intended course of Civil Community will minister continual occasion of offence, and will be as fuel for that fire, except you diligently quench it with brotherly forbearance. And if taking offence causelessly, or easily, at men's doings be so carefully to be avoided, how much more heed is to be taken that we take not offence at God himself, which yet we certainly do, so oft as we do murmur at his Providence in our crosses, or bear impatiently such afflictions as wherewith he pleaseth to visit us. Store we up therefore patience against the evil day! without which, we take offence at the Lord himself in his holy and just works.

"[4] A fourth thing there is carefully to be provided for, to wit, That with common employments, you join common affections truly bent upon the general good, avoiding (as a deadly plague of your both common and special comfort) all retiredness of mind for proper [*i. e.* for one's own personal] advantage, and all [persons] singularly affected any manner of way. Let every man repress in himself, and the whole body, in each person (as so many rebels against the common good) all private respects of men's selves not sorting with the general conveniency! And as men are careful not to have a new house shaken with any violence before it be well settled, and the parts firmly knit, so be you, I beseech you, brethren, much more careful that the House of God, which you are, and are to be, be not shaken with unnecessary novelties, or other oppositions, at the first settling thereof.

"[5] Lastly, whereas you are to become a Body Politic, using amongst yourselves Civil Government, and are not furnished with any persons of special eminency above the rest to be chosen by you into Office of Government, let your wisdom and godliness appear, not only in choosing such persons as do entirely love, and will diligently promote, the common good; but also in yielding unto them all due honour and obedience in their lawful administrations. Not beholding in them the ordinariness of their persons, but God's ordinance for your good, nor being like unto the foolish multitude, who more honour the gay coat than either the virtuous mind of the man, or glorious ordinance of the Lord.

"But you know better things, and that the Image of the

Lord's power and authority, which the Magistrate beareth, is honourable in how mean persons soever. And this duty you both may the more willingly, and ought the more conscionably to perform, because you are, at least for the present, to have only them for your ordinary Governors which yourselves shall make choice of for that work.

"[Conclusion] Sundry other things of importance I could put you in mind of, and of those before mentioned in more words, but I will not so far wrong your godly minds, as to think you heedless of these things, there being also divers among you so well able to admonish both themselves and others, of what concerneth them.

"These few things, therefore, and the same in few words, I do earnestly commend unto your care and conscience, joining therewith my daily incessant prayers unto the Lord, that he (who hath made the heavens and the earth, the sea and all rivers of water, and whose Providence is over all his works, especially over all his dear children for good) would so guide and guard you in your ways (as inwardly by his Spirit, so outwardly by the hand of his power) as that both you, and we also for and with you, may have after matter of praising his name, all the days of your, and our, lives.

"Fare you well in him in whom you trust, and in whom I rest!

"An unfeigned well-willer of your happy success in this hopeful voyage,

"I[OHN] R[OBINSON]."

This letter "had good acceptation with all and after fruit with many." It is not too much to say that some part of Bradford's own charitableness in judgment and equable temper in the face of many provocations was due to the influence of John Robinson upon his character, exerted through such teaching as this letter embodies. The need and pertinence of the advice here given is made manifest by the letter of Robert Cushman from Dartmouth quoted below.

The Pilgrims had occasion at once to exercise the power of election to which Robinson refers. They "chose a Governor and two or three Assistants for each ship to order the people by the way and see to the disposing of the provisions and such-like affairs."

At last they weighed anchor and dropped down

Southampton Water to the Channel, " about the 5th of August." But they had not got far on their voyage before Reynolds, Master of the *Speedwell*, reported that she was so leaky that he durst not face the open sea with her till she was mended. Christopher Jones, the Master of the *Mayflower*, was consulted, and it was resolved to put into Dartmouth. Here the *Speedwell* was " thoroughly searched from stem to stern," and some leaks repaired. All this meant loss of time, further expense to the Pilgrims, and loss of a favourable wind. While the repairs were in execution at Dartmouth, Cushman wrote a long letter to Edward Southworth in London. He felt impelled to pour out an account of their troubles to some sympathetic ear. It was a grief to Cushman that they started on their venture under a cloud of misunderstanding and ill-feeling between Weston and other of the Adventurers and themselves. The poor man was ill and disheartened. Here is his vivid letter—

" To his loving friend, Ed. S., at Henige House, in the Duke Place, these—

" Loving Friend,

" My most kind remembrance to you, and your wife,[1] with loving E. M.,[2] etc., whom in this world I never look to see again. For, besides the eminent dangers of this voyage, which are no less than deadly, an infirmity of body hath seized me, which will not in all likelihood leave me till death. What to call it, I know not. But it is a bundle of

[1] Southworth married Alice Carpenter on May 28, 1613, at Leyden. He was now living at Heneage House in Duke's Place, Aldgate Ward, London. The house had belonged to the Abbots of Bury St. Edmunds, and had passed from them to Thomas Heneage. It had a special advantage for Separatists, for it stood in the parish of the Priory of Holy Trinity. This religious house was dissolved in 1531 and granted to Sir Thomas Audley, through whose daughter it came to Thomas, Duke of Norfolk. Hence the title Duke's Place. Those dwelling there, says Stow, " became utterly destitute of any parish church," so the Separatists in that parish escaped indictment under the Act enforcing attendance at one's parish church. A new church, built on the site of the old Priory, was consecrated January 2, 1622, by George Abbot, assisted by Sir Henry Martin, the Bishop's Vicar-General in Spirituals.

[2] I think these initials refer to Experience Mitchell.

lead, as it were, crushing my heart more and more these fourteen days, as that, although I do the actions of a living man, yet I am but as dead. But the will of God be done!

"Our pinnace will not cease leaking, else, I think, we had been half way at Virginia. Our voyage hither hath been so full of crosses as ourselves have been of crookedness. We put in here to trim her, and I think, as others also, if we had stayed at sea but three or four hours more she would have sunk right down. And though she was twice trimmed at Hampton, yet now she is as open and leaky as a sieve, and there was a board, two feet long, a man might have pulled off with his fingers, where the water came in as at a mole hole.

"We lay at Hampton seven days in fair weather, waiting for her, and now we lie here waiting for her in as fair a wind as can blow, and so have done these four days, and are like to lie four more,[1] and by that time the wind will happily [haply] turn, as it did at Hampton. Our victuals will be half eaten up, I think, before we go from the coast of England, and if our voyage last long, we shall not have a month's victuals when we come in the country.

"Near £700 hath been bestowed at Hampton upon what I know not. Master Martin[2] saith, He neither can, nor will give any account of it. And if he be called upon for accounts, he crieth out of unthankfulness for his pains and care, that we are suspicious of him, and flings away, and will end nothing. Also he so insulteth over our poor people with such scorn and contempt, as if they were not good enough to wipe his shoes. It would break your heart to see his dealing, and the mourning of our people. They complain to me, and alas, I can do nothing for them. If I speak to him, he flies in my face as mutinous, and saith, 'No complaints shall be heard or received but by himself,' and saith, 'They are froward and waspish, discontented people, and I do ill to hear them.'

"There are others that would lose all they have put in, or make satisfaction for what they have had, that they might depart; but he will not hear them, nor suffer them to go ashore lest they should run away.

[1] Four days more would bring them to August 21. Captain John Smith, in *New England's Trials*, says, "They left the coast of England on August 23."

[2] Bradford, on inserting this letter into his *History*, gives this note on Martin: "He was Governor in the bigger ship and Master Cushman Assistant." As Cushman had remitted the money "adventured" in London to Martin at Southampton he wanted an account.

"The sailors also are so offended at his ignorant boldness in meddling and controlling in things he knows not what belongs to, as that some threaten to mischief him. Others say they will leave the ship, and go their way. But at the best, this cometh of it, that he makes himself a scorn and laughing-stock unto them.

"As for Master Weston, except grace do greatly sway with him, he will hate us ten times more than ever he loved us, for not confirming the *Conditions.* But now since some pinches have taken them, they [*i. e.* the opponents of the altered *Conditions*] begin to reveal the truth and say, Master Robinson was in the fault,[1] who charged them never to consent to those *Conditions* nor choose me into Office; but, indeed, appointed them to choose them they did choose. But he and they will rue too late. They may now see, and all be ashamed when it is too late, that they were so ignorant, yea, and so inordinate in their courses. I am sorry, as they were resolved not to seal those *Conditions,* I was not so resolute at Hampton [as] to have left the whole business, except they would seal them. And better the voyage to have broken off then, than to have brought such misery to ourselves, dishonour to God, and detriment to our loving friends, as now it is like to do.

"Four or five of the Chief of them which came from Leyden, came resolved never to go on those *Conditions.* And Master Martin, he said, '*He* never received no money on those *Conditions.* He was not beholden to the Merchants for a pin. They were bloodsuckers,' and I know not what. Simple man! He, indeed, never made any *Conditions* with the Merchants, nor ever spake with them. But did all that money[2] fly to Hampton or was it his own?

"[*Firstly*]—Who will go and lay out money so rashly and lavishly as he did, and never know how he comes by it, or on what conditions?

"*Secondly*—I told him of the alteration long ago, and he was content.

"But now he domineers, and said, I had betrayed them into the hands of slaves! He is not beholden to them! He can set out two ships himself to a voyage! When, good man! he hath but £50 in [*i. e.* invested in this

[1] Bradford adds a note here: "I think he was deceived in these things." Robinson was clearly opposed to the altered *Conditions,* but he would hardly nominate in Leyden those to be elected into office on shipboard at Southampton.

[2] The £700 invested by the London merchants and remitted by Cushman to Martin and Carver.

venture], and if he should give up his accounts, he would not have a penny left him,[1] as I am persuaded, etc.

"Friend, if ever we make a Plantation God works a miracle! specially considering how scant we shall be of victuals, and, most of all, ununited amongst ourselves and devoid of good tutors and regiment. Violence will break all. Where is the meek and humble spirit of Moses? and of Nehemiah, who re-edified the walls of Jerusalem, and the State of Israel? Is not the sound of Rehoboam's brags daily heard amongst us? Have not the philosophers and all wise men observed that, even in settled Common Wealths, violent Governors bring, either themselves or people, or both, to ruin? How much more in the raising of Common Wealths, when the mortar is yet scarce tempered that should bind the walls?

"If I should write to you of all things which promiscuously forerun our ruin, I should overcharge my weak head and grieve your tender heart: only this I pray you, Prepare for evil tidings of us, every day! But pray for us instantly! It may be the Lord will be yet intreated, one way or other, to make for us. I see not, in reason, how we shall escape, even the gasping of hunger-starved persons, but God can do much, and his will be done!

"It is better for me to die, than now for me to bear it, which I do daily, and expect it hourly, having received the sentence of death, both within me and without me. Poor William Ring and myself do strive who shall be meat first for the fishes; but we look for a glorious resurrection, knowing Christ Jesus after the flesh no more, but looking unto the joy that is before us, we will endure all these things and account them light in comparison of that joy we hope for.

"Remember me in all love to our friends as if I named them, whose prayers I desire earnestly and wish again to see, but not till I can, with more comfort, look them in the face. The Lord give us that true comfort which none can take from us!

"I had a desire to make a brief Relation of our estate to some friend. I doubt not but your wisdom will teach you seasonably to utter things, as hereafter you shall be called to it. That which I have written is true, and many things more, which I have foreborne. I write it as upon my life

[1] Bradford notes here in the margin, "This was found true afterward." In *A Relation . . . of the Proceedings of the English Plantation . . . at Plymouth*, 1622, we read: "Saturday, January 6 [1621], Master Martin was very sick, and to our judgment no hope of life, so Master Carver was sent for to come aboard to speak with him, about his Accounts."

and last confession in England. What is of use to be spoken of presently, you may speak of it, and what is fit to conceal, conceal! Pass by my weak manner! for my head is weak, and my body feeble. The Lord make me strong in him, and keep both you and yours!

"Your loving friend,

"ROBERT CUSHMAN.

"*Dartmouth*,

"*August* 17, 1620."

The repairs at Dartmouth being finished, they again put to sea, and the two vessels kept together well out into the Atlantic; but again the *Speedwell* proved leaky—"they could scarce free her with much pumping." Jones and Reynolds, after consultation, resolved that both ships should "bear up back again and put into Plymouth." The fact that the *Mayflower*, having got thus far, did not proceed with her voyage, but turned back with the *Speedwell*, indicates that the latter was in a dangerous condition, and that it was desirable to stand by her to render help in case of need. The root of the trouble seems to have been that the *Speedwell* was not in fit trim for the Atlantic voyage. She was overmasted, and when her canvas was spread the strain on the hull was too great and opened her timbers. After she was sold and put back into her former trim she made many profitable voyages in safety. It is also alleged that Reynolds and his crew were none too eager to face the voyage, as they were hired to stay with the Planters in New England for a year.

The two little ships made Plymouth Sound without mishap and came up into Sutton Pool, where the *Speedwell* was searched, but no special leak could be found. It was concluded she was not equal to the voyage, and accordingly it was resolved to send her back to London with those least willing and least fit "to bear the brunt of this hard adventure." Robert Cushman and William Ring were amongst those who returned. "Thus, like Gideon's army, this small number was divided, as if the Lord, by this work of his providence, thought these few too many for the great work he had to do." Such of the stores as could be stowed in the *Mayflower* were transferred to her, together with some of the passengers from the *Speedwell*. The *Mayflower* thus had one hundred and two souls, men, women and children, belonging to this "Pilgrim company," crowded between her decks, besides the Master, Christopher Jones; the ship's surgeon, Giles Heale; the two pilots, and the crew. She was dangerously crowded, and it was a mercy that sickness did not break out on board. So far as we know only one of the crew died on the voyage, and one of the Pilgrim company, William Butten, a man-servant, died as they drew "near the coast." To Elizabeth Hopkins, wife of Stephen Hopkins, was born a son on the *Mayflower*, to whom the name Oceanus was given.

I am confident that Jones and his pilots would take the opportunity of their enforced visit to the port of Plymouth to make inquiry of the seamen and ship-masters there about the coast and harbours of the New England shore for which they were bound. Captain Dermer had returned to Plymouth, in Devon, from the very district where the *Mayflower* was shortly to make her landfall, but a few months before this time. It is not impossible that Carver, a quiet, undemonstrative, but far-seeing man, who could keep his own counsel, gained some information from friends in Plymouth about the locality visited by Dermer, where the Pilgrims eventually seated themselves. If the Hudson River district, at which they aimed, should prove impracticable this other region might afford them a home.

The Second, or Plymouth Virginia Company, to which some of the leading men in Plymouth, Devon, belonged, was interested in these more northerly parts of the American coast, and the question of the most fitting destination for the Pilgrims was bound to be discussed amongst them. One man in Plymouth, we may be sure, was interested in the *Mayflower* and

MEMORIAL STONE ON THE BARBICAN JETTY AT PLYMOUTH, DEVON.

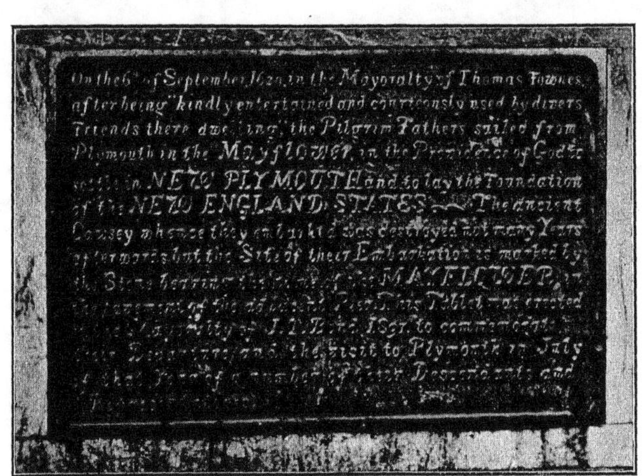

TABLET COMMEMORATING THE SAILING OF THE "MAYFLOWER" FROM PLYMOUTH.

her venture, and that was David Thomson, a Scot by birth, but domiciled in Plymouth. He married Amyas Colle at St. Andrew's, Plymouth, July 18, 1613. He secured a grant, November 16, 1622, of 6000 acres in New England, and a month later contracted with the Plymouth merchants, Abraham Colmer, Nicholas Sherwill and Leonard Pomeroy, for the transport of himself and five of his men on the *Jonathan* and the *Providence* to New England. He settled at the mouth of the Piscataqua River. Abraham Jennens,[1] of Plymouth, was also interested in the New England trade and seated a plantation at Monhegan Isle in 1622. Did these friends talk matters over with Carver and Brewster?

At last, according to their own relation, on—

"Wednesday, the sixth of September, the wind coming East-North-East, a fine small gale, we loosed from Plymouth, having been kindly entertained and courteously used by divers friends there dwelling, and, after many difficulties in boisterous storms, at length, by God's providence, upon the 9th of November following, by break of the day, we espied land, which we deemed to be Cape Cod, and so afterward it proved."

They thus made their landfall far to the north of the territory over which the First, or London Virginia Company, had jurisdiction, and for which their "patent" was drawn. They accordingly tacked and put to the southward, "to find some place about Hudson's River for their habitation." But the *Mayflower* soon got into dangerous waters off Monamoy Point, and it was resolved to bear up again for the Cape. If the map of the New England coast drawn by Captain John Smith is consulted, it will be seen that the eastern shore of the Cape Cod peninsula below its northern point is not charted. These were strange waters, and Jones prudently put about and got the *Mayflower* round the Cape into the snug harbour

[1] Apparently his son, *Gulielmus Jennens, Anglus, Plimutensis,* matriculated at Leyden University November 1, 1628.

encircled by its hook-like terminal promontory. Smith had marked this bay upon his map as " Milford hauen "; it is now known as Provincetown Harbour. The eyes of the Pilgrims were refreshed with the sight of land; there would be eagerness to get ashore; the season of the year was late; it was needful to act at once if any shelter against the winter was to be provided, but the coast upon which they now rested their eyes was in territory covered by the charter of the Second, or Plymouth Virginia Company, to which their "patent" gave them no rights. Moreover, there were indications that some of the party were " not well affected to unity." They " gave some appearance of faction." To be boxed up together on shipboard for a long voyage is a bit trying, even for saints. What was to be done? With the Englishman's usual genius for ordered self-government, and with the words of Robinson, " you are to become a Body Politic, using amongst yourselves Civil Government," still fresh in their memory, they met in the cabin of the *Mayflower* and entered into a memorable compact. They were equal now to the work of erecting a Commonwealth as they had been equal to the task of building themselves by covenant, in 1606, into a Church of Christ—

> " It was thought good there should be an Association and Agreement that we should combine together in one body, and to submit to such Government and Governors as we should, by common consent, agree to make and choose."

So the following document was drawn up and signed—

> " In the name of God, Amen. We, whose names are underwritten, the loyal subjects of our dread Sovereign Lord King James, by the grace of God, of Great Britain, France, and Ireland King, Defender of the Faith, etc.
>
> " Having undertaken for the glory of God, and advancement of the Christian faith, and honour of our King and country a Voyage to plant the first Colony in the northern parts of Virginia do, by these presents, solemnly and mutually,

in the presence of God and one of another, covenant and combine ourselves together into a CIVIL BODY POLITIC for our better ordering and preservation, and furtherance of the ends aforesaid, and by virtue hereof to enact, constitute, and frame such just and equal laws, ordinances, acts, constitutions, offices, from time to time, as shall be thought most meet and convenient for the general good of the COLONY, unto which we promise all due submission and obedience.

"In witness whereof, we have hereunder subscribed our names. Cape Cod, 11th of November, in the year of the reign of our Sovereign Lord King James, of England, France, and Ireland, 18 and of Scotland 54. Anno Domini 1620.

"John Carver
William Bradford
Edward Winslow
William Brewster
Isaac Allerton
Miles Standish
John Alden
Samuel Fuller
Christopher Martin
William Mullins
William White
Richard Warren
John Howland
Stephen Hopkins
Edward Tilly
John Tilly
Francis Cooke
Thomas Rogers
Thomas Tinker
John Ridgdale
Edward Fuller
John Turner
Francis Eaton
James Chilton
John Craxton
John Billington
Moses Fletcher
John Goodman
Degory Priest
Thomas Williams
Gilbert Winslow
Edmund Margeson
Peter Brown
Richard Britteridge
George Soule
Richard Clarke
Richard Gardiner
John Allerton
Thomas English
Edward Dotey
Edward Leister."

The signatures of heads of families were evidently deemed sufficient to cover sons and men-servants. The question of woman's part in civil government had not yet risen above the horizon of politics. The women were covered by their husbands' names.

The drawing up and signing of this Compact must not be taken as an indication that these pioneers sought to dissociate themselves from the English State. Far from it. They desired the support of

England in their loneliness. As soon as the *Mayflower* arrived at London again, in May 1621, and reported as to the situation of the new Plantation, steps were taken to regularize the position of the Planters with regard to the English Government. The "grant" or "patent" taken from the London Virginia Company, with which they sailed, was of no use, so application was made to the authority having jurisdiction over the territory where they had seated themselves.

The position was somewhat complicated here in England also, because the Second, or Plymouth Virginia Company had been superseded, soon after the *Mayflower* left the shores of England, by a "Council for New England," constituted on November 3, 1620. To this Council, therefore, the London Adventurers interested in the Pilgrim Colony had to apply for a "patent" to give their Plantation a colourable legal standing. On June 1 such a "patent" was granted by the "Council for New England" to "John Peirce and his Associates," in behalf of the Adventurers and Planters. This document was sent off by the little ship *Fortune*, which carried Robert Cushman and a further small contingent of Leyden friends to join the new colony. She called at Plymouth on her way down Channel, and made a good passage, arriving at New Plymouth on November 9, 1621. This "patent" gave the colonists some sort of legal title and recognition by the English State. It secured them from the intrusion of interlopers, prevented other patentees from getting authority over them or dispossessing them, and gave them a ground of appeal to the English Government in case they were interfered with by Frenchmen, Spaniards or Dutchmen. They were still amenable to English law, and they themselves had the right of turning to the Courts of the Motherland for protection and redress of injuries.

CHAPTER XXIII

ROBINSON AND THE PLYMOUTH PLANTATION

It does not come within the scope of our study of the life and influence of John Robinson to deal in detail with the struggles and hardships of the Pilgrim Fathers in laying the foundations of their new colony. For that story the remarkable *History of Plimouth Plantation*, by William Bradford, one of the classic narratives in our tongue, should be consulted. Suffice it to say that after exploration the Pilgrims eventually fixed on Patuxet, or New Plymouth,[1] as the site of their settlement. They had no time to provide adequate protection against the rigours of the New England winter, and though the season was really a mild one as winters go in that region, yet, owing to sickness and exposure, no less than forty-seven of the colonists had died before the *Mayflower* left for the Homeland on April 5, 1621. Fortunately, the real leaders in the venture for the most part survived.

We can imagine the anxiety with which Robinson and the Leyden friends would await news of their brethren. With Robert Cushman it would be almost like hoping against hope to hear of their safety, and when the *Mayflower* got back into port he would send the letters she brought post-haste to Leyden.

When the *Fortune* sailed Cushman went with her and carried the following letter, addressed by Robinson to the portion of his flock in distant Plymouth. It

[1] The name *Plimouth* appears on the map of "New England observed and described by Captayn John Smith" in 1614, for this spot, and the Pilgrims retained it, noting the coincidence that Plymouth was the last port they left in Old England.

is one of the three letters that have survived from the "mail" she carried. Robinson was anxious to join his friends in the New World, but, like the good pastor he was, he felt responsible for the wives and children left behind at Leyden under his spiritual oversight. He recognized that the first contingent of his little army had won a victory over adverse circumstances, and, like a brave leader, he does not mourn unduly over losses, but comforts his brethren. He exhorts them to peace and unity. We do not know what the "token" of love sent by the Leyden friends was—perhaps a parcel of cloth or goods to meet the Pilgrims' special needs.

To the Church of God in Plymouth, New England

"Much-beloved Brethren,

"Neither the distance of place nor distinction of body, can at all either dissolve or weaken that bond of true Christian affection in which the Lord by his Spirit hath tied us together. My continual prayers are to the Lord for you; my most earnest desire is unto you; from whom I will not longer keep (if God will) than means can be procured to bring with me the wives and children of divers of you and the rest of your brethren, whom I could not leave behind me without great injury both to you and them, and offence to God and all men.

"The death of so many, our dear friends and brethren, oh! how grievous hath it been to you to bear, and to us to take knowledge of; which, if it could be mended with lamenting, could not sufficiently be bewailed; but we must go unto them, and they shall not return unto us. And how many, even of us, God hath taken away here, and in England, since your departure you may elsewhere take knowledge. But the same God has tempered judgment with mercy, as otherwise, so in sparing the rest, especially those by whose godly and wise government you may be, and (I know) are so much helped. In a battle it is not looked for but that divers should die; it is thought well for a side if it get the victory, though with the loss of divers, if not too many, or too great. God, I hope, hath given you the victory, after many difficulties, for yourselves and others; though I doubt not but many do and will remain for you and us all to strive with.

"Brethren, I hope I need not exhort you to obedience unto those whom God hath set over you in church and commonwealth, and to the Lord in them. It is a Christian's honour to give honour according to men's places; and his liberty to serve God in faith, and his brethren in love, orderly, and with a willing and free heart.

"God forbid! I should need to exhort you to peace, which is the bond of perfection, and by which all good is tied together, and without which it is scattered. Have peace with God first, by faith in his promises, good conscience kept in all things, and oft renewed by repentance, and so, one with another, for his sake who is, though three, one; and for Christ's sake, who is one, and as you are called by one Spirit to one hope.

"And the God of peace and grace and all goodness be with you, in all the fruits thereof plenteously upon your heads now, and for ever. All your brethren here remember you with great love; a general token whereof they have sent you.

"Yours ever in the Lord

"JNO ROBINSON.

"*Leyden, Holland, June* 30, *Anno* 1621."

When this letter was written the Leyden friends were not aware of the death of John Carver, the first "Governor" of the new Plantation. The colonists re-elected him to that office as "a man well approved amongst us,"[1] on March 23, 1621, some thirteen days before the *Mayflower* sailed for home. But a few weeks later he came in from working on the land complaining of his head, lay down, lost consciousness, and died in a few days. It was a grievous loss to the little colony. Carver's skill in husbandry and farm management, gained by his experience in earlier days at Sturton, would have been of great value to the Planters. A few weeks later, in June 1621, his widow, Catherine, the sister of Bridget Robinson the Pilgrim Pastor's wife, also died. They were not long divided. The records of the Church at Plymouth, in referring to Carver, say—

"This worthy gentleman was one of singular piety, and rare for humility, which appeared, as otherwise, so by his

[1] *A Relation or Journal . . . of the English Plantation . . . at Plymouth*, 1622.

great condescendency, whenas this miserable people were in great sickness, he shunned not to do very mean services for them—yea, the meanest of them. He bare a share likewise of their labor in his own person according as their great necessity required. Who, being one also of a considerable estate, spent the main part of it in this enterprise, and from first to last approved himself not only as their agent in the first transacting of things, but also all along to the period of his life, to be a pious, faithful, and very beneficial instrument. He deceased in the month of April in the year 1621, and is now reaping the fruit of his labor with the Lord."

While the *Fortune* lay at New Plymouth Cushman exercised his gifts on one Sunday in their meeting by preaching a sermon " On the Sin and Danger of Self-love," based on the text, " Let no man seek his own, but every man another's wealth." The subject was pertinent to the main object of Cushman's visit. He was the one man amongst them who was sincerely convinced that the communistic principle of ordering their society would be best for all concerned if given a fair trial. Unfortunately, Weston and other of the Adventurers in London made use of Cushman's strong convictions on this point to further their own prospects of personal gain. He was commissioned to get the assent of the colonists to the altered *Conditions* which they declined to sign at Southampton. In this he was successful. The great need in which the colonists stood of further supplies compelled them to assent to those hard terms in the hope and expectation of the good-will and continued support of the company of Adventurers and merchants in London.

The *Fortune* was loaded up with such goods as the colonists had managed to get ready for shipment, in spite of their hardships—clapboard, or rough-sawn timber, and some hogsheads of beaver skins. She sailed for home about December 11, 1621, carrying letters and a *Relation* of the Planters' proceedings, written by Bradford. As she drew near to the mouth of the Channel a French man-of-war, captained by Fontenau de Pennart, a Breton, took her as a prize. She and her company, thirteen souls all told, were detained thirteen days and then released, and with loss of some of their lading and personal belongings they got back to London on February 14, 1622. Thus Robinson would get further news of the distant section of his flock in New England.

In Weston's letter to Carver, sent by the *Fortune*, dated London, July 6, 1621, he said, "I pray you write instantly for Mr. Robinson to come to you." [1]

But Robinson's intention of joining them, with the rest of the Leyden Church, was frustrated, and mainly for two reasons.

First—on account of poverty. The Pilgrim company were not rich in this world's goods. They had not sufficient capital of their own to pay for the equipment and transportation of their Church as one body. Nor had they enough whole-hearted supporters in England with sufficient means to set them out. The fact that they had received support for the initial venture from sundry London merchants not of their religious fellowship was already involving them in difficulty. To some extent it put the Pilgrims in the power of these unsympathetic strangers.

Secondly—hostility to Robinson's convictions in regard to Church government and order was a great barrier in the way of his removal. There was an extraordinary and unreasonable prejudice against his religious movement on account of its affinity with "Brownism," which had been made odious to the public mind by ridiculous slanders. Brownism was the whipping-stock alike of Puritans and Prelatists. God forbid that respectable London merchants should do anything to further it—at a less rate than twenty per cent.!

Weston himself, who had promised to stand by the new colony, early contemplated breaking away, and for his greater gain starting a colony of his own. A letter of his, dated April 10, 1622, sent to New Plymouth by a fishing-vessel called the *Sparrow*, which

[1] Bradford, MS. *History*, fol. 67.

he and Beauchamp, a "salter," had bought and fitted out, reveals something of the feeling in London—

"Most of them [*i.e.* the Adventurers] are against ye sending of them of Leyden, for whose cause this bussines was first begune, and some of ye most religious (as m^r^. Greene by name) excepts against them, so y^t^ my advice is (you may follow it, if you please) that you forthwith break of [f] your joynte stock, which you have warente to doe both in law and conscience, for ye most parte of ye adventurers haue given way unto it by a former letter."[1]

When the *Charity* and the *Swan*, the vessels fitted out by Weston for his own new colony, arrived at New Plymouth, June 1622, they brought a letter sent privately by Cushman to Bradford, putting him on his guard against Weston and his people, but speaking hopefully of the prospect of their Leyden friends joining them.

"Our friends at Leyden are well, and will come to you as many as can this time. I hope all will turn to the best; wherefore I pray you be not discouraged, but gather up yourself to go through these difficulties cheerfully and with courage in that place wherein God hath set you, until the day of refreshing come. And the Lord God of sea and land bring us comfortably together again, if it may stand with his glory."

These hopes of Cushman were not realized in 1622, but the next year a further contingent from Leyden went out, though Robinson's way was still barred.

[1] Bradford, MS. *History*, fol. 75.

CHAPTER XXIV

OPPOSITION TO ROBINSON'S MIGRATION—HIS CONCERN FOR THE INDIANS—HIS LAST LETTERS

PREPARATIONS were in hand in the spring of 1623 for sending reinforcements and supplies to the infant colony. A letter was sent to the Planters, dated April 9, 1623, stating, "We have agreed with 2 merchants for a ship of 140 tunes called y^e^ *Anne* which is to be ready ye last of this month to bring 60 passengers and 60 tune of goods." The *Anne* arrived at Plymouth "about the later end of July and the *James* a fourthnight after."[1] The *Little James*, a fine new pinnace, was to remain in the colony for fishing and trade. By the *Anne* came a letter in which excuse is made for the absence of Robinson from the party.

"We have in this ship sent shuch women as were willing and ready to goe to their husbands and freinds, with their children, etc. We would not have you discontente, because we have not sent you more of your old freinds, and in spetiall (J. R.) him, on whom you most depend, farr be it from us to neclecte you, or contemne him. But as ye Intente was at first, so ye evente at last shall shew it that we will deal fairly, and squarly answer your expectations to the full."[2]

The initials J. R. placed by Bradford in the margin indicate the pastor of their Church. Among those who went out in the *Anne* and the *Little James* were George Morton and his family; Alice, the widow of Edward Southworth, who shortly after arrival was

[1] MS. letter of Bradford and Allerton, dated September 8, 1623, discovered by Mr. R. G. Marsden in Public Record Office.
[2] Bradford, MS. *History*, fol. 101.

married to William Bradford, and Experience Mitchell, together with two of William Brewster's daughters, "Patience" and "Fear" by name. William Hilton, Robert Hickes, Thomas Flavell and William Palmer, who had crossed in the *Fortune*, were now joined by their wives. Bridget Fuller, wife of the good deacon who sailed in the *Mayflower*, and Barbara, who became the second wife of Miles Standish, were also of this company, so there must have been a joyful reunion on the landing from the *Anne* and the *Little James*.

Bradford arranged with William Pierce, the master of the *Anne*, "to lade him back for a . 150 . pounds,"[1] and with her he sent "one of our honest freinds Edward Winslow by name . . . unto whom we refferr you in all partickulars . . . expecting his returne by the first fishing-shipes." In the letter from Bradford and Allerton, dated "Plimouth, September 8, 1623" (two days before the *Anne* sailed), they say—

"For our friends in Holland we much desired their company and have long expected the same. If we had had them in the stead of some others we are persuaded things would have been better than they are with us, for honest men will ever do their best endeavour, whilst others (though they be more able of body) will scarce by any means be brought to [do so]. But we know many of them [at Leyden] to be better able, either for labour or counsel than ourselves. And indeed if they should not come to us we would not stay [her]e, if we might gain never so much wealth. But we are glad to take knowledge of what you would write touch[ing] them, and like well of your purpose not to make the general body bigger, save only to furnish them with useful members for special faculties.

"Touching those *Articles of Agreement*, we have taken ourselves bound by them unto you, and you unto us. Being by Mr. Weston much pressed thereunto we gave Mr. Cochman [*i. e.* Robert Cushman] full commission to conclude and confirm the same with you. For anything further thereabout we refer you to our Messenger [Winslow]; though in any bond made or to be made between you and us we take our friends at Leyden to be comprehended in the same, and as

[1] MS. letter in the Public Record Office.

much interested as our selves; and their consents to be accordingly had. For though *we* be come first to this place, yet *they* are as principal in the action and they and we to be considered as one body." [1]

The return of the *Mayflower*, the *Fortune* and the *Anne* to London undoubtedly quickened interest in the colonization of New England, and the news from the Pilgrim colony led many to turn their eyes in that direction. There was something like a scramble to secure grants and patents for the more desirable sites for settlement. But with the increased popular interest, the opposition to Robinson amongst the Puritan and Anglican section of the Company of London Adventurers for Plymouth Plantation seems to have sensibly hardened.

Some of those who had gone over in the *Anne*—notably a little group of settlers under John Oldham—had gone on their own footing, as "particulars," to use Bradford's phrase, that is to say, they were not incorporated in the "general" company on the accepted conditions for a seven-years' co-partnership. They were received in a friendly manner and allotted lands, but sent home complaints, and some returned in discontent. They said, amongst other things, that in the Plymouth colony there was "wante of both the Sacrements." To this the colonists justly replied—

"The more is our greife that our pastor is kept from us, by whom we might Injoye them, for we used to haue the Lord's supper every saboth, and baptisme as often as ther was occasion of children to baptize." [2]

The opposition to Robinson is referred to in a letter from himself to William Brewster, written when Winslow was preparing to return from England to the colony. In it his judgment on the question of the Sacraments is given. It was his settled conviction

[1] MS. letter of Bradford and Allerton, 1623, in Public Record Office, London.

[2] Bradford's MS., *History*, fol. 112.

that they pertained to the ministerial office alone. Here is the letter—

"Loving and dear Friend and Brother,

"That which I most desire of God in regard of you, namely the continuance of your life and health and the safe coming of those sent unto you, that I most gladly hear of and praise God for the same. And I hope Mrs. Brewster's weak and decayed state of body will have some repairing by the coming of her daughters and the provisions in this and other ships sent, which I hear are made for you; which makes us with the more patience bear our languishing state, and the deferring of our desired transportation, which I call desired, rather than hoped for, whatsoever you are borne in hand with by others.

"For, first, there is no hope at all that I know nor can conceive of, of any new stock to be raised for that end; so that all must depend upon returns from you, in which are so many uncertainties, as that nothing with any certainty can thence be concluded.

"Besides, howsoever, for the present the Adventurers allege nothing but want of money, which is an invincible difficulty; yet if that be taken away by you, others without doubt will be found.

"For the better clearing of this, we must dispose the Adventurers into three parts; and of them some five or six (as I conceive) are absolutely bent for us above others. Other five or six are our bitter professed adversaries. The rest, being the body, I conceive to be honestly minded and lovingly also towards us; yet such as have others, namely the forward preachers nearer unto them than us, and whose course so far as there is any difference they would advance, rather than ours.

"Now what a hank these men [*i. e.* the forward Puritan preachers] have over the professors you know, and I persuade myself that for me, they, of all others are unwilling I should be transported, especially such as have an eye that way themselves, as thinking, if I come there, their market will be marred in many regards. And for these adversaries, if they have but half the wit to their malice, they will stop my course when they see it intended, for which this delaying serveth them very opportunely. And as one restie jade can hinder, by hanging back, more than two or three can (or will, at least if they be not very free) draw forward, so will it be in this case.

"A notable experiment of this they gave in your messenger's presence, constraining the Company to promise that none of the money now gathered should be expended or employed to the help of any of us [in Leyden] toward you [in New England].

"Now, touching the question propounded by you, I judge it not lawful for you; being a ruling elder (Rom. xii. 7–8 and 1 Tim. v. 17) as opposed to the elders that teach and labor in word and doctrine to which [office] the sacraments are annexed—to administer them, nor convenient if it were lawful.

"Whether any learned man will come unto you or not, I know not. If any do come you must *consilium capere in arena*.

"Be you most heartily saluted, and your wife with you, both from me and mine. Your God and ours, and the God of all his, bring us together if it be his will, and keep us in the meanwhile and always to his glory, and make us serviceable to his majesty and faithful to the end. Amen."

James Sherley [1] wrote to the colonists on January 25, 1623–4—

"We have some amongst vs which undoubtedly aime more at their owne private ends, and ye thwarting and opposing of some hear, and other worthy Instruments of God's glory elswher, then at ye general good and furtherance of this noble and laudable action." [2]

In transcribing the letter into his *History* Bradford explains who was the "Worthy Instrument" thus thwarted, by adding the note "he means m^r. Robinson."

The Puritan element amongst the London Adventurers succeeded in blocking the way for Robinson and in securing the transportation of a more pliant minister to the colony—one John Lyford. He struck Cushman as being "none of the most eminent and rare," and he says—

"About choosing him into office use your own liberty and discretion. He knows he is no officer among you, though

[1] The name is frequently given as Shirley, but he himself used the form Sherley. He was a goldsmith, and carried on a profitable business at the sign of "The Golden Horseshoe" on London Bridge. His town house was near by, in "Crooked Lane," a thoroughfare still bearing that name. Later on we have a glimpse of him in his house at "Clapham," to which he withdrew when the plague was hot, and there busied himself with the accounts of this Colonial venture.

[2] Bradford's MS., *History*, fol. 110.

perhaps custom and universality may make him forget himself. Mr. Winslow and myself gave way to his going to give content to some here; and we see no hurt in it, but only his great charge of children."

As a matter of fact, John Lyford [1] was one of those unctuous hypocrites who are too often found battening upon fervent religious movements. A sensual, unprincipled rogue, he was a disgrace to his profession. When aboard the *Charity* at Gravesend in readiness to sail, and while Winslow was busied about final preparations, Lyford's eye caught sight of two letters in the cabin. He slyly broke the seals of both, took copies and sealed them up again. One was a letter from Winslow addressed to Robinson at Leyden, telling him how their affairs stood in England on the eve of his return to New Plymouth. Lyford little thought that by the same trick played upon himself a few months later in warrantable circumstances, his own roguery would be exposed. On arrival at the colony, Lyford soon entered into intrigue with the discontented "particulars," who urged that "mr. Robinson and his company may not goe ouer, to our plantation, unless he and they will reconcile themselves to our church by a recantation under their hands, etc." [2]

Lyford sent home letters by the return of the ship *Charity* from New England in which he advised his partisans and backers in London—

"that ye Leyden company (Mr. Robinson and ye rest) must still be kepte back, or els all will be spoyled. And least any of them should be taken in priuatly somewher on ye coast of England (as it was feared might be done) they must chaing

[1] So far as I know, Lyford has not been identified. I fancy he was the John Lyforde of Magdalen College, Oxford, admitted B.A. December 16, 1597, licensed M.A. June 26, 1602, and that the correspondent in England to whom he wrote his disparaging account of the Pilgrim Church at Plymouth was John Pemberton from county Durham, who matriculated March 8, 1604-5, at Broadgate's Hall, Oxford. Cf. Clarke's *Register of the University of Oxford*, vol. ii. pp. 206, etc.

[2] Bradford's MS. *History*, fol. 134.

the mr of ye ship (mr. William peirce) and put another allso in Winslow's stead for marchante or els it would not be prevented."

Though the effort to impose "the French Discipline" or "Presbyterianism" or a modified "Anglicanism" upon the Church of the infant colony failed, the opposition to Robinson and his democratic principles of Church government was sufficiently strong to prevent his ever joining his friends and his flock in New England.

Robinson's Concern for the Indians

Robinson's missionary spirit and concern for the natives of America were evinced in one of the last of his letters that have come down to us. It will be remembered that Thomas Weston made an attempt to plant a colony at Wessagusset. His men were of the wrong stamp for colonizing, and soon got into difficulties with the Indians. This led to a general conspiracy against the English settlers, both at Wessagusset and at Plymouth. Through the friendliness of their ally "Massacoyte," the Plymouth Planters were warned. Let Bradford tell what followed—

"We went to reskew the lives of our countrie-men, whom we thought (both by nature and conscience) we were bound to deliver, as also to take vengeance of them [the Indians] for their villanie entended and determened against us, which never did them harme, weaiting only for opertunite to execute the same. But by the good providence of god they were taken in their owne snare, and ther wickednes came upon their own pate; we kild seven of the cheife of them, and the head of one of them stands still on our forte for a terror unto others." [1]

News of this affray was brought over by Winslow, and it caused Robinson much uneasiness. His letter of remonstrance does credit to his heart and shows his

[1] MS. letter from Bradford, September 8, 1623.

humane feeling. Had he been on the spot he might have realized more fully the peril in which the Pilgrim Colony then stood. Yet we may be sure his moderating word would not be without good effect in the councils of the infant state.

"My Loving and Much-beloved Friend, whom God hath hitherto preserved, preserve and keep you still to his glory and the good of many; that his blessing may make your godly and wise endeavours answerable to the valuation which they [the colonists] there [in New England] set upon the same.

"Of your love to and care for us here we never doubted; so we are glad to take knowledge of it in that fullness we do. Our love and care to and for you is mutual; though our hopes of coming unto you be small and weaker than ever. But of this at large in Mr. Brewster's letter with whom you—and he with you mutually—I know, communicate your letters, as I desire you may do these.

"Concerning the killing of those poor Indians of which we heard at first by report, and since by more certain relation, oh! how happy a thing had it been if you had converted some before you had killed any! Besides where blood is once begun to be shed, it is seldom stanched of a long time after. You will say they deserved it. I grant it: but upon what provocations and invitements by those heathenish Christians! [*i. e.* by the crew of Planters sent out by Weston]. Besides, you being no magistrates over them, were to consider not what they deserved, but what you were by necessity constrained to inflict. Necessity of this, especially of killing so many (and many more it seems they would if they could) I see not. Methinks one or two principals should have been full enough, according to that approved rule 'The punishment to the few, and the fear to the many.' Upon this occasion let me be bold to exhort you seriously to consider the disposition of your Captain [Miles Standish] whom I love, and am persuaded the Lord in great mercy and for much good hath sent you him, if you use him aright. He is a man humble and meek among you and toward all, in ordinary course: but now, if this be merely from a human spirit [if there is no divine quality about his humility] there is cause to fear that, by occasion especially of provocation, there may be wanting that tenderness of the life of man, made after God's image, which is meet. It is also a thing more glorious in men's eyes than pleasing in God's or convenient for Christians, to be a terror to poor barbarous people, and, indeed, I am afraid lest, by these occasions, others should be drawn to affect a kind of ruffling course in the world.

"I doubt not but you will take in good part these things which I write, and, as there is cause, make use of them. It were to us more comfortable and convenient that we communicated our mutual helps in presence, but seeing that cannot be done, we shall always long after you and love you, and wait God's appointed time.

"The Adventurers, it seems, have neither money, nor any great mind of us [at Leyden] for the most part. They deny it to be any part of the covenants between us that they should transport us; neither do I look for any further help from them, till means come from you. We here are strangers in effect, to the whole course; and so both we and you (save as your own wisdom and worth have interested you further) of principals, [as was first] intended in this business, are [now become] scarce accessories.

"My wife, with me re-salutes you and yours. Unto him who is the same to his in all places, and near to them who are far from one another I commend you and all with you.

[*Leyden*]

"*December* 19, 1623." [JOHN ROBINSON.]

CHAPTER XXV

ROBINSON'S HOUSEHOLD AT LEYDEN—LATER CONTROVERSIES—ROGER WHITE

WE must turn away from the fascinating story of the activities of that portion of Robinson's Church now planted in New England to deal with the publications of Robinson himself in his last years, and the history of the Leyden section of his religious society.

The last five years of Robinson's life must have been busy years both for him and for his good wife Bridget. They brought both sorrows and joys. The eldest girl Ann (named after her grandmother at Sturton), now grown to woman's estate, married Jan Schetter of Utrecht before 1622, but was left a widow by the autumn of 1625. John, the eldest son, was quickly growing to manhood. His father designed him for the ministry, and would doubtless give a personal oversight to his studies.

What Church, however, was open to the son of the Separatist pastor? It appears that Robinson favoured his preparation for the ministry of the Dutch Reformed Church rather than for the pulpits of those English congregations in Holland which still kept in touch with the Episcopal Anglican Church. The other alternative was that fresh churches might be built up in America, on the principles which Robinson laid down. To one or another of such churches young John Robinson might be joined as a member, then be called to exercise his gifts in prophesying, and finally be ordained either as a pastor or teacher. That is the interpretation I give to the following document, discovered by Dr. Dexter among the papers of the English Reformed Church at Amsterdam, and thus translated—

"I, the undersigned, hereby certify that D[omine] Rubbensonus, pastor of the English Church here which is called the Brownists', has at divers times conversed with me concerning the separation between their congregation and the other English congregations in this country, and that he has at divers times testified that he was disposed to do his utmost to remove this schism; that he was also averse to educating his son for the work of the ministry in such congregations [English Puritan congregations], but much preferred to have him exercise his ministry in the Dutch Churches; that to this end, by the help of Domine Teellinck and myself, he had also begun to move some good people in Middelburg to provide some decent support for his son's studies for a few years; that he, moreover, at divers times assured me that he found in his congregation so many difficulties in connexion with this [Query, the proposed education of his son for the ministry in the Dutch Church] that he, with a good part of his congregation, was resolved to remove to the West Indies, where he doubted not he should be able to accomplish his desires.

"This has passed between us at divers times.

"Given at Leyden, May 25, 1628.

"ANTONIUS WALAEUS.

(Professor of Theology in the University).

"That which is above testified concerning the union of the English Churches in this country, I, the undersigned, likewise certify that I have divers times heard from the late D[omine] Robinson.

"At Leyden, May 26, 1628.

"FESTUS HOMMIUS,[1]

(Rector of the Theological College)."

This document bears testimony to Robinson's friendly intercourse with those on the professorial

[1] Festus Hommius was incorporated of the University of Oxford, June 6, 1620; perhaps it was to that year of the *Mayflower's* sailing that the following incident is to be referred—

"When proposals were made to put Dr. Ames into a Professor's Chair at Leyden, the motion was stopped by the English Prelates. Festus Hommius took the occasion of a visit to England to wait upon the Archbishop of Canterbury to beg him not to obstruct the appointment of Ames, but he told him 'that upon his own particular knowledge Dr. Ames was no obedient son unto his mother, the Church of England.'" Quick's *Icones Sac. Angl.* MSS., D.W.L., p. 33.

staff of the University and with the Rev. William Teelinck, who, it is well to remember, was keen in championing the cause of Thomas Brewer in 1619 against the demand of King James for his extradition.

The educational career of young John Robinson, like that of his father, covered a long period. Perhaps it was interrupted by his father's death. It was not till April 5, 1633, that "Joannes Robinsonus, Nordovico-Anglus" [Englishman born at Norwich], graduated at Leyden. Research in the archives of the Dutch Church might throw further light upon his career.

A few other details concerning the history of the Pilgrim Pastor's household in the last years of his life have been recovered.

On February 1, 1621, "the English preacher" living in the Pieterskerkhof, undoubtedly Robinson, buried one of his children in St. Peter's. The town census of October 15, 1622, gives his place of residence as Zevenhuysen, in the same ward of the city, and mentions his wife Bridget with the children, John, Bridget, Isaac, Mercy, Fear and James, with their maid-servant, Mary Hardy. It was a good long family, but one of these children of "the English preacher dwelling by the Bell Tower" was buried on March 27, 1623. This was probably the little girl Mercy, of whom there is no further record. In a subsequent section we shall set out what is known as to the after career of the survivors and connexions of the Robinson household.

The pen of Robinson in these last years was partly engaged on a controversial work[1] entitled—

"A / DEFENCE / of the Doc / trine Propovn / ded by the Synode / at Dort / Against / IOHN MVRTON and / his ASSOCIATES in a / Treatise in[ti]tuled A Description / what God, etc. / with / THE REFVTATION of / their Answer to a Writing touching / BAPTISM / by IOHN ROBINSON / Printed in the year 1624."

[1] Preface, p. ii., the book, p. 203.

A note on the last page excuses misprints on the ground of "the Author being absent"; the work therefore was not printed at Leyden.

To understand the circumstances which called forth this work we must look back for a year or two, and take up once again the threads of the story of the group of English refugees who gathered round John Smith. Through the influence of that remarkable man the main body of the Church that he gathered abandoned Calvinism and adopted a theology akin to that professed by the Mennonites. They proclaimed the doctrine of general redemption as opposed to particular redemption. They asserted that the efficacy of the redemptive work of Christ extended to all men and not to the elect alone. Thomas Helwys and John Murton, or Morton, accepted these views when propounded by Smith, and submitted to the baptism which he revived. They returned to England full of zeal for their convictions, and made London the centre for their propaganda. Robinson had some controversy with them in 1614, and in 1615, when issuing their "Objections answered by way of Dialogue, wherein is proved . . . that no man ought to be persecuted for his religion," they took the opportunity of pointing "at the principal things of Mr. Robinson's late book till further time."[1]

Helwys soon died, but Murton and his friends continued their work by issuing a book entitled *Truth's Champion* in 1617, which upheld the Arminian scheme of doctrine; and by publishing in 1618 *A Plain and Well-grounded Treatise concerning Baptism*, translated from the Dutch. Robinson, in opposition to these old friends, upheld the practice of baptizing infants one or both of whose parents were Church members. He argued that baptism by any one not a Minister or not specially deputed for the duty by the Church was invalid, and printed a leaflet setting forth his views on this point. Murton puts a reference

[1] Postscript to *Objections Answered*, 1615.

to this leaflet into the mouth of an objector in the dialogue now to be noticed—

"Ereunetes (*loquiter*). I am every way satisfied in this [*viz.* in the point that infant baptism is a late invention] only Iohn Robinson, Preacher to the English at Leyden, hath printed half a sheet of paper, who laboureth to prove that none may baptize but Pastors and Elders of a Church (for other officers to baptize I conceive not that he meaneth) and consequently that you [John Murton] and all your companies in England wanting Pastors are unbaptized."[1]

This "half a sheet" by Robinson received attention in a spirited little book by Murton in 1620, entitled: "*A Discription* (sic) *what God hath Predestinated concerning Man in his creation, transgression, regeneration . . . as also an Answere to John Robinson touching Baptisme.*"

The book, greatly daring, applies the principles of common sense and common affection governing the thought and feeling of the ordinary layman to the deep problems which the Synod at Dort essayed to solve. It is written in dialogue form, and livens up towards the end, when it comes to deal with the "little printed writing of John Robinson's touching baptism."

No copy of Robinson's pamphlet has so far come to light, but we can gather its drift from the references made to it in other works. It contained two main propositions—

(1) "That there is no lawful Baptism but by him that hath a lawful calling to baptize.

(2) "That only he hath an ordinary lawful calling to baptize who is called thereto by the Church."

These "grounds" Robinson supported by six "proofs." He argued that, as John Smith, "their first baptizer," had no ordinary lawful calling to baptize, John Murton and his associates were not "lawfully baptized, and so, by the verdict of their own

[1] *A Description what God hath Predestinated*, 1620, p. 154.

quest, [were] unbaptized persons." This controversy between the followers of Smith and John Robinson had shown singular vitality. It went on for more than a dozen years. Murton's intimate acquaintance with Robinson's writings enabled him to turn some of the latter's arguments in favour of the Separatist position against himself on this point of infant baptism. For example, Robinson, in support of his separation, quoted[1] the opinion of William Perkins—

"If in Turkey, or America, or elsewhere, the gospel should be received of men, by the counsel and persuasion of private persons they shall not need to send into Europe for consecrated ministers, but they have power to choose their own ministers from within themselves; because where God gives the word he gives the power also." [2]

Murton, in 1615, argued in the same way—

"Many famous men, as Mr. Perkins and others, confess that if a Turk should come to the knowledge of the truth in Turkey, he might preach the same to others, and converting them, baptize them, though unbaptized." [3]

Again, in his *Manumission*, Robinson had argued against Ames that it was needful to renounce his so-called "orders," received in the Anglican Church, and to be rightly "ordained" by the Church which called him to the pastoral office in Holland. Murton skilfully framed a similar argument to show that Robinson ought also to renounce his baptism received in England, and submit to baptism according to the New Testament order.

In his reply to "Murton and his Associates," Robinson, according to his plan in answering Bernard, followed his adversaries through the many subjects touched on by the way—

"As he that will overtake and hold a malefactor," he says, "must follow him, not only in the high and beaten way, whilst he keeps it, but in all the out-leaps also, and turnings

[1] *Works*, vol. ii. chap. 3, *Justification of Separation*, 1610, also *Works*, vol. i. p. 468.

[2] *Perkins on Galatians*, 1604, p. 35.

[3] *Objections Answered*, 1615.

which he makes, so, God assisting me, purpose I, though it be troublesome, to follow and prosecute these adversaries in this, and other their particular stragglings, if any way pertinent to the general controversy." [1]

The effect in the subsequent discussion of predestination, election, falling away, free-will, and the original state of mankind is tedious. Robinson is at too great pains to set his adversaries right in every detail. The Synod of Dort, which had met at his doors with the benediction of King James, had tuned up the Calvinistic system of theology to a pitch which Calvin himself would not have recognized, and Robinson in general assented to its conclusions. To put the matter shortly, Murton, approaching the subject from the layman's standpoint, looked at the problems at issue in the light of his faith in God's love and his own sense of justice and liberty; while Robinson, from the position of the trained theologian, viewed them in the light of God's sovereignty. The difference in the way of approach to these questions led to divergent conclusions respecting them.

There is one point touched on in the latter portion of his book which had a practical bearing upon the position of affairs in the section of Robinson's Church under the oversight of Brewster as ruling elder in New England. Murton argued that any man making a convert might, according to examples given in the New Testament, forthwith baptize him. Now, if that position were conceded, might not Brewster equally well baptize such infants as were presented to the Church in New Plymouth, and so remove one of the objections brought against the Plymouth Plantation? From what Robinson says in explanation of his position that only one lawfully called by the Church can baptize, it is clear that he attached the function of baptism to the office of the "teaching elder," or the pastor, but he left a loophole for the possible appointment of his "ruling Elder," Brewster, as "a member able to teach," to perform that duty—

[1] *Works*, vol. i. p. 274.

"My meaning was not to deny, that a church wanting pastors may appoint a member able to teach (though out of office) to baptize: for which much may be said, and hath been by some so minded. Which though I do not simply approve of; yet, neither did, neither had I occasion to deal there against, but only against the wild course of these All-alikes; of whom any that can wrest a few Scriptures intended of men of years only, against the baptizing of infants, to the corrupting of some simple man, or woman, thinks himself another John Baptist, as their practice and profession manifests."[1]

Among the events in his congregation during the last years of his life Robinson would be specially interested in the marriage of his brother-in-law, Roger White, who was now beginning "to make good" in Leyden. He was a younger brother of Bridget Robinson, born at Sturton, probably in 1589, and as a youth went over to Leyden. He eventually started business as a grocer. Not till he was thirty-two years old did the way seem clear for him to marry. He was betrothed at Amsterdam on February 20, 1621, to Elizabeth Wales, aged twenty-two, and married at Leyden on the following March 14. Two years later (May 5, 1623) he was admitted to citizenship on the guarantee of Edmund Chandler and Anthony Clement, and thenceforth took a leading part in the affairs of the congregation and the English colony in Leyden. He, in turn, guaranteed others for admission to citizenship, amongst them his brother-in-law, Francis Jessop, on May 5, 1625, who was also a shopkeeper in Leyden. As late as May 26, 1631, he guaranteed William Jackson. I discovered a reference to him in the will of his eldest brother, Charles White, drawn up in 1633, wherein is the bequest, "to my brother Roger ffower pounds."

[1] Robinson's *Works*, vol. i. p. 446.

CHAPTER XXVI

LETTERS OF THE LEYDEN CHURCH—ROBINSON'S ESSAYS—HIS DEATH

Two letters from Robinson and his Church at Leyden of the year 1624 may be briefly noticed here. The earlier of the two, dated April 5, 1624,[1] was addressed "To our Beloved in the Lord, the Church of Christ in London," and was printed in 1634 as an appendix to Robinson's *Treatise on the Lawfulness of Hearing Ministers in the Church of England.* The circumstances were as follows: In the old Separatist Church of Barrowe and Greenwood, which still kept up some sort of meetings in London, trouble had arisen over a maid who had attended worship at the meetings of the Independent Church gathered by Henry Jacob in London in 1616. The more rigid members of this older Separatist Church carried things to such a pitch that they regarded Jacob's Church as, in effect, idolatrous, because its members did not utterly renounce the Church of England. The erring maid was brought before the Separatist Church to which she belonged and admonished. She promised to give up going to the meetings in Jacob's Church, and was accordingly retained as a member in fellowship. The extremists were not satisfied. St. Paul had plainly laid it down (1 Cor. v. 11) that if any called a brother be an idolater they were "not to keep company" with him, "no, not to eat" with such a one. The girl ought to have been excommunicated. Feeling on the matter ran high. The

[1] See above, chap. xiv.

" teacher " of the old Separatist Church, with some of the brethren, renounced communion with those who retained the maid in fellowship and, though they were in a minority, claimed still to be the " Church " on the ground that they held the " truth."

It was felt that outside advice might smooth over the difficulty. Accordingly a letter was sent from the more moderate section of the London Church to the sister Churches of Amsterdam and Leyden containing six inquiries. The letter went first to the Amsterdam Church, which was now, after Ainsworth's death, under the guidance of Elders. There this missive acted with explosive force. The rigid London Separatists found their counterpart in Amsterdam. The kernel of the matter was as to the standing of the Congregational or Independent Church founded by Henry Jacob. In the Amsterdam Church Sabine Staresmore and his wife were in fellowship. They had first been members of Jacob's Church in London, and in virtue of that membership had been received into Robinson's Church at Leyden, and thence had been commended to the Amsterdam Church. This was tantamount to a recognition of Jacob's congregation as a true Church of Christ. When the question put by the Londoners as to " whether Mr. Staresmore and his wife are received and retained . . . by that covenant which they made with God in Mr. Jacob's Church, or whether they have renounced it as false and made another," was brought up for consideration at Amsterdam it led to heated disputes. A series of " interrogatories " was put to Staresmore on his position, and when he declined to answer them he was censured and " cast out." The matter led to correspondence between the Churches at Amsterdam and Leyden.

When it became evident that there was no possibility of the Churches at Leyden and Amsterdam returning a joint reply to London, as there was a hopeless divergence between them on the points at issue, Robinson wrote this letter in answer, which was "read in public, and by the whole consent of the Church was sent to London."[1] It is too long to quote in full, but we may extract from it the six questions upon which the London Separatists sought advice.

"(1) Have we done well in retaining the maid about whom the difference was, she leaving off her attendance at the meetings of Jacob's congregation according to her promise?

"Robinson answered yes. Even 'though she had continued her practice upon occasion, and without neglect of the Church whereof she was a member,' they would have done well to retain her.

"(2) Whether Mr. Jacob's congregation be a true Church or no?

"(3) Whether Mr. Staresmore and his wife are received and retained in the Leyden and Amsterdam Churches by that covenant which they made with God in Mr. Jacob's Church or whether they have renounced it as false and made another?

"(4) How ought we to carry ourselves towards our 'Teacher' and other brethren renouncing communion with us?

"(5) Whether their pretence of having the truth be sufficient to make them the 'Church' and to warrant their above-mentioned dealing, [*i. e.* their renunciation of communion with the majority of the old members]?

"(6) Whether women have voices [*i. e.* votes] with men in the judgments of the churches?"

To the last question Robinson replied that "if a woman may not so much as move a question in the Church for her instruction, how much less may she give a voice or utter a reproof for censure." John Smith took up a more liberal position in regard to this question. In his *Principles and Inferences* of 1607 he left the matter open with a "*Quære*," but in his *Paralleles* of 1609 he decided it in the affirmative, and gave allowance to women members to take part in the "Censures" of the Church. The general tenor of the letter, however, manifests the moderate and sensible temper of Robinson and his associates.

[1] *Works*, vol. iii. p. 379.

The second letter of the year 1624, dated September 18 from Leyden, is addressed to the Amsterdam Church, and deals with Staresmore's case. It appears that, after Staresmore had been censured and cast out, some steps had been taken to review the judgment of the Church in the matter, but this course was broken off on the ground that the decision, once given, must stand.

Whereas Leyden acknowledged the congregation gathered and covenanted together under Henry Jacob as a true Church, Amsterdam took the opposite view, and agreed to support those Londoners who desired the excommunication of the maid resorting to its services. Staresmore, dissenting from this judgment, greatly daring, had written a letter on his own account from Amsterdam to London "in opposition to the Church's agreement." This was regarded as a grave offence and a mark of rebellion. Robinson supported Staresmore's position, and in his letter pleaded for a more moderate and reasonable course to be taken by the brethren at Amsterdam. There is a note of tiredness and disappointment in this letter at the bickerings which marked the Church "nearliest united" unto his own religious society. The Separatist movement had more than a fair share of self-sufficient and impossible saints. Robinson showed remarkable patience in dealing with them—

"To our Beloved, the Elders and Church at AMSTERDAM, grace and peace from God the giver thereof, and in him our salutations.

"We received your letter, brethren, but not answering either our expectation or the weightiness of the business in hand; and are withal rather driven to gather your meaning out of it, than finding the same in it expressed. Only we see plainly your intent of imputing special blame to one [Sabine Staresmore], by you accounted the chief adversary, as offering boastingly (as you say), to prove that he doth *worship the God of his fathers* in writing a letter in opposition to the church's agreement, and in 'rebellious refusing and despising of the same Church.'

"First, touching the person intended by you. It should not seem strange to any, if he were most forward, who was deepliest interested in the business; and *that* so far, as his church estate and membership must necessarily stand or fall with that covenant [*i. e.* the covenant of the Church founded in London by Jacob in 1616] impugned by you, as the branch with the root. As Zilpah was not, nor could be, rightfully Leah's handmaid, except she had been Laban's first, rightfully (Gen. xxix. 24) by whose gift she was transmitted and conveyed unto her; so neither could he [Staresmore] be truly a member there [in Amsterdam] with you but by transmission, dismission, or conveyance (call it as you will) from this church [Leyden] to that, and so from that at London first to us here, by virtue of that first covenant there made by profession of faith; which covenant, howsoever by some light person accounted no better than the Turks might make, was by the churches both there [in London] and here also [in Holland], in the time of those worthy governors [Jacob and Ainsworth] now at rest in the Lord, esteemed truly Christian.

"[Secondly] The party intended by you should, by your grounds, not have been cast out, but left out of the church.

"[Thirdly] And for the things by you imputed unto him, we are certified by many eye and ear witnesses that his speech was as followeth: 'As Paul in his case when he was accused unjustly, said, *In the way they call heresy, worship I the God of my fathers*, so haply I in this, that which you call and have censured for faction, or *a factious action tending to the breach and division of the Church*, I judge to be nothing less, but rather a Christian duty, tending to love and not to division in the Church in the least, either in action or intention. And if way may be given to speak our minds freely, without interruption, as hath been solemnly granted, it may and will so appear, I doubt not, to the heart, etc., etc.'

"And that this speech he [Staresmore] used not till all hope was taken away of any moderate course of proceeding, or of [any] other [way of satisfying the Church] than by simple confession of the sin of faction.

"And surely, brethren, it is not credible that he would speak of the worshipping of the God of his fathers, or that any one endued with common sense would offer to prove unto others that he worshipped God by that which he knew they esteemed sinful and evil. If he had proved that he had *so* worshipped God, what else had it been, but to have proved that he had worshipped God by doing evil in their conscience, with whom he had to do? This had been an offer fit for *him* to make that meant to prove himself guilty, and so to persuade others that he was; but not for him who means, as he did, to avow his innocency in the thing.

"Brethren, let us be mindful, as we ought, that no relation of a cause, nor plea for or against it, can make either ours the better, or our adversaries' the worse, in the eyes of the Supreme Judge both of our persons and judgments and all other our actions.

"And whereas the course, well begun and tending to pacification, was (as we understand) interrupted and broken off upon a ground [or reason] taken from the course of not calling again into question civil judgments once passed by the Judge according to right; let it not be grievous unto you if we a little warn you of that dangerous foundation, upon which, it seems, you too much build your manner of proceeding in the church. And to let pass that it were more for the true peace of the Judges of the world with God (though some diminution of their credits in the eyes of vain men) if they not only revised, but often, upon better information or advice, even reversed their former sentences. We pray you call to mind how grievous it was unto the body of you [followers of Ainsworth] and dangerous in itself, when some of place [Francis Johnson and his Elders] amongst you, a few years since, would pattern the government of the church now, by the government of the elders in Israel, which is in truth to transform a service into a lordship.

"More specially for the matter in hand. When the *civil* Judge hath passed sentence, and that execution is done accordingly, and that every one hath his due, there is an end of the matter; but in *spiritual* judgments there is a further thing which the Magistrate meddles not with—the repentance of the censured to follow in time by God's blessing. The end of excommunication is not that the person might be excommunicated, but that repentance might follow; for the furthering whereof many things may and ought to be done in Christian discretion by the church towards the excommunicated, as being, as it were, the church's prisoner (1 Cor. v. 5), by which he and his sins are bound upon earth, as our Lord teacheth (Matt. xviii. 18). And a larger extent of discretion this way, few cases in an age can persuade to, than this in hand, considering both the ground and carriage of the thing, and the number of the persons opposite, and with these the interest of all other churches in the business.

And now understanding, brethren, that competent satisfaction for the *manner* of the carriage hath been tendered by the parties censured, for the *matter* (to be reduced, as we conceive, to these two heads following) we can do no less, in honour of the truth, discharge of our own consciences before God, and due respect unto them in their distressed state, than to signify and profess.

"1. That in a matter of mere counsel and advice, more than which neither the church of London required nor you could afford them, any particular persons advised with and having their reasons of difference from the church's persuasion, may, and, in cases of weight, such as this was, ought by speech or writing as there is occasion, signify that their different judgment and advice to them whom it concerns, provided the same be done in good manner and with due respect to the church. Solomon saith (Prov. xi. 14), that 'in the multitude of counsellors there is safety'; and every man's common sense teacheth, that he who propounds a thing to others for counsel, should hear every man's opinion, and the reason thereof for his help and direction. To deny this is to deprive him of liberty that should give counsel, and him of help that should receive it. The church was not in this case to use authority, but to show reason.

"2. That, seeing both Moses in the law (Deut. xix. 15), and Christ in the gospel (Matt. xviii. 15–17) ordains that every matter should be established by two or three witnesses, and that, in that order the church should be told or complained to of a brother; for the officer to traduce or complain of a brother to the church, without witness of an offence done, and to proceed with him by questions and interrogatories, tending to his prejudice, and for the church to censure him for refusing to answer such interrogatories so ministered, is both against Moses and Christ, and the law of nature itself (Acts xxiv. 8, 13; and xxv. 15, 16), which taught the wise of the heathen not to proceed in judgment with any but by way of accusation and proof of evil against him. And these persuasions of the things and defence of our own and all other Christians', yea, of all men's lawful liberty, we are willing and able, by the grace of God, to justify against all gainsayers.

"And now, brethren, what shall we say more unto you? Our and all other churches' advice you reject, in confidence of your own unerring judgment and proceeding in this matter.

"In your letter you mention the great weakness of the church. Oh, that you would indeed manifest such persuasion of yourselves! Then would you not proceed with that confidence in a matter and manner before unheard of in the churches; then would you both be glad of and desire the advice and counsel of others, able and willing, in the fear of the Almighty and in a good conscience, to afford you the best help they can; and not so carry things as if the Word of God either came from you or unto you alone. And for the church here, which is nearliest united unto you, what other use have you had of us, since the death of your wise and modest governors, in all your differences and troubles, save to help to bear part of that scandal and opprobry wherewith, specially in the public carriage of matters, you have laden the ordinances of God and professors of the same in the eyes of all, within and without. But in vain we speak unto you, whose ears prejudice hath stopped. We purpose not henceforth to trouble you any more in this kind; but taking part on occasion in the good things amongst you, and professing ourselves innocent of the things amiss, will bewail your state, which is indeed to be bewailed, and commend it, as we do, to the Lord for bettering. His grace be with you always more and more.

" Your loving brethren,

" The Pastor and Church at Leyden,

" JOHN ROBINSON.

"*Leyden, September* 18, 1624."

It will be remembered that there was issued from the Pilgrim Press of Brewster at Leyden in 1619 a Defence or " Apologia " of Robinson's Church and its opinions, in Latin, compiled by Robinson himself. This book gave a useful account of the position taken up by his congregation. It was felt that an English edition would be helpful in spreading the light and removing prejudices. Robinson accordingly prepared a translation for the press, and this was issued in 1625 with the title " A / IUST AND NECESSARIE / APOLOGIE / OF CERTAIN CHRISTIANS / no lesse contumeliously then commonly called / Brownists or Barrowists / By MR. IOHN ROBINSON, Pastor of the Eng/lish Church at Leyden, first published in Latin in his and the / Churches name over which he was set, after translated into / English by himself, and now republished for the / speciall and common good of our / own Countrimen // Psal. 41. 2 / O Blessed is he that prudently attendeth to the poore weakling // Printed in the yeare of our Lord / M.DC.XXV."

The work runs to seventy-two pages. It is printed

in good, clear type, similar to that used by Brewer and Brewster in earlier days. My own conjecture is that Brewer had recovered possession of the type impounded in the University of Leyden at the instance of the English Ambassador, and now, in conjunction with the members of his congregation, procured the publication of this work as a pious duty immediately after Robinson's death.

Robinson was probably engaged in seeing through the press his volume of *Essays* when he was seized with his last illness. The volume seems to me to have had his careful oversight for the most part, and has a brief preface from his own hand. Whether he lived to see a completed volume is doubtful. His name is printed as " Robbinson " on the title page of the first edition and in the signature to the preface—the latest portions to be set up, which looks as though they had not been submitted for his revision. The title of the first edition runs as follows: " OBSERVATI/ONS DIVINE / AND MORALL / FOR THE FURTHERING / of knowledg, and vertue / By John Robbinson / Prov. 9. 9. / Give Instruction to a wise man, and he will be yet / wiser : teach a just man and he will en / crease in learning / Printed in the year M.DC.XXV." The volume is a quarto of 324 pages, with a preface of four pages, and at the end is " The table Conteyning the Contents of everie Chapter," two pages. This volume was frequently re-issued. Its solid merit and its practical treatment of a variety of subjects of perennial interest commended it to a wide public. The fact that it contained a large amount of valuable sermon matter was not without influence on its circulation. A second issue appeared in 1625, another came out in 1628, with an expanded title based on Robinson's preface, " New Essayes or Observations Divine and Morall collected out of the Holy Scriptures, Ancient and Modern Writers, both divine and human; as also out of the great volume of men's manners tending to the furtherance of knowledge and virtue." It appeared again in a volume of smaller page in 1638, styling itself "The second edition." Again in 1642 and in 1654 as "Essayes and Observations Theologicall and Morall, by a Student in Theologie," without Robinson's name. The labour lovingly spent on these essays was not labour in vain, though the author did not live to see the fruits of his work. They testify to Robinson's wide reading, his unflagging industry, and his care in noting anything which had a bearing upon those points in life and manners in which he was specially concerned. His preface shows that in this line of work he took real pleasure and delight. It would be a relief to turn from the field of controversy to this labour which he loved. Here is his preface—

"In framing these mine Observations, Christian Reader, I have had, as is meet, first and most regard to the Holy Scriptures; in which respect I call them divine: next, to the memorable sayings of wise and learned men, which I have read or heard, and carefully stored up as a precious treasure for mine own and others' benefit; and lastly, to the great volume of men's manners, which I have diligently observed and from them gathered no small part thereof; having also had, in the days of my pilgrimage, special opportunity of conversing with persons of divers nations, estates and dispositions in great variety. The names of the authors, specially known, out of whom I gathered anything, I have, for the most part expressed: partly to give them their due; and partly, that the authority of their persons might procure freer passage for their worthy and wise sayings, with others; and make the deeper impression of them in the reader's heart.

"In the method I have been neither curious nor altogether negligent, as the reader may observe. Now, as this kind of study and meditation hath been unto me full sweet and delightful, and that wherein I have often refreshed my soul and spirit, amidst many sad and sorrowful thoughts unto which God hath called me, so, if it may find answerable acceptance with the Christian Reader, and a blessing from the Lord, it is that which I humbly crave, specially at his hands, who both ministereth seed to the sower, and fruit to the reaper. Amen.

"JOHN ROBINSON."

The essays, sixty-two in number, range over a wide field, from the opening one on "Man's Knowledge of God," to that on "Death," which closes the book. Such topics as "Labour," "Sobriety," "Prayer," "Flattery," "Conscience," "Anger," "Modesty," "Marriage," "Envy," "Peace," receive special and separate treatment. Robinson is fond of balancing qualities one against another, or dealing with a pair of either related or opposed subjects, *e. g.* "Truth and Falsehood," "Wisdom and Folly," "Speech and Silence," "Authority and Reason," "Contempt and Contumely," "Books and Writings," "Knowledge and Ignorance." This gave him the opportunity of elucidating his subject by way of contrast, of which he took full advantage. The essays vary considerably in length; on such topics as "Religion, and the Differences and Disputations thereabout," and "The Holy Scriptures," Robinson has a good deal to say, while of such subjects as "Health and Physic," "Zeal," "Rewards and Punishments," he completes his study in a page or two.

In his essays, while giving many references to books and authors, Robinson makes but few references to persons. Twice he quotes sayings of Lord Willoughby, whom I take to be Robert Bertie, Lord Willoughby, born in 1582, who went up to Corpus Christi College, and must have been well known to Robinson. His allusion to "the wily fox who being once caught hath his skin plucked over his ears, wherewith every fool will have his cap furred," remained in Robinson's memory, and was used in illustration of the downfall waiting on craftiness. We may note that John Jegon sent a letter[1] to Robert, Lord Willoughby, October 9, 1601, dated from Corpus Christi College, condoling with him on the death of his father, and referring to Robert himself as one who "lived so longe with me in such excellent moderation."

The essay on "Riches and Poverty" has an incidental allusion to Robinson's University days in these terms—

[1] MSS. of the Earl of Ancaster, *Hist. MSS. Com.*, 1907, p. 351.

> "A friend of mine in the University was wont to tell me merrily and wittily, that surely there was something in this money more and better than he and I saw; seeing such a great, wise and learned man, whom he would name, loved it so well; and such another, as wise and learned as he, as well as he; and so a third, and a fourth. He knew well enough it was not any good in it, which we saw not; but lust and filthy covetousness in them, whose learning and wisdom should have taught them to despise and hate such base-mindedness." [1]

In another place Robinson makes a casual reference to the "many dangers and calamities" to which in his "afflicted state" he had been exposed, counting it in one way a mercy that he had not had many bosom friends to be thrown into "excessive sorrow" by the "misery" that had befallen him. But in general the allusions to his own condition are indirect and indefinite. We have a shrewd contrast between the esteem in which labour was held in England and Holland respectively in the following passage, but the places are not named—

> "This difference I have observed . . . that whereas in plentiful countries, such as our own, it is half a shame to labour: in such others, wherein art and industry must supply nature's defects, as in the country where I have last lived, it is a shame for a man not to work and exercise himself in some one or other lawful vocation." [2]

Here and there Robinson's humour and sense of fun peeps out, and here and there we come upon proverbial sayings which have the tang of the soil in them, *e. g.* "He that makes a bridge of his own shadow, cannot but fall into the water." "Living springs send out streams of water, dead pits must have all that they afford drawn out with buckets." "He that hath but half an eye, is a king amongst them that are blind." Make a friend of a man after you have "eaten a bushel of salt together." But the essays are most noteworthy for their plain good sense and the firm ethical note which is struck throughout them.

[1] *Works*, vol. i. p. 122. [2] *Ibid.*, p. 114.

Robinson's Death and Funeral

These gleanings from his ministry and meditation were garnered by Robinson just in time for posterity. To his friends he seemed in quite his usual health, but probably he himself had an instinctive feeling that his time was short. He died on March 1, 1625. We have a touching account of his last days by Roger White of Leyden, in the following letter—

To his loving Friend Mr. William Bradford, Governor of Plymouth, in New England, these be, etc.

"Loving and kind Friends, etc.,

"I know not whether ever this will come to your hands, or miscarry, as other of my letters have done; yet in regard of the Lord's dealings with us here, I have had a great desire to write unto you, knowing your desire to bear a part with us, both in our joys and sorrows, as we do with you.

"These, therefore, are to give you to understand that it hath pleased the Lord to take out of this vale of tears, your and our loving and faithful pastor, and my dear and reverend brother Mr. John Robinson, who was sick some eight days, beginning first to be sick on a Saturday morning; yet the next day, being the Lord's day, he taught us twice, and the week after, grew every day weaker than other, yet felt no pain, but weakness all the time of his sickness. The physic he took wrought kindly in man's judgment, yet he grew every day weaker than other, feeling little or no pain, yet sensible to the very last. He fell sick the twenty-second of February, and departed this life on the first of March. He had a continual inward ague, but I thank the Lord was free of the plague, so that all his friends could come freely to him; and if either prayers, tears, or means would have saved his life he had not gone hence.

"But he having faithfully finished his course, and performed his work, which the Lord had appointed him here to perform, he now rests with the Lord in eternal happiness; we wanting him, and all church governors, not having one at present that is a governing officer among us.

"Now for ourselves here left (I mean the whole church) we still, by the mercy of God, continue and hold close together in peace and quietness, and so I hope we shall do, though we be very weak, wishing (if such were the will of God) that you and we were again together in one, either there or here; but seeing it is the will of the Lord, thus to dispose of things, we must labour with patience to rest contented, till it please the Lord otherwise to dispose of things.

"For news at present here, [there] is not much worth the writing; only, as in England we have lost our old King James, who departed this life about a month ago, so here we have lost Grave Maurice the old prince here, who both departed this life since my brother Robinson. And as in England we have a new king, Charles, of whom there is great hope of good, so here likewise we have made Prince Hendrick, general in his brother's place, who is now with the Grave of Mansfield with a great army, close by the enemy, to free Breda, if it be possible, which the enemy hath besieged now some nine or ten months, but how it will fall out at last is yet uncertain. The Lord give good success, if it be his will. The king is making ready about one hundred sail of ships; the end is not yet certain, but they will be ready to go to sea very shortly. The king himself goes to see them once in fourteen days.

"And thus fearing lest this will not come to your hands, hoping as soon as I hear of a convenient messenger, to write more at large and to send you a letter which my brother Robinson sent to London, to have gone to some of you, but coming too late, was brought back again. And so for this time I cease further to trouble you and rest

"Your assured loving friend,

"ROGER WHITE.

"*Leyden, April* 28, 1625."

Robinson was buried on March 4 in St. Peter's Church, as the record discovered by Mr. Sumner in the register of burials discloses—

"4 Maart Jan Roelends Predicant van de Engelsche Gemeente by het Kloekhuijs—begraven in de Pieters Kerk."

That is, "John Roelends [Robinson] Preacher of the English Congregation by the Belfry—buried in Peter's Church."

We have it on the authority of Edward Winslow that—

"The University and ministers of the city accompanied him to his grave with all their accustomed solemnities, bewailing the great loss that not only that particular church had whereof he was pastor, but some of the chief of them sadly affirmed that all the churches of Christ sustained a loss by the death of that worthy instrument of the Gospel."

Making some allowances for the natural tendency to give as impressive and dignified an account as possible of the obsequies of his beloved minister, we may, I think, take Winslow's account as substantially correct. It was a laudable custom to pay a tribute of respect for the memory of friends by attendance at the funeral, and in all likelihood some of Robinson's acquaintances in the University and amongst the ministers of the city were present at his burial. The fact that the low fee [1] of nine florins only, was paid on the following Monday, in discharge of the cost of opening and hiring the grave for his interment, has been taken as pointing to a ceremony of quite a different type from that suggested by Winslow's words. No doubt simplicity and absence of needless expense would be in keeping with Robinson's own feeling, but Dexter has pointed out that nine florins was the usual fee for funerals at the accustomed time, *i. e.* before half-past one, and that in the case of such a distinguished preacher as Arminius the fee paid was only six florins. It would not trouble Robinson or his friends that the hired grave in which his body was laid would be used again and again for burials in successive periods; "the dust returns to dust, and the spirit unto God who gave it."

From Governor William Bradford's *Dialogue, or the Sum of a Conference between some Young Men born in New England and sundry Ancient Men that came out of Holland and Old England*, compiled in 1648, and subsequently transcribed into the records of the Plymouth Church by Nathaniel Morton, we have a pen-picture of Robinson's character as viewed by a devoted disciple in the light of a long experience of men and manners—

[1] [1625] } Openen en huer van Jan Robens.
10 Mart. } Engels predekant—9 florins.

"Mr. John Robinson," he says, "was pastor of that famous Church of Leyden, in Holland; a man not easily to be paralleled for all things, whose singular virtues we shall not take upon us here to describe. Neither need we, for they so well are known both by friends and enemies. As he was a man learned and of solid judgment and of a quick and sharp wit, so was he also of a tender conscience and very sincere in all his ways, a hater of hypocrisy and dissimulation, and would be very plain with his best friends. He was very courteous, affable and sociable in his conversation, and towards his own people especially.

"He was an acute and expert disputant, very quick and ready, and had much bickering with the Arminians, who stood more in fear of him than any of the University.

"He was never satisfied in himself until he had searched any cause or argument he had to deal in thoroughly and to the bottom; and we have heard him sometimes say to his familiars that many times, both in writing and disputation, he knew he had sufficiently answered others, but many times not himself; and was ever desirous of any light, and the more able, learned, and holy the persons were, the more he desired to confer and reason with them.

"He was very profitable in his ministry and comfortable to his people. He was much beloved of them, and as loving was he unto them, and entirely sought their good for soul and body.

In a word, he was much esteemed and reverenced of all that knew him and his abilities—both of friends and strangers. But we resolved to be brief in this matter, leaving you to better and more large information herein from others." [1]

News of Robinson's death did not reach the Pilgrim colony for over a year. It was carried by Captain Miles Standish, who had been sent by the colonists to England in the summer of 1625, with a view to settling up affairs with those "Adventurers" in London still interested in the colony. When he got to London the plague was raging, and the most he could do was to put things in train for a general composition. He had brought with him letters for friends at Leyden, one in special inquiring their mind and their prospects as to migrating to New England, and expressing the

[1] *Chronicles of the Pilgrim Fathers*, Alexander Young, 1844, p. 452.

desire to have Robinson with them soon. The members of the Church in New Plymouth longed for the presence and fellowship of their Leyden brethren. To this letter the leading members of the Leyden congregation wrote the following reply, sending it over to Standish in London in good time for his return—

The Leyden people to Bradford and Brewster

"To our most dear and entirely beloved Brethren, Mr. William Bradford and Mr. William Brewster, grace, mercy, and true peace be multiplied from God our Father, through our Lord Jesus Christ. Amen.

"Most dear Christian Friends and Brethren, as it is no small grief unto you, so is it no less unto us, that we are constrained to live thus disunited each from other, especially considering our affections each unto other, for the mutual edifying and comfort of both in these evil days wherein we live, if it pleased the Lord to bring us again together, than which, as no outward thing could be more comfortable unto us, or is more desired of us, if the Lord see it good, so see we no hope of means of accomplishing the same except it come from you; and therefore must [we] with patience rest in the work and will of God, performing our duties to him and you asunder; whom we are not any way able to help but by our continual prayers to him for you, and sympathy of affections with you for the troubles which befall you; till it please the Lord to reunite us again.

"But, our dearly beloved brethren, concerning your kind and respective letter (howsoever written by one of you, yet as we conceive with the consent, at least in affection, of you both) although we cannot answer your desire and expectation, by reason it hath pleased the Lord to take to himself out of this miserable world our dearly beloved pastor, yet for ourselves we are minded as formerly to come unto you, when, and as, the Lord affordeth means; though we see little hope thereof at present as being unable of ourselves; and that our friends will help us, we see little hope.

"And now, brethren, what shall we say further unto you? Our desire and prayer to God is (if such were his good will and pleasure) we might be reunited for the edifying and mutual comfort of both, which, when he sees fit, he will accomplish. In the mean time, we commit you unto him and to the word of his grace, whom we beseech to guide and direct, both you and us, in all his ways according to that his Word,[1] and to bless all our lawful endeavours for the glory of his name and the good of his people.

"Salute, we pray you, all the church and brethren with you, to whom we would have sent this letter, if we knew it could not be prejudicial unto you, as we hope it cannot; yet, fearing the worst, we thought fit either to direct it to you [Bradford and Brewster], our two beloved brethren, leaving it to your godly wisdom and discretion to manifest our mind to the rest of our loving friends and brethren, as you see most convenient.

"And thus entreating you to remember us in your prayers, as we also do you, we for this time commend you, and all your affairs, to the direction and protection of the Almighty, and rest,

"Your assured loving friends
"And brethren in the Lord,
"FRANCIS JESSOP.
"THOMAS NASH.
"THOMAS BLOSSOM.
"ROGER WHITE.
"RICHARD MAISTERSON.

"*Leyden, November* 30, A.D. 1625."

Of the signatories to this letter, Jessop and White were brothers-in-law of Robinson. The latter has already been noticed. Jessop, according to Dexter, was from Rotherham and Sheffield, and a son of Richard Jessop. But Worksop was probably his birthplace, for I find he was baptized there on November 12, 1568. He married Frances White, the youngest sister of Bridget Robinson, at Worksop, January 24, 1604–5. Charles White, the eldest brother of his wife, was still under obligation to him in 1633 for some of the moneys left to little Frances White by her father and mother. The will of Charles White, proved October 9, 1634, has the direction "for that fifteene pounds per annum due to my Cosen Jessopp for eight yeares to come, my will is that it shalbe paid out of the Castle Rents [*i. e.* rents of Greasley Castle Farm] if Mr. Poole soe long live, but if hee dye before those yeares be expired my wife shall discharge

[1] There is an echo here of the terms of their Church Covenant. Notice the hesitation about publicly addressing the Plymouth Colonists as a "Church" lest it should bring trouble upon them from England.

it out of my goods." It also contains the bequest, "*Item* to my brother Jessops children I give Tenn pounds."[1] This proves they had a family. They were still in Leyden in 1624, when, on October 27, Frances Jessop witnessed the betrothal of Thomas Nash. Returning to England they settled at Beccles in Suffolk. Frances died in 1636, and her husband married again the next year.

Thomas Nash is first heard of in connexion with the Pilgrim Church in 1620, when he went over to Holland with the pilot for the *Speedwell*. His first wife was Margaret Porter. His second wife, whom he married November 11, 1628, was Margaret Stuart, widow of Simeon Stuart, a niece of Roger White's wife. Nash was connected with Leyden for at least twenty years. There is a record of his witnessing, on March 17, 1640, the betrothal of his stepson Simon Stuart, a tobacco-pipe maker, born at Yarmouth, to Mercy Jennings at Leyden.

Richard Masterson was one of the Kentish group of Separatists, who attached himself to Robinson's Church soon after its formation in Holland. He was a "wool-carder" by trade, and probably worked in close association with Robert Cushman, for whom he stood surety on his buying a house, April 19, 1612. Two years later (January 2, 1614) Masterson himself bought a house on the Uiterstegracht for 800 gilders from Robert Wilson, who, like Masterson, hailed from Sandwich. On November 8, 1619, Masterson was betrothed to Mary Goodale of Leicester. They both migrated to Plymouth, New England, in 1630. It appears from the letter of Sabine Staresmore, September 4, 1618, dated from prison in Wood Street, London, that "brother Maistersone" stood in similar peril to the writer, and would "have tasted of the same cup had his place of residence and his person been as well known."

[1] Extracted from the *Register of Wills* in the Probate Registry at York, vol. xlii. fol. 306. The term "cousin" was used for connexions by marriage and other ties of relationship.

Thomas Blossom we have already referred to as from Cambridge. He was living in Leyden in the first year of the Pilgrim's settlement in that city, for when George Rogers matriculated as a student in medicine, October 27, 1609, he stated that he lived with Thomas Blossom. He was one of the little colony of English folk in the Pieterskerkhof, whence, on April 12 in 1617, he buried one of his children. Blossom and his wife with their sons, Thomas and Peter, crossed to New England in 1629. He was intimate with Robinson, for whom he had a high regard, as the following letter shows—

Thomas Blossom to Governor Bradford

"Beloved Sir,

"Kind salutations, etc.—I have thought good to write to you, concerning the cause as it standeth both with you and us. We see, alas, what frustrations and disappointments it pleaseth the Lord to send in this our course, good in itself, and according to godliness taken in hand and for good and lawful ends, who yet pleaseth not to prosper [us] as we are, for reasons best known to himself; and which also nearly concerns us to consider of, whether we have sought the Lord in it as we see, or not.

"That the Lord hath singularly preserved life in the business to great admiration giveth me good hope that he will (if our sins hinder not) in his appointed time, give a happy end unto it.

"On the contrary, when I consider how it pleaseth the Lord to cross those means that should bring us together, being now so far off, or farther than ever in our apprehension; as also to take that means [John Robinson] away which would have been so comfortable unto us in that course, both for wisdom of counsel, as also for our singular help in our course of godliness; whom the Lord (as it were) took away even as fruit falleth before it was ripe, when neither length of days, nor infirmity of body did seem to call for his end. The Lord even then took him away, as it were in his anger, whom, if tears would have held, he had remained to this day.

"The loss of his ministry was very great unto me, for I ever counted myself happy in the enjoyment of it, notwithstanding all the crosses and losses otherwise I sustained. Yet indeed the manner of his taking away hath more troubled me, as fearing the Lord's anger in it, that, as I said, in the ordinary course of things might still have remained, as also the singular service he might have yet done in the Church of God.

Alas! dear friends, our state and cause in religion by his death, being wholly destitute of any that may defend our cause as it should [be defended] against our adversaries; that we may take up that doleful complaint in the Psalm [74.] that 'there is no prophet left among us, nor any that knoweth how long.'

"Alas! you would fain have had him with you, and he would as fain have come to you. Many letters and much speech hath been about his coming to you, but never any solid course propounded for his going. If the course propounded the last year had appeared to have been certain, he would have gone, though with [but] two or three families. I know no man amongst us knew his mind better than I did about those things. He was loth to leave the church, yet I know also, that he would have accepted the worst conditions, which in the largest extent of a good conscience could be taken, to have come to you.

"For myself, and all such others as have formerly minded coming, it is much-what the same—if the Lord afford means. We only know how things are with you by your letters; but how things stand in England we have received no letters of anything, and it was November before we received yours. If we come at all unto you, the means to enable us so to do must come from you. For the state of our Church, and how it is with us, and of our people, it is wrote of by Mr. [Roger] White.

"Thus praying you to pardon my boldness with you in writing as I do, I commend you to the keeping of the Lord, desiring, if he see good and that I might be serviceable unto the business, that I were with you.

"God hath taken away my son, that was with me in the ship when I went back again. I have only two children, which were born since I left you. Fare you well.

"Yours to his power,

"THOMAS BLOSSOM.

"*Leyden, December* 15, anno 1625."

The letters from New Plymouth to the friends at Leyden referred to by Blossom as coming to hand in November 1625 were penned before the news of Robinson's death had reached the colony. Amongst these letters was one from Bradford, probably addressed to Robinson, asking advice as to the desirability of allowing himself and Allerton to be elected as Governor and Assistant year after year; and earnestly pleading that Robinson and the remaining members of the Church at Leyden should cross to join their brethren in America.

Roger White, after the Church had drawn up its official reply on Sunday, November 30, to the greetings from New Plymouth, wrote a private covering letter in answer to Bradford's inquiries. He and others were dubious whether it would be possible to maintain the liberty of exercising their religion, according to their conviction and present practice, in New England under the sway of King Charles, so soon had their hopes of the new king begun to droop.

Roger White to Governor Bradford

"To his very loving friend Mr. William Bradford, Governor of Plymouth in New England, these be, etc.

"My loving, kind Friend and Brother in the Lord,

"My own and my wife's true love and hearty salutations to yourself and yours and all the rest of our loving friends with you; hoping in the Lord of your good health, which I beseech him long to continue for the glory of his name and good of his people.

"Concerning your kind letter to the Church, it was read publicly; whereunto (by the Church) I send you here enclosed an answer. Concerning my brother Robinson's sickness and death and our practice, I wrote you at large, some five or six months since; but lest it should miscarry, I have now written to Mr. Brewster thereof, to whom I refer you.

"Now concerning your course of choosing your Governors yearly, and in special of their choosing yourself year after year (as I conceive they still do) and Mr. Allerton your Assistant; howsoever, I think it the best way that can be, so long as it please the Lord to continue your lives and so good governors offer you, yet, considering man's mortality, whose breath is in his nostrils, and the evils of the times wherein we live, in which it is ordinarily seen that worse follow them that are good, I think it would be a safer course for after time, [if] the government was sometime removed from one to another; so the Assistant one year might be Governor next, and a new Assistant chosen in his place, either of such as have or have not been in office; sometimes one, sometimes another, as it shall seem most fit to the Corporation. My reasons are—

"First, because other officers that come after you, will look (especially if they be ambitiously minded) for the same privileges and continuance you have had; and if he have it not, will take great offence, as though [thought] unworthy of the place and, so greatly disgraced, whom to continue might be very dangerous, and hazard (at least) the overthrow of all; men not looking so much at the reasons why others were so long continued as at the custom.

"Secondly, because others that are unexperienced in government might learn by experience, and so there might be fit and able men continually, when it pleaseth the Lord to take any away.

"Thirdly, by this means you may establish things begun or done before; for the Governor this year that was Assistant last, will in likelihood rather ratify and confirm and go on with that he had a hand in the beginning of when he was Assistant, than otherwise, or persuade the new to it; whereas new Governors, especially when there are factions, will many times overthrow that which is done by the former, and so scarcely anything goeth forward for the general good; neither, that I see, can this be any prejudice to the Corporation; for the new may always have the counsel and advice of the old for their direction, though they be out of office. These things I make bold to put to your godly wisdom and discretion, entreating you to pardon my boldness therein, and so leaving it to your discretion to make use of as you see it fitting, not having written the least inkling hereof to any other.

"Now, I entreat you, at your best leisure to write to me how you think it will in all likelihood go with your Civil and Church estate: whether there be hope of the continuance of both or either: or whether you fear any alteration to be attempted in either.

"The reason of this my request is, the fear of some amongst us (the which, if that hinder not, I think will come unto you), occasioned partly by your letter to your father-in-law, Mr. May,[1] wherein you write of the troubles you have had with some, who it is like (having the times and friends on their sides) will work you what mischief they can; and that they

[1] Henry May, from Wisbech, Cambridgeshire, whose daughter, Dorothy, Bradford married.

may do much many here do fear; and partly by reason of this king's proclamation, dated the 13th of May last, in which he saith that his full resolution is : to the end that there may be one uniform course of government in and through all his whole monarchy—that the government of Virginia shall immediately depend on himself, and not be committed to any Company or Corporation, etc., so that some conceive he will have both the same civil and ecclesiastical government that is in England, which occasioneth their fear.

"I desire you to write your thoughts of these things for the satisfying of others. For my own part and some others we durst rely upon you for that, who (we persuade ourselves) would not be thus earnest for our Pastor and Church to come to you if you feared the danger of being suppressed.

"Thus desiring you to pardon my boldness and remember us in your prayers, I for this time and ever commit you and all your affairs to the Almighty, and rest,

"Your assured loving friend and brother in the Lord,

"ROGER WHITE.

"*Leyden* [*Monday*] *December* 1, *Anno* 1625.

"P.S.—The Church would entreat you to continue your writing to them, which is very comfortable."

CHAPTER XXVII

AFFAIRS IN PLYMOUTH COLONY

WE are apt to think of the Pilgrim colonists as so absorbed in battling with the difficult conditions of establishing their Plantation that they would have little time for books or for the discussion of those religious problems which were of supreme interest to them in Leyden. It comes almost as a surprise, therefore, to find a reference to Ainsworth's and Robinson's books being available for the perusal of visitors to New Plymouth in the infant days of the colony. Yet such was the case, as we learn from a letter, dated " August 28, 1622," from John Pory to Governor William Bradford.

Pory was a man of affairs, and a graduate of Cambridge University. On April 18, 1610, he was also incorporated at the University of Oxford. He was returned to Parliament for Bridgwater in 1605, and had travelled extensively in Europe. Pory became closely concerned with affairs in Virginia. He was at " James City " in the summer of 1619 when the representative " General Assembly " of Virginia met, and he sent an account of its proceedings to Sir Dudley Carleton, with whom he had an acquaintance. Several times he passed to and from the homeland and Virginia. A warrant bearing the sign manual of King James still exists, dated July 20, 1624, granting him £150 in payment of his expenses and " as [1] a reward for his service when employed in Virginia about the King's special affairs." Now Pory put into New Plymouth on one of his voyages, and had some time to stay there

[1] *Cal. of Colonial Papers*, p. 65.

while his ship watered and made ready to continue her Atlantic passage. The friend of Carleton meets in the New World Brewster, the Leyden printer, whom Carleton three years before had sought in vain. How strangely the threads of life are crossed!

Here was an opportunity to remove misunderstandings and overcome prejudices. Pory's intercourse with level-headed men like Brewster and Fuller and Bradford would be helpful to both sides. Here was a visitor who could appreciate the contents of those weighty cases of Elder William Brewster's books with which the *Mayflower* had in part been ballasted. Leisure time at Plymouth was pleasantly employed by Pory in looking over Brewster's library and dipping into the books that had come from the press of the Separatists at Leyden and Amsterdam. A present of spare copies of Robinson's and other volumes at parting did not come amiss. Hence this postscript to his letter—

"To yourself and Mr. Brewster I must humbly acknowledge myself many ways indebted, whose books I would have you think very well bestowed, who esteems them such jewels. My haste would not suffer me to remember, much less to beg Mr. Ainsworth's elaborate work on the five books of Moses; both his and Mr. Robinson's do highly commend the authors, as being most conversant in the Scriptures of all others; and what good who knows it may please God to work by them through my hands, though most unworthy, who find such high content in them. God have you all in his keeping.

"Your unfeigned and firm friend,

"John Porey."

The close association of Pory with Virginian affairs made his friendliness towards the Pilgrim colony all the more valuable. One of the earliest descriptions of the Plymouth Colony that has come down to us is by him. It gives us a glimpse of the Planters and their Fort in the summer of 1622. Bradford gratefully notes "the credit and good that he procured unto the plantation of Plimouth after his return, and that amongst those of no mean rank." In 1624 he was active in securing a commission for a "Council in Virginia." "Mr.[1] Pory," we read, "has spared no attendance nor diligence in the matter." He settled in London, and died in 1635.

The desire on the part of the Pilgrims at New Plymouth that their Leyden friends should join them in America was not lessened by Robinson's death. From the letters given above it is clear that the members of the Church at Leyden saw but little prospect of arranging for the passage by themselves. But Bradford and his associates kept that end steadily in view. The Plantation was gradually disengaging itself from the entanglement with the odd lot of Adventurers in London. The "composition" suggested to the Londoners by Standish was furthered by Allerton in the next year (1626), and was at last happily concluded in 1627. By this voluntary agreement, the joint-stock company of Adventurers was wound up. They agreed to accept £1800 in nine annual instalments of £200 in full discharge of the moneys they had ventured to equip, transport and supply the colonists.[2] While this placed a heavy obligation on the young colony—honourably met—it gave the colonists greater freedom of action. Stumbling-blocks could not now so easily be thrown by fanatical and fearsome Anglicans and Puritans in the way of transporting the people from Leyden.

Before sending Allerton over to England to act for them again in 1627, the colonists not only considered how they might best discharge their debts and engagements, "but also how they might (if possibly they could) devise means to help some of their friends and brethren of Leyden over unto them, who desired so much to come to them and they desired as much of their company."

[1] Secretary Conway, *State Papers, Colonial*, p. 69.

[2] Captain John Smith contrasts this arrangement favourably with the issue of Ventures in Virginia, where, after an expenditure of more than £200,000, the Adventurers or Investors "had not sixpence."—*Advertisements*, 1631, p. 19.

James Sherley, the London goldsmith, one of the few Adventurers who was heart and soul with the Planters, had brought maledictions upon his head for supporting them in this matter. He says, "ye sole cause why they maligne me (as I & others conceived) was y^t I would not side with them against you & the going over of ye Leyden people." [1]

When Allerton got back to New England, in the spring of 1628, and gave an account of his stewardship he was not only able to tell of satisfactory financial arrangements, but of the intention of their true London friends "to send over to Leyden for a competent number of them to be here the next year without fail—if the Lord pleased to bless their journey."

Eagerly and hopefully those at New Plymouth awaited their coming. It was not till August 1629 that the first considerable batch of those left at Leyden managed to reach their destination. They had a tedious journey. There were, says Bradford, "thirty-five of our friends, with their families." They first crossed to England, and then "shipped at London in May, with the ships that came to Salem, which bring over many pious persons to begin the churches there. So that their being long kept back is now recompensed by heaven with a double blessing; in that we not only enjoy them beyond our expectation, when all hope seemed to be cut off, but with them many more godly friends, as the beginning of a larger harvest for Christ, in the increase of his people and churches in these parts of the earth, to the admiration of many and almost the wonder of the world."

Arrived at Salem, it was some weeks before this party could be transported to New Plymouth. There they had to be supplied with corn "above thirteen or fourteen months before they have a harvest of their own production."

It is noteworthy that most of this party were on the old *Mayflower*, which thus for a second time carried

[1] Bradford's MS., reverse of fol. 154. Sherley's letter, dated December 27 [1627].

over a company of the Pilgrim Church. Sherley, writing May 25, 1629, says—

"Here are now many of your and our friends from Leyden coming over, who, though for the most part be but a weak company, yet herein is a good part of that end obtained which was aimed at, and which hath been so strongly opposed by some of our former adventurers. But God hath his working in these things which man cannot frustrate. . . . These come in the *May Flower*."

Some "servants" for the Plymouth colony had been sent, he says, in the "*Talbut* that went hence lately."

The next year another party from Leyden made the voyage. Sherley, writing from London on March 8, 1629–30, to Bradford, says, "Most of those who came in May last unto you, as also of these now sent, though (I hope) honest and good people are not like to be helpful to raise profit, but must somewhile be chargeable to you and us." This further company from Leyden also came with a large body of Puritan planters under the Massachusetts Company. They and their goods were set ashore in the Bay, and arrangements had to be made to fetch them thence to the Plymouth Plantation. They arrived "at the latter end of May" 1630, and in their case their maintenance had to be provided for sixteen months before they reaped a harvest of their own.

The twelve "Undertakers" in America and London met the heavy costs and charges of these two transportations.[1] It is testimony to the strength of the tie which bound the members of the Leyden Church in religious fellowship that those who had migrated to America should make such sacrifices to help their weaker brethren and fulfil their promise to assist them across the Atlantic. Bradford, with just pride, referred to it as "a rare example of brotherly love and Christian care in performing their promises and covenants to their brethren." Sherley was rather disappointed with this last batch of Leyden friends. He added a postscript to his letter of March 8,

[1] For these Undertakers consult the Index.

1629–30, to Bradford, in which he expressed his feeling in regard to their long wait in London and their equipment for the voyage—

"Indeed, they have been unreasonably chargeable, yet grudge and are not contented. Verily their indiscreet carriage here hath so abated my affection towards them, as, were Mrs. Robinson well over, I would not disburse one penny for the rest."[1]

Sherley evidently had regard for Robinson's widow, and probably talked over with her the possibility of her migrating to New Plymouth during his lengthy visit to Holland and Amsterdam on business in the preceding summer, but he did not think much of the rank and file. Bradford, with more kindly judgment, says, "This offence was given by some of them, which redounded to the prejudice of the whole."

A short catechism prepared by Robinson to explain the distinctive features of his teaching in regard to the constitution of a true Church of God was reprinted more than once after his death. I conjecture that he issued it first with a view to sending copies over to New England for the use of his followers there. The texts chosen for the title page and set out separately support this opinion. Here is the title of the edition of 1642—

A Briefe / Catechisme / concerning / CHVRCH / Government / By / That Reverend Divine Mr. IOHN / ROBINSON and may fitly be / adjoyned to Mr. Perkins six Prin / ciples, as an Appendix thereto.

1 Tim. iii. 14.

"These things I write hoping to come unto thee shortly."

1 Tim. iii. 15.

"But if I tarry long that thou mayst know how thou / oughtest to behave thy selfe in the house of God which is / the Church of the living God the pillar and ground of the truth."

London
Printed in the year 1642.

[1] See Bradford's *Letter-book* 1, Mass. Hist. Coll., vol. iii. p. 69.

A manuscript note to Robinson's name in the British Museum copy of this work identifies him as "a Separist at Leyden." The preface gives us a picture of Robinson as the faithful pastor catechizing the youthful part of his flock in private, and grounding them in the principles of religion by the use of William Perkins's Catechism on *The Foundation of the Christian Religion gathered into six Principles,* issued in 1606. It was a work designed to make "ignorant people . . . fit to hear sermons with profit, and to receive the Lord's Supper with comfort." The additions by Robinson may be illustrated by quoting the teaching concerning the Church and its officers—

"*Q.* What is the church?

"*A.* A company of faithful and holy people with their seed, called by the Word of God into public covenant with Christ and amongst themselves, for mutual fellowship in the use of all the means of God's glory and their salvation.

. . . .

"*Q.* How many are the offices of ministry in the church?

"*A.* Five, besides the extraordinary offices of apostles, prophets and evangelists, for the first planting of the churches, which are ceased with their extraordinary gifts.

. . . .

"*Q.* Show me which those offices be, with their answerable gifts and works?

"*A.* (1) The pastor (exhorter), to whom is given the gift of wisdom for exhortation. (2) The teacher, to whom is given the gift of knowledge for doctrine. (3) The governing elder, who is to rule with diligence. (4) The deacon, who is to administer the holy treasure with simplicity. (5) The widow or deaconess, who is to attend the sick and impotent with compassion and cheerfulness."

The little tract occupied sixteen pages, and bore the name "I. Robinson" at the end.

A curious metrical piece, entitled "*The Spy discovering the Danger of Arminian Heresie and Spanish Trecherie,* written by I. R.," appeared at Strasburgh in 1628. Mr. Sayle, in the *Cambridge University Library List of Early English Printed Books,* vol. iii.

p. 1563, asks if this was not by John Robinson, and points out that an edition of his *New Essays* appeared in the same year from the same press. Mr. Sayle assumed that Robinson was living in that year, whereas he died in 1625; and the signature to the address "To the zealous Professors and all true-hearted Patriots in Great Britaine," which runs—

"Strasborgh Aug. 23 sty. vet.
"Your affectionate though afflicted
"Servant and Countreyman
"J. R.,"

does not point to Robinson with any clearness.

Here is a sample of the verse—

"Yet though Arminius *Holland* had infected,
Since we his poysonous doctrine had detected,
And that blest King most learnedly repell'd
Those false positions seduc'd Vorstius held:
What madnes was't for vs to foster here
Those errours that our *Church* condemned there?"

The British Museum catalogue assigns this book to John Rhodes, minister of Enborne, near Newbury, who issued volumes of topical verse in 1602 and 1606.

CHAPTER XXVIII

THE INFLUENCE OF ROBINSON ON THE THOUGHT OF HIS AGE

THE influence of Robinson's work was felt long after his death in both hemispheres. It was exerted mainly in three directions: through his books, through the practical example of Congregational Church order which the religious societies at Leyden and New Plymouth afforded, and through the democratic ideals with which he had inspired his friends and connexions.

I. We have already noticed that Robinson's volume of *Essays* and his brief catechetical pamphlet on *Church Government* were several times reprinted after his death. His *IVSTIFICATION OF SEPARATION from the CHURCH OF ENGLAND* was re-issued, in an edition "printed in the yeere 1639," when the question handled was again coming prominently to the front, and again in 1644. The Puritans, who had formerly treated the Separatists with scant consideration, were driven to review their position as Laud tightened up the machinery of the Anglican Church. Their hope of capturing this Church and reforming it from within had been rudely dashed. Churches on the model of Robinson's congregation seemed to do very well in New England. After all there might be something to be said for the "Congregational way," when the State Church allowed no deflection from the high-road of Laudian ceremony and doctrine, which appeared to be heading straight for Rome. They were prepared to read *A Justification of Separation* through fresh spectacles. The

THE OLD CHAPEL AT GAINSBOROUGH.

booksellers, with their fingers on the pulse of the market, were ready to meet the need. Since the days of the Pilgrim Press at Leyden, a large traffic had grown up between Holland and England in political and religious books and pamphlets, which it was inconvenient to print under the eye of the Bishop of London and His Grace of Canterbury. When Matthew Simmons was over in the Low Countries in November 1637 he gathered information about English books printed there. Amongst them he notes a Scottish book, entitled *The English-Popish Ceremonies;* many Bibles in quarto and folio " with notes "; the *News from Ipswich* in Dutch, and intended to be printed in French, " to make the bishops' cruelty known to all nations," and a tract on *The Practice of Piety*, printed by ten thousand at a time.

> " Robinson's *Justification of Separation*," he informs us, " is going in hand. All the shipmasters are engaged in the traffic, and they have a way, as they say, to cozen the devil. They strike upon the sands at Queenborough and send away their passengers and deliver all their prohibited goods in some small boats, and then come off the sands without danger." [1]

Thus the printers and booksellers got Robinson's book out of hand and into general circulation again.

Not long after this the English Parliament discarded episcopacy as the form of government for the State Church, and the question as to the most appropriate form of Church order to take its place arose. There was a conflict of opinion between those who favoured the Presbyterian and the Congregational ways of Church government respectively. Here again Robinson was appealed to by the latter and opposed by the former. His painstaking study of the question from the New Testament standpoint,

[1] *State Papers, Domestic*, Charles I, 1638.

in answer to Richard Bernard, proved to be a useful armoury from which the controversialists of the next generation drew effective arguments.

Samuel Rutherfurd, Professor of Divinity at St. Andrew's, in his work on *The Due Right of Presbyteries*, 1644, turned his attention to Robinson, and tells us that in his book "the arguments of Mr. Robinson in his *Justification of Separation* are discovered, and his treatise called *The Peoples Plea for the Exercise of Prophecy* is tryed." Rutherfurd used the reprints of Robinson's books. He noted the coincidence of the brethren in New England with the teaching of Robinson.

In another direction the work of Robinson exerted a moderating influence on those who would otherwise have gone to the extremes of "rigid separation." Perhaps his spoken word, his personal example and the general tone of his later writings had as much to do with this as his actual arguments written to this end, but the publication of his treatise on the *Lawfulness of Hearing the Ministers in the Church of England* in 1634 was not without effect. It helped to bridge the gulf between the Separatists and the "forward preachers" in the Puritan party, and to pave the way for the formation of a strong Congregational party in the Commonwealth period to serve as an effective check upon the drastic and sweeping plans of the Presbyterians.

About half a century later this treatise of Robinson was re-issued under very different conditions. It was a period of bitter persecution of the Dissenters. They were not allowed to hold office in the State unless they took the Communion in the Anglican Church, and when they occasionally resorted to their parish church for the Communion they were charged with deserting their principles and acting as hypocrites. In these circumstances some one bethought him of this treatise by Robinson and another on similar lines by Philip Nye, and reprinted them under the following title—

"The / LAWFULNES / of / Hearing the Publick Ministers / of the / Church of England, / proved, /

By { Mr. Philip Nye
and
Mr. John Robinson }

Two Eminent Congregational Divines.

. . . . . .

London: Printed for Jonathan Robinson at the Golden Lion in St. Paul's Church Yard 1683."

The object of the reprint is explained in the following prefatory note—

ADVERTISEMENT

"To stop the Mouths of many especially those Ministers that continually from Press and Pulpit do maliciously, as well as ignorantly, tell the People that the Dissenters (especially Independents and Anabaptists) do act contrary to their own Principles in Communicating sometimes with the Church of England and that they do so meerly to qualifie themselves for an Office to serve a Turn (as they spitefully phrase it) or to save themselves from the penal Laws, I have here inserted in what follows, the Opinion not only of the Independents, but even of the Brownists themselves, many years since about this matter."

It must not be supposed that Robinson would have countenanced the use of his treatise for the purpose of bolstering up the practice of occasional conformity with the Communion Office of the Anglican Church. He argued for the legitimacy of occasional hearing, but did not sanction participation in the parochial Communion services. To participate in order to qualify for office would have been abhorrent to him.

Another of Robinson's books was called for almost as soon as the Long Parliament got to work and made it safe to issue such publications. I refer to his spirited little defence of lay preaching in *The People's Plea for the Exercise of Prophesie.* The pent-up feelings of the people found vent in an outburst of lay preaching on the fall of Laud and the restriction of the power of the Bishops, and in Robinson's book was to be found a reasoned argument, supported by ample Scriptural quotations, upholding the practice.

II. The second direction in which Robinson's influence was felt in after times was in the organization of Congregational Churches in England and America. There was direct intercourse between Henry Jacob and John Robinson, and the Congregational Church gathered by the former in London in 1616 owed not a little to the ideas concerning Church government which Robinson expounded and followed. It may be noted also that the Baptist Churches which sprang, in course of time, from Jacob's congregation followed the same principles of Church order, while the old General Baptists, derived more directly from the movement started by Smith and Helwys, evolved a system of Church government virtually episcopal in form, by which an order of "Messengers," ordained to supervise and serve the churches of a wide district, was set up.

In New England the effect of the example of the Church at Plymouth was most striking, and there the principles of Church order enunciated by Robinson were widely adopted. When John Endicot, Charles Gott and others from the Dorchester district went over in 1628 to Naumkeak (afterwards called Salem) as pioneers for the Massachusetts Bay Company, they found Roger Conant, who had recommended the site, holding on there with the remnants of a previous colonizing venture, at the adjacent Cape Ann, till their arrival. Now Conant already had some acquaintance with the Church and Planters of New Plymouth, and was able to contrast their dependableness with the instability of John Lyford. Lyford, on his disgrace and expulsion from New Plymouth, had become minister of the Cape Ann settlers and those "lately removed out of New Plymouth out of dislike of their principles of rigid separation," but on receiving "a loving invitation" to Virginia he induced the main part of them to go off with him, "for fear of the Indians and other inconveniences,"[1] and thus left Conant in the lurch to stay at the hazard of his life. He might well begin to think the Planters of Plymouth, in spite of their separation from the Anglican Church, were more desirable neighbours and friends than men of the Lyford stamp. He would tell Endicot on his arrival that the Brownists, after all, were not so black as they had been painted. Endicot soon had a chance of judging for himself. Sickness broke out amongst his company of Planters, and in his need he sent over to New Plymouth for help. Samuel Fuller, deacon of the Plymouth Church, had some skill in medicine, and was accordingly sent to Salem on a healing mission. He was also skilled in the Scriptures, and well grounded in the principles of Church order set forth by his pastor at Leyden. The questions at issue in respect to Church government came up for discussion between him and Endicot, and it was soon made plain that they both held practically identical views. The following letter from Endicot to Bradford speaks for itself. It was preserved especially because it showed "the beginning of their *Christian fellowship*."

"Right Worshipful Sir,

"It is a thing not usual, that servants to one master and of the same household should be strangers. I assure you I desire it not. Nay, to speak more plainly, I cannot be so to you. God's people are all marked with one and the same mark, and have, for the main, one and the same heart guided by one and the same spirit of truth; and where this is, there can be no discord, nay, here must needs be a sweet harmony. And the same request with you I make unto the Lord, that we may, as Christian brethren, be united by an heavenly and unfeigned love, binding all our hearts and forces in furthering a work beyond our strength, with reverence and fear, fastening our eyes always on Him that is able to direct and prosper all our ways.

"I acknowledge myself much bound to you for your

[1] Leonard Bacon, *Genesis of the New England Churches*, p. 448.

kind love and care in sending M[r]. Fuller amongst us, and rejoice much that I am by him satisfied touching your judgment of the outward form of God's worship; it is, as far as I can gather, no other than is warranted by the evidence of truth, and the same which I have professed and maintained ever since the Lord in mercy revealed himself unto me, being far from the common report that hath been spread of you touching that particular, but God's children must not look for less [than misrepresentation] here below, and it is a great mercy of God that he strengtheneth them to go through with it.

"I shall not need, at this time, to enlarge unto you, for (God willing) I purpose to see your face shortly. In the meantime I humbly take my leave of you, committing you to the Lord's blessing and protection: and rest,

"Your assured loving friend,

"JOHN ENDICOT.

"*Neamkeak, May* 11, 1629."

When this letter was being written reinforcements on a large scale were already on the way from the Mother Country to the new colony at Naumkeak. The supporters of the movement in England had secured (March 4, 1629) a Royal charter confirming their "patent," and incorporating their society under the title of "The Governor and Company of Massachusetts Bay in New England," and they were planning big things. Three ministers were sent over to serve the colonists, Francis Higginson, Samuel Skelton and Francis Bright. With these ships there also travelled several members of Robinson's old Church at Leyden with their families, and one Ralph Smith, a Separatist minister, who was granted a passage before "his difference in judgment in some things from our ministers" was understood. The intercourse on shipboard would do something to overcome the prejudices between the Puritans and Separatists thus embarked on a common venture. Higginson and Smith were together on the *Talbot.*

"When they came to the Land's End M[r]. Higginson, calling up his children and other passengers unto the stern of the ship to take their last sight of England, said, We will not say as the Separatists were wont to say at their leaving of England, Farewell, Babylon! farewell, Rome! but we will say Farewell, dear England, farewell the Church of God in England and all the Christian friends there."

Higginson put into the mouth of the Separatists at this juncture the sentiment he thought appropriate to the character as popularly conceived, and as pictured in his own imagination. I think he soon realized that he had done them an injustice. In the course of the voyage a day of fasting and prayer was kept, and the two ministers joined together in the solemnity. "There being two ministers in the ship," says Higginson, "Mr. Smith and myself, we endeavoured, together with others, to consecrate the day as a solemn fasting and humiliation to Almighty God, as a furtherance of our present work." They spent seven Sundays together on board, time enough to get to understand one another. On June 29, 1629, they safely entered Salem harbour and landed from their voyage.

Ralph Smith, after trying the ground at Nantasket amongst a few "straggling" settlers, found his way to Plymouth. Here he joined the Church as a member, and assisted Brewster in the exercise of "prophesying." When the Church had made sufficient trial of his gifts he was duly appointed minister.

Meanwhile the newly arrived colonists, together with the settlers already at Salem under John Endicot, proceeded to set their ecclesiastical affairs in order. It was just here that the example of the Plymouth Church as a self-governing, reformed Christian society had telling effect. The colonists were bent on "settling a reformed congregation." The Bishops of England were now far away, and there was a clear field for a fresh start. After conference on the matter and looking into the New Testament for guidance the majority came to conclusions very similar to those at which Robinson had arrived. We are fortunate in having a contemporary letter describing the first steps taken to lay the foundation of their new Church order. It was not to be expected that all would be satisfied with the changes made. Francis Bright withdrew to Charlestown, and after a year returned to England; the Browne brothers, John and Samuel, " men of parts and port in the place," stood out for the use of the Book of Common Prayer and the customary Offices for Baptism and Communion. As they were creating a faction in the infant colony Endicot promptly shipped them back to England on the return of the vessels in which they had come. The election and ordination by the people of Skelton as " pastor " and Higginson as " teacher " was a close approach to the practice of the Plymouth Church. Gott reports the matter for us from the spot—

" To the worshipful, his worthy and much respected friend, Mr. Bradford, Governor of Plymouth, these:

" I, with my wife, remember our service unto you and yours, thanking you most humbly for your great kindness when we were at Plimouth with you.

" Sir—I make bold to trouble you with a few lines, for to certify you how it hath pleased God to deal with us since you heard from us, [and] how, notwithstanding all opposition that hath been here and else where, it hath pleased God to lay a foundation, the which I hope is agreeable to his Word in everything.

The 20th of July it pleased the Lord to move the heart of our Governor to set it apart for a solemn day of humiliation for the choice of a pastor and teacher; the former part of the day being spent in prayer and teaching, the latter part about the election which was after this manner.

" The persons thought on (who had been ministers in England) were demanded concerning their callings. They acknowledged there was a twofold calling; the one an inward calling when the Lord moved the heart of a man to take that calling upon him and fitted him with gifts for the same; the second was an outward calling which was from the people, when a company of believers are joined together in covenant to walk together in all the ways of God and every member (being men) are to have a free voice in the choice of their officers, etc.

" Now, we being persuaded that these two were so

qualified, as the apostle speaks of to Timothy where he saith 'a bishop must be blameless, sober, apt to teach,' etc., I think I may say, as the eunuch said unto Philip, 'what should let him from being baptized seeing there was water and he believed'; so these two servants of God clearing all things by their answers (and being thus fitted) we saw no reason but we might freely give our voices for their election after this trial.

"Their choice was after this manner. Every fit member wrote in a note his name whom the Lord moved him to think was fit for a pastor, and so likewise whom they would have for teacher. So the most voice was for Mr. Skelton to be pastor and Mr. Higginson to be teacher, so Mr. Skelton was chosen pastor and Mr. Higginson to be teacher; and they accepting the choice, Mr. Higginson, with three or four more of the gravest members of the church, laid their hands on Mr. Skelton, using prayer therewith. This being done there was imposition of hands on Mr. Higginson also.

"Then there was proceeding in election of elders and deacons[1] but they were only named and laying on of hands deferred, to see if it pleased God to send us more able men over; and since that time, Thursday (being as I take it ye 5 August[2]) is appointed for another day of humiliation for the full choice of elders and deacons and ordaining of them.

"And now, good Sir, I hope that you, and the rest of God's people (who are acquainted with the ways of God) with you, will say that here was a right foundation laid and that these two blessed servants of the Lord came in at the door and not at the window.

"And thus I have made bold to trouble you with these few lines, desiring you to remember us to Mr. Brewster, Mr. [Ralph] Smith, Mr. Fuller and the rest of the church; so I rest,

"At your service in what I may till death,

"CHARLES GOTT.

"*Salem, July* 30, 1629."

Whether the Plymouth people made any suggestion as to laying the foundation more truly and securely does not appear, but it is noteworthy that the Salem

[1] Henry Houghton was selected as "ruling Elder" and Gott himself was eventually ordained deacon of Salem Church.

[2] Gott was a day out in his reckoning. Thursday was August 6 in 1629.

people advanced yet another step nearer to the polity advocated by Robinson before they completed their Church organization. I think it quite likely that there had already been some discussion about the covenant of Robinson's Church. In the formation of the Separatist Church at Gainsborough under John Smith, and in the Leyden Church under Robinson, the members had first constituted themselves as a Church by mutual covenant with God and one another. Not until that was done did they proceed to elect and ordain officers from among their members. The Church came before the officers. Membership in the true Church was a pre-requisite to bearing office in the Church. These points were now discussed at Salem. It was a question whether the colonists were in true Church order when they first elected and ordained their pastor and teacher. The defect ought to be remedied. It was therefore agreed to constitute the Church by covenant and repeat the ordination, imperfectly effected on July 30, on another day. For this purpose August 6 was set apart, and notice of the event sent to the Church of Plymouth. The settlers at Cape Ann and Naumkeak under Conant and Endicot had certainly met together from time to time for religious worship, but up to now they were merely a congregation and not a "Church." Francis Higginson, at the request of those who held this view, wrote out thirty copies of a simple Church covenant, which was owned on the appointed day by as many persons, and the business of electing and ordaining pastor, teacher and other Church officers was then proceeded with in order. William Bradford and other delegates from the Plymouth Church set out with the intention of joining the friends at Salem on this historic occasion, but they "coming by sea were hindered by cross winds that they could not be there at the beginning of the day, but they came into the assembly afterward and gave them the right hand of fellowship, wishing all prosperity and a blessed success unto such good beginnings."

From the outset, therefore, the New England Churches constituted by the Puritan refugees were influenced by the example and practice of the Plymouth Church. The very covenant adopted at Salem was based on that formulated by John Smith, and taken as the basis of his Church by John Robinson—

> "We covenant with the Lord and one with another; and doe bynd our selves in the presence of God to walke together in all his waies, according as he is pleased to reveale himself unto us in his Blessed word of truth."

The Church formed in the next year (July 30, 1630) at Charlestown followed the same lines as that at Salem. Here again the influence of Samuel Fuller of Plymouth was felt, and his advice was reinforced by Endicot, who had become an ardent advocate of the Congregational way. Fuller, writing on June 28, 1630, to Bradford, says, "The Governor [John Winthrop] hath had conference with me both in private and before sundry others." These conferences bore fruit. A few weeks later, on Sunday, July 25, after "the evening exercise," a letter arrived at Salem from Winthrop asking the advice of the friends there as to the best course of procedure for setting themselves in Church order in view of the mortality afflicting the newly-landed colonists. Now, when this letter came to hand at Salem, it happened that Fuller, Edward Winslow and Isaac Allerton of the Plymouth Church were present. The Salem friends at once took them into consultation in the matter, and it was resolved to advise Winthrop and the Charlestown settlers to set apart—

> "the 6 day (being Friday) [July 30, 1630] of this present week . . . that they may humble them selves before God and seek him in his ordinances; and that then also such godly persons that are amongst them and known each to other may publicly at the end of their exercise make known their godly desire, and practice the same, *viz.* solemnly to enter into covenant with the Lord to walk in his ways."

The Church at Plymouth, also, was asked to specially observe the same day on their behalf. The following covenant was accordingly adopted by the Charlestown-Boston Church. It is still in use in the First Church, Unitarian, in Boston, the direct descendant of that religious society—

"In the name of our Lord Jesus Christ and in Obedience to his holy Will and divine Ordinance—

"We whose names are hereunder written, being by His most wise and good Providence brought together into this part of America in the Bay of Massachusetts, and desirous to unite ourselves into one Congregation or Church under the Lord Jesus Christ our Head in such sort as becometh all those whom He hath redeemed and sanctified to himself, do hereby solemnly and religiously (as in his holy presence) promise and bind ourselves *to walk in all our ways according to the Rule of the Gospel, and in all sincere conformity to his holy Ordinances and in mutual love and respect each to other, so near as God shall give us grace.*"

William Bradford in his *Letter-Book* noted the course of affairs with approval. He pointed out how the new-comers in 1629 "quickly grew into Church order, and set themselves roundly *to walk in all the ways of God.*"

Salem and Plymouth friends also advised the Charlestown people not "rashly to proceed to y[e] choyce of officers" on the day of covenanting. It was not till August 27, 1630, that officers were chosen from the covenanted members and set apart for their duties by laying on of hands. John Wilson was set apart to the office of "teacher," but he stipulated that this appointment was not to be taken as a renunciation of his orders received in the Anglican Church. Two years later (November 22, 1632) he was chosen "pastor," an office which he held till his death (August 7, 1667). In consulting with the people at New Plymouth about their Church affairs the Puritan colonists were following the advice of an eminent minister, John Cotton, who was soon to join them. At their leaving England he urged them to "take the advice of them at Plymouth," and when he himself came over and was chosen as colleague with John Wilson in the Boston Church he followed the principles which Robinson had advocated, and was duly ordained to his new post of teacher by the imposition of the hands of the pastor and elders and special prayer (October 10, 1633). It was in virtue of this ordination, and not of that received in the Episcopal Church at home, that he henceforth carried on his ministry.

It was not only in the matter of setting up and ordering the "Church" that the new-comers coincided with the practice of Robinson and his followers. Morton tells us, in his *New England's Memorial*,[1] that Higginson and Skelton took into consideration "the state of their children." Were they members of the Church along with their covenanted parents? "Concerning which letters did pass between Mr. Higginson and Mr. Brewster, the reverend elder of the Church at Plimouth, and they did agree in their judgments, namely, concerning the Church membership of the children with their parents; and that baptism was a seal of their membership; only, when they were adult, they being not scandalous, they were to be examined by the Church officers, and upon their approbation of their fitness, and upon the children's public and personal owning of the covenant they were to be received unto the Lord's Supper." This course was followed in the case of Higginson's son John, then about fifteen years old. In practice "the parents, owning and retaining the baptism which they themselves received in their infancy in their native land, as they had any children born, baptism was administered unto them, namely, to the children of such as were members of that particular Church." This is precisely the position which Robinson laid down and defended.

Seeing that there was such a close agreement between

[1] Sub Anno 1629.

Plymouth and the other Churches of New England, it is strange to find how touchy the latter were upon the point. They did not like being reminded of the fact. They argued that they were simply following the plain teaching of the New Testament—which argument, by the way, only served as a fine vindication of Robinson and his followers.

Puritans and Presbyterians at home soon saw which way the wind was blowing in New England. As a writer put it in 1659—

> "Mr. Hildersam did much grieve when he understood that the Brethren in New England did depart from the Presbyterian Government and he said: 'This mischief had been prevented if my counsel at Mr. Higginson's going over had been taken, which was that brethren driven thither by Episcopal persecution should agree upon Church Government before they depart from hence.' And it is well-known that many presbyterian non-conformists did by a letter sent into New England bewaile their departing in practice (as they heard) from the way of Church Government which they owned here." [1]

Cotton and Winslow, in rebutting the charge brought against them on this head, in which there was nothing to be ashamed of or to make apologies for, in effect admit the truth of the statement made about the influence of the Plymouth Church on those Churches subsequently formed in New England.

Robert Baillie had declared "the congregation of Plymouth did incontinently leaven all the vicinity." To this Cotton rejoined there was no vicinity to leaven. "Salem itself, that was gathered into Church order seven or eight years after them, was above forty miles distant from them. And though it be very likely that some of the first comers might help their theory by hearing and discerning their practice at Plymouth, yet therein the Scripture is fulfilled, 'The kingdom of heaven is like unto leaven, which a

[1] *Irenicum, or an Essay towards a brotherly peace . . . between those of the Congregational and Presbyterian Way,* "Epistle to the Reader." London, 1659.

woman took and hid in three measures of meal till all was leavened.' "[1]

Winslow, for his part, concedes all that I wish to claim. He, like Cotton, took up his pen in 1646 against Baillie, and this is what he said—

> "For the many Plantations that came over to us upon notice of God's blessing upon us, whereas 'tis falsely said they took Plymouth for their precedent, as fast as they came; 'tis true, I confess, that some of the chief of them advised with us (coming over to be freed from the burthensome ceremonies then imposed in England) how they should do to fall upon a right platform of worship, and desired to that end, since God had honoured us to lay the foundation of a Commonwealth and to settle a Church in it, to show them whereupon our practice was grounded; and if they found, upon due search, it was built upon the Word, they should be willing to take up what was of God. We accordingly showed them the primitive practice for our warrant, taken out of the Acts of the Apostles and the Epistles written to the several churches by the said Apostles, together with the commandments of Christ the Lord in the Gospel and other our warrants for every particular we did from the book of God. Which being by them well weighed and considered, they also entered into covenant with God and one another *to walk in all his ways revealed or as they should be made known unto them, and to worship him according to his will revealed in his written word only, etc.*
>
> "So that here also thou mayest see they set not the church at Plymouth before them for example, but the primitive churches were and are their and our mutual patterns and examples, which are only worthy to be followed, having the blessed Apostles amongst them, who were sent immediately by Christ himself, and enabled and guided by the unerring spirit of God. And truly this is a pattern fit to be followed of all that fear God, and no man or men to be followed further than they follow Christ and them."[2]

In other words, the Puritan settlers recognized the form and order of the New Testament Church when it was indicated for them by members of the Plymouth Church who had been schooled in the teachings of

[1] Cotton's *Way of the Congregational Churches Cleared*, p. 16.

[2] Winslow's "Narration" appended to his *Hypocrisie Vnmasked*, 1646.

Robinson, and when they saw it exemplified in the Plymouth Plantation.

There was a reaction from New England upon the religious life of Old England under the tolerant sway of Cromwell, and thus the fundamental ideas of the Congregational Church order, which Robinson had done so much to bring out into strong relief, gained a firm footing in his Homeland. Let one example suffice.

John Phillip, beneficed at Wrentham, who had married (January 6, 1611–12) Elizabeth Ames, became obnoxious to the clerical authorities on account of his Puritan proclivities, and was deprived of his living in 1638. Now, Joan Ames, the widow of his brother-in-law, William Ames, had gone over to America in 1637 and settled at Salem; to that place John Phillip followed her, crossing the Atlantic in 1638. When news of the great turn of affairs and the election of the Long Parliament came to hand Phillip resolved to return to Old England, and took ship on October 26, 1641. After a perilous voyage he went back to his old post at Wrentham, and began to model the Church affairs in his parish on lines with which he had become familiar in New England. When, on May 29, 1644, a move was made in Norwich by certain Congregationals, "to incorporate into a Church," they "gave notice thereof to Mr. John Phillip," and desired his assistance. It was only "infirmity of body" that hindered his attendance at this "inchurching" of a Congregational society amidst the scenes of Robinson's first ministry. Phillip was appointed a member of the Westminster Assembly of Divines in 1643, where he acted with the Congregationals.

After William Ames, son of William Ames, the friend of Robinson, had graduated at Harvard, in 1645, he, too, returned to the Mother Country, and went down to Wrentham to help John Phillip in his ministerial work. Here, in due course, he was made "Teacher" of the "Church" which his uncle served as "Pastor," and on February 1, 1649–50 the Church itself was reconstituted on more definitely Congregational lines in accordance with the model followed by the English Churches set up in Holland and New England. The Wrentham people were careful to disclaim any implication of censure on others who did not see their way to follow this method of reform. They sought to prevent "misconstructions of medling with or censuring any churches by o^{r} course the grounds whereof we doe shewe." But they used their liberty to reform the Church order in their parish, and they desired their action to be understood only "as ye reforming of o^{r}selves according to that Church estate, the patterne whereof is set before us in the words of Ct. according to ye measure of o^{r} enlightening therein." The point, however, to which I would specially draw attention is, that the members banded themselves together in a covenant, which, both by its brevity and its terms, reminds us of the covenants of the Church of Robinson and that at Salem—

> "Wee doe agree to give up ourselves unto ye Lord in p'fessed subiection to his gospell; and promise by the help of his grace whereupon wee trust, *to walke together in his holy ordinances and wayes, to watch over one another in love, and submit to the government of Christ in this society.*"

The Brewsters of Wrentham Hall were patrons of the living, of Wrentham, and throughout the seventeenth century presented preachers of Puritan type to that rectory. One cannot help suspecting that there was some connexion, more than that of name, between these Suffolk Brewsters and the families of the Pilgrim Elder, seated in Nottinghamshire at Scrooby, and of James Brewster, the incumbent of Sutton-cum-Lound, adjacent to Scrooby.

Robert Brewster, who presented Thomas King to the living, after John Phillip "fell asleep ye 2 of September 1660," was apparently the *Robertus Brewster, Anglus*, who matriculated at Leyden University "22 Maij 1619." When the Act of Uniformity was passed Thomas King was ejected. Then, in 1664, Henry Wotton became rector, on the presentation of Francis Brewster, apparently the *Franciscus Brewster, Anglus,* who matriculated at Leyden "1 Mart. 1645." Ames and his flock enjoyed the protection of this influential family, and Wotton showed a politic "forbearance towards the wandering sheep of his own parish."[1]

Though William Ames the younger was ejected from the benefices he held when the Act of Uniformity came into force, he continued in the neighbourhood under the shelter of the Brewsters and exercised his "office of Doctor," *i. e.* teacher, in the Congregational Church here till his death. In 1672 he was licensed as a "Presbyterian teacher," an indication that the term "Presbyterian" was already loosely used in England and without care for exactness. On July 21, 1689, he died, and is described on his tombstone as, "TEACHER . OF . A . CONGREGATIONAL . CHURCH . IN . WRENTHAM." He carried the traditions of Holland and New England on to the period of the Revolution. Thus he affords a notable link in the religious history of the East Anglian district, besides illustrating the way in which the principles of Church order and government put into practice in the "plantations" in New England reacted on the religious life of the Old Country.

Enough has been said to show that the influence of Robinson's ideas upon the right ordering of Christian Churches was felt as a potent and constructive force in the religious life of England and America long after his death.

III. A third direction in which Robinson's influence was exerted in after years—less obvious perhaps, but none the less real—was through the democratic ideals with which he inspired his friends and connexions. His example and teaching remained as an abiding and stimulating memory with men like Brewster, Brad-

[1] *Edm. Bohun's Diary,* quoted by Browne, *History of Congregationalism in Norfolk and Suffolk,* 1877, p. 431.

ford, Allerton, Blossom, Winslow and others, who had been closely associated with him. It was not without effect also on kinsfolk and connexions at home.

His wife's nephew, Charles White, the younger, took a prominent part on the side of the Parliament in the great Civil War. Bridget Robinson's eldest brother, Charles White, took up his residence at Beauvale Abbey in the parish of Greasley, which was more convenient for the county town of Nottingham than his old home at Sturton.[1] He continued at Beauvale till, " sicke in body but of perfect memory," he made his will in 1634 and died. To his son of the same name he left his " lease of Beavall."

When the Civil War broke out this Charles White the younger actively bestirred himself in the Parliamentary interest. He is frequently mentioned by Lucy Hutchinson in her *Memoir of Colonel Hutchinson*, but was not in her good books. She did not like him, and did him less than justice, speaking of him in rather disparaging terms. With Lucy Hutchinson her husband was the only hero. No one could be allowed to shine near him or diminish his glory, so when she mentions White she uses him as a foil to show up the virtues and graces of Colonel John Hutchinson. Still less did she like Charles White's choice of a wife. She says that he and Gilbert Millington, the Member for Nottingham in the Long Parliament, picked up with " a couple of ale-house wenches." Well, the choice of Millington seems to have satisfied not only himself, but his constituents, for we find the Corporation of Nottingham making a present to Mrs. Millington, and we may take it that White's choice also turned out pretty well. We must read Mrs. Hutchinson's character-sketch with caution. She tells us White " was of mean birth and low fortunes, yet had kept company with the underling gentry of his neighbourhood." Furthermore " he

[1] He was still described as " of Sturton " in 1620, when he was appointed " Treasurer " for the north part of Notts for the fund raised for the relief of " maymed souldiers."

gave large contributions to Puritan preachers," but she unkindly imputes this to a desire "to keep up a fame of godliness." She could not deny his popularity, but declared he won it "by a thousand arts."

"This man," she continues, "called Charles White, at the beginning of the Civil War got a troop of dragoons, who armed and mounted themselves out of devotion to the Parliament's cause, and, being of his neighbourhood, marched forth in his conduct, he having procured a commission [1] to be their captain."

He did good service in the war and saved Nottingham at one critical juncture by his timely arrival with troops from Leicester and Derby.

Here is a despatch of his, hitherto unpublished, addressed to that resolute soldier, Francis Thornhagh [2] of Fenton, in the parish af Stvrton, with which the Whites and Robinsons were connected. Thornhagh and White were closely associated in their campaigning—

Add. MS. 34,253, f. 38.

"ffor the Honble Col. Thornhagh
at the Kings Head
in the Strand
theis
wth my hu^m^ble
service.

[Sealed with dark red wax coat of arms]

"Since yor depture hence Parties have beene sent out every night but the enemie have drawne into thiere Guarrisons continually that nothing could be attempted onely on Friday morning last Corporall Crofte who is one of my Corp^ls^ wth 20 Horse of Capt Pendocks and mine did fall into Bridgeford long mour whither the Queens Regmt were newly come and all mounted, they charged through them routed the whole Regmt killed 8 beside what were wounded and brought off 16 prisoners and 28 Horse w^th^out loss of one man And on

[1] He was "one of the Captains appointed by the Earl of Essex." See a letter of Francis Pierrepont, December 13, 1642, *Hist. MSS. Comn. Report* 13, Pt. I. p. 79.

[2] Francis Thornhagh was killed August 17, 1648, in the pursuit of the Scots after the Battle of Preston. His body was taken to Sturton for burial.

Saturday following my L^{d} wth 42 men going to secure the markett fell into Langer where the Earl of Northtons Regimt were drawing out to a Randervous being about 200 Horse. 30 of o^{r} men charged about 80 of them and routed them and falling into the Towne wth them they killed betwixt 20 and 30 and a Capt they tooke a Maj^{r} 9 others and 27 Horse wthout loss of one man I desire that God may have the praise of all for he is worthy.

"On Sunday Capt Pendock and my L^{d} with 150 Horse went to Ekrin [Eakring] to gain Intelligence and the king quartered at Tuxford Laxton and Egmonton [Egmanton] wth his whole Army but they wanted men to fall upon any Quarte^{rs} I am just now sending a small pty to Ekrin.

[1] ["Since I begun this lttre I heare y^{t} the king quart^{rs} this night about Welbeck and Worksopp and (as Report gives it) he is for the North.

"S^{r} be pleased to pc̄ure some Armes if it be possible and some money for the country is impoverished and the souldiers in great wante. S^{r} I have noe more but to assure y^{u} that I am

"S^{r}

"Yo^{r} humble servant

"CHA: WHITE.

"*Nott. Oct.* 13. about 8 at night

"S^{r} I beseech yo^{u} psent my service to m^{r} Millington and excuse my not writing to him."][1]

With Millington, who was his neighbour at Felley Priory in Greasley parish, White was on terms of intimate friendship. From 1654 to 1656 White was knight of the shire. He served on many County Committees and took his full share in public work. Apparently he had some offer of service about this time in Russia, for on March 26, 1655, he sought a passport for himself, his wife Deborah, and their child Sarah, with a maid and two menservants, "to repair to Moscow." If he took the journey his stay was short, for on June 4, 1656, he was approved as an "elder" for Greasley parish, and signed his name,[2]

[1] This part is written along the side of the page.

[2] A facsimile of the signatures to this document is given in the *Transactions of the Unitarian Historical Society*, vol. i., 1917.

next after Millington, to the agreement to form a "Classis" or "Classical Presbytery" for Nottingham.

Charles White fell in with the Presbyterian system of Church order as then adopted in England, and not with the Congregational way. He was one of those Presbyterians who were disappointed at the outcome of the war on the practical side, and at the breakdown of Parliamentary government. He came to feel that the best hope for settled peace in England lay in the restoration of the King and the summons of a Parliament free from the domination of the Army. When Sir George Booth made his premature rising on behalf of Charles II in Cheshire, White, according to Mrs. Hutchinson, "thinking he could sway the scales of the country, raised a troop, brought them into Derby, and published a declaration of his own for the King."

His action created such a stir that the day was long known in Derbyshire as *White-Friday.* It was an abortive movement, and brought him and his friends into serious danger. Those implicated were summoned to appear before the County Committee of Notts. on November 26, 1659, or in ten days thereafter. On December 5 the Committee returned the name of Colonel Charles White amongst those who did not appear, but there was a reason, "Col. White, we hear, is prisoner at the Gatehouse, Westminster."[1] Already, in October, information had been sent up as to some of White's possessions: he "rented a coal delph of the Earl of Rutland . . . there are many coals on the bank which winter will prevent the carrying away of."[2] His property was to be sequestered.

But meanwhile the tide of popular feeling was fast turning. White had only anticipated by a few months a general movement throughout the country. The power of the old Parliamentary party was crumbling away. It had done its work, and lost favour the longer it now clung to office. A letter[3] from Major James

[1] *Calendar of the Proceedings of the Committee for Compounding*, ed. by M. A. Green, p. 769.

[2] *Ibid.*, Letter of James Fulwood, October 7, 1659, p. 756.

[3] *Ibid.*, p. 773.

Fulwood, one of the County Commissioners for Derby, dated January 14, 1659–60, shows how things were going in that locality. He reports that Colonel Thomas Sanders, who had been an eye-witness of White's "rebellion" in Derby, had actually given power to Captain Greenwood and Captain Samuel Doughty to secure all the arms of the county and send the soldiers home, which left the Parliamentary Commissioners bereft of authority. He goes on to say that both Greenwood and Doughty—

"were notorious in the rebellion raised by Col. White at Derby . . . where there were cries for a king and for a free Parliament and for the Cheshire Declaration . . . that Col. Sanders should give such power to these men has discouraged many that were faithful to Parliament."

At the Restoration, according to Mrs. Hutchinson, White "was rewarded for his revolt with an office, which he enjoyed not many months, his wife and he and some of his children dying altogether in a few days of a fever little less than a plague." He died in 1661, and was buried at Greasley.

So ended the life of Bridget Robinson's militant nephew—a man ready to strike a blow for civil and religious liberty, ready to adventure his life for what he esteemed a worthy cause.

If we turn from "Notts. and Derby" to the neighbouring shire of Lincoln, we there find a nephew of John Robinson taking an equally prominent part on the Parliamentary side in the Civil War. Mary Robinson, sister of the pastor of the Pilgrim Church, married William Peart. Peart evidently won the affection and confidence of the Robinson family. Old John Robinson, the father of the Leyden pastor, appointed him "overseer" of his will. His widow, Ann Robinson, in the absence of her eldest son in Holland, made her son-in-law Peart her executor. This was in 1616, and already there was a brave little family of grandchildren, for she left to every one of Peart's four sons, "William, Thomas, Originall, and John Pearte everye of them the some of xx^{s}."

The surname Peart is itself unusual, and conjoined with Original it makes a singular combination. This lad made his way in the world. He was apprenticed in the summer of 1620, at the age of fifteen, in Lincoln. When his seven years' apprenticeship was over in 1627 he married.

The clerk put him down as prosaic "Reginald" in the licence—it was the best he could make of Original. In 1640 he was Sheriff, and went out in his official capacity to meet King Charles on his visit to Lincoln. Unfortunately the minutes of the Lincoln Corporation are missing for the Commonwealth period, so the materials for a full-length portrait of Peart are lacking. He held a commission as "Captain" in the army under Fairfax, and saw service with Cromwell in the north in 1648. During his absence there was a Royalist raid on Lincoln. Edward Reyner of St. Peter at Arches, appointed Corporation Lecturer in 1627, a post once held by John Smith, was attacked in this raid, and Peart's house, in the parish of St. Peter at Gowts, was wrecked. He received a grant from Parliament in compensation out of moneys derived from the sale of Bishop's lands, and built himself "a delicate fine house, which cost him about £900." The citizens chose him as Mayor for 1650–51, and he represented Lincoln both in the "Short Parliament" (September 3, 1654–January 27, 1655); and in the second Parliament of the Protectorate (1656–58). After the Restoration and the return of a Bishop to the See of Lincoln he was soon turned out of his house. He is said to have interceded successfully with Cromwell for the preservation of the magnificent Lincoln Cathedral, in which the citizens took a just pride.

These examples from amongst the kinsfolk of John Robinson of the second generation show us how the ideals that stirred the minds of Englishmen in his day lived on and worked themselves out. A study of the family history of those prominent in the strife between Crown and Parliament goes to show that the causes of the struggle were of no sudden growth. The principles inculcated in the Puritan households of England in the days of Elizabeth and James came to fruition in the time of the Long Parliament. Through much striving and blood and tears those principles were at length recognized and embodied in the working constitution of the country. The leaven had long been at work in silence. There were those who thought the principles of absolutism in politics and religion were going to be a success in England. William Laud had spent his tireless energy in compelling the clergy to toe his own special ecclesiastical mark. Outwardly he got things in some measure to his satisfaction. Open opposition seemed to die down. But nothing convicts Laud more completely with narrowness of vision than the fact that he mistook the lull before the storm as evidence of the triumph of his policy of repression. Sincere and devout though he was, yet he was incapable of recognizing the intensity of religious conviction in those who could not keep step with him in matters of ritual and doctrine. In the great Civil War in England, by means of which great constitutional issues were decided, the driving force in the conflict was religion. The ideals and principles, drawn out into definite shape by such men as Robinson, in regard to the rights of the individual Christian, "the visible saints" in the Church, reacted upon the current ideas of the rights and privileges of the citizen in the State, and gave the stiffening for the struggle.

CHAPTER XXIX

THE FORTUNES OF THE ROBINSON FAMILY AND THE AFTER-HISTORY OF THE PILGRIM CHURCH—A PARALLEL RELIGIOUS DEVELOPMENT IN OLD AND NEW ENGLAND

Of the members of Robinson's own family we have but little information beyond what has already been given in these pages. In a paper on "The Descendants of the Rev. John Robinson," by William Allen, D.D., prefixed to Ashton's reprint of Robinson's *Works*, it is said that his eldest son John "settled at or near Cape Ann, and had a son Abraham, who died at the age of one hundred and two." This, though often repeated, has not been substantiated. And as John Robinson junior matriculated at Leyden, April 5, 1633, the statement that he came "to Plymouth, Mass., in 1630,"[1] can hardly be correct.

Ann, the eldest of Robinson's children, seems to have married into a Dutch family.

Bridget, born in 1608, the year of migration to Holland, was twice married—

(*a*) First, to John Greenwood, born in London about 1605. He matriculated at Leyden University in philosophy July 9, 1625, at which time he boarded with John Keble, and thither also he took his young bride after the wedding, on May 26, 1629, for he was still living in Keble's house when, on May 22, 1634, he matriculated in theology at the University, giving his age then as twenty-eight. Before long, however, he died, and his young widow married—

(*b*) William Lee of Amsterdam on July 25, 1637.

[1] *The Robinson Family*, New York, 1902, Paper by W. A. Robinson, p. 29.

The next in age in John Robinson's family was Isaac, born in 1610. Of him more is known, for he crossed over, when he came of age, to Massachusetts in the good ship *Lion* in the year 1631, and then made his way to the Plymouth colony to the old friends of his father. He did not take a very prominent part in colonial affairs. He was busied in making his footing good in the New World, and when that was done he married, in 1636, Margaret Hanford. On her death, after bearing him five children, he married a second wife in 1649, who bore him other four. It is his descendants who carry on the line of the Pilgrim Pastor in New England. He settled first at Scituate, where in 1633 he was on the list of freemen. In 1639 he removed to Barnstable. It is of interest to note that Isaac Robinson moved on to the Quaker position in religion. When the Quakers turned their attention to New England as a field for missionary enterprise, in 1656, they found Plymouth more congenial ground for their message than Massachusetts. The tradition of the place was in their favour. The mother Church had long been served by the ministration of laymen, and the members were encouraged to exercise their gifts. There was not quite the same view of the ministry as an exclusive and peculiar class which prevailed in the Puritan colonies. Writing to Margaret Fell from Barbadoes in 1657 Henry Fell says, "In Plimouth patent there is a people not soe ridged as the others of Boston, and there are great desires among them after the Truth." Indeed there had already been "a crying downe of minnestry and minnesters" in Plymouth Colony.[1] But having said this, we must not suppose that the Quakers, with their then extravagant methods, were welcome visitors. Indeed "the General Court" of the colony, in order to stem the tide of Quakerism, appointed in 1659 Isaac Robinson, J. Smith, J. Chipman and J. Cooke to attend the Quakers' meetings, "to endeavour to reduce them from the error of their ways." It was a good thing

[1] *Colony Records*, vol. ii. p. 156.

to put the son of their old pastor on to the deputation. He, if any one, ought to be well grounded in their principles. Besides, he was a solid sort of man, who had served the Governor twice as Assistant, and would not easily be rattled. The upshot, however, was that Robinson himself was "convinced" of "truth," and became a member of the Society of Friends. He, like his father, was ready to suffer for his convictions. He and Cudworth, the "assistant" from Scituate, where Timothy Hatherley, one of the original London Adventurers for the colony, had also joined the Quakers, were left out of office and disfranchised. Under the governorship of the Hon. Josias Winslow (elected June 3, 1673) their rights as "freemen" were given back to them.

Isaac Robinson, with thirteen other colonists, founded the town of Falmouth, in Plymouth Colony, and took the lead in a small Quaker meeting in that place.[1] He lived to a great age. Prince, who was born at Sandwich, New England, in 1687, remembered him as "a venerable man," whom he had often seen. When Judge Sewell was on circuit in the old colony in 1702, he visited Isaac, and made the following entry in his Journal under date April 4—

> "Visit Master Robinson, who saith he is 92 years old; is the son of Master Robinson, Pastor of the Church of Leyden, part of which came to Plymouth. But, to my disappointment, he came not to New England till the year in which Master Wilson was returning to England after the settlement of Boston.
>
> "I told him [I] was very desirous to see him, for his father's sake and his own. Gave him an Arabian piece of gold, to buy a book for some of his grandchildren."[2]

That is the last picture we have of him—the aged grandfather with the little ones about him. Did no one think it worth while to gather his reminiscences of the life at Leyden and his recollections of his

[1] For these details I am mainly indebted to an excellent work by Rufus M. Jones, *Quakers in the American Colonies*, pp. 60–64.

[2] Quoted in Arber's *Pilgrim Fathers*, p. 160.

father? Isaac Robinson died at Barnstable, full of years and honour.

The next child, Mercy Robinson, ten years old at the census of 1622, was probably the child of Robinson buried in 1623. Of her younger sister Fear more can be said, thanks to the researches of Dr. Dexter and his son.

Fear Robinson, born in 1614, remained in Leyden for life. She was in no hurry to marry, and would be a help and comfort to her mother during her widowhood. At last, on August 21, 1648, she was betrothed to John Jennings the younger, a wool-comber by trade, whose father, of the same name, had been connected with the congregation from its earliest days in Leyden. The witnesses at the betrothal were Elias Arnold, a watchmaker, and Rose Jennings. The marriage of John and Fear took place on September 8. For sixteen years they lived together, then John Jennings fell ill. He drew up his will, December 1, 1664, a necessary act, as he was leaving three little children behind. Six days later his body was carried out from his house on Molesteeg for burial in St. Peter's Church.

Fear Jennings was not left altogether unprovided for, and by the death of Rose Jennings, her mother-in-law, in 1668, further property came to her in right of her husband, in the shape of a house on Coepoortsgracht. Having inherited this property, she in turn made a will, March 20, 1669, and added a codicil in the following January. Before May 31, 1670, she was dead, and on that date the guardians of her three children, still under age, sold her house for 3790 gilders. It is noteworthy that John Butterfield, one of the English colony in Leyden, was the purchaser.

James, or Jacob, Robinson (the name was recorded as "Jacobus"), the youngest surviving son, barely lived to man's estate. He died in May 1638, and was buried from Engelschepoort on the 26th of that month in St. Peter's.

Bridget Robinson still lived on in the Pieterskerkhof, where her husband had spent the best years of his life. She was there in 1635, ten years after John Robinson's death. The last notice of her recorded by Dexter is as a witness at the betrothal of George Matersee̋ to Elizabeth Loder, April 6, 1640. She spent her declining years with her kinsfolk in the fair city of Holland which had given them asylum in earlier days. Only within the last few weeks, through the diligent research of Professor Eckhof, her Will has come to light.

The indications are that she remained in Holland and identified herself more and more with the Dutch Church, as her husband's Church departed from his liberal principles, and became too weak to sustain a regular pastorate. In a work on the *Sum of the Controversies of Religion,* issued in 1658, by John Hoornbeck, a professor at Leyden University, it is recorded that after Robinson's death "contention and schism having arisen in his congregation about communion with the Anglican Church in hearing the word, his widow, children, and the rest of his kindred and friends were received into the communion of our Church." [1] We may be sure that at times her thoughts would go back to the old homestead at Sturton, the green fields of Fenton, the flowing waters of the Oswald Beck, running down to the river of Trent, and to the scenes amidst which her girlhood was spent.

Of John Robinson's younger brother William, and of his younger sister, who married Roger Lawson, I can get no further information than that contained in the wills of their father and mother. The Christian name of William Robinson's wife was Ellen, and by 1612 they had a family, for old John Robinson in that year left "to everie of their children xx^{s}." I do not think he remained in Sturton. As a younger son he went out into the world, possibly to Hull or Gainsborough. Hunter pointed out [2] that "in the reign

[1] Oborta in cœtu contentione et schismate super communione cum Ecclesia Anglicana in auditione verbi D. Robinsoni vidua, liberi, reliquique propinqui et amici in communionem ecclesiæ nostræ recepti fuerunt. *Summa Controversiarum Religionis,* 1658, p. 42.

[2] *Collections Concerning the Founders of New Plymouth,* 1854, p. 93.

of Charles II Robinsons were chief persons among the Dissenters " in the latter town. Possibly further research may establish some connexion between these Robinsons and the family from which the pastor of the Pilgrims sprang; but to identify with certainty one bearing the designation William Robinson is only a degree less difficult than the identification of any particular John Smith.

No doubt there were those in the Gainsborough, Sturton, Retford and Worksop district who treasured the memory of John Smith and John Robinson after their removal into Holland, and continued to act on their principles. When Hanserd Knollys held the post of usher, from 1625 to 1629, in the Gainsborough Grammar School, he became acquainted with one of these "Separatists," and sometimes resorted to his house to hear him expound and preach. The fact that these house-meetings were open to an outsider indicates that there was a group of religious folk in the place holding kindred views with those of Smith and Robinson, the originators and leaders of the Separatist movement in the locality.

When the era of toleration came a General Baptist Church sprang into being at Retford, embodying some of the principles advocated by John Smith. At Gainsborough the Dissenters met in the house of Matthew Coats, when the brief Indulgence of 1672 gave them liberty to gather together. After the Toleration Act was passed, they felt free to set their Church affairs in order and build a chapel. This Church has continued down to the present time, its direct representative to-day being the Unitarian congregation in Gainsborough. Among the records of this congregation is an interesting document [1] giving a list of preachers and the fees paid to them for the period Dec. 1698 to May 1700, when Ambrose Rudsdell

[1] A facsimile of this document is given by Rev. W. R. Clark-Lewis in his *Foundation and History of Beaumont Street Church, Gainsborough*, 1912. I have consulted the original. Through the courtesy of Mr. Lewis we are able to reproduce it here.

settled as pastor, and a list of contributors to the expenses. The name of "Mr. Quip"[1] occurs more than once among the former. No doubt he was a descendant of the Quipps beneficed at Sturton, Littleborough and Leverton in the days of John Robinson. Amongst the contributors the names of "Robisson" and "Hopkinson" are prominent, while a payment appears to "Thomas Robinson, 4 Nights' Grass 1–4," for grazing the horse of the preacher.

The Hopkinson family, which was closely associated with the parish of Sturton,[2] presented this congregation with two silver chalices, which bear the inscriptions—

H
E A and E.H.
1697

The latter has the London date-letter of 1709–10, the initials being those of Elizabeth Hopkinson. The trust deed (dated July 12, 1701) of the building "lately erected in a place called the Ratten Row in Ganesburgh aforesaid, now used and intended to be used as a Chappell or meeting-house as by the lawes of this kingdom the same is now permitted and authorized," indicates that the congregation was of that broad inclusive spirit which John Robinson exemplified in his later years. Using the current nomenclature of the time for the English Nonconformists, the deed sets apart the building "for such Protestant Dissenters,

[1] This was William Quipp, who was minister of Newton-on-Trent in 1664. He was constantly in hot water with his Bishop for nonconformity. He was articled against for officiating in the churches of Marton and Torksey without a licence. In 1673 and 1679 he was articled against for non-observance of certain rubrics, and in 1685 "as a revolter from the doctrine and discipline of the Church of England." The Register of Marton, under date December 10, 1707, has the entry of the burial of "Mr. Wm. Quipp, Minister." Palmer's *Nonconformist's Memorial*, London, 1775, vol. ii. p. 166, and letter from Mr. A. R. Corns, City Librarian of Lincoln, *penes me*, September 3, 1919.

[2] Humphrey Hopkinson, son of John Hopkinson, dwelt in a messuage adjoining the east side of Sturton churchyard in 1655. His father's will was executed April 1, 1652. *Notts. County Records*, Copnall, p. 62, and information from Mr. S. Ingham. Sarah Leggatt, widow, by will in 1730 left part of the rent of a close of land in Morton for the support of a "preacher or teacher" of this Gainsborough congregation, *Transactions of the Unitarian Historical Society*, Dec. 1919, p. 21. Any connexion with the family into which Catherine Carver married ?

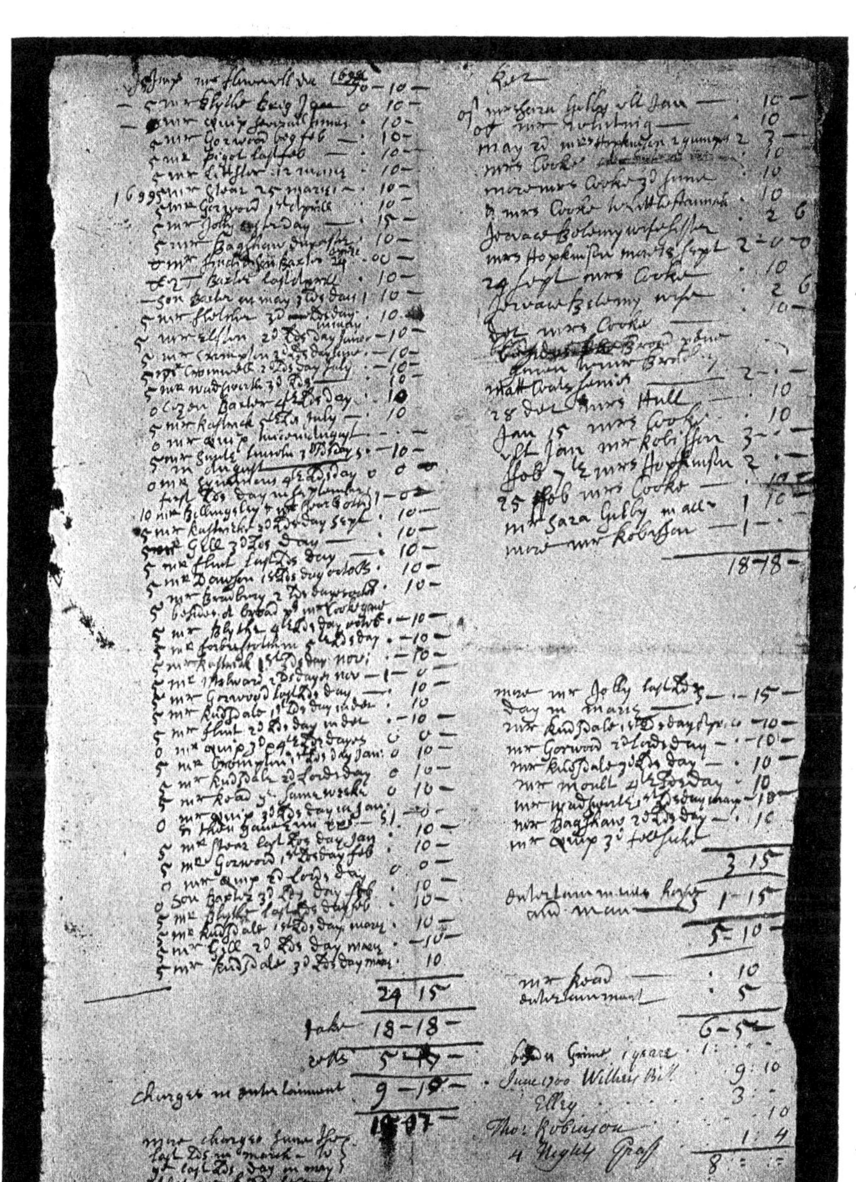

A LIST OF PREACHERS TO THE GAINSBOROUGH PROTESTANT DISSENTERS 1698–1700.

persons or people to meet, assemble and worshipp God in or [? as are] distinguished or goe under the names of Congregationall Independents or Presbyterians"; which means that the Congregation assented to the "Happy Union" of the Congregational and Presbyterian sections of Dissent which took place after the Toleration Act. This union persisted longer in the country than in London, where it was first mooted. Amongst the trustees we find Francis Hopkinson, mercer, and Nathaniel Robinson, mercer, both of "Ganesburgh."

Francis Hopkinson left a bequest to this congregation on his death in 1728, and it is noteworthy that he did not forget the old association of his family with Sturton and its neighbourhood, for he founded a charity there to provide clothing for the poor, which still continues its beneficent work. Elizabeth Hopkinson, his widow, was also a benefactor to this congregation. "Nathaniel Robinson, Senior," was described on his tombstone as "wholesale mercer in Gainsburgh." He died January 31, 1730, aged fifty-nine; Mary, his wife, died June 11, 1743, aged sixty-seven years. It remains for some local antiquary to discover whether or no he was a descendant of William Robinson of Sturton or any connexion of the family from which our John Robinson was derived.[1]

To exemplify the persistence of a deep concern for civil and religious liberty in the same families through several generations, I may instance a document preserved amongst the papers of the Earl of Ancaster relating to the stir caused by the Jacobite rebellion of 1745, when the work of the "Glorious Revolution," as the Whigs termed it, seemed to be endangered. On October 1, 1745, a "general and numerous" meeting was held at Lincoln Castle, a loyal address voted to the King and a resolve made to raise "A Voluntary

[1] There is in Gainsborough a "John Robinson Memorial Church," but its association with Robinson's name is simply a matter of sentiment, as the congregation for which it was built only came into being during the Evangelical Revival of the eighteenth century. It was opened on June 11, 1902, by the Hon. Francis T. Bayard, the United States Ambassador.

Subscription for the security of his Majesty's person and Government and for the payment of such forces as shall be raised within the county of Lincoln." Among the contributors are the names of several families whose interests had been enlisted on the side of progress and reform from the days of Elizabeth and James and the period in which John Robinson lived and wrote, *e.g.*—

> "John Peck, £15.
> John Robinson, £15.
> Joshua Peart,[2] £10.
> Cranwell Coats, £25.
> J. Crompton, £25.
> Benjn. Bromhead, £20.
> Nathl. Robinson, £10 10*s*.
> F. Flower, £50.
> Fitz. White, £21.
> Jonathan Rudsdell, £10.
> John Baxter, £4 4*s*.
> John Smith, £10.
> Jno. Disney, £80."

The history of Robinson's Church at Leyden after his death is obscure. The remnant of his congregation evidently held together for some years, but they were never able to appoint another minister. With the removal of many of the members to Plymouth in New England the Leyden Church was greatly weakened, and by the year 1634 its roll of members was reduced to a fifth of what it had been in Robinson's time. Moreover, on the withdrawal of Robinson's moderating influence differences had broken out amongst the members themselves, leading to a "breach." The occasion of this "rent in the Church" is explained by the "printers" of Robinson's treatise on the *Lawfulness of Hearing Ministers in the Church of England*, which they issued in 1634. They tell us that "some, though not many, were contrary minded"

[1] Hist. MSS. Com., *Report on MSS. of the Earl of Ancaster*, 1917, pp. 444–5.

[2] As late as October 23, 1783, I notice Edward Peart, from the county of Lincoln, graduated at Leyden.

to Robinson's judgment on this point. While "their chief if not their only teacher" adhered to the opinion of their late pastor, some "four or five men" in the congregation leaned to the stringency observed by the Amsterdam Separatists. When they heard that two of their fellow-members in the Leyden Church had on occasion "heard some of the ministers in England preach" they demanded that the Church should straightway deal with them "as for sin," and if they did not repent, after the admonition of the Church, that the delinquents should be excommunicated. The majority in the Church were so far true to the tradition set by Robinson that they were "not willing to consent" to this drastic procedure. Accordingly the minority who stood out for the stiffer course withdrew, made a "rent in the Church," and apparently joined themselves to the Separatist Church at Amsterdam. We soon find John Canne, the minister of that Church, taking up his pen in defence of the position held by these seceders from Leyden, and in opposition to the treatise in which Robinson argued that hearing the sermons of godly Anglican divines was on occasion quite permissible. His *Stay against Straying* put a ban upon all attendance at the services or sermons in the Anglican Church.

Samuel Gorton has a singular reference to the relations between the "Church in Holland" and the "Church at Plimouth" about the year 1636. He was mistaken in regarding the Church in Holland to which he refers as the "mother" of the Plymouth Church, for the incident he relates evidently concerned the Amsterdam Church—high, dry and rigid; but it shows the disfavour which the Leyden-Plymouth Church had drawn upon itself in the eyes of the strict Separatists on account of the more liberal spirit and practice it had displayed, in accordance with the example of its beloved pastor in his later years. We have a glimpse here, too, of the kindly William Brewster interpreting the matter in the better part and dealing skilfully with a difficult situation.

This is what Gorton wrote, in 1669, to Nathaniel Morton, the historian of New England—

"I would say some thing of the foundation of your Church at Plimouth if I thought it were not a matter too low to talke of, for when suit was made to the Church in Holland, out of which your Church came, to procure a dismission of a sister there to the Church of Plimouth, though the Gentlewoman vpon ocation had bin in New England diuers yeares: yet a dismission would not be granted. Their preaching minister then with them, I knew to be a godly man and was familiarly acquainted with him now aboue halfe a hundred yeares agoe, in Gorton [Lancashire] where I was born and bred and the fathers of my body for many generations. . . . The ruling Elders when this dismission was earnestly sought for, as I take it, were frenchmen [Jean de l'Ecluse] zealously affected, the Church vnanimously being against a dismission, the Elders gave this ground and reason, that they could not dismisse their sister to the Church of Plimouth in New England because it consisted of an Apostatized people fallen from the faith of the Gospell; and when, through much importunitie, a writing was procured, properly of advice to their Sister how to carry her selfe among them, being already married there, her husband being the Solicitor [*i. e.* the one who desired the dismission] whom you know I need not to name. And I thinke you know after what manner the writing was read in your Church by your ancient Elder—part concealed and part expounded to the best. If you know not I doe for I was then present."

To be stigmatized as an Apostate Church was to be ranked about on the same level, thought Gorton, as that on which the Plymouth people would place the Church of Rome. Though this testimony is evidence of the singular strictness of the Church of refugee English Separatists in Amsterdam, it is at the same time testimony to the more liberal spirit of the first Church in Plymouth, New England.

The lack of regular pastoral oversight told heavily against the already diminished Church at Leyden, and the stream of refugees from England with which it had been refreshed in the time of Robinson slackened as the power of Laud began to wane, and the fitness of

New England for permanent settlement became better known.

Nor did all of those English members of the Church who remained in Leyden continue faithful to its fellowship. The minutes of the Church Council of St. Peter's have an entry under date June 17, 1639, concerning an application for membership from John Masterson, a native of Henley, and his wife Catherine (Lisle), and Stephen Butterfield from Norwich, who, after earning his living for a time as a "say weaver," had become a bookseller—

> "John Meester and his wife, also Steven Butterfield,—English, from the congregation of the sainted Robinson, complaining of a lack of appropriate exercises since his death, so that they cannot be edified in the way they might be were they members of some other Church provided with a pastor; request that they may be allowed to become members of our Church.
>
> "Their request is granted by the brethren."

These two families became absorbed by the Dutch. Butterfield bought property in Leyden and settled down as a citizen. He was buried in St. Peter's December 24, 1652. Morton Dexter gives references to his descendants at Leyden down to 1672.

As late as 1644 there is a reference to this congregation of "Brownisten" at Leyden. In that year it is recorded they took a collection at their meeting in Vrowencamp on behalf of the Protestants in Ireland who had suffered at the hands of the "Papists." Possibly the small remnant of Robinson's Church met at this time either in the house of Peter Wood or in that of John Keble, both of whom lived in that part of Leyden and were actively interested in the affairs of the Church.

Of the Church at New Plymouth a more satisfactory account can be given. It has had a continuous existence down to the present time, and its story has been told by more than one writer. The original covenant of 1606 remains to-day as the basis of its fellowship, but, in common with many of the old New England Churches, in the exercise of the liberty the founders won, this Church has gone through a gradual doctrinal development to the Unitarian position, while preserving its continuity. In this respect it affords a remarkable parallel to the old congregation of Puritan origin at Gainsborough and similar Churches of a kindred type in Old England.

The Pilgrim Church was admirably served by its "elder," William Brewster, and its deacons, John Carver and Samuel Fuller. After the death of the latter there were appointed to the deacons' office "Richard Masterson and Thomas Blossom, two experienced saints, the former especially a man of rare abilities, a second Stephen to defend the truth against gainsayers, and one who had expended most of his estate for the publick good." [1]

Brewster died on April 16, 1644, but it was not till five years afterwards (April 6, 1649) that the Church ordained his successor to the eldership in the person of Thomas Cushman. He had come over with his father in the *Fortune*, and was left in the charge of Brewster and Bradford on his father's return. Robert Cushman's last letter to the colony, written in 1626, is full of manly and tender solicitude on behalf of his son. He begs that he may be afforded time and opportunity for exercise in writing. The example of the father was not lost, as the following account by John Cotton will show—

"After Mr. Brewster's decease, the church chose Mr. Thomas Cushman as his successor in the office of ruling elder, son of that faithful servant of Christ, Mr. Robert Cushman, who had been their chief agent in transacting all their affairs in England both before and after their leaving of Holland till the year 1626. And this his son inheriting the same spirit, being competently qualified with gifts and graces, proved a great blessing to this church, assisting Mr. Reyner not only in ruling, catechising, visiting, but also in publick

[1] "*An Account of the Church of Christ in Plymouth, the first church in New England* . . . by John Cotton, Esq., Member of said Church," written in 1760, Mass. Hist. Soc. Coll., vol. iii. p. 107.

teaching as M[r]. Brewster had done before him. It being the professed principle of this church in their first formation 'to choose none for governing elders but such as are able to teach.' Which ability (as M[r]. Robinson observes in one of his letters) other reformed churches did not require in their ruling elders."

The Mr. Reyner here referred to was John Reyner, who became pastor of the Pilgrim Church, after an interval, in succession to Ralph Smith. I believe Reyner was connected with a family of that name closely associated with Rampton, and the locality immediately to the south of Sturton in Old England. The colonists were anxious to supplement the moderate abilities of Ralph Smith by appointing a dependable "teacher" as his colleague. The brilliant Roger Williams did them good service for a time by way of supply, but Brewster deemed him too unstable to be elected and ordained to office. Accordingly Edward Winslow, on his next visit to England, was commissioned "to procure them a teaching elder to be joined with Mr. Smith." He agreed with one "Mr. Glover, an able dispenser of the word, to come over to them, but he ended his life in London before he came on board."[1] Winslow, however, returned in the same ship with John Norton, and treated with him "about supplying Plymouth." They landed together at Plymouth, and Norton preached for that winter to them, but "declined settling."

Then it was that Reyner became pastor. With him in 1633 there was associated as colleague Charles Chauncy. Though he remained three years he declined an invitation to become the regular "teacher" of the Church.

Reyner was succeeded in the pastoral office by John Cotton, son of the famous John Cotton, whose life-work was bound up with the Churches at Boston, both in England and America. John Cotton junior, after his gifts had been duly tested for a period, was ordained at Plymouth June 30, 1669. We need not

[1] Cotton's *Account*, etc., p. 110.

carry the succession of the ministry in this Church further, but a reference to one or two events in Cotton's time will show how the old traditions and customs of the Leyden period persisted.

On August 1, 1669, Robert Finney and Ephraim Morton were elected deacons and ordained. The catechism adopted by Robinson was then still in use, for under date November 1669 we read, "began catechizing of the children by the pastor (constantly attended by the ruling elder) once a fortnight, the males at one time and the females at the other. The Catechism then used was composed by the Rev. Mr. William Perkins." [1]

On December 11, 1691, Thomas Cushman, "the good elder," died, aged eighty-four. He had married Mary, a daughter of Isaac Allerton, and their son, Isaac Cushman, carried on the family tradition of the "Pilgrims," and its interest in religious work, by becoming the first minister of the daughter Church at Plympton, in Plymouth colony.

It is perhaps more than a coincidence that six months after Cushman's death there was a proposal to supplement the Psalm-book brought from Holland by the one in vogue in the Massachusetts Churches. Here is the record—

"June 19, 1692, the pastor propounded to the church that, seeing many of the psalms in Mr. Ainsworth's translation which had hitherto been sung in the congregation had such difficult tunes that none in the church could set [them], they would consider of some expedient that they might sing all the psalms. After some time of consideration on August 7 following, the church voted, that when the tunes were difficult in the translation then used they would make use of the New-England psalm-book, long before received in the churches of the Massachusetts colony, not one brother opposing this conclusion. But, finding it inconvenient to use two psalm-books, they at length, in June 1696, agreed wholly to lay aside Ainsworth, and with general consent introduced the other, which is used to this day. . . . It

[1] Cotton's *Account*, etc., Mass. Hist. Soc. Coll., vol. iii. p. 124. The Catechism of the Westminster Assembly was afterwards introduced.

was their practice from the beginning till October 1681 to sing the psalms without reading the line; but then, at the motion of a brother, who otherwise could not join in the ordinance (I suppose because he could not read), they altered the custom and reading was introduced; the elder performing that service, after the pastor had first expounded the psalm, which were usually sung in course, so that the people had the benefit of hearing the whole book of psalms explained." [1]

Thus the laudable custom of expository preaching, upon which Robinson and Brewster set such store, was long continued in the Church of their foundation; but the old Psalm-book gave place to a new one. We may take this as symbolic of the gradual change which takes place in a living Church in its practice and its doctrine according as new needs arise and fresh knowledge is opened up for man.

There was implicit in Robinson's system of thought a strong vein of what we may describe as religious rationalism. He felt that if men and women would but apply their reason and common sense to the interpretation and understanding of the Divine message enshrined in the Scriptures, they would soon grasp the truths it conveyed. It is true he limited the exercise of the reasoning faculties, so far as the elucidation of religious truth was concerned, almost entirely to the canonical books of the Bible. Reason was to be applied in a reverent way to the rich field of the Biblical writings, and a harvest of truth in regard to life, duty, and God was the reward to be reaped.

The limitation to Scripture was the common axiom of nearly all Protestant leaders in the seventeenth century. From the standpoint of the twentieth century that may seem somewhat narrow, but we must judge Robinson by the standards of his own age. And the limitation to Scripture interpreted by reason as the final court of appeal in matters of religion carried with it the advantages of concen-

[1] Cotton's *Account*, etc., Mass. Hist. Soc. Coll., vol. iii. p. 127.

tration and definiteness. Robinson and his friends drew from this source a scheme of religious thought which gave coherence for them to life as a whole, and left their minds free for the tasks of the world.

In course of time, as fresh problems rose over the horizon of the mind of the average man and fresh realms of knowledge were opened up for his consideration by the discoveries of science and the study of other races and religions, the question came to be put as to whether the reason of man was not competent to elicit the Divine message from these fresh fields.

If Robinson was justified in declaring that man, by the exercise of right reason, could arrive in some measure at a true apprehension of the light that is enshrined in the Divine Word of the Scriptures, was not man also capable, by the same means, of gathering some part of the Divine light and truth which the facts of nature, science and history express? The reverent use of reason, valid for drawing truth from the field of Scripture, must be valid also for the larger book of life and nature.

The high place and responsibility which Robinson accorded to every member of his Church, rich or poor, high or low, was a feature in his system noteworthy, on account of its reaction upon the political thought of his followers. It was a recovery of the New Testament ideal. Every member of the Church was responsible for its good name, and had the right to participate in its affairs and its government. Churches based on the model laid down by John Smith and John Robinson (according to their interpretation of the relevant passages in the New Testament) indirectly fulfilled an important function as training places for the cultivation of gifts of administration which proved of good service when applied to civic affairs. The Independent or Congregational Churches of Old England and New England, as well as those designated as Baptist, were the nurseries of British and American democracy.

They trained the champions of civil and religious liberty. They helped to draw out into explicit form those principles of political and religious freedom which have at last been embodied in the Covenant of the strongest League of Nations the world has ever seen. Robinson and his associates were pioneers in a great venture, the end of which they could but dimly discern. If, in accordance with his spirit, we read into his utterance concerning the revelation of truth the widest possible meaning, and interpret it of the book of nature, as well as of the Sacred Book of the Christian Church, it will still serve to voice the conviction of men of the forward-look and the open-mind. "He was very confident the Lord had more truth and light yet to break forth out of his Holy Word."

APPENDICES

DOCUMENTS ILLUSTRATING THE LIFE OF STURTON IN JOHN ROBINSON'S TIME

APPENDIX I

SUITS AT LAW OF THE TIME OF QUEEN ELIZABETH AND KING JAMES, ILLUSTRATING THE LIFE OF STURTON IN JOHN ROBINSON'S DAY

In the Record Office are to be found some depositions made in one or two legal cases, which throw light on the life of Sturton and the neighbourhood in John Robinson's time. These documents bring matters home to us more vividly than pages of descriptive writing. They show the customs of the locality about pasturing cattle on the commons and reveal to us the occupations of the people. For many purposes the village community acted together, and the parishioners were quite familiar with the practice of levying a "rate" to meet a common expense. There is the additional advantage in quoting these documents, that the father of John Robinson was personally interested in three of the cases to be cited.

The first case [1] relates to lands in Littleborough, or lying between that parish and Sturton. It appears from the evidence that about the year 1541 the people of Littleborough, finding it inconvenient to tether their cattle on the lands in question, by a joint consent resolved to enclose them "for a cowe pasture for them to eate in common." Accordingly they ran a ring fence round these lands, taking in at the same time a smaller lot of about four acres known as "The Hermitage and Demmes." It was remembered that "Sir John Hearcye did give certayne wood towards the first takinge in thereof." The

[1] Exchequer Depositions, 33 Eliz. Notts., Easter Term, 14. In the Public Record Office.

whole thus enclosed was known as "Barcroft," or "Littleborough Rayles,"[1] and consisted of about forty acres. The enclosure did not extinguish the rights of the owners of certain strips and patches of land embraced within it, but a working agreement was come to by the village community of Littleborough for the common use of this land, which met the general convenience. At length, about the year 1589, one Leonard Dennis claimed three acres scattered about in patches in this enclosure as his absolute property, and desired to take the profit of those three acres severally to himself. He objected to the cattle of the Littleborough people roaming over what he considered to be his own particular plots. As David Harrison (one of the witnesses, who described himself as a "labourer,") put it, Dennis disturbed the inhabitants "by offeringe to drive their Cattell out of the said pasture wth a pyke staff." It was the women of the place who offered a spirited resistance. Robert Gringley of "Littleborowe," a "laborer," aged seventy years, deposed that when Dennis "went about to have put out the cattell of the said inhabitants out of the pasture called Barcroft . . . he was lett of his purpose by the women of the Towne of Littleborrow." The dispute grew warm. Leonard Dennis brought a suit at common law against William Harpur, Jeffry Harpur, Nicholas Wryght, William Harrison, David Harrison, John Nicholson and Robert Gringley, all of Littleborough, "touchinge the use of the said common." This did not end the matter. William Harrison, "clerke," the incumbent of the parish, joined with others in lodging a complaint against Dennis, and in consequence a commission was issued out of the Queen's Court of Exchequer to George More, Esq., Henry Norwall and Michael Bland, gents., to inquire into the facts of the case.

[1] Mr. S. Ingham, who has kindly examined the modern Enclosure Award Map of Littleborough for me, says, the names Horse Rails, Cow Rails and Hermitage still appear on it. The Hermitage is marked as an old enclosure. This is an example of the persistence of English field-names.

Accordingly, these gentlemen sat and examined witnesses at East Retford on " the xvj[th] daye of Aprill," 1591. From the interrogatories administered to the witnesses and the evidence given we have first-hand information about the matters in dispute. The people of Littleborough claimed that this enclosure was managed in the following way. From the feast of the " Annunciation of our Lady " (March 25) up to Pentecost it was " layed severall as a cowe pasture " by the tenants, inhabitants and freeholders of Littleborough; then (as " Brian Ricrofte of Litleborowe fysher " deposed), " between Whitsunday or thereabouts, and Lammas " (August 1) those who owned ground within the compass of Barcroft were entitled " for every acre that they had there to put on twoe beaste, or one horse, to feede there till Lammas," and in the same period the general inhabitants of the village, also, were entitled to put on their kine at the rate of one cow for every house or cottage. After Lammas Day the ground was thrown open for the villagers to pasture not merely their cows, but " all manner of cattle commonable until the feast of the Annunciation of our Lady next following."

Now it is clear that this amicable arrangement between owners and commoners for the joint use of this enclosure would be upset if any of those who had rights there in strips of land claimed the privilege of ploughing or mowing their plots and taking for themselves the crop of corn or hay which their particular strips produced. If that were allowed, the inhabitants of Littleborough would have to tether their cattle on the other parts of the enclosure till the crops of corn or hay on the patches of land claimed by individual owners were gathered in. With the passage of time, however, rights in certain pieces of land in this enclosure had passed to those who no longer lived in Littleborough. Thus, George Dickons of Sturton, yeoman, " of the age of fyftie yeeres, or thereabout," testified " there are divers freeholders dwelling out of Littleborough which have ground in the ground called Littleborowe Rayles." He himself had come into three acres there and had passed them by "demise" (according to Brian Ricroft) to Leonard Dennis, who was now asserting that he had a right to take the profit of his own particular pieces exclusively. Outsiders could not go down to Littleborough conveniently to look after their cattle. They wanted to cut and carry off their hay. The villagers, for their part, wanted the old joint arrangement, which had worked fairly well for fifty years, to continue. The dispute was further complicated by some uncertainty as to whether "Barcroft," or "Littleborough Rayles," was not after all in Sturton parish. Brian Ricroft asserted it was in the "lordship of Littleborough and Sturton," others declared that such tithes as had been paid upon the produce of this land had gone to "the farmer of the parsonage of Sturton"—that is, to the lay impropriator of the tithes of that parish. Amongst the witnesses called was John Quipp "clarke," the vicar of Sturton, whom John Robinson must often have seen and heard. He gave his age as about fifty-four years. According to his testimony, "the ground called the Rayles lyeth wthin the p'she of Sturton." He said he had "heard that one Willm More and one Turnell of great Markham have ground within the Rayles, he knoweth that More did demyse some there unto George Eaton of Fenton for years, which he passed on to George Dickons of Sturton, and that it was demysed either all or some part thereof to the now defendant [Dennis]."

Quipp in his evidence gives a curious story of a wager laid with Thomas White (presumably the grandfather of Robinson's wife). The question arose as to whether the land in dispute, or any part of it, had ever been ploughed. Quipp said he had—

"knowne one pte of the ground within the Rayles plowed and sowen by Thomas Burton of Littleborowe, or his assignes, in one year, and that he sayth that he heard the said Burton saye he did so plowe and sowe yt by reason of a wager of x^{li} layde wth one Thomas Whytt, then Baylyff there, that he, the said Thomas Burton, would plowe and sowe the same grounde before Mydsomer daye to his remembraunce and the said Thomas Whyte layde he should not, and that this said wager was about xviij yeares synce."

But, after all, John Quipp had to confess "that, to his knowledge, the said Burton received not any p'fitt by that plowinge and sowinge." He declared he had seen some part of the land "mowen and in heye coks betweene Maydaye and Lamas" in two recent years, and that Walter Popp and John Deane "did one time about viii or ix yeares synce plowe and sowe some pte of the said ground . . . and of any more plowinge, soweinge, moweing, or tethering he cannot tell."

William Harrington of North Leverton, husbandman, aged sixty, said "the ground called the Rayles lyeth within the parishe of Sturton, as he verylye thinketh, for he saith that he hath seene the p'ambulacon of Sturton goe to the myddest of Stafforde bridge." [1]

No doubt John Robinson in his boyhood had been an interested participator in the annual perambulation of the parish boundaries in Rogation week. He refers to the "parishional assemblies" in England as being "gathered by their parish perambulation" (*Works*, vol. iii. p. 131).

The people of Littleborough certainly had the best case, if customary usage was to count for anything. But the dispute was not altogether a new one, and seems to have been smouldering for years, for Brian Ricroft testified that—

[1] In 1607 the people of Littleborough were ordered to repair Stafford Bridge before Michaelmas Day. In 1611 they were indicted because "its use by the King's subjects" was not possible, but the jury acquitted them. Early in 1615, on the petition of the inhabitants of Littleborough, the Lord Chief Justice Coke ordered that this bridge, "leading from very many northern parts into and towards the several counties of Lincoln and Norfolk," was to be repaired by the whole county. This order was reversed in 1635, and the charge of maintaining the bridge "for ever" was placed on the people of Sturton, Fenton, and Littleborough.

"between xxxiiij and fortie yeares agoe the Rayles of the said pasture of Barcrofte were cut downe, as he hath heard say, by mr Brian Lassells and others and that the same was set up agayne by the Inhabitants of Litleborowe."

Those, said Ricroft, who "hyred any gates there" usually contributed to the making and maintenance of the fence "by a comon laye . . . reatablye accordinge to their beaste-gates."

It is reasonable to suppose that John Robinson heard this case discussed in his father's household. It gives us incidentally some light upon the life and people of Sturton, and shows us the relation in which they stood to the neighbouring parish of Littleborough.

When in after years the colonists of Plymouth Plantation became the possessors of cattle they remembered the customs of the homeland in regard to joint ownership and pasturage in common.

One of the witnesses in this case was "Alexander Rycroft of Littleborowe, fisher of the age of eighty yeares." He and Brian Rycroft fished the Trent and supplied the neighbourhood with fresh-water fish. Even a little place like Scrooby had its "fisher," Thomas Justice [1] by name, who in his will, dated May 16, 1601, left to his son "all . . . my beste new nette not yet fynished." [1] The inland fisheries were of value in Tudor times; no one could get a living in that way to-day in England.

Elizabeth, Countess Dowager of Rutland, and Roger, Earl of Rutland *v.* Leonard Dennis

After evidence had been taken on April 16, 1591, in reference to the dispute between the Littleborough people and Leonard Dennis, the same Commissioners sat again at East Retford on the next day to inquire into charges brought against Dennis by "Elizabeth, Countess Dowager of Rutland, and Roger, now Earl of Rutland, and others," [2] touching his execution of

[1] Vol. xxviii. fol. 540, York Registry.

[2] Exchequer Depositions, Notts., 33 Eliz., Easter, 22.

the office of deputy bailif for the manor of Oswaldbeck Soke. There seems to have been an effort to get rid of Dennis. Amongst the witnesses examined was "John Robynson of Sturton in the countye of Nott., yoman of the age of thirtie vj yeares, or thereabouts." This was the father of the pastor of the Pilgrim Fathers. He testified that he knew Dennis and "the mannor of Osweldbecke Sooke, and that Jeffrey Harpur of Grantham in the countye of Lincoln, was baylyff for the same Sooke." Dennis executed the office of bailiff under Harpur. Robinson said that Dennis some three years before collected such yearly rents, profits, fines, issues and amerciaments of Court as happened and grew within that Soke, and continued to do so for a year and a half; but he could not depose as to the value or amount of such rents and fines. He also testified that Dennis, in virtue of his office, "did take one saddell and a brydell, a payer of Boots and spurres, and a Cloake bagge of ffelons goods wthin the said Sooke about ij yeres synce, but to whose use he knoweth not." This was the sum of his evidence. Another witness from Sturton was Henry Ridley, aged fifty-five years, a tailor, who himself appears to have once held the office of deputy bailiff for Oswaldbec Soke, and asserted that he knew both the Dowager Countess of Rutland and Roger, the then earl. He gave evidence as to certain "estrayes" which Dennis had received from his hands, and declared his judgment as to the amount of rents, fines and amerciaments which Dennis had collected during his time of office. He notes by the way that Dennis received "from George Netleshipp about twoe yeres synce for a fould breach made in Sturton wthin the Sooke about three pounds and three shillings and fourpence."

Dennis, for his part, was able to call some good witnesses. He had been under-bailiff successively to Francis Barker, gentleman, of East Retford, and Robert Southworth of "Wellom," both of whom had held the office of bailiff of Oswaldbec Soke under the

Right Honourable Edward, Earl of Rutland. Barker himself and Thomas Southworth, son of Robert (who was now dead), testified that the accounts of Dennis while he served in this way were all in order, and they held "acquittances" from the "Auditor or Receivor" of the Earl for these accounts. Dennis apparently had not been able to work under "Jeffrey Harpur" without friction.

A Burglary near Sturton

The next case,[1] which also touched the lives of Sturton people, is of a singular nature. One "Ruben Wright," who "dwelt in the personage house in Burton" (that is, West Burton, the next parish to the north of Sturton) and occupied the land thereunto belonging, was arrested on suspicion of having committed, "about fryday at night in the week before Easter 42 Eliz." (1601), a burglary upon one "wydowe ffoxe" at Drayton.

He was brought before John Thornhagh, senior, one of the nearest Justices of the Peace, and examined in his house at Fenton, "in the presence of Mr. Thornhagh's clerk, one John Turnell, and others." Afterwards Mr. Thornhagh examined him privately, when he confessed his guilt. Now, the goods of any one convicted of felony were forfeit to the Crown, or to the overlord. The Sheriff for the county of Nottingham, who happened that year to be Brian Lassells of Sturton, a neighbour of John Thornhagh, would have to seize the goods of the felon if they were on "Crown land"; but if they were in the township of Sturton, or liberty of Oswaldbec Soke, they would be forfeit to Roger, Earl of Rutland, who was then lord of that liberty.

Thornhagh appears to have desired to help Reuben Wright out of the mess and save him from the extreme penalty of the law. It was alleged that, after Wright confessed his guilt, Thornhagh told him—

[1] Exchequer Depositions, 43–44 Eliz., Notts. and York, Mich. 3.

"That yf his goodes were within that Townshipp of Sturton and libertye of Oswaldbecke Soake belonging, as he sayd, unto the Earl of Rutland that then he could and would helpe the sayd Ruben Wright so as he should be well delte withall."

Then "John Cowper and Hunter's son-in-law" came to Wright to persuade him to bring his goods into Sturton liberty, "for yf he [Lassells] the said Sheryf once seased them, he, beinge a hard man, would do hym no favour." Wright, in order to save something from the wreck of his fortunes, fell in with the suggestion. John Cowper and James Harpam, the Burton blacksmith, fetched Wright's cattle and stock into Sturton, where "they were praysed by the order of the Baylyf of the libertie of Oswaldbec soake by one John Robinson," father of the Pilgrim pastor, with the help of "Olyver Gybson" and two others,[1] "to the valewe of xxvj^{li}, or thereabouts . . . and were afterwards disposed into the hands of John Thornhagh the younger."

Reuben Wright at the time of his apprehension was possessed of—

" Syxtie yeowes, twenty-seaven lambes, then thought to be worthe . .	£20
ffoure oxen	£14
Syxe horses and mares	£17
Syxe kyne	£23
Syxe yonge Cattle	£6
One Bull	£1 6*s*.
And tenne Swyne	£3 6*s*. 8*d*."

Some of this stock was over at Gringley, and we have a graphic picture of the way it was brought in by "John Jackson of Sawnby [Saundby] laborer," servant of Reuben Wright. He said he was driving it from Gringley to Mr. Lassells' when—

"he receaved worde from his Master by one Barmby that he should dryve them to Sturton whiche he dyd accordynglye and putt them into Cowper's ffolde. And as [he] was

[1] The membrane is damaged here, and the other names are not clear.

returnynge from Sturton towards West Burton the said Cowp. dyd take from this deponente one blacke baye mare of the Cattle of the said Ruben."

Jackson then had to tramp home on foot. The next step in the case we learn from the testimony of Wright. He had his "mittimus" made out committing him to prison—

"and he goynge towards the gaole the said John Cowp. dyd take this deponent into his yarde where the Cattle of this deponent then were and dyd pswade hym to make a deed of guyfte to such psons as hee Cowp. woulde nomynate wheruppon this Depon^{t} did delyver a horse and twelve pence in money to the hands of one George Knagge and for the use of hym George Knagge in the name of the reste of the goods and Chattels of hym" (Reuben Wright).

Knagge, it should be noted, was brother-in-law to Reuben, and said he had advanced money to him. George Lassells, son of the sheriff, declared that—

"John Thornhaghe had some of the said Cattle for that the wief of Ruben Wright had the mylke of twoe of the kyne whiche were the goods of the said Ruben Wright by the permyssion of the said John Thornhaghe."

It was not likely that the sheriff would allow things to be thus "managed" under his very nose. He lodged a complaint against "John Thornehaghe the father and John Thornehaghe the sonne, George Gilbye Esquires and William Noddle and Martyn Challendge" in the matter. A Commission, dated July 1, 1601, was accordingly issued from the Court of Exchequer to Gervase Neville, Gervase Eyre, Gervase Helwys and John Marshall, "to four, three or two of them" to inquire into the case and take evidence. The two first-named accordingly held an inquiry at East Retford on the "xxiiijth day of Sept. in the xliijth year" of Elizabeth's reign, and it is from the depositions then taken that the information given above is gathered. Besides the witnesses already mentioned the following gave evidence—

"Gregory Starkye of Burton, gent, 38 years

"Dorothy Wright, wife of Reuben, late of Burton, aged 40 years (her husband gave his age as "30 years or thereabout");

"Robert North of Sturton, laborer;

"William Mylnes of West Burton, laborer, 45 years old;

"John Quippe of Sturton, clerke, of the age of lx yeares or thereaboute and Edward Southworth of ffenton yeoman aged 34 years."

It will be remembered that an Edward Southworth was one of the Pilgrim company in Leyden, who there married, in 1613, Alice Carpenter. Their sons Constant and Thomas went over to Plymouth in New England, the former in 1628, the other soon after. I venture to identify this Edward Southworth of Fenton with the Edward Southworth of Leyden. The will of "Robert Sowthworthe of Wellam in the parishe of Clarebrowghe," who I take to have been the father of this Edward Southworth, is an interesting document. It is dated November 20, 1580, and besides bequests of lands in East Retford, Ordsall and "Gringley in the hoole," to his son Edward Southworth, it contains this clause—

"I make the right worshipfull m^r^. Thornaghe of ffenton esquier Gardiner unto the said Edward my sonne yf yt would please his worshippe to take the paines."

He also bequeathed "to the foresaid m^r^. thorneaighe for his paines an angell of gould." This relation of guardianship will account for Edward Southworth's presence at Fenton, where he would make the acquaintance of the Robinsons. It may be of interest to give the testimony of Edward Southworth in full, as it throws light upon the life and the local administration of the district—

"Edward Southworth of ffenton in the Countie of Nott. yeoman of the age of xxxiiij yeares or thereabouts saieth he doth knowe the Manno^r^ or Soake of Oswaldbecke in the Countye of Nott. and that the same soake doth extende as well into the towne of Sturton as into dyvers other townes and that the same doth belong to her Matie in the righte of her highnes crowne of England and that the said soak ys accompted to be a specyall libtie or Baylywick exempt from the Sherif. And that the Baylyffe of the said libtie, or his deputy (by reason of the said Baylywicke) have vsed to take or seaze wayves, estrayes, felons goods and such like usuall pffyts happenynge w[th]in the same. And hath not knowen or heard that the sherif hath vsed to doe the like there. And that her Ma[tie] hath graunted or comytted the said soake to Roger Earl of Rutlande or his predecessors. And that the said Earle hathe appoynted John Thornhaghe the yong[r] Esquier as a pryncipall offycer under hym in the said Soake. He saith that in the weeke before Easter in the 42 yeare of her Ma[ties] raigne [1601] the said John Thornhagh the yonger was at the Castle of Belvoyre in the Countye of Lyncolne and there stayed aboute a fortnighte and that the said Castle ys about xxiiij myles distante from the towne of Sturton. And sayeth that the said John Thornhaghe the yonger had no knowledge or gave any direction towchinge the examynynge of Ruben Wright for the Burglarie or ffelony w[ch] he and others had than comytted in the towne of Drayton, or towching the seasynge of any of his goods in Sturton at or before the tyme of the said examynacon or seazinge; and doe verilie thynke that the said John Thornhaghe the yonger was altogether vnacquaynted therew[th] for that he wente to the said Castle of Belvoyre before the said Burglarie was comytted and came not home agayne till after the said Ruben Wright was sent to the gaole. . . . He saith that the said Burglarye and ffelony was comytted in the towne of Drayton by the said Ruben Wright and others vppon ffrydaye at nyghte in the weeke before Easter in the xlij[th] yeare of the Quenes M[aties] raigne. And that Ruben Wright came before John Thornhaghe the elder to his howse at ffenton wth the constable of west burton vppon mondaye nexte after the said burglarie was comytted. And saith that he was p'sente when the said John Thornhaghe the elder did examyn the said Ruben Wrighte towchinge the same and wrytt downe his examynacon.

"And saith that the said John Thornhaghe the elder presentlie vppon the said Wright's confession of the offense dyd cause a *Mittimus* to be made for the sendynge of hym to the gaole w[ch] this ex̄amte did wryte, and as sone as the *Mittimus* was made the said John Thornhagh the elder did delyver the said Ruben Wrighte to the constable there and did charge hym (as his manner is in that case) to take heede and looke well to hym and to carrye hym saffe to the gaole or to the like effecte. And saith that to his remembraunce the said Constable and Wrighte did not staye wth the said John Thornhaghe the elder after that he was delyvered to the Constable and had receaved his *Mittimus*. But howe longe they stayed at his howse this exa̅n̅te knoweth not, but thinketh yt was aboute halfe an hower. And the reason of this staye was (as he verelie thynketh) to make a deede of guyfte to Knagge of all his goods for that this exa̅m̅te was entreated to make the same wch he refused by reason he knew not howe to make the same substancyallie. But lent them pen Incke and pap. to make the same and sayeth that he wente from thence to the towne of Sturton.

"He thinketh that Willm̅ Hunter did firste enforme the said John Thornhagh the elder of the Wrights goods that they were in the Soake, but what direction he gave for the seasynge of the same he knoweth not, nor how muche was seased in the righte of the said soake this examte certeynlie knoweth not, nether knowethe by whom they were seased and thynketh they were indyfferentlie and accordinge to their true values prysed. And that they were prysed by foure men. And sayeth that there were foure oxen prysed at ix^li^, ffoure kyne a Bull and a Calfe at vij^li^, ffyftie olde sheepe and xviij lambes at viij^li^, A Blynde mare and two old horses at iij^li^, All which amounted to the Sume of xxvij^li^ or thereabouts. And this he knoweth for that the prysers did entreat hym to set downe their prysement in wrytinge. And lastlie saieth that he thynketh that dyvers of the sheepe did myscarrye or prove worth lytle or nothynge. And the reason that moves hym to thynke so ys, for that this exa̅ı̅a̅te hath hearde one John Harryson a Butcher say that he dyd buy the moste or all of them, the beste for three shillynges a peece, others for two shyllyngs a peece, and some for twentye pence a peece. And many of them, as he said, were Rotten and died." [1]

Besides the sheriff of the county and the bailiff of Oswaldbec Soke there was another authority which had an eye on Wright's goods. "The Bailywicke of Bassettlawe accompted p[ar]cell of her Maties Honor of Tickhill in the countye of Yorke pcell of her highnes Duchye of Lancaster," extended to parts of West Burton and Sturton. In virtue of this "George Gilbye" of Bole, to whom this bailywick was entrusted, by and through his deputy, William Nodell, seized "one cowe and fyve calves" of the goods of Reuben

[1] Exchequer Depositions, *ut supra*, Membrane 5 *dorso*.

Wright after he was committed to gaol. The sheriff disputed his authority to do this. Evidence was given by William Wright of Stirrop, yeoman, aged sixty, who deposed that "Noddle seized the ffyve calves in the yarde of one Robt. ffytzwillms [1] at Sturton."

"Thomas Wylton of Sawneby yeoman," aged twenty-eight years, said, "Noddle seized the cow nere vnto one Ryalls yarde in Westburton wch ys accompted to be w^th^in the libtie of the Baylywicke of Bassetlawe." He himself was present at the seizing of this cow and the calves. "He, this deponent, by the appoyntment of George Gilbye did re-delyver vnto the wief of Ruben Wrighte one of the sayd Calves for that she said it was her daughters calfe." "Robert Syms of Sturton labourer aged xxx yeares or thereabouts" was also examined, and said that, being then the "freeboroughe of Sturton," he was "wth the sayd Noddle at the seazynge of the Calves and that the sayd Calves came to the dysposynge of George Gylbye." [2]

The matter did not end with this inquiry, for a further Commission was issued in Easter term in the following year, 1602, to "Johe Hellves, Jervasis Eyre ar., Robt. Eyre armiger, and George Nevill generoso," to determine to whose hands the cattle of Reuben Wright had come and their right value. Accordingly an inquiry was held and witnesses examined before Robert Eyre and George Nevile [3] which elicited one or two fresh points. In addition to the cattle which came to the hands of John Thornhagh the younger and George Gilbie, it was deposed by "Thos. Lasselles of Sturton gent. (aged 34)" that "one red-cow and two couples of the said Ruben his Shepe came to the hands and possession of John Cowp together with one horse and tenn swine wch horse and Swine the said Cowp sould vnto one Stokham of Retford." Lassells valued this red cow at five nobles,

[1] An inquisition into the possessions of John Fitzwilliam, dated September 21, 14 Henry VIII, says he, "had long possessed the Manors of Styrton and Heyton."

[2] Exchequer Depositions, *ibid.*, Membrane 7 *ultimo.*

[3] Exchequer Depositions, Notts., 44 Eliz., Easter, No. 29.

and "tow couple of Shepe wch Cowp had thirteene shillings fourpence and the said horse three poundes ten shillings." Dorothy Wright lets us know that Martin Challendge was associated with Cowp in seizing her husband's goods "about Sturton." "She saieth she had of M$^{r.}$ Thornhaghe the younger thirtie shillings forth of the sd goodes towards the Reliefe of her sd husband in his imprisonm^{t}." She, too, gave an estimate of the value of the cattle seized.

What the upshot of the case was does not appear. I do not know whether the sheriff made good his case, and compelled the value of the goods seized to be handed over to the Crown, or whether the bailiffs of Oswaldbec Soke and the Bassetlaw Liberty of the Duchy of Lancaster established their right to seize felons' goods in Sturton and West Burton, or whether any compensation was paid to poor old widow Fox of Drayton, who had suffered from the burglary. I have instanced the case as one in which old John Robinson was interested. He is mentioned in the evidence. And it is a case which brings vividly before us some of the Sturton and Fenton people with whom John Robinson the pastor must have been well acquainted.

Dispute as to Land between Littleborough and Fenton

The records of another case[1] to which I would draw attention relate to a dispute between the people of Littleborough and those of the hamlet of Fenton, in the parish of Sturton, as to common rights and rights of way, and as to whether the lands in question were really in Sturton or Littleborough. The documents are rather voluminous in this case, but they illustrate the social economy of the locality. John Robinson, the father of the "Pastor Pilgrim," was a witness, and from his depositions one or two details concerning his life can be gathered.

The evidence informs us that Littleborough was

[1] Exchequer Depositions, Notts., 1 James I, Michaelmas Term, No. 14.

"parcel of the manor of the Soke of Oswaldbec." John Harewood of Lea, in the county of Lincoln, wheelwright, aged seventy years, who was born at Littleborough, took it to be the chief manor of the Soke, "for the King's Leet is kept there"; while Alexander Robson, husbandman, about eighty-seven years of age, said "the great Leete for the King is there houlden." He testified that the "King hath viij ferme houses over and besides his Ma[ties] frehoulds" in Littleborough, and that the place had "xxij households at the least and above seaven score Inhabitants." With the growth of the population of the district there was a tendency to overstock the commons.

The people of Littleborough complained that the men of Fenton, "under the countenance of Mr. Thornhey," had barred them from their right of way over Breamore Syck for ten years past, and had driven their own "herdshippe of cattell into the common of Littleborough" between May Day and Midsummer Day, when it was reserved for the cattle of the people of Littleborough alone. They asserted that Nicholas Fenton, Robert Poole, Oliver Gibson, William Farra and Seth Woode "did fourcably put their herdshippe of ffenton into the com̄on of Littleburgh, sekinge and endeavoringe by stronge hande to kepe them there," and they alleged that "Mr. Thornhey hath of late yeares brought a flocke of shepe thither eatinge therewith so neare and bare that the cattell of Littleburgh can hardly lyve thereupon." They declared that the perambulation in Rogation week for their parish encompassed the disputed lands.

Acting in virtue of a Commission issued from the Court of Exchequer, and dated "xiij July 1603," Sir Henry Ayscough and Sir George Gilbie, knights, together with Thomas Mountfort and Henry Broome, gentlemen, sat at Gainsborough on the last day of October 1603 to inquire into the matter. The complainants were Robert Cherbery, John Deane, Thomas Burton and Nicholas Wright. The defendants were

Sir John Thornhagh, Nicholas Fenton, Robert Poole, Oliver Gibson, William Farra and Seth Woode. It was an occasion when the testimony of the old men was called upon. We can picture them journeying in to Gainsborough on that October morning. There was "Bryan Rycrofte," fisherman, whom we have met before; he testified that between March 25 and May Day, in which period Littleborough Common was "layed" (that is, either left for the grass to grow, or pastured only by those who had special rights of ownership), "ye Pinder of Littleburgh used to ympound all such horses and other cattell as came upon ye comon which wear not the townes of Littleburgh . . . he knoweth this to be true because he hath beene sworne the pinder in the Leet and hath knowne it ever since he was of discresion."

David Harison of Littleborough, described as "badger," *i. e.* a corn dealer, and sixty-six years old, gave evidence, and so did John Robson of "Skellingthorpp," Lincolnshire, labourer, aged seventy-four years or thereabout. He was born, he said, at Littleborough, "and after, kept the herdshipp of Littleburgh wth his father." William Cowly of Habstropp (Habblesthorpe), Notts., yeoman, aged seventy, thought the people of Littleborough would not be able to live and pay rent without the use of these common lands. Antony Spencer of Gamston, laborer, an old native of sixty years, and Richard Rawlyn of Littleborough, husbandman, came forward to give evidence, the latter asserting that he had "paid tythe to the vicar of Littleburgh for his cattel goinge on the comon on the easte syde of Sudcrofte Lews," and "John Deane thelder ffisherman lx yeares" testified in the same sense. Another witness described as "fisherman" was Alexander Turner of Coote. Old John Nicholson, a "laborer of the age of lxxviij years," said the people of Littleborough only had one other piece of common besides those referred to, and that was "lowe ground wch they eat wth their swyne and goest" (goats), and "that there belongeth scarce xl acres of arrable land " to the said town, which must have been a very low estimate. " Richard Harington of Gainsburgh glover of the age of liiij " said he knew the parties, " and hath knowne most of them longe tyme for that he was in Sturton and heretofore hath dwelt in Littlebroughe."

The answer of " Sir John Thornhagh esquire and Nicholas ffenton, gent.," with the other defendants to the bill of complaint, was that the parcels of ground in dispute lay within " the bounds and precyncts or perambulacon of the parishe of Sturton," that the inhabitants of Sturton and Fenton had the right of turning their cattle on the waste ground or common in dispute from May Day until Midsummer, as well as after that date until Lady Day, and they had done so " without disturbance until now of late "; that the alleged right of way granted by the Littleborough people to Stafford bridge and the Trent was a highway for all other strangers and passengers to pass to the River of Trent; that as to the parcel of ground called Horse Leys, the men of Sturton and Fenton had used it " as their common, and staffe hearded their cattell there, from Midsummer yearly until the Annunciacon of our Lady," and that the Littleborough cattle used to run or go there no " otherwyse than by rake " during that time. If the people of Littleborough were freeholders and tenants of the King, those of Fenton and Sturton were so likewise, and that the commons of Littleborough besides the grounds in question " for the number of households there before it was soe increased, and the quantitie of theire tillage was more then the comons of ffenton and Sturton are for th'inhabitants there and the quantity of theire tillage with the said grounds in question." They alleged that the Littleborough cattle had been impounded when found on some of the grounds in question and that they had no rights of pasturage " in the Upper Inge of Sturton other wayes than by waye of rake."

The witnesses called on this side were John Dammes of Askham, yeoman, aged fifty, who used to live at

Sturton; George Smyth, aged forty years, of Gringley on the Hill, yeoman, who knew the places in question, "for y[t] he was borne in Sturton"; Robert Shacklock of Misterton, labourer, aged eighty-five years, who was "born in Sturton, and contynued there until he was xx[tie] years of age"; John Poole of Everton, yeoman, sixty years or thereabouts, and Thomas Copland of Sturton, labourer, of the same age. This last witness, who had known the "several parcels of ground" for the previous forty years, gave important evidence. He "and one Leonard Cockes underbailiffe at that tyme of the socke of Oswelbecke . . . about xi yeares last part" impounded some of the Littleborough cattle "for depasturing on Horse Leas after Mydsomer in the open tyme of the year, and the owners did compound with M[r.] John Thorney [1] for their said cattell."

Anthony Richardson of Littleborough, "Taylior," aged fifty years, gave a lively account in his evidence of the fray, which brought the dispute to a head. This is what he said—

"Nicholas Fenton, Robert Poole, William Farra and Seth Wood the first day of May in the 43rd year of the reign of our late sovereign Lady Queen Elizabeth did drive their cattle into some part of the common adjoining the parcel of ground called Fenton Thornhill [2] as the herdsmen of Fenton did use to do the like at other times, and that the Complainants and others [of Littleborough] did resist and drive back the said cattle which Nicholas Fenton and the rest did drive into the said common and that they were resisted and their cattle driven back again by John Deane the younger and his wife, and Thomas Burton his wife's son, and Nicholas Wright and one of his sons, and Richard Rowland and his daughter. And that they did drive and burke the said cattle with staves; . . . and Nicholas Fenton did serve process upon some of them for the same."

[1] Thorney was an alternative spelling of the name Thornhagh. Among the Adventurers who invested money to send out the Pilgrim Colony, was one John Thorned or Thornell. Was he of this family? Bradford, in his *Letter-book*, refers to him in 1625 as prominent amongst the opponents of the religious aims of the Plymouth Plantation.

[2] The road from Littleborough to Cottam and Leverton is still known as "Thornhill" Road.

This must have been an exciting May Day. It evidently led up to the bill of complaint from Littleborough which was now being considered.

The next witness called was John Robinson, the father of the Pilgrim Pastor. His evidence was regarded as important. He is described as of Sturton, in the county of Notts., yeoman, "of ye age of liij^{tie} yeares or thereabout." On being sworn and examined he gave testimony as follows—

Imprimis . . . he saith he knoweth all ye pties pl[aintiffs] and def[endants] and y^{t} he hath knowne the moste of them xxx^{tie} yeares and doth know ye townes of Littlebroughe and Sturton and hamlett of ffenton in ye county of Nott. and doth know evrie of them because he was borne at Sturton."

He supported Thomas Copland's testimony that the grounds in dispute were really in Sturton parish, and said further—

"y^{t} he hath heard ye late viccar of Sturton called John Quipp confesse y^{t} he hath had one rowe and a halfe of hey ground of John Quipp now pson of Littlebroughe in Liewe and satisfacon of ye renewes and tythes wch did fall and was due on ye ground in variance and hath also heard the p[ar]son of Littlebrough confesse ye payment thereof."

He further testified—

"y^{t} the Inhabitants of Sturton and ffenton have used to keep sheepe and other cattell upon the grounds in variance called Sudcrofte and horselews from mydsom^{r} untill Thannuncon of o^{r} lady and y^{t} the said Inhabitants of Sturton and ffenton have Stockhirded their cattell on ye said grounds in all that tyme . . . he saith y^{t} he hath heard his ffather and others say that the Inhabitants of Littlebroughe kept no herdshipp of Cattell upon the comon wch lyeth on the weste syde of Stafford Bridge or Cartbridge when ye said Inhabitants did eat severally or by way of tetheringe Sudcrofte lewes, savinge y^{t} after Mydsom^{r} the Inhabitants of Littlebroughe had rake wth their cattell on ye said ground called Sudcrofte . . . he saith y^{t} ye Cattell of Littlebroughe have beene impounded after Mydsomer and in the open tyme of the year of some of ye said grounds in controversie by some of ye servants of m^{r} Thorney and that the owners thereof have paid poundshipp for them, some of them i^{d} and some ij^{d} accordinge to the nomber of their cattell impounded . . . he saith y^{t} John Thorney Esquire and the Inhabitants of Sturton and ffenton keepeth sheepe now upon the said comon no other wyse then they have formerly used to doe. . . . he saith y^{t} the Inhabitants of Littlebroughe never at any tyme had any use of comon in the Over Inge of Sturton neyther did he ever hear y^{t} they did make any clayme or title thereunto and that he knoweth upon his owne knowledge that their Cattell have been impounded and paid poundshipp if they have beene taken there by way of rake."

The next witness called was "Christopher Fielden of Sturton, clerke of ye age of xxxiiij^{tie} years or thereabout," the vicar of the parish. He knew the plaintiffs and some of the defendants and had so known some of them "ye space of ten yeares" and the localities in question for a like time. He said—

"y^{t} John Quipp now vicar of Littlebroughe hath dyverse tymes of late and namely upon Mychaelmas even last paste offrede him composicōn for the renewinge of all such Cattell belonginge to the towne of Littlebroughe as eyther did or should depasture and renue of any of those grounds on the West syde of Stafford water sayinge further y^{t} all such tythes except corne and hay as did renew or fall on the West syde of Stafford Water was due unto the vicare of Sturton and y^{t} ye said John Quipp did heretofore give a certaine porcōn of medowe ground unto the laste vicar of Sturton for the yearly composition thereof."

The next witness to be sworn and examined was "John Quipp, Clerke of the age of xxxiij^{tie} yeares," who had known the persons and places "by the space of eight yeares." As to the parcel of ground between the "Cartbridge and Sudcrofte leaes," he did not certainly know in which parish it was, but had heard Robert Cherbury say "y^{t} the Renewinge wch fell in y^{t} place came to Littlebroughe." As to—

"Sudcrofte, Burcrofte and horse leaes the tythe hay, if there were any, went to ye pson of Sturton or his fermer to the said deponents knowledge, for other renewinge of cattell belonging to the p[ar]ishioners of Littlebroughe fallenge wthin ye pishe of Sturton he beinge Mynister at Littlebroughe for ye space of eight or ix yeares last past did agree wth the vicar of Sturton by letting hym have medowe for them . . . he saith yt he did see a copie of an agreement in ye church [Bible ?] of Littlebroughe betwixt Willm Harison Mynister of Littlebrough deceased and John Quipp ministr of Sturton deceased for ye renewinge wthin Sturton pish . . . for ye pmbulac [perambulation] he said yt he wth ye rest of his neyghbours went about all the said pcelles yearly to his knowledge for the space of viii or ix yeares or thereabout last paste, when they could for water, exceptinge in the year as he remembreth 1602 when they were phibited by ii of Mr. Thorneyes men at ye Cartbridge."

William Twelles, a labourer of Fenton, aged sixty, corroborated the statement that the vicar of Sturton had from the vicar of Littleborough one acre of meadow by way of composition for the "tythes and renewes" of the parcels of ground in variance. Then the herdsman of Fenton, William Harington, aged sixty years, who had lived there for eight years, was called. It was he who at divers times had impounded cattle of the Littleborough men found straying on "Sudcrofte and Horseleaes," for which some of them had "paid poundship to the pinders within this three years." George Toppyn of Thrumpton and William Cooke of Fenton, both of them "labourers," also gave evidence.

The upshot of the case does not appear.

The Littleborough Ferry

The next case to which I would draw attention is of interest both because it brings before us several of the inhabitants of the district and deals with one of the chief means of communication of the locality, and also because old John Robinson again came forward to give evidence. His gifted son, it is true, had left the country for Holland by this time, but the evidence refers to the conditions in which the Trent was crossed in the preceding years. The ferry over the Trent usually landed travellers, passengers, packhorses and other horses and cattle with their packs and burthens on the Lincoln side of the river, at "the great highwaye called Marton Streete," which was in the parishes of Marton and Burton, in the county of Lincoln. This was the old Roman road. But when this highway was "overflowen or daungerously covered either by spring tydes from the sea or by meanes of the swellings of fresh watters," the ferrymen and boatmen, "when they thought good or convenyently might wth safetye, used to sett on land and disburden and also to take in and loade at a bancke or place known by the name of Marton Bancke and the passengers after that they have been there sett on shoare quyetly passed uppon the same banke with their horses or other cattell withoute interrupcon." Of late, however, the Marton people had blocked up this way. They said there was an alternative passage at "a place called Red Hill neere adjoyning to Littlebroughe ferrie," and that the ferryboat was usually kept there when the "great ordinarie Calsey or highwaye was wth waters overflowen," and that the ferrymen had "there made to themselves for shilter a Cabbin or Lodge under the said Red hill." They further asserted that when both these places were inundated the ferry used to land passengers and goods "at a place called the street yate or streete end lyinge at the East end of the calsey in Marton." They recognized no obligation on their part to keep Marton Bank in repair, and the ferryman had only been allowed to land people there on terms which he had not observed. He was to keep the bank in repair in order to protect Marton Marsh, and put a "sufficient Slewce" with a door to keep out the water from the marsh, and clean the ditch alongside the bank, receiving "a halfpenny for every Roode of the said ditche soe often as he did skower the same," and this agreement was only for eight years.

Edward Howley, who rented the ferry (of which, by the way, the King was part owner), lodged a bill of complaint against "Edward Fletcher, Roger Smith the elder; Willyam Harryson, Clarke; Roger Smith the younger, John Sherieffe and Henry Rogers of Marton." A Commission[1] was accordingly issued from the Court of Exchequer to investigate the case, in virtue of which witnesses were examined and depositions taken at "Gainsburgh" on April 19, 1609, before "Sir John Thornagh, knight, Sir John Thorold, knight, Sir Thomas Darell, knt., and ffrancis Bussye, esquier."

The first witness was "David Harrison of Littlebrough, laborer of the age of threscore years or thereabouts." He testified that the farmers of the ferry (*i. e.* those who rented it) had been at great charges "to maintaine and repaire great staires chardgable ferry boats and servants to attend and labor in them." He knew this because he had been "many tymes used as a workman for repairing of the same."

The second witness was "John Robinson of Sturton in the County of Nott. yeom̄. of thage of threscore years or thereabouts." He deposed that he knew the parties to the suit. The towns of Marton and Littleborough he had known by the space of forty years. He also knew Marton Bank, and described it as "neare adioyning to the great highway and served wth a dike of the North side of the said Banck." Further he said—

"that the farmers and ferrymen of the ferry of Littlebrough and their servants and boatmen when the great highway called Marton Street hath bene overflowne wth water had used, as nede did require, to sett on land, disburden and also to take in and load as well all or any of the passingers at the said ferry passing either on horseback or on foote as also all or any packhorses or other horses or catle wth their Packes and their Burdens upon the said Banck or place called or knowne by the name of Marton banck. And that he hath knowne it soe used by the space of 40^ty^ years. And that the passingers have quietly passed upon the said Banck to and fro wth their horses and other cattle and their packes and other Burdens w^h^out Interrupc̄on̄ to his knowledge at such tymes."

[1] Exchequer Depositions, 7 James I, Easter, No. 12, Lincs. and Notts.

The next witness was old "Brian Rycroft" of Littleborough, aged 88 years, and there is a pathetic touch in his evidence, that he—

"knoweth not what the defend^{ts} have latly done bycause he hath bene six years blind but saith the said passage was never before that tyme stopped to his knowledge and that he knoweth this to be true because he hath alwaies lived in Littlebrough as an Inhabitant and hath many tymes bene used as a ferryman."

The next witness was Richard Thornton of North Leverton, aged seventy years, and then came "William Sowbye of Haplesthorpe yeoman of the age of fowerscore yeares or thereabouts," who for threescore years had never known the passage by Marton Bank to be interrupted, "and this he knoweth to be true for that he hath most comonly in ye winter tyme weekly gone on that Banke wth his horses loaded wth Corne to Gainsburgh M^{r}kett." In the last two or three years, however, "stoopes and rayles was sett" by some of the defendants, as he thought. The remaining witnesses were John Harewood of "Leigh," in the county of Lincoln, and Robert Cherebury, a yeoman of Littleborough, aged sixty years, whom we have met with before.

It seems to me likely that the fact that Sir John Thornhagh had been granted a lease of the Manor of Oswaldbec by Letters Patent dated August 15, 4 an. James I, to which the ferry rights were attached, had something to do with this endeavour to put things on a satisfactory footing. In the State Papers there is a petition [1] from Sir John Thornhagh, assigned to December 3, 1608, addressed "To the righte honourable Robert Earle of Salisbury Lord Highe Treasuror of England." The following extract throws some light on the matter—

"In all humblenes sheweth to yor good Lo^{p}, John Thornhagh of ffenton in the countie of Nott. Knighte. That where it hath pleased his Matie of late under the great seale

[1] *State Papers, Domestic*, James I, vol. xxxviii.

of England to demyse to yor Lo^ps^ supp^lt^ the Manno^r^ of Oswardbysoke in the said countye for fortie yeares under the yearly rente of xxxiiij^li^ a great parte of wch rente is cheefely raised yearely out of the profitts that aryse of an oulde decayed house called the Manno^r^ house and some other poor oulde houses and of the passage over the River of Trente by twoe fferry boates as well for cartes as for horses and fotemen out of the said countie of Nott. into the countie of Lyncolne and soe back againe from the one countie to the other. . . ."

The petitioner goes on to say that the houses are ruinous . . . "also the saide boates are both so rotten and utterly decayed y^t^ they must be p'sntly new made," and he therefore prays for a grant of timber for the needful work from the Royal forests. A note is endorsed on the petition, "Lett Mr. Baron Altham consider of this suitor and certifie me his opinion. R. Salisbury." Accordingly James Altham got the opinion of two local Justices of the Peace, Sir Richard Williamson and Mr. Symcocke, on the matter. He then reported in favour of a grant, pointing out, however, that the King was in "no way tyed unto yt by any clawse in the lease." The upshot was that a warrant was issued for 150 tons of timber to be delivered from Sherwood Forest to Sir John Thornhagh for the repair of the Manor House and Ferry Boats.

From another source [1] I find that the remainder of this lease of Oswaldbec Soke and the ferry rights was made over by Sir John Thornhagh to his son Francis on October 29, in the third year of Charles I, by "act and deede." Christopher Fielding, clerk, of Treswell and Sturton, and Godfrey King witnessed the "deed of gift."

[1] Exchequer Depositions, Notts., 13 Charles I, Michaelmas.

APPENDIX II

RESIDENTS IN STURTON AND FENTON IN THE SIXTEENTH AND SEVENTEENTH CENTURIES

SEVERAL good lists of residents in Sturton, the neighbours of the Robinson family, are extant, from the time of Henry VIII down to the reign of Charles. Most of these I have transcribed, but the space at my disposal only permits the printing of a selection. Here is a Muster Roll for the parish headed as follows—

"Certyfycate of Musters takyn the xxiiij^te daye Marche the xxx^te yere of oure sufferand Lord Kyng Henry VIIIth by Gerves Clyftone, John Hercy, John Babyngton, George Wastenes, Antony Nevyll, Chareles Morton esquiers commyssyoners of oure sufferand Lorde the kyng by v'tue of hys commyssyon to them derectyd ffor the Northe claye p'cell off the Wapyntake of Barsett-Law for the county of Nottynghm̄ accordyng to the devytyon of syd the commyssyoners unto y^em allottyd

Sturton cum Fenton

b[1] George Lassells harnes for iij men
a[2] Antonye thorney harnes for a man
a Thom̄s ffenton harnes for a man
a Rauffe hogson harnes for a man
b John Drap com̄an harnes for iij mē

[1] *b* stands for billman.
[2] *a* stands for archer, Harness = armour or fighting equipment.

b Thomā Stourton	
b James Tomson	
b John chadkerye	
b John corbrygge	
b Wyllm̄ Hawton	
b Robt Sturton	
a Wyllm̄ Sowbe	
b Rychard shakloke	
b Robt Haworth	horse & harnes for a man
b Robt Wolley	
b Robt hynd	
b John Stene	
b Thom̄s baleme	
b Andye dykcons	
a Rychard Smyth	
a An'y harynton	
a John Smythe	

b Wyllm̄ Stort	
b Wyllm̄ Kechyng	
b And Tomson	
a Rychard Saunbe	
b gylles browyll	horse and harnes for a man
a Thom̄s Saunbe	
a Wyllm̄ kyrkbe	
b Thom̄s bynghm̄	
b henry fflowe[r]	

Vidua clarke	
b Wyllm̄ bynghm̄	
b george Nysyo^{r}	
a Thomas Rake	
b John Smythe	
b Wyllm̄ Lawcoke	
b olyv' Boythe	horse and harnes for a man
b Wyllm̄ Atton	
a John legett	
b John corver	
b Rauffe cawthorne	
b Robt Smyth	

b Thom̄s Smythe
b Rychard cawtorn
a Henry browne
a Rychard dogeson
b Matthewe Roger
b Wyllm̄ Crofte
a Thomo^{s} Whyt
b John Shawe
b Rychard Alyn
b george cawtorne
b Roger yewett
b John powyll
b Wyllm̄ Wyvyll
b Wyllm̄ ffenton
b Wyllm̄ Eyton
b george cosyn } horse and harnes for a man
b Thoms Wensley
b Wyllm̄ bee [?Lee]
b Wyllm̄ byrkyll
b Ric. Mare
a hugh unvyn
b Thom̄s spense
a Thom̄s Joye
a Edward Orwene
a Wyllm̄ Atkynson
a Thom̄s catlyn
b Rychard carver [?]
b Robt Stafforth
a Ryc bylle
a george dewyt

Som̄e of ye harnes ys for xiij men
Som̄e of ye archers ys xxij^{ti}
Som̄e of ye byll men ys xxxvij^{ti}."

The clerk has made an error in the addition. The list gives fifty billmen who, with the twenty-two archers and the widow Clarke, give a total of seventy-three names. If we multiply the total of able-bodied men by six to give the women, children and aged men, we get a population for the parish of 432, as compared with an estimated population for the present year of 455.

The names in this list may be checked by an

excellent list of Sturton taxpayers for the thirty-fourth and thirty-fifth years of King Henry VIII, containing sixty-two names.[1] Forty-one of the names in this second list correspond with names given above, seven others merely show a change of Christian name, leaving a balance of only fourteen entirely fresh names since the muster roll was compiled. Widow Clarke is again the only woman in the list, and we get her full name "Eliz. Clerke." She paid a subsidy of 6*s*. 8*d*. on goods valued at £10. In both lists the names of Thomas White, the grandfather of John Robinson's wife, and John Legatt, the father of Catherine White's first husband, occur. The John Corver or Carver mentioned in both lists I take to have been the father of John Carver, the second husband of Catherine White and the first Governor of Plymouth Colony.

In a list [2] of *Sturton* residents who contributed to a "*benevolence*" [3] for King Henry VIII in the thirty-sixth year of his reign we have the following names and the respective amounts which were given. Old John Carver joined in this loyal gift—

"Antony Thorney off Sturton		xx^{s}
Thomas Fenton	de ead.	xxiij^{s} iiij^{d}
John Legatt	de ead.	xx^{s}
Geo. fflowere	de ead.	vj^{s} viij^{d}
Andr. Dickson	de ead.	iiij^{s}
Wyllm̃ Eyton	de ead.	ix^{s}
John Cawver	de ead.	viij^{s}
Thom@ Bynghm̄m	de ead.	v^{s}
Elizabethe Clerke	de ead.	vj^{s} viij^{d}
Wyllm̃ Wolley	de ead.	iij^{s} iiij^{d}
Wyllm̃ Kyrkbye	de ead.	xiij^{s} iiij^{d}
Wyllm̃ ffenton	de ead.	x^{s}."

John Carver's name also appears in the roll [4] for the thirty-seventh year of Henry VIII as paying a tax of

[1] Lay Subsidies, Notts., Bassetlaw, $\frac{159}{147}$, Record Office.
[2] *Ibid.*, 36 Henry, Notts., Bassetlaw Hundred, $\frac{159}{160}$.
[3] Benevolence from the inhabitants of Notts. town and county, Membrane 1.
[4] Lay Subsidies, 37 Henry VIII, Notts., Bassetlaw $\frac{159}{164}$.

13*s*. on goods (not lands) of the value of £13. This roll is the first in which I have noted the Robinson family name in connexion with Sturton parish. Christopher Robinson paid 2*s*. 8*d*. on lands of the annual value of £1 6*s*. 8*d*.

There is a good list of names[1] for the first year of Elizabeth's reign—

" Bryan Lassells	in lands	xiij^{li} xiij^{s} iiij^{d}	— xvjj^{s} x^{d}
Larance fenton	in lands	iiij^{li}	— v^{s} iiij^{d}
Thomas Sturton	in lands	iiij^{li}	— v^{s} iiij^{d}
Thomas White	in lands	iij^{li}	— iiij^{s}
Edmunde Mering	in lands	xl^{s}	— ij^{s} viij^{d}
George Dyckons	in lands	iij^{li}	— iiij^{s}
Raffe Dyckons	in lands	xl^{s}	— ij^{s} viij^{d}
George flow^{er}	in lands	xl^{s}	— ij^{s} viij^{d}
Robert Sturton	in lands	xl^{s}	— ij^{s} viij^{d}
George Motson	in guds	v^{li}	— v^{s}
George Eaton	in lands	xl^{s}	— ij^{s} viij^{d}
*Xρ*ofer Robbinson	in lands	xxvj viij	— xxj$^{d\,ob}$
George kyrkeby	in lands	xxvj viij	— xxj^{ob}
Ryc. Smyth	in lands	xx^{s}	— xvj^{d}
Cicilly Smyth	in lands	xx^{s}	— xvj^{d}
Antony Powle	in lands	xx^{s}	— xvj^{d}
Henry Sturton	in guds	v^{li}	— v^{s}
Sm̄a	iij^{li} vij^{s} iiij^{d}."		

It will be noticed that the assessment on Bryan Lassells was not quite exact, and that the odd half-penny in the charge on John Robinson's grandfather (the obolus) was apparently neglected in collection, as it is not included in the sum total. The rate was sixteen pence in the pound on lands and a shilling in the pound on goods.

On the roll[2] for the subsidy of the thirteenth year of Elizabeth we have another good list of "Sturton-cum-Fenton" inhabitants. The clerk in this instance affected the Latin form for Christian names—

[1] Lay Subsidies, 1 Eliz. $\frac{160}{198}$, Notts., Bassetlaw.
[2] *Ibid.*, $\frac{160}{208}$, Notts., Wapen. de Bassetlawe.

" Brianne Lassells, Armig^{r}	in terr.	xx^{li}	— liii^{s} iiij^{d}
Johes Thornagh	in terr.	viij^{li}	— xx^{s} iiij^{d}
Thomas Sturton	in terr.	v^{li}	— xiij^{s} iiij^{d}
Georgius Eyton	in terr.	xl^{s}	— v^{s} iiij^{d}
[Rob]tus Sturton	in terr.	xl^{s}	— v^{s} iiij^{d}
Rādus Dicons	in terr.	xl^{s}	— v^{s} iiij^{d}
Lawrence Smith	in terr.	xl^{s}	— v^{s} iiij^{d}
*Xρ*oferus Robinson	in terr.	xl^{s}	— v^{s} iiij^{d}
Jaina Mering	in terr.	xl^{s}	— v^{s} iiij^{d}
Georgius Sturton	in terr.	xx^{s}	— ii^{s} viij^{d}
Antonius Poole	in terr.	xx^{s}	— ij^{s} viij^{d}
Dionisius Barneby	in bon.	vj^{li}	— x^{s}
Wiłłus Sturton	in bon.	iij^{li}	— v^{s}
Henr : Sturton	in bon.	iiij^{li}	— vj^{s} viij^{d}
Johes Smith	in bon.	iiij^{li}	— vj^{s} viij^{d}
Jacob^{us} Wakefeld	in bon.	iij^{li}	— v^{s}
Lawrenc ffenton	in terr.	iij^{li}	— viij^{s}
Thomas White	in terr.	xl^{s}	— v^{s} iiij^{d}
Rādus Wastnes	in bon.	iiij^{li}	— vj^{s} viij^{d}
Willo Bennington	in terr.	xl^{s}	— v^{s} iiij^{d}
Georgius Dicons	in terr.	xl^{s}	— v^{s} iiij^{d}
Georgius fflower	in terr.	xl^{s}	— v^{s} iiij

Giving a total of [i]x^{li} xiiij^{s} viij^{d}."

The roll [1] for 1585 gives one or two unusual details. It indicates that Sturton had suffered from some epidemic, and notes that the raising of the subsidy in East Retford was " greatly hindered by casualty of fyer." It will be noted that the names of " John Smyth, John Robynson and Alexander Whyte " here actually occur in juxtaposition, and that the vicar of the parish is included in the list. The heading to this roll runs as follows—

" Nottingham

"North-claye. The Taxacion for the first payment of the Subsidye graunted to the Queenes Matie in the xxvijth yeare of her highnes Raigne p'sented and taxed before us

[1] Lay Subsidies, 27th Eliz. $\frac{254}{25}$, Notts., Bassetlaw.

Sir Willm Hollis knight and Robert Markam esquier two of the Queenes Maties Commissioners appointed for the same taken at Estretford the xxviijth day of maye in the sade xxvijth y^{r} of her highnes Raigne for the wapentake of Bassetlawe 1585."

The Commissioners appointed Edward North of Walkeringham, gent., as "high collector" for the Wapentakes of Bassetlaw and Newark and for Newark Town, and granted an allowance for the "petty collector" and to the clerk for engrossing the roll, according to Act of Parliament. The list for Sturton is as follows—

"Sturton com
ffenton vissited
wth sicknes

John Thorney Ar.	in terr.	x^{li}	— xxvj^{s} viij^{d}
Willm Remington	in terr.	v^{li}	— xiij^{s} iiij^{d}
Thomas Sturton	in terr.	v^{li}	— xiij^{s} iiij^{d}
George Dickens	in terr.	iiij^{li}	— x^{s} viij^{d}
George Eaton	in terr.	xl^{s}	— v^{s} viij^{d}
Rādus Dickens	in terr.	iij^{li}	— viij^{s}
Nicus ffenton	in terr.	iij^{li}	— viij^{s}
Johnes Smyth	in terr.	iij^{li}	— viij^{s}
John Robynson	in terr.	xl^{s}	— v^{s} iiij^{d}
Alexander Whyte	in terr.	iij^{li}	— viij^{s}
Bryanus Sturton	in terr.	xl^{s}	— v^{s} iiij^{d}
Ricus Smyth	in terr.	xl^{s}	— v^{s} iiij^{d}
Laurance Smyth	in terr.	xl^{s}	— v^{s} iiij^{d}
Anthony Poole	in terr.	xx^{s}	— ij^{s} viij^{d}
George fflower	in terr.	xl^{s}	— v^{s} iiij^{d}
Dennes Barnebye	in bon.	vj^{li}	— x^{s}
John Barneabye	in bon.	iiij^{li}	— vi^{s} viij^{d}
Johes Turnell	in bon.	v^{li}	— viij^{s} iiij^{d}
Johes Cowper	in bon.	iiij^{li}	— vj^{s} viij^{d}
Willms Walker	in bon.	iij^{li}	— v^{s}
weadowe Halton and her sonn	in bon.	iij^{li}	— vj^{s} viij^{d}
Nicus Dickens	in bon.	iij^{li}	— v^{s}
John Quipe, Clarke	in terr.	xx^{s}	— ij^{s} viij^{d}

Som — ix^{li} xx^{d}."

In the roll[1] of subsidy payers dated October 7th, 36 Elizabeth (1594), we find another excellent list of Sturton names. The name of John Robinson's father is not far away from that of Alexander White, the father of his wife (Bridget White), while next to this name comes Brian Smith, the oldest brother of John Smith, of Christ's College, Cambridge, who led the Separatist movement in this district.

STURTON CUM FFENTON

"Johannes Thornehaghe ār	in ter.	xx^{li}	iiij^{li}
Georgius Lassells gen̄	in ter.	v^{li}	xx^{s}
Thomas Sturton gen̄	in ter.	v^{li}	xx^{s}
Wm. Rm̄mington	in ter.	v^{li}	xx^{s}
Nic̄us ffenton	in ter.	v^{li}	xx^{s}
Allexaund^{r} White	in ter.	iij^{li}	xij^{s}
Brianus Smithe	in ter.	iij^{li}	xij^{s}
Georgius Dickons	in ter.	xl^{s}	viij^{s}
Rādus Dickons	in ter.	xl^{s}	viij^{s}
Johannes Robinson	in ter.	xl^{s}	viij^{s}
Laurentius Smithe	in ter.	xl^{s}	viij^{s}
Ricus Smith	in ter.	xl^{s}	viij^{s}
Thomas Markham ār for the lands of George Eaton	in ter.	xl^{s}	viij^{s}
Robte Sturton	in ter.	xl^{s}	viij^{s}

Sm̄a xij^{li}."

These payments were for the second of three entire subsidies granted to the Queen in the Parliament of 1593. The Commissioners "appointed for assessing, rating and taxing" this part of Notts. for this subsidy were "Sir John Holles, knight, Peter Roos, Brian Lasseles and John Thornhagh esquiers."

After a considerable gap we come upon another good list of Sturton names in the subsidy roll[2] for the thirty-ninth year of Elizabeth's reign as follows—

[1] Lay Subsidies, Roll 35, Eliz. Notts., Bassetlawe $\frac{160}{236}$, Membrane 6.
[2] Lay Subsidy $\frac{160}{251}$, Bassetlaw, 39 Eliz.

“ Sturton cū
ffenton

Johēs Thornhagh Ar	in Terr.	xx^{li}	iiij^{li}
Georgius Lassells gen	in Terr.	v^{li}	xx^{s}
Thomas Sturton	in Terr.	v^{li}	xx^{s}
Nichus ffenton	in Terris	iiij^{li}	xvj^{s}
Charolus White	in Terr.	iij^{li}	xij^{s}
Brianus Smith	in Terr.	iij^{li}	xij^{s}
Robtus Pennington	in bon.	xl^{s}	viij^{s}
Georgius Dickons son	in ter.	xl^{s}	viij^{s}
Radus Dickons	in Ter.	xl^{s}	viij^{s}
Johes Robinson	in Terris.	xl^{s}	viij^{s}
Robtus Sturton	in Terr.	xx^{s}	iiij^{s}
Thomas ffox	in Terris.	xx^{s}	iiij^{s}
Johes Barmeby	in bonis.	iij^{li}	viij^{s}

Sum x^{li} viij^{s}.”

This subsidy of four shillings in the pound on lands was taken up at one collection. Frequently a subsidy was taken up in instalments. This roll is signed at the foot by Brian Lassells and John Thornhagh.

When we reach the reign of James I we have further lists. Parliament granted this King “ three entire subsidies ” in the third year of his reign. The “ Commissioners for assessing, rating and taxing of the first payment of the third subsidy ” [1] in the Bassetlaw Wapentake in Nottinghamshire were “ Henry Pierpoint, Bryan Lassells and John Thornhagh knights and William Coop esqr.” Two of these were connected with Sturton and Fenton, and thus we may be sure the assessment in that parish would be carefully made. They appointed Gervase Bellamy of Laneham their “ high collector.” We can picture him going round for the tax and drawing up his roll, which is dated March 10 in the sixth year of James I.

[1] Lay Subsidy $\frac{160}{274}$, Bassetlaw, Notts. 3, James I. The rolls for the first two of these subsidies are missing.

“ Sturton cum
Fenton

Johēs Thornhagh, miles	in terr.	xx^{li}	liij^{s} iiij^{d}
Geor. Lassells, miles	in terr.	xx^{li}	liij^{s} iiij^{d}
Roger Sturton, sesso	in terr.	iij^{li}	viij^{s}
Carolus White, sessor	in terr.	iij^{li}	viij^{s}
Richo et Willm̄ ffenton	in terr.	iij^{li}	viij^{s}
Tho : Dickons, sesso^{r}	in terr.	xl^{s}	v^{s} iiij^{d}
Johes Robinson, sesso^{r}	in terr.	xl^{s}	v^{s} iiij^{d}
Johēs Cowp	in terr.	xx^{s}	ij^{s} viij^{d}
Johēs Barmeby	in terr.	xx^{s}	ij^{s} viij^{d}
Robtus Sturton	in bonis.	iij^{li}	v^{s}
Grego Steedman	in bonis.	iij^{li}	v^{s}

Sum̄^{a} xxj^{s} viij^{d}.”

We also have the names of those assessed for this subsidy[1] who paid their second instalment in the following year (seventh James I), 1610. The name of Robinson's father still appears—

“ Sturton with ffenton	Johes Thornhagh miles
	Georgius Lassels miles
	Roger Sturton
	Carolus White
	Rich et W. ffenton
	Thomas Dickons
	Johes Robinsonne
	Johes Coop
	Johes Barmeby
	Robtus Sturton
	Gregorius Steedman.”

All were assessed on lands except the last two, who were assessed on goods (in bonis). The roll is damaged at the edge, so the individual payments cannot be recovered. The sum total from the parish was iij^{li} x^{s}.

When we come to the next available list of inhabitants and landowners in Sturton in a subsidy roll[2] of the eighteenth year of James I, we notice that the name of Robinson has died out, though that of

[1] Lay Subsidies $\frac{160}{277}$, Bassetlaw, 3 James I.
[2] *Ibid.*, $\frac{160}{279}$, Bassetlaw, Notts, 18 James I.

Charles White, the brother-in-law of the pastor of the Pilgrim Fathers, still appears—

"Sturton cū
ffenton

Johannes Thornhagh mil.	in ter.	xxli	—	xxxvj^{s} viij^{d}
Willms ffenton	in ter.	xl^{s}	—	ij^{s} viij^{d}
Carolus White	in ter.	xl^{s}	—	ij^{s} viij^{d}
Gregorius Steedman	in ter.	xl^{s}	—	ij^{s} viij^{d}
Robtus Byshopp	in ter.	xx^{s}	—	xvj^{d}
Vidua Briani Smith	in ter.	xx^{s}	—	xvj^{d}
Robtus Sturton	in ter.	xx^{s}	—	xvj^{d}
Willms fflower	in ter.	xx^{s}	—	xvj^{d}
Thomas ffox	in ter.	xx^{s}	—	xvj^{d}
Nicus White	in ter.	xx^{s}	—	xvj^{d}
Thomas Nayler	in bon.	iij^{li}	—	iij^{d}

Sma xlv^{s} viij^{d}."

For the names of leaseholders and tenants-at-will in the Sturton of Robinson's day other sources must be consulted. For example, a family of Lamberts is disclosed in the will of William Lambert of Sturton, dated October 9, 1592.[1] This document is witnessed by Robinson's father-in-law, "Alexander Whyte," and by the vicar, "John Quipe," amongst others. Its provisions indicate the custom of leases and one of the quarterly terms for wage-paying.

"The lease of Willowes Farme I give unto Robt. Lambert, Edward Lambert, Thomas Lambert my children.

"Whereas yt hath pleased my good and worshipfull maister of his good and benevolent will to grant unto me the disposinge of the farme wherin I now dwell for and duringe his naturall lyef, I give and bequeathe the same farme during the tearme and tyme unto William Lambert George Lambert and Ralfe Lambert three of my eldest sonnes.

"My servants to have ther quarters wages payde duely unto them att Martinmas nexte.

"I humblely desyre my good maister, Maister Bryan Lassels and Mr. Jarvase Lassels and Mr. Alexander Whyte to be the supervisors of this my last will."

[1] Probate Registry at York, Vol. 25, f. 1192.

It seems to me that the Whites were more closely associated with the Lassells family and the Robinsons with the Thornhagh family in the parochial and public affairs of Sturton.

A bequest in the will of "Henrie Broomehead," clerk or parson of North Wheatley, dated 20 October, 20 James, *i. e.* 1623, may help local antiquaries to determine the site of the Robinson holding in Sturton. "I give unto my brother Henrie Bromehead (*sic*) [apparently there were two brothers Henry in one family] one acre and a halfe of meadow lyeinge in Storton overinge, thre Rood lyeinge in littlemarsh at Littlebrough bancke, one Rood above little marsh furlonge, 1 half acre buttinge on Robinson close nooke."[1] Can this last spot be identified?

NOTE.—In the Subsidy Roll for 1585 only two taxpayers are mentioned under Scrooby and Ranskill, one of whom was the father of William Brewster, the "Elder" of the Pilgrim Fathers' Church.

"Scrobe cum Raskall" } "Willim Bruster in bonn. vj^{li}–x^{s}
John Danson in terr. xx^{s}–ij^{s} viij^{d}."

Among other names in this roll for the parish of Ragnall we have a reference to Robert Neville, the father of Gervase Neville. He had recently died, and his children were under age.

"Robtes Nevell . in terr.
beinge deade & his childerne infants } xl^{s}–v^{s} iij^{d}."

[1] York Probate Registry, Vol. 37. f. 157.

APPENDIX III

A STATEMENT AND EXPLANATION BY JOHN BURGESS

DR. AUGUSTUS JESSOP contributed a good account of John Burgess to the *Dictionary of National Biography*. He had in his possession a manuscript of the sermon preached by Burgess at Greenwich. He tells us that while Convocation was deliberating on the "Canons," Burgess "was called upon to explain the ground he took, and to preach before the King at Greenwich on June 19, 1604. Burgess chose his text from Psalm cxxii. 8–9: *For my brethren and companions' sake I will now say Peace be within thee. Because of the house of the Lord our God I will seek thy good.*

"The sermon," says Jessop, "was a poor performance and somewhat offensive in its tone, but one passage seems to have provoked the king beyond measure, though it is difficult to say why. Burgess likened the ceremonies to Pollio's glasses 'which were not worth a man's life or livelihood,' and for this and other expressions he was sent to the Tower."—Article on "Burgess, John" (1563–1635), in *Dict. Nat. Biog.*

The following document in the State Papers in Burgess's handwriting refers to this occasion. It illustrates the position of one who opposed John Robinson's separation from the Anglican Church, and yet was far from comfortable himself within her borders—

"I doe thinke & beeleive touchinge the gôvernmente of the churche by Bishops as wth us in Englande, or by rulinge elders as in other churches of god: that neither of them was prescribed by the apostles of Christ, neyther of them is repugnant to the woorde of god, but may be well & profitably used if more faulte bee not in the persons then in the orders themselfes

"I doe houlde & am pswaded of the crosse in baptisme & the surples that as our church useth them, they bee not unlawfull; though in some men & places so inexpedient, as I think no man's ministery lykely to doe so much good as some mens sodeyne use of theis thinges mighte doe hurte

"ffor the subscription to the articles of 62 [*i.e.* 1562] as the lawe requireth it, & to his Maties supremacie, I approve it wthout any deception or qualification: And touchinge the thirde article about the book of common prayer & booke of ordination doe houlde that howsoever they have some thinges in them wch cannot simply bee allowed as false translations &c yet considered in the porpose & entention of the churche of Englande, & reduced to the .prositions [propositions] & doctrines wch it publiquely pfessethe, they conteyne nothing contrary to the woorde of god.

"And in witnes that this is my unfayned iudgment in the prmisses I have sett to my name this 2 of July 1604

"† and will be allwayes reddy to pfesse by any meanes at his Maties commande †[1]

"JOHN BURGES

"ffor my sermon preached before his excellent Matie [I] doe take god to witnes, that I was not incited advised or moved thereto, by any but myne owne hearte, that I had no porpose to glaunce at such pticulareties, as his Matie (very pbably) conceived me to ayme a[t] that I had not so wicked a thought in me, as to compare his Matie to any evel example wch I alleaged, no porpose to gall or discipher pticuler psons, that I spake nothinge but out of the deernes & integretie of my affections to his Matie and the state & out of opinion that it was such a dutie, as I ought to psew to all myne owne hopes or possibilleties of prferment, or els let the god of truth cut me of from his favour for ever

"JOHN BURGES."[2]

The paper is endorsed in a later hand "Mr. Burgess his profession."

[1] The words between daggers were evidently interlined after the signature was appended.

[2] *State Papers, Domestic*, James I, vol. viii. No. 86.

And in witness that this is my unfeigned judgment in these
premisses I have set to my name this 2 of July 1604
and will bee allwayes ready to confirme by any meanes at his Matie commande
John Burges

For my sermon preached before his excellent Matie, I doe take god
to witness, that I was not invited, advised, or moved thereto, by any
but myne owne hearte, that I had no purpose to glance at
such particularities, as his Matie (very probably) conceived me to ayme at,
that I had not so wicked a thought in me, as to compare his
Matie to any evil example which I alleaged, no purpose to
gall or disgrace particular persons, that I spake nothing
but out of the doctrine & integritie of my affections to his Matie
& the state, & out of opinion that it was such a dutie, as
I ought to prefer to all myne owne hopes or possibilities of
preferment; or els let the god of truth cut me of from his
favoure for ever
John Burges

THE HANDWRITING OF JOHN BURGESS. COMPARE WITH THE FACSIMILE ABOVE AT PAGE 99.

APPENDIX IV

DID JOHN SMITH THE SE-BAPTIST SPRING FROM STURTON?

THERE was another family in Sturton with a member of which our story concerning Robinson is intertwined: I refer to the Smiths, Smyths or Smythes—the name is one, though the spelling varies. There were indeed two families of Smiths in Sturton with various branches, the one in quite a humble station, the other a trading and yeoman family in comfortable circumstances and of equal station with the Whites and Robinsons. It is of the latter I write.

In 1537 Richard Smyth and John Smythe appear in the list of "archers" for Sturton. In 1544 "John Smythe" was assessed on a substantial amount of goods in the same parish. The name is still there in 1571. This John Smith, who paid tax in that year, had a goodly family of boys. There was Brian, the eldest, so named perhaps in honour of the local magnate Brian Lassells, then came George, born about 1563, who went to a farm at Gringley-on-the-Hill. He testified at Gainsborough in 1603[1] that he was then forty years old and born at Sturton. Next came Thomas Smith. The fourth son was John Smith, and I venture to identify him with John Smith the pioneer in the Separatist movement in this part of England, who took the lead in moulding distinct "Churches of Christ" on the New Testament model, apart from the Anglican and Catholic Churches. The last boy in the family was Anthony, and there

[1] Exchequer Depositions, Notts., 1 James I, Michaelmas Term, No. 14.

was one girl, Katherine, who, we may be sure, had a lively time amongst her brothers. If I am right in my identification John Smith, the fourth son, was sent up to Cambridge, and matriculated as a sizar at Christ's College early in 1586, when John Robinson was about ten years old. Two years later (June 1, 1588) John Smith of Sturton, yeoman, made his will. To Brian Smith, his heir, he left "lands and tenements," to his other children "40li apece," and to each of his four sons, other than Brian, "xxs yerely after the death of Alice Smith," his wife; to her he left a third of his lands and a third of his lease of Torksey, a few miles up the Trent, on the Lincolnshire side of the river, the port of the cathedral city. To the "poor people of Sturton" he left xls, to John Quipp, the vicar, who witnessed the will, xs and "to Brian Lassels, Esq., xxs." As young John Smith had a year or two to run before he came of age his father entrusted him to the guardianship of his eldest brother, Brian, while for him there was a special bequest which would help him with his expenses at Cambridge: "To John Smith my son xls yerely out of a close called Intake Close."

Though the five younger children (if Brian renounced the duty) were nominated as executors, yet when the will was proved (October 9, 1589) it was only George and Thomas who acted. John was away at Cambridge and still under age, but power was reserved to him, with Anthony and Katherine, the other executors. In due course young John Smith took his degree, was elected to a Fellowship in his college, and was then ordained by Wickham, Bishop of Lincoln. When he married the problem arose as to where he and Mary his wife should settle. Now Brian Smith, his eldest brother, had married into another family of Smiths connected with Welton and Lincoln. This leads to a multiplication of Smiths, and is rather confusing, but a careful study of the adjoining tables (Smith pedigrees II., III., IV.), will help to make the matter clear. Brian's wife was Jane Smith, eldest

SMITH PEDIGREES

I.—Smith of Honington and the Close of Lincoln

Thos. Smith, *d.* 1541. = Margaret, daughter of Richard Clarke of Welbourne.

Issue:

- William of Honington, Lincs., *d.* 1551. = Katherine, daughter of Augustine Porter of Belton. She married as second husband Thomas Disney of Carlton-le-Morland. Issue by both husbands.
  - William, twice married, issue by both wives. Mentioned in will of his sister, Eleanor White.
  - Elizabeth = Edward Saltmarshe.
  - Eleanor Smith = Alexander White of Sturton.
    - (1) Catherine, *m.* (*a*) George Leggatt. (*b*) John Carver.
    - (2) Charles, *m.* Elizabeth.
    - (3) Bridget, *m.* John Robinson, Pastor of the Pilgrim Fathers.
    - (4) Thomas.
    - (5) Roger, *m.* Elizabeth Wales at Leyden, 1621.
    - (6) Edward.
    - (7) Jane, *m.* Randall Thickins of London at Leyden, 1611.
    - (8) Frances, *m.* Francis Jessop at Worksop, 1605.
- Alban.
- Thomas.
- Robert of the "Black Monks by Lincoln." = a daughter of one Simcotts of Co. Hunts.
  - (1) Bartholomew.
  - (2) Robert.
  - (3) Edward, of the Castle, Lincoln, *m.* Frances, daughter of Geoffrey Harper of Co. Notts. and had large family.

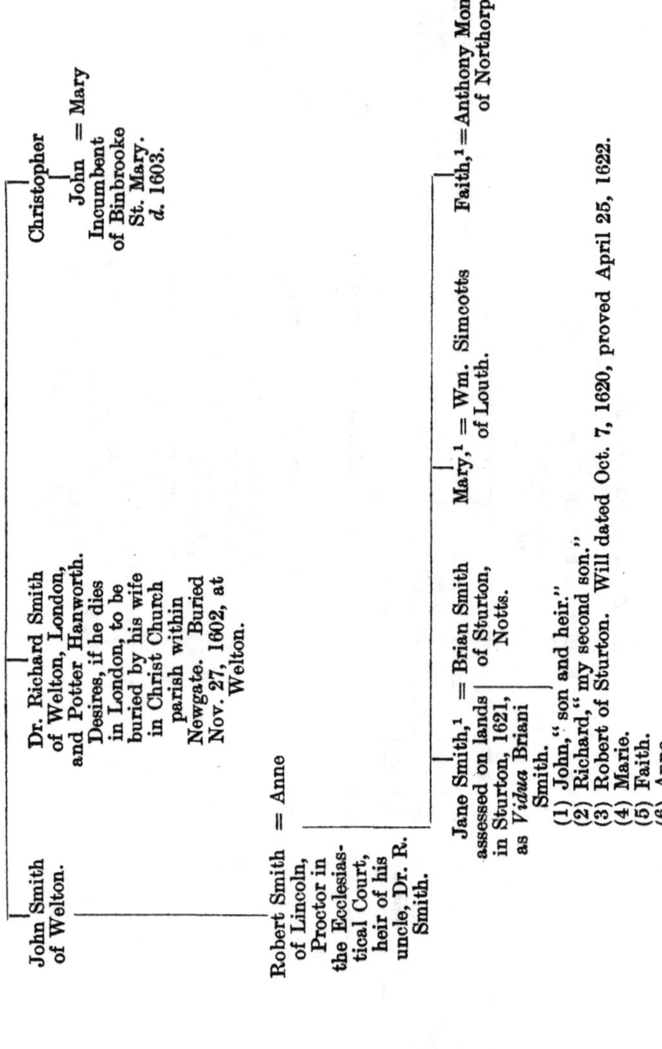

[1] From an inquisition taken at the Castle of Lincoln, Sep. 27, 1611, I find that Dr. Richard Smyth was a "meanes of the p'fermt in mariage of the said ffaithe Marie and Jane and out of his bountie and benevolence paied theire mariage porcons."

III. Smith of Sturton-le-Steeple

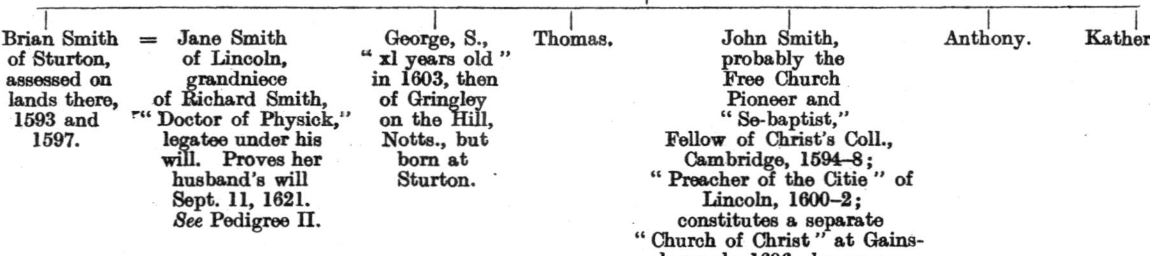

IV. Smith of Lincoln

(Arms, argent, a chevron between three roses gules)

Richard Smith, Attorney and Town Clerk of Lincoln, Warden of St. Peter's at Arches, Executor of Dr. Richard Smith. Mentioned in will of Brian Smith of Sturton, 1621. = Mary, daughter of Wm. Bayley of Louth, at St. Margaret's, Lincoln, Oct. 21, 1576.

Robert Smith of Lincoln, Attorney. Appointed "City Attorney-General" in the room of his father, 1618. = Susan, daughter of Gervase Wastneys of Headon, Notts., 1609.

(1) Robert, *d.* s.p., 1627.
(2) Elizabeth, *m.*, 1627, Sir Charles Dalyson, Recorder of Lincoln.

daughter of Robert Smith of Lincoln, a nephew of the Richard Smith of Welton and London who had amassed a fortune in the metropolis as "Doctor of Physick." This marriage of Brian Smith with Jane Smith of Lincoln brought him into touch with a group of prominent citizens of that city actively interested in civic affairs.

Dr. Richard Smith [1] died in 1603, without children. He left munificent bequests, which to this day help the education of the boys of Potter Hanworth and Lincoln, and in his will he remembered the children of his grand-niece Jane, the wife of Brian Smith of Sturton.

One more point. He appointed a namesake (though no apparent blood relation), as executor of his will, a Richard Smith, attorney and town clerk of Lincoln, one whose legal knowledge ought to have been of service in settling the educational trusts of the will. This Richard Smith was also Warden of the Church of St. Peter at Arches, which the Corporation of the City of Lincoln attended. The indications are that

[1] In a list of *Recusants in and about London committed to Prison*, dated 1592, I find "Richard Smith of Christ Church, Doctor of Physic." Is it the same man? *Calendar of Salisbury Papers*, Pt. IV, p. 267.

Brian Smith was acquainted not only with Richard Smith the physician, whose relative he married, but also with Richard Smith the attorney. He certainly had intercourse with him on legal business.

What more natural than that Brian Smith should suggest his younger brother, John Smith, to the warden of St. Peter's as a suitable candidate for the post of "lecturer" or "preacher to the City of Lincoln"? It is a fact that with the powerful backing of the clan of Smiths, and others in Lincoln, John Smith was elected to that office on September 27, 1600, though not without strong opposition. His forceful and searching sermons made for him both friends and enemies. The ecclesiastical authorities came down upon him and he lost his post. Moving to Gainsborough, within easy reach of his brother George at Gringley, he took upon him to expound the Psalms to the congregation in the parish church in the absence of Jerome Phillips, the vicar. In this good work too he was stopped. It was out of order. Then it was that, following the example of Francis Johnson, his Cambridge tutor, he deliberately severed his connexion with Anglicanism and gathered a separate Church at Gainsborough, of which he was made "Pastor." Toleration for his movement was not accorded, and he removed with his followers to Amsterdam, where he advanced to the theological position of the liberal Mennonites, practised physic for a livelihood and died of consumption. His books show him to have had an intimate knowledge of the Sturton district. He was aware of the clerical gossip of the locality, and refers to Richard Bernard's "vehement desire" to secure the living of "Sawenbie," *i. e.* Saundby, between Gainsborough and Sturton. He had some knowledge of the state of feeling in regard to religion among the people of Worksop. He was intimate with the Helwys, Hamerton and Neville families, which had connexions with Broxtowe, Askham, Habblesthorpe, Saundby and Ragnell. When Richard Clifton was deprived of his living at Babworth, the arguments of John Smith won him to his side. He was intimate with Hugh Bromehead, "curate" of North Wheatley, the next parish but one to Sturton, and induced him to break with Anglicanism and join the new "Church of Christ" in its migration to Holland. Last, but not least, he exerted a marked influence upon John Robinson, the Pastor of the Pilgrim Church, who writes of him as of one with whom he had been long acquainted.

Dr. W. T. Whitley, in his recent biography of "John Smyth," is baffled by the problem of his identity. What other John Smith meets the requirements of the case so well as this one? The evidence is not decisive, but the indications point to this John Smith of Sturton as the one who stands in the ranks of the originators of the Free Churches of the English-speaking world; the one who left the mark of his thought upon the minds of his followers and the sweet influence of the gracious Christian temper of his last days as a wholesome leaven in their hearts.

A paragraph from the will of Brian Smith, the eldest brother of John Smith, illustrates and confirms part of what I have said. It is dated at Sturton. June 20, 1621—

> "To Marie and Faith Smith my daughters £50 a piece . . . in consideration of a legacy bequeathed unto them amongst my other children by . . . Richard Smith late of Welton . . . Doctor of Phisicke deceased and since his death was ordered unto the said Marie and Faith . . . by the charitable disposition of Richard Smith of the Cittie of Lincoln, Gent., . . . unto whom I stand bound in the sum of £300 to pay and discharge the same."

One more point. I discovered the will of a son of Brian, and nephew of John Smith of Sturton, in the Probate Registry at Lincoln. It was proved in that diocese because the young man apparently died at the house where his Aunt Faith (*née* Smith), his mother's sister, who married Anthony Monson of Carlton in Lincolnshire, had resided. Remember there was a tendency to consumption in the family. "Robert Smith of Sturton in the County of Notts. sonne of Bryan Smith yeoman, sicke in body but whole of minde," made his will October 7, 1620. I only cite one sentence of this document—

> "*Itm* I give and bequeath the Cli pound wch my uncle George Smith did give unto me wch now remayneth in my father's hands and my uncle John Smith's exequtors to my uncle George Smith."

The reference to the *executors* of John Smith accords with our provisional identification; because the Free Church pioneer (called for the sake of distinction John Smith the Se-baptist) had died at the end of August 1612,[1] leaving young children to be provided for. Pending further discoveries I suggest that John Smith and John Robinson were natives of the same village.

[1] The will of Nicholas White of Sturton, dated December 14, 1638, refers to lands "which I lately purchased of William Smyth and the heires of John Smyth . . . as also all and singular Muniments touching and concerning the same." It also refers to a piece of land "in the lowe ffield" of Sturton abutting on "the lande of Mary Smyth." This date, however, allows time for another generation of Smyths to have come on the scene.

CHRONOLOGICAL TABLE OF THE WRITINGS OF JOHN ROBINSON

SOMETIME FELLOW OF CORPUS CHRISTI COLLEGE, CAMBRIDGE

THE extent and range of the writings of Robinson which have survived afford ample testimony to his industry and scholarship. He was thoroughly well versed in the theological literature of his day and a keen student of Biblical and theological topics to the end of his life. We may note that he accepted and made use of the Authorised Version of the Bible almost as soon as it appeared. The Genevan Version had previously been favoured by the Puritan wing in the Anglican Church.

1. Controversy with John Burgess embodied in Jones MS., 30, in the Bodleian Library, Oxford . . 1608–9
2. „ An Answer to a Censorious Epistle." A "pamphlet" replying to a "monitory letter" from Joseph Hall, then Rector of Halstead . . 1609
3. " A Justification of Separation from the Church of England." A reply to Richard Bernard . . 1610
4. Letter to the Church at Amsterdam concerning Dismission of Members and method of handling cases of Discipline. 14 Nov. 1610
5. Letter on Christian Fellowship to William Ames, printed in *The Prophane Schism of the Brownists* 1611
6. "Testimonie of the Elders of the Church at Leyden." This was by Robinson and Brewster jointly 1612
7. A Brief Answer to the Exceptions of Francis Johnson against points in Robinson's *Justification of Separation.* This is printed in Ainsworth's *Animadversion to Mr. Richard Clyfton,* 1613 1612

8. A volume of Five Tracts :—
   (*a*) Of Religious Communion Private and Public.
   (*b*) Of Flight in Persecution.
   (*c*) The Outward Baptism received in England Lawfully retained.
   (*d*) Of the Baptism of Infants.
   (*e*) A Survey of the Confession of Faith published in certain Conclusions by the remainders of Mr. Smyth's Company . . . 1613–14
9. " A Manumission to a Manuduction or answer to a Letter inferring public communion in the parish Assemblies upon private communion with godly persons there " 1615
10. *Admonitio ad Lectorem* prefixed to Robert Parker's *De Politeia Ecclesiastica Christi* 1616
11. *Seven Articles* sent to the Privy Council giving the judgment of the Leyden Church on matters of religion, occasioned by their proposal to migrate to Virginia 1617
12. Letter to Sir Edwin Sandys by Robinson and Brewster, Leyden, 15 Dec. 1617
13. Letter to Sir John Wolstenholme with *Two Declarations*, Robinson and Brewster. Feb. . 1618
14. " The People's Plea for the Exercise of Prophecy against Mr. John Yates " 1618
15. *Apologia Justa et Necessaria quorundam Christianorum . . . per Johannem Robinsonum, Anglo-Leidenensem, suo et Ecclesia nomine, cui praeficitur* 1619
16. Letter to John Carver. June 14 1620
17. " The Wholesome Counsel Master Robinson gave that part of the Church whereof he was Pastor at their Departure," reported by Edward Winslow. July 1620
18. Letter to John Carver. Dated Leyden, 27 July . 1620
19. " Certain useful Advertisements sent in a Letter . . . unto the Planters . . . at their first setting sail from Southampton." July 1620
20. Letter " to the Church of God in Plymouth." 30 June 1621
21. Letter to William Brewster on the faint prospects of Robinson joining him and giving advice on church matters 1623
22. Letter to William Bradford pleading for a moderate and Christian course with the Indians. 19 Dec. 1623

23. A Briefe Catechism concerning Church Government, an appendix to Mr. Perkins' Six Principles of the Christian Religion . . . . (?)1623
24. " A Defence of the Doctrine propounded by the Synod at Dort " 1624
25. A Letter to the Church of Christ in London. 5 April 1624
26. " An Appeal on Truth's Behalf," being a Letter " to the Elders and Church at Amsterdam." 18 Sept. 1624
27. " Treatise on the Lawfulness of Hearing the Ministers of the Church of England " (not printed till 1634) 1624
28. " Observations Divine and Moral " 1625
29. " A Just and Necessary Apology of certain Christians . . . commonly called Brownists or Barrowists." English Translation by Robinson . 1625

INDEX

ABBOT, Archbishop George, 257
Act of Supremacy, 42, 216
Adventurers, 225, 249; composition with, 316
Ainsworth, Henry (1570–1622), scholar of Gonville and Caius Coll., Cambridge, 1587–1591, son of Thos. Ainsworth, yeoman, of Swanton Morley, where he was educated by Mr. Clephamson for three years. Went first to St. John's Coll., Camb.; transferred to Caius. Left without a degree. Ministered for a time amongst religious refugees in Ireland. Appears at Amsterdam in poverty. Married there March 29, 1607, to Margery Appleby, a widow. Elected "teacher" of the Separatist Church of which Francis Johnson was pastor, 85; reply to Bernard, 112, 128, 188, 192, 202; death of, 203 *note*, 291, 315, 362
Alden, John, 246
Aldrich, Henry, bequest of, 33
Allerton, Isaac, 229, 316, 333, 362
—— John, 108, 246
—— Mary, 362
Ames, Elizabeth, 338
—— Joan, 338
—— Wm., 123, 165, 173, 283 *note*, 338
—— Wm., jun., 338
Amsterdam, 71, 79; refugees at, 85, 93; letter from, 196, 391
Articles of Association for the Plantation, 226, 259, 274
Argall, Captain Saml., 221
Arminius, 159
Austerfield, 3
Aylmer, Bishop, 44

BABWORTH, 68, 71, 188, 190 *note*
Baillie, Robert, 141, 336
Bancroft, Richard, 44, 64
Baro, Peter, 49
Barrett, William, 49
Baslyn, Thos., 86
Baynes, Paul, 69
Beauvale Abbey, 7, 20, 46, 341
Belvoir Castle, 6, 380
Benet (Benedict) Church and College, 33, 39, 146
—— Sir John, 184
Benevolence to Henry VIII, 10, 398
Bernard, Richard, 71, 94, 111 *note;* his *Plaine Evidences*, 113; rhyming rhetoric of, 118
Best, Wm., 125
Billericay, 236
Blackwell, Francis, 202, 219, 221
Blossom, Thos., 307, 309, 360
Bontius, Dr. Wm., 171
Boston, 83
Bradford, Wm., 3, 56, 161, 265; his *History of Plimouth Plantation*, 267; opinion of Robinson, 305, 332
Bradshaw, Wm., 128
Brewer, Thos., 109, 157, 171 *seq.*
Brewster, James, 83, 188, 339
—— Jonathan, 164
—— Mary, 81, 103
—— Robert, 339
—— William, the Pilgrim Elder, 67, 79, 102–3; his press, 164, 209, 357
—— Wm., senior, 80, 406
Bright, Francis, 330
Bromehead, Hugh, 71
Broome, John, 190 *note*
Brouckhoven, Jacob von, 170, 177
Browne, Robert, 66, 146 *note*
Burgess, John, 97, 406
Burton, William, 98
Busher, Mark Leonard, 154
Butler, Silvester, 90
Butten, Wm., 262
Butterfield, Stephen, 359
Buttes, Henry, 40, 46

CAMBRIDGE, 29; Life at, 35
Canne, John, 357
Canons, Book of, 45
Cape Cod, 263
Carleton, Dudley, 162, 314
Cartwright, Thos., 165
Carver, Catherine (White), 269
—— John, 212, 225, 251, 269, 398
Castle Combe (Wilts), 90
Cathkin, James, 166
Chaderton, Laurence, 47, 50, 55
Charlestown, 333
Chauncy, Charles, 361
Church Order, 337
Clapham, Enoch, 85
Clarke, John, 231, 245
Clifton, Richard, 71; arrives at Amsterdam, 84, 110, 187, 190
Coats, Matthew, 353
Common Apologie, A, 96
Conant, Roger, 326
Conditions of Association of Plymouth Plantation, 249
Coppin, Robert, 245
Corpus Christi College, 32, 45; Fellows of, 46
Cotton, John, 141, 334
—— John, jun., 361
Covenant of the Pilgrim Church, 115, 215, 241, 332, 339
Crabe, Master, a minister, 243
Cullimer, Thos., 89
Cushman, Isaac, 362
—— Robert, 157, 212, 220, 225, 230, 236, 261
—— Thomas, 360

DARTMOUTH, 257, 261
Davison, Wm., 80
Delftshaven, 237, 248
Dermer, Captain Thos., 262
Disney, John, 256
—— Thos. 19, 25
Dort, Synod of, 160, 288
Drakes, Thos., 139, 204, 207

EMDEN, 202
Endicot, John, 326
English, Thos., 246
Episcopius, 159, 161
Euring, Wm., 204, 207

FALMOUTH, New England, 350
Fenton, 383
—— family of, 7
—— Hall, 30
Fenton, Wm., 14
Fielding, Christopher, 12, 389, 394
Forbes, John, 142
Fuller, Samuel, 229, 327, 333. He is referred to by an opponent as one that "had taken the oath of abjuration" (Morton's *New English Canaan*). This means that on account of his nonconformity he had to abjure the realm and was banished from the homeland on the expiration of three months after sentence of the Court.

GAINSBOROUGH, 27, 67, 75, 353, 384, 386, 415
Goade, Roger, 50, 55
Gorton (Lancs.), preacher at, 358. Mr. Ernest Axon suggests to me that the "preaching minister" here referred to may have been Thomas Paget, sometime curate of Blackley, Manchester, who was suspended for nonconformity and withdrew to Amsterdam.
—— Samuel, 357
Gott, Charles, 326; letter to Wm. Bradford, 330
Gouda, 160
Greasley, 20, 46, 307, 343
Greenwood, John, 348
Gringley-on-the-Hill, 387
Guiana, 211
Gurnay, Edmund, 39, 40

HABBLESTHORPE, 5, 385, 393
Hall, Joseph, 38, 64, 94, 146
Halton, John, shoemaker, 27
Hampton = Southampton, 258
Harrison, David, 385
—— Richard, 66
—— William, 370, 390
Hatherley, Timothy, 350
Heale, Giles, 246
Heinsius, Daniel, 179, 184
Helwys, Thomas, 77, 82, 143, 285
Heneage House, 257
Hetherington, John, 143
Higden, Marlian, 40, 46
Higginson, Francis, 328, 335
Hildersham, Arthur, 336
Hommius, Festus, 161, 283
Honington, 18
Hopkins, Elizabeth, 262
—— Oceanus, 262

Hopkinson, Francis, 354
—— Wm., 28
Hudson River, 262
Hunt, Clement, 66

INDIANS, 211, 279

JACOB, Henry, 137, 140, 212, 291
James, King, 159, 166, 175, 183, 303
Jamestown, 314
Jegon, John, 29, 40, 50, 61, 300
—— Thos., 46
Jennens, Abraham, 263
Jepson, Henry, 108
—— Rosamund, 107
—— William, 106
Jessop, Francis, 289, 307
Johnson, Francis, 79, 87–9
Jones, Christopher, 245, 257
Justice, Thos. (of Scrooby), 374

KEBLE, JOHN, 359
Knollys, Hanserd, 353

LALAING, Johann de, 107
Lambeth Articles, 49
Lassells, Brian, 376, 399, 402–3
—— family of, 6
—— Thos., 12, 382
Laud, Archbishop Wm., 104, 347
Lawne, Christopher, 189
Lawson, Roger, 14
Legate, Bartholomew, 180
Leggatt, George, 22, 25
Leigh, Captain Charles, 211
Leverton, North, 28
—— South, 29
Leyden, 100; letter from, 197
Lincoln, 28, 414
Lyford, John, 277, 326

MAISTERSON (Masterson), John, 359
—— Richard, 307–8, 360
Manners, Roger, 29, 374
Marriage, form of, 103
Martin, Christopher, 169, 236, 258
Martin, Sir Henry, 184, 257 *note*
Marton, 392
Mason, Francis, 65
Mattersey, 5
May, Henry, 312
Mayflower, 230, 238, 244; log of, 245; compact and signatories, 265, 267
Middelburg, 283
Millenary Petition, 44
Millington, Gilbert, 341
Mitchell, Experience, 257, 274
Monson, Wm., 19
More, John, 59
Morton, George, 273
Mullins, Priscilla, 246
—— William, 246
Murton (Morton), John, 143, 154, 180, 285

NASH, Thos., 227, 307
Naumkeak, *vide* Salem
Naunton, Sir Robert, 167, 215
Nelson, John, post of Scrooby, 81 *note*
Neville, Anthony, 5
—— Gervase, 72 *seq.*
—— Robert, 72, 406
Newhouse, Thos., 59
Norton, John, 361
Norwich, 58 *seq.*, 204

OCCUPATIONS of the Pilgrims, 104
Oldham, John, 275
Ormerod, George, 26
Oswald Beck, 27
Overall, Dr. John, 50

PAGET, JOHN, 125, 136
Parker, Matt, 33
—— Robert, 135
Patent for the Colony, 266
Patuxet, 267
Pearte, Original, 346
—— Wm., 15, 345
Pecke, Anne, 102
—— Robert, 103
Peirce, John, 235, 266
—— William, 275–9
Penry, John, 86
Perkins, William, 48, 59, 320, 362
Perth Assembly, 166
Phillip, John, 338
Pickering, Edward, 186, 233
Piggott, Thos., 151
Pillowbeeres, 24. This word was carried to Plymouth, N.E., where it occurs in a Will of the year 1633.
Plymouth (Devon), 261
—— (New England), 241, 266, 267 *note*, 314; Church at, 326, 332, 358–9
Polgeest, 107
Polyander, John, 57, 158, 171, 179, 185
Pomeroy, Leonard, 263

Porter, Katherine, 19
Pory, John, 314–16
Powell, Thos., 88
Psalm Book, 362

QUAKERS, 349
Queenborough, 323
Quick, John, 283 *note*
Quipp, John (of Littleborough), 388–9
—— John (of Sturton), 12, 373, 379, 401, 409
—— William, 354, 388

RAGNELL (Notts), 73
Rampton (Notts), 361
Religion, disputations on, 51 *seq.*
Reyner, John, 361
Reynolds, Captain, 231, 257
—— John, printer, 165
Rhodes, John, 321
Ring, William, 260
Robinson, Ann, junior, 282, 348
—— Ann, senior, will of, 15, 345
—— Bridget the younger, 348
—— Bridget (*vide* Bridget White), 15, 108, 307, 352
—— Christopher, 10, 399, 400
—— Ellen, 15, 352
—— Fear, 351
—— Isaac, 349
—— John, junior, 15, 348
—— John, senior, 9, 12, 375, 377, 388, 392, 401, 403, 404; will of, 13
—— John, the Pilgrim Pastor, 11; admission to College, 34; takes his degree, 37; elected Fellow, 38; signs letter to Cecil, 39; resigns Fellowship and marries, 46; religious discussion by, 56; at Norwich, 58; revisits Cambridge, 67; leaves Anglican Church, 70; conference with John Smith, 93; controversy with Hall and Burgess, 95–7; house at Leyden, 106; replies to Bernard, 113; opinion on Church order, 116; follows Smith, 117; discussion with forward Puritan preachers, 123; his *Manumission*, 129; on baptism, 143; limits of religious liberty, 152; matriculates at Leyden University, 158; his advice sought, 192; plea for lay preaching, 204; intercourse with the Dutch, 224; letter to Carver, 232; parting counsel of, 239, 251; letter to colonists, 268; to Brewster, 276; concern for Indians, 279; his household in 1622, 284; letter to Amsterdam, 293; essays, 298; death of, 302; Bradford's appreciation of, 304; his *Catechism*, 319, 362; books reprinted, 323
Robinson, Mary, 11, 16, 355
—— Mercy, 351
—— Nathaniel, 355
—— William, 11, 352–3
Rogers, Thos., 236
Rutherfurd, Samuel, 324

ST. ANDREW'S CHURCH, Norwich, 58, 98
—— Plymouth, 263
St. Benet's (Benedict's), Cambridge, 33
St. Botolph's, Cambridge, 33
Salem (Naumkeak), 317, 327–9, 333, 338
Saltmarshe, Edward, of Strubby, Lincs., 19
Sandys, Sir Edward, 212; letter to, 214, 217
Saundby, 377, 382, 415
Scrooby, 3, 70, 75, 80, 104, 374
Sherley, James, 277, 317
Sherwill, Nicholas, 263
Ships:—
Anne, 81, 109, 273, 275
Charity, 272, 278
Fortune, 266; captured, 270, 360
James, or *Little James*, 109, 273
Jonathan, 263
Lion, 349
Mary Rose, 8
Mayflower, 1, 19, 105, 244, 264, 266, 275
Providence, 263
Sparrow, 272
Speedwell, 233, 261
Swan, 272
Talbot, 349
Simmons, Matt., 323
Skelton, Samuel, 328
Slade, Matthew, 97, 160, 174, 190
Slaughterford, identified with Sechtenfort, 88
Smith, Brian, 402, 409, 415

Smith, Captain John, of Lincs., navigator, 235, 263
—— George, 387, 417
—— John, senior, of Sturton, 400, 401
—— John, the Sebaptist, 67; his *Paralleles*, 112, 126; death of, 144; *Confession of Faith*, 151; influence on Clifton, 188, 285, 292; did he spring from Sturton?, 409
—— Mary, wife of John the Sebaptist, 410
—— Ralph, 328, 331
—— Richard, of Sturton, painter, 27
—— Richard, of London and Welton, Lincs., Doctor of Physic, 413–415
—— Richard, Town Clerk of Lincoln, 414–16
—— Robert, 417
—— Thomas (deacon at Amsterdam), 157
—— Wm. (Bradford-on-Avon), 87
—— Wm. (Honington, Lincs.), tomb of, 18
—— Wm. (Honington, Lincs.), jun., 25
—— Wm. (Sturton), 28
Southampton, 237
Southworth, Alice, 273
—— Edward, 9, 104, 257, 379
—— Robert, 110
Stafford Bridge, 27, 373
Standish, Miles, 274, 280, 305
Staresmore, Sabine, 140, 203 *note*, 217, 291, 293
Studley, Daniel, 195
Sturton-le-Steeple (Notts.), 4; infectious sickness at, 11; life at, in Elizabethan times, 369; residents in, 395

Teellinck, Wm., 283
Testimonie of Leyden Elders, 192
Thickins, Randall, 107
Thomson, David, 263
Tithes, 5, 389
Thornhagh family, 8
—— Francis, 9
—— John, senior, 9, 20, 376, 378, 384
—— Sir John, 20, 378; petition of, 393
Thorpe, Giles, 174
Trevore, Wm., 246
Turner, John, 231

Undertakers, 318. This was the name given to the eight leading colonists in Plymouth Plantation and the four London merchants who undertook to be responsible for the debts of the Colony under the Composition Deed of November 1626. In return they were granted the privilege of managing the trade of the Plantation. They were sometimes called the "Purchasers." The four in London were Richard Andrews, Timothy Hatherley, John Beauchamp, James Sherley. Beauchamp was a drysalter and a grantee of land in New England; Hatherley subsequently crossed to the Plymouth Colony; Sherley was treasurer of the Plymouth Adventurers.
Unitarian Church, Boston, Mass., 334; Gainsborough, 353; New Plymouth, Mass., 359

Virginia, 202, 208–9, 241, 258, 313
—— Company, 220, 225
Vorstius, Conrad, 159, 321

Walæus, 179, 283
Watkins, Nicholas, 102 *note*
Watson, Anthony, 40, 45
Wessagusset, 279
Weston, Thos., 186, 224–8, 234, 249, 259, 271
Whitgift, John, 42, 49
White, Alexander, 17; marriage, 18; will of, 20, 401
—— Bridget, 21, 25, 46–7, 402
—— Captain Charles, 341; dispatch from, 342
—— Charles, 16, 22, 25, 289, 307, 403–5
—— Catherine, 19, 24
—— Edward, 19, 24
—— Eleanor, 22; will of, 23
—— Frances, 19, 25, 307
—— Jane, 19, 23, 104, 107
—— Nicholas, 107, 417 *note*
—— Roger, 19, 24, 289; letters from, 302, 307, 311
—— Thos., of Sturton, 17
—— Thos., of Slaughterford, 88, 91
Willet, Thos., 109
Williams, Roger, 361
Williamson, Mr., 245
Willoughby, Lord (Robert Bertie), 300

Wilson, John, 334
—— Roger, 105
Wincob, John, 222
Winkburn, 9
Winslow, Edward, 229, 247, 303
Winthrop, John, 333
Wolstenholme, Sir John, 216
Women in the Church, 293
—— of Littleborough, 370
Wood, Henry, 105, 108
Worksop, 5, 71, 415
Wrentham, 338
Wright, Reuben, 376
Wrington, 157

YATES, JOHN, 204

ZOUCHE, SIR WILLIAM, 181

NOTE

For an account of the relation between the work of John Smith and John Robinson and the influence of their respective churches the reader is referred to the author's little volume on *John Smith, the Sebaptist, Thomas Helwys and the first Baptist Church in England, with fresh light upon the Pilgrim Fathers' Church*, 1911.

www.ingramcontent.com/pod-product-compliance
Lightning Source LLC
LaVergne TN
LVHW020518100826
845148LV00010B/1270

* 9 7 8 1 6 0 6 0 8 5 1 3 4 *